FOCUS ON SUCCESS

Erweiterte Ausgabe

3rd edition

von

Angela Diermayr

Thomas English

Siegfried Meinunger

Josef Strasser

Wolfgang Towara

sowie Megan Hadgraft

unter Mitarbeit
der Verlagsredaktion

Verfasser/innen:	Angela Diermayr, Berufliche Oberschule Regensburg Thomas English, M.A., Berufliche Oberschule Krumbach Siegfried Meinunger, Berufliche Oberschule Krumbach Josef Strasser, Berufliche Oberschule Regensburg Wolfgang Towara, Berufliche Oberschule Würzburg Megan Hadgraft (Webcodes)
Beraterinnen:	Ellen Baderschneider, Fachoberschule Karlsfeld Sabine Lauber, Staatliche Fachoberschule und Berufsoberschule Landshut-Schönbrunn
Projektleitung:	Merlene Griffin
Außenredaktion:	James Abram
Redaktionelle Mitarbeit:	Gemma Duggan, Alice Gleeson Oliver Busch (Wörterverzeichnisse)
Bildredaktion:	Gertha Maly
Umschlaggestaltung:	werkstatt für gebrauchsgrafik, Berlin
Layout und technische Umsetzung:	Oxana Rödel, Absatz DTP-Service, Teltow
Illustrationen:	Oxford Designers & Illustrators

http://www.cornelsen.de

Die Mediencodes enthalten ausschließlich optionale Unterrichtsmaterialien; sie unterliegen nicht dem staatlichen Zulassungsverfahren.

1. Auflage, 2. Druck 2014

Druck: Stürtz GmbH, Würzburg

ISBN 978-3-06-450650-3

VORWORT

Focus on Success – Erweiterte Ausgabe 3rd edition ist für Lernende und Unterrichtende an Fachoberschulen, Berufsoberschulen, Höheren Berufsfachschulen und Beruflichen Gymnasien konzipiert. Das Lehrwerk baut auf den mittleren Abschluss auf und führt zur Fachhochschulreife bzw. zur (fachgebundenen) Hochschulreife. Dabei führt es von Stufe B1 des Gemeinsamen europäischen Referenzrahmens zu Stufe B2.

Focus on Success – Erweiterte Ausgabe 3rd edition besteht aus zwölf auf Lehrplan und Abschlussprüfung abgestimmten Kapiteln. Die Themen (wie z. B. *Travelling the world*, *Individual freedom*, *Spreading the news*, *Clashes of interest*, *The globalized world* und viele weitere) folgen lehrplanbezogenen Kriterien.

Jedes Kapitel beginnt mit einer meist visuellen Hinführung zum Thema (**Focus**). Im Mittelpunkt stehen drei Texte unterschiedlicher Länge, Textsorte und Perspektive, wobei darauf geachtet worden ist, dass sie sowohl Motivation für die Lernenden bieten als auch einen klaren Lehrplanbezug besitzen. Die Texte innerhalb eines Kapitels sind von unterschiedlichem Schwierigkeitsgrad, wodurch auf die Bedürfnisse der jeweiligen Lerngruppe besser eingegangen werden kann. Eine intensive Wortschatzaufarbeitung erfolgt anhand eines zusätzlichen **Words in Context**-Textes pro Kapitel, der *topical vocabulary* enthält, sowie durch vielfältige, gezielte Wortschatzübungen.

Der Aufgabenapparat ist klar kompetenz- und prüfungsorientiert, sowohl in Form authentischer Prüfungsaufgaben wie auch anhand hinführender Übungen, die die für die Prüfung notwendigen Fertigkeiten aufbauen. Solche Übungen finden sich häufig auf den stärker prüfungsorientierten **Further activities**-Seiten. Zur Schulung der Schreibfertigkeit dienen einerseits aktuelle Bilder, Cartoons, Statistiken und Graphiken, andererseits motivierende Schreibanlässe mit realistischem Situations- und Adressatenbezug. Jedes Kapitel enthält zudem Themenstellungen zur Förderung der Sprechfertigkeit und Vorbereitung auf die mündliche Gruppenprüfung sowie abwechslungsreiche Aufgaben zur Schulung des Hörverstehens.

Zur Festigung der Grammatik dient der **Grammar check**, der jedes Kapitel abrundet. Dieser *Grammar check* fördert das eigenständige Verbessern von Fehlern und weist auf Probleme hin, die bei deutschsprachigen Lernenden häufig auftreten. Außerdem finden sich in jedem Kapitel zahlreiche Querverweise zum Anhang, um den individuellen Lernprozess zu unterstützen.

Der Anhang enthält ergänzende Materialien; neben den **Files** sind dies vor allem:

Exam practice: eine Musterprüfung zur Vorbereitung der Abschlussprüfung,

Language study skills: ein anwendungsbezogener Leitfaden zu Lernstrategien, auf den im Verlauf der Kapitel durchgehend verwiesen wird,

Grammar summary: eine übersichtliche Zusammenfassung der wichtigsten Grammatikstrukturen

sowie umfangreiche Wörterverzeichnisse.

Zur Differenzierung und selbstständigen Weiterarbeit stehen zu jedem Kapitel des Lehrwerks **Webcodes** zur Verfügung, die mit klaren Verweisen gekennzeichnet sind und von den Lernenden auf www.cornelsen.de/webcodes/ abgerufen werden können.

Wir hoffen, dass Ihnen die Arbeit mit **Focus on Success – Erweiterte Ausgabe 3rd edition** Freude bereitet und das Lehrwerk zu einem gelungenen und erfolgreichen Unterricht beiträgt.

Die Autoren und der Verlag 2013

CONTENTS

Appendix

1

What is happiness?

FOCUS

1 There is only one happiness in this life, to love and be loved.

(George Sand)

2 Happiness lies in the joy of achievement and the thrill of creative effort.

(Franklin D. Roosevelt)

3 *Happiness is gratitude for the simple things around you: family, friends, children and nature!* *(jonjamy21)*

4 Happiness consists of freedom: having the freedom to speak, think and do anything you want.

(suzieque08)

Look at the photos and quotes and do these tasks.

1 Which photo illustrates each quote best? Justify your choices.
2 Which photo do you think expresses the idea of happiness best? Why?
3 What makes you happy? Or unhappy?
4 Write a short quote on happiness that you could post on a website.
Start like this: *Happiness is ...*

A Are you happy?

BEFORE YOU READ

The British newspaper *The Guardian* asked its readers if they were happy. The contributions on the next three pages are from a glider pilot, an ice cream seller and a climate change campaigner. What might make each of them feel happy? Which of them do you think will be the happiest?

Adrian Hobbs, glider pilot

I came to gliding quite late. I was 50 and slightly lacking in confidence. It immediately gave me a feeling of achievement. There was the camaraderie of the gliding club and the feeling of climbing up through the smooth, still air. I've flown over Mont Blanc. Perhaps the word gets overused, but there is a privilege that comes with such an experience – of doing something few others can even attempt, of using currents of rising air to reach huge distances and great height.

I have three children, and they think I'm a bit potty. They've flown with me a couple of times. I get told, "You be careful up there." Golf, I hear, is a very compelling activity. Fine, but my first flight solo was a real feeling of achievement. I was yelling out, "I've done it!" I wanted to fly well. I wanted to make the perfect landing.

Gliding suits my independent streak. You're making decisions for yourself. This independence has been one of the largest reasons for happiness throughout my life. I've been fortunate in my career: I'm not a well-known photographer, but I've made a living out of something I like. I haven't had to deal with a boss. In the sky you are alone. You can be happy if you follow your own course. (218 words)

The Guardian, 22 September 2007

1 SHORT-ANSWER QUESTIONS / SENTENCE COMPLETION > Skills p. 178

Answer the questions or complete the sentences with information from the text.

1 Apart from the feeling of freedom, what else does Adrian like about his sport? (*3 aspects*)
2 Adrian says that flying over the highest mountain in Europe was ... that not too many people have ever experienced.
3 For him, gliding is a real thrill and the perfect match for his ... which is also apparent in his job, where he has done without ... . This characteristic has (according to him) always been ... .

2 WORKING WITH WORDS

A Find synonyms from the text to complete the table.

1	rather	pretty	...
2	needing	being without	...
3	success	accomplishment	...
4	several	a few	...
5	fascinating	gripping	...
6	go with	fit	...
7	vein	characteristic	...
8	during	over	...

B Complete the text using the new words from the table on page 7.

Some sports and jobs can really be ...[1]. Bungee-jumping might give you the thrill of a lifetime, but you can also get the same feeling from a real ...[2] that proves your worth. Only ...[3] weeks ago, I finally got the promotion I knew I deserved. However, it was ...[4] a nerve-wrecking time before my boss actually told me. ...[5] my life, I haven't really been very patient, so you could say I have an impatient ...[6] in me. I don't mind what people think because what works for other people doesn't necessarily ...[7] me. There had been rumours that I was looking for a new job. So it was no surprise when my boss called me into his office to talk to him. I told him that I wasn't ...[8] ambition, but that I had no intention of quitting my job just yet.

Kate Drummond, ice cream seller

I can hear them running down the prom shouting, "Ice cream, ice cream!" The kids want chocolate sauce and raspberry sauce. Older people want plain vanilla. They remember what ice cream used to be, and a lot of the appeal is in the memories they have of the seaside.

I like old things. I wanted an old car, but an old ice cream van is just as good. I saw an advert and bought it two and a half years ago. I came to Morecambe* because my best friend moved here and I wanted to be close to my godsons. I moreover needed to be part of the traditional seaside scene.

What I do in the van is a simple transaction. I give people ice cream. They go away happy. I'm happiest on those days that aren't frantically busy. When it's slow, I can sit and look out at the water, the different light and the Lake District in the background. Happiness comes in the accumulation of little things – a nice hot bath or spending time with my godsons. Toppings make people happy. Children love to add toppings. Some people charge extra for them. Charging for toppings means you must be in a sorry state of affairs.

Ice cream is a good indicator of happiness. You know when it's made children happy. It's dribbling down their chins. (226 words)

The Guardian, 7 June 2008

*Morecambe = a seaside town in NW England

3 MEDIATION ENGLISH-GERMAN

> Skills p. 178

Beantworten Sie die folgenden Fragen stichwortartig auf Deutsch.

1 Welche Gründe hatte Kate, in den Badeort Morecambe zu ziehen?
2 Was meint Kate mit „when it's slow" (ll. 14–15)?
3 Welche Dinge tragen dazu bei, dass Kate glücklich ist? (*3 Aspekte*)
4 Was meint Kate mit dem Ausdruck „in a sorry state of affairs" (l. 21)?
5 Woran erkennt Kate, dass die Kinder glücklich sind?

4 WORKING WITH WORDS

> Skills p. 172–174

Rewrite the following sentences so that their meaning doesn't change. Use phrases from the text to replace the underlined parts.

1 Many people find it difficult to remember what ice cream <u>tasted like in former times</u>.
Many people can't remember what the taste of ice cream ... .
2 <u>They are attracted by what they remember of</u> past holidays at the seaside.
For them, the ... of past holidays at the seaside.
3 Kate <u>can easily see when</u> ice cream <u>makes a person feel good</u>. *For Kate ice cream is ... .*
4 In Kate's view, <u>lots of everyday things</u> contribute to her happiness.
According to Kate, ... makes her feel happy.

Fiona Dear, climate change campaigner

It's easy to be happy when you're younger. You're not as bothered by issues such as this. I'm pretty happy now, although I can feel the effects of climate change around me. I trained as an ecologist and for years worked on scarlet macaw* conservation in Costa Rica. Climate change was becoming an issue for parrots, with the wet winters affecting breeding habits.

I lived relatively simply in Costa Rica and I'm trying to be green in the UK, but I do consume more. There's a lot of focus put on changing our lifestyles. A change of behaviour can make people happy, but they must be given incentives. Bus and train fares? Still horrendous. I'm getting better at accepting the bad news and not letting it make me unhappy. You'll hear about some company getting their wicked way despite going against the general consensus of the people, but any hopelessness is balanced by knowing I'm doing what I can.

Happiness doesn't seem to be related to the GDP or to consuming more. People living simpler lives get on with it. It's less complicated. I'm happy being surrounded by people I trust and love: my sisters, my family. To have fun but not feel as if you're letting go of your principles – that's happiness. (213 words)

The Guardian, 26 April 2008

*scarlet macaw = name of a bird

5 GAPPED SUMMARY

> Skills p. 177

Fill in the missing words from the text. Use one word only for each gap.

Fiona, a professional ...[1] who worked in Costa Rica with parrots for a while, is more ...[2] by climate change now than she used to be. She has seen the impact climate change has had on the ...[3] ...[4] of birds. Fiona believes that people won't change their lifestyle unless they get the right ...[5]. Now that she is back in Britain, she has changed her lifestyle, but she thinks it is slightly worse because she has taken to ...[6] more. However, she admits that this probably has nothing to do with being happy. There has been another change in her life: she has learned to accept defeat without getting depressed. Enjoying her family and sticking to her ...[7], those are the things that really make her feel happy.

6 WORKING WITH WORDS

> Skills p. 172–174

With words from the text match these definitions?

1 to be worried, to be concerned
2 an important topic that people are discussing or arguing about or a problem/ worry that somebody has with something
3 a scientist who studies the relations of plants and living creatures to each other and to their environment
4 protection of the natural environment
5 to use something, especially fuel, energy, clothes or food
6 the money you pay to go by bus, taxi, etc.
7 an opinion that all members of a group agree with
8 connected with sb./sth. in some way

7 TALKING

Discuss which of the three people in the texts on pages 7–9 is the happiest. Is that the same person you chose at the beginning? If not, what made you change your decision?

B Are we becoming happier?

BEFORE YOU READ

Match the words/expressions (1–10) with the correct synonyms and paraphrases (a–j).

1	bliss	**a**	trying to achieve sth.
2	crammed with sth.	**b**	the well-being of people
3	paraphernalia	**c**	the act of buying and using products
4	affluence	**d**	subdued
5	consumption	**e**	saying
6	muted	**f**	prosperity
7	welfare	**g**	personal possessions or equipment needed for an activity
8	striving	**h**	happiness
9	elaborate	**i**	full of sth.
10	adage	**j**	detailed and well-prepared

THE BLISS WE CAN'T BUY

A In 1974, economist Richard Easterlin pointed out that beyond a certain point – presumably when people's basic needs for food, shelter, public order and work are met – greater wealth does not generate more national happiness. The America of 2007 is far richer than the America of 1977. Life expectancy is 78 years, up from 74 years. Our homes are bigger and crammed with more paraphernalia (microwave ovens, personal computers, flat-panel TVs). But happiness is stuck. In 1977, 35.7 percent of Americans rated themselves "very happy," 53.2 percent "pretty happy" and 11 percent "not too happy," reports the National Opinion Research Center at the University of Chicago. In 2006, the figures are similar: 32.4 percent "very happy," 55.9 percent "pretty happy" and 11.7 percent "not too happy." Likewise, in most advanced countries, self-reported happiness has been flat for decades.

B Hordes of scholars are asking why. Economist Robert H. Franks argues that rising affluence condemns us to self-defeating consumption contests. People want ever-bigger homes, because their friends have ever-bigger homes. But the extra pleasure of owning these grander homes is muted, because (yes) all our friends have them, too. Meanwhile, the added debt to buy the house may make us more anxious; and we may regret sacrificing some leisure – working harder to buy the bigger home.

Greater individual wealth does not bring greater collective welfare. Moving farther out into suburbia for a bigger home increases traffic congestion and our commutes. Roads grow more clogged, pollution worsens. We engage in "behaviors that are smart for one, dumb for all," Franks claims.

C The psychology of prosperity – striving, taking risks – feeds on ambition and insecurity. Our system often seems an insane rat race. But over time, it has created huge gains in material well-being. Air conditioning may not have made people in the South and elsewhere happier. But it surely has made them more comfortable.

D True, there's an economic disconnect today. Despite obvious prosperity, including 8 million new jobs since mid-2003, consumer confidence is subdued. But the explanation, I think, lies neither in Franks' elaborate theory nor in several popular culprits – higher gasoline prices and the housing slump. Instead, I'd cite two underlying causes.

E First, economic insecurity has increased. Companies are quicker to fire. Median job tenure for men aged 45 to 54 dropped from about 13 years in 1983 to eight years in 2006, reports economist Rob Valletta of the San Francisco Fed. People have more cause to worry – and they do. Second, Americans compare the present with the immediate past. The economic boom of the late 1990s conditioned people to expect a blissful future. Clearly, that hasn't arrived. People are disappointed because reality doesn't match the promise.

F Still, even the 1990s economic boom didn't produce a happiness boom; the survey figures barely budged. Nor has the growing income inequality since the 1970s produced an unhappiness boom. Between the richest and poorest Americans, happiness gaps have always been large. But income differences in the middle class involve modest or nonexistent differences in happiness. The old adage is true: money can't buy happiness.

G We ultimately get satisfaction from our relations with family and friends, the love we give or receive, the meaning we find in work, service, religion or hobbies. The strongest survey finding is that married people are happier than singles, particularly widowers and divorcees, says Tom Smith of the National Opinion Research Center. An estimated 42.5 percent of married couples say they are "very happy," compared with 18 percent of the divorced.

H The popularity of happiness research suggests that economists and other social scientists think they can devise public policies to elevate the nation's feel-good quotient. This is an illusion. Happiness depends heavily on individual character and national culture. Some people will complain no matter how great their fortune; others will smile through the worst of times. In international comparisons, the United States ranks lower in happiness than some smaller nations (Denmark, Ireland, Sweden) but much higher than many large countries with paternalistic welfare states (France, Germany, Italy). Governments can provide health care. But they cannot outlaw despair or mandate euphoria. It is novelists and philosophers, not social scientists, who provide a deeper understanding of happiness. For better or worse, there are limits to re-engineering the human spirit. (704 words)

Newsweek, July 2007

1 SHORT-ANSWER QUESTIONS / SENTENCE COMPLETION > Skills p. 178

Answer the questions or complete the sentences with information from paragraphs A and B of the text.

1 Once their bare necessities are satisfied, people don't become happier despite enjoying even ... .
2 The results of surveys done in the USA in 1977 and in 2007 show that Americans have become more prosperous and that ... has increased.
3 A comparison of happiness levels during the same period of time shows that the ... and these findings correspond with the majority of ... .
4 Why don't greater wealth and more purchasing power result in greater happiness in the end? (*3 aspects*)
5 How does Franks' example of the location of our bigger homes explain why it might be "smart for one, dumb for all"? (*3 aspects*)

2 MULTIPLE CHOICE

> Skills p. 176

Choose the most suitable option.

1 When the author calls the American system a "rat race" (paragraph C) he … .
- a refers to the Darwinian idea of the survival of the fittest
- b wants to say that only smart and educated people will succeed
- c disapproves of their tough and competitive way of life
- d refers to the fact that Americans like to gamble

2 Which of the following reasons for the discrepancy between wealthier but less confident consumers is not mentioned in paragraph D?
- a the wish to keep up with the Joneses
- b declining American bank accounts
- c more expensive petrol and diesel
- d plummeting real estate prices

3 Which reason does the author give in paragraph E for the missing consumer confidence?
- a the fear of being made redundant
- b the fact that the promise came true
- c people have always been anxious about the future
- d the fact that older males are fired more easily

4 According to paragraph F, the real relationship between happiness and money is … .
- a not apparent
- b unproven
- c doubtful
- d pretty clear

5 According to paragraph G, happiness is most closely related to … .
- a marital status
- b emotions
- c job satisfaction
- d gender

6 The belief that experts can think up steps to boost happiness levels is … .
- a inspiring
- b misleading
- c promising
- d universal

7 With regard to happiness, the USA is … .
- a on the same level as Germany
- b on the same level as Denmark
- c on a lower level than Sweden
- d on a lower level than France

8 When the author says governments cannot "mandate euphoria" (l. 90) he wants to say that … .
- a they weren't elected to feel happy
- b governments are never happy
- c they can't pass laws to make us feel happy
- d they pass laws to make us happy

3 WORKING WITH WORDS

> Skills p. 175

A Which word from the text completes each group of collocations?

1	to prove a …	to get to the …	beside the …	up to a certain …
2	a beauty …	to enter/win/ lose a …	a … for the leadership of a party	to be no …
3	to be in sb.'s …	to pay off a …	to get into …	to stay out of …
4	to take sb. into your …	to gain/lose …	a lack of …	to have … in sb./sth.
5	to keep/make/a …	to show great …	to be full of …	to break a …

B Rewrite the following sentences so that their meanings don't change. Use phrases from the text to replace the underlined parts. You may have to adapt them to fit.

1 The results of many surveys show that people don't feel happier. Their mood stays more or less the same.
According to some surveys, people's ... at the same level.

2 There are plenty of scientists who have worked on the issue of happiness.
... have worked on the issue of happiness.

3 It is true that in the last two decades most people have become richer.
It is true that the last two decades have brought ... .

4 A scientist found that people act in ways that are pretty strange.
According to one scientist, people ... that are pretty strange.

5 Americans sometimes feel deeply worried because they desire new things.
Their desire for new things sometimes ... .

6 Although it is plain to see that people have become richer, they still complain.
People still complain ... .

7 Americans feel less and less sure that their income will rise.
... among Americans.

8 Unfortunately, governments can't order people to be in high spirits.
Unfortunately, governments can't ... .

4 PROJECT

> Skills p. 190

You and your friends want to join an organization that offers a convincing way of making the world a better place. You have the following organizations in mind:

- > Amnesty International
- > Greenpeace or Friends of the Earth
- > Oxfam
- > Attac
- > Médecins sans frontières

Split into five groups. Each group collects information on one of the organizations listed above. Prepare a fact sheet on 'your' organization which gives a comprehensive but not too detailed overview (who they are, members, activities, successes, etc). Present your fact sheet (PowerPoint presentation; don't forget to properly visualize your findings) to the class.

5 GROUP DISCUSSION

> Skills p. 187

Work in groups of five, so that each member of the group has information on a different organization from exercise 4.

Phase 1: individual (= one-minute speech)
Although your organization has already been presented to the class, just focus in your one-minute speech on the most important facts.

Phase 2: interactive (= group discussion)
Exchange arguments. On the basis of your fact sheet, try to convince your friends that your organization is the most attractive one to join. Try to win them over but also be ready to compromise. In the end, decide which organization you will join and choose a runner-up.

C Words in context

Defining happiness

What is happiness? Which people, things or events in our lives make the heart sing or send us to seventh heaven? Or, in scientific terms, which factors provide the basis for our "subjective well-being"? Unfortunately, there doesn't seem to be one common denominator for what makes us feel good. Happiness simply means different things to different people. For some people, bliss is a sunny autumn day or a coffee with a good friend, while other people get ecstatic about a shining SUV or a brand new coffee maker.

Pop groups, politicians and psychologists all agree that money can't buy you happiness, although many people would argue that some additional cash can add a little extra joy to our lives and create some short-term satisfaction. However, happiness is a state that is measured over years or decades rather than in hours or days; it is a fundamental emotional state rather than a temporary emotional high. When the pendulum of our emotions swings from ecstasy to depression, as it does in everybody's life at some stage, the norm, the default setting as it were, is our basic level of contentment.

It is generally agreed that a sense of contentment comes from a few common aspects in our lives: a stable relationship, family and friends, good health and perhaps a fulfilling job. Other individual factors can be added to this equation: financial success or spiritual wellbeing, interesting hobbies or an active lifestyle. However, happiness can also be enhanced by simple everyday pleasures: meeting with friends, spending time with one's family, enjoying good food, keeping fit or avoiding stress.

But happiness is not a static state. Even the most cheerful and light-hearted person feels blue, downcast or miserable at times. Studies show that traumatic events, such as the death of a loved one, the loss of a job or serious illness, can cause even the most contented person to fall into a state of gloom or despair. For many people, a feeling of happiness is connected to accepting things as they are, having peace of mind and not worrying too much. One interviewee says he feels content "when I am OK inside about where I am and who I am". Discontent on the other hand occurs when our expectations haven't been met or we are at odds with ourselves. However, by changing our perspective we can often affect our level of contentment. Scientists claim you can raise your spirits by doing exercises, such as writing down three things that went well and why. There is some proof that this makes people less depressed or dispirited. Or as the old saying goes: "Change what you can, accept what you cannot and have the wisdom to know the difference". (455 words)

First of all, make sure you understand the meaning of each of the highlighted words or phrases used in the text above. If you are not sure, look them up in your dictionary. Then complete the tasks on page 15.

1 WORDFIELDS

> Skills p. 176

A **Copy the table. List all the highlighted words in the text which belong to the wordfields "happy/happiness" and "unhappy/unhappiness". One example is given for each.**

Wordfield	
"happy/happiness"	*"unhappy/unhappiness"*
happiness, ...	*depression, ...*

B **Add as many other words or phrases as you can to the table.**

2 IDIOMS

A **Add the following idioms to the "happy" or "unhappy" columns in your table.**

1 to have a face like a wet weekend
2 to be down in the dumps
3 to be/feel on top of the world
4 to be over the moon
5 one's heart sinks
6 to be on cloud nine
7 to feel let down
8 to be thrilled to bits

B **Work with a partner: how could you say these idioms in German?**

C **Add more words/phrases of your own to your list.**

3 WORD FORMATION

> Skills p. 173

Use a member of the word family of the word in brackets to complete the gap.

For some people, a small everyday ...[1] (please) can provide an almost ...[2] (spirit) sense of well-being. However, when it comes to ...[3] (happy), most people rank their partners, their family and friends and their job ...[4] (satisfy) at the top of their list of the most important factors. The ...[5] (die) of a loved one or the ...[6] (loose) of a job are considered to be two major causes of ...[7] (depressed). However, no-one expects to be ...[8] (cheer) every day of their lives and we can experience ...[9] (feel) of extreme ...[10] (ecstatic) and strong ...[11] (discontent) in quick succession. This ...[12] (emotion) pendulum is completely normal and doesn't say anything about our basic state of ...[13] (content).

4 COLLOCATIONS

> Skills p. 175

A **Find the English equivalents of these German expressions in the text.**

1 gemeinsamer Nenner
2 Grad der Zufriedenheit
3 alltägliche Freuden
4 innerer Friede
5 Erwartungen erfüllen
6 mit sich selbst uneins sein

B **Match the verbs on the left with the words and phrases on the right to make collocations. Sometimes more than one answer is possible.**

feel | experience | get | have | make sb. | raise | suffer from

content | contentment | depressed | depression | ecstatic | happiness | happy | peace of mind | sb.'s spirits

D Further activities

1 LISTENING

> Skills p. 179

You are going to hear a former Asia correspondent for National Public Radio talk about how China can become happier.

1 3 **A Listen once and say whether these statements are true or false.**

1 Eric Weiner has written a book about happiness in China.
2 Weiner has travelled a lot to find out about the happiest country.
3 Weiner gives advice to China about how it can become happier.
4 Weiner criticizes Chinese policies.
5 Weiner lists examples of happy countries.
6 All the happy countries are in Europe.

1 3 **B Listen to the podcast again. Copy and complete the table with the correct information.**

	Weiner's recommendations	Proof that they work
1	Lower	... shows that this works.
2	Cultivate	Psychologists have found that happiness comes when you believe in ... , ... and ... .
3	Embrace	... has successfully done so after its ... and ... problems.
4	Make happiness	... has a policy of Gross National Happiness. The first question the government there asks itself is "Will it ... ?"
5	Don't ... too much.	Happiness is a ... of a life lived well.

2 DESCRIPTIVE WRITING

> Skills pp. 183–186

A Describing photos: Describe what you see in the photo. Write about 80 words.

> Webcode: FOSEAU0101

B Interpreting statistics: Describe and analyse this bar chart. Write about 100 words.

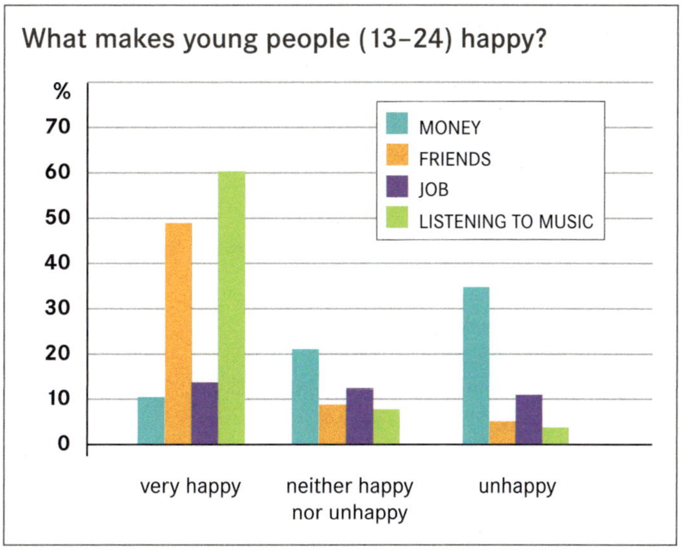

C Interpreting cartoons: Describe and interpret the cartoon on the right. Write about 100 words.

3 ARGUMENTATIVE WRITING

Choose one of the following topics and write at least 200 words. > Skills p. 181

1 Do you agree with the saying "Money can't buy you happiness"?

2 "The grand essentials of happiness are: something to do, something to love and something to hope for." (Allan K. Chalmers). Do you agree? Give reasons for your opinion.

4 GROUP DISCUSSION > Skills p. 187

Work in groups of four or five students.

You are members of the editorial staff of your school newspaper. You want to publish a special issue on "Happiness" as you have noticed that many students seem to be worried or preoccupied. In preparation for the staff meeting everyone has to present ideas on how to lead a happier life. You and your team members then have to decide which of the ideas you are going to publish.

Turn to File 1 on page 158 for some ideas.

Phase 1: individual (= one-minute speech)
First, describe your idea to the rest of the group. In about one minute, explain why you think your idea is the best and therefore worth publishing.

Phase 2: interactive (= group discussion)
Discuss the various possibilities and try to convince the others that your choice is the best one. If you think other suggestions are better, be ready to make a compromise.

E Grammar check

SIMPLE PRESENT – PRESENT PROGRESSIVE

> Grammar summary p. 193

SPOT THE MISTAKES

Spot the mistakes and correct them. Explain why they are wrong.

1 ~~In the photo a boy digs a hole in the garden.~~
2 ~~Is the pie tasting good?~~
3 ~~John always go to work by bus.~~
4 ~~Hi, Jill. What do you do at the moment?~~
5 ~~Joe is having a house in Bristol.~~

A Complete the sentences using the *simple present* or the *present progressive*.

1 Jackie is American. She ... (work) for an IT company and ... (live) in Silicon Valley.
2 Look, Sally ... (leave) her parents' house to go to work.
3 Brian usually ... (study) hard, but at the moment he ... (play) an online game.
4 I ... (be) sure he ... (enjoy) his holiday in the USA.
5 Mary and her mother ... (live) in Cornwall, but this week they ... (stay) in London with her sister.
6 They often ... (play) soccer, but right now they ... (work) on a physics project.

B Read the following cartoon description and decide which is correct: the *simple present* or the *present progressive*.

The cartoon shows / is showing [1] a couple in the wilderness. The location is / is being [2] a river valley, framed left and right by a forest with a mountain range in the background. A man blows / is blowing [3] up a mattress. He sits / is sitting [4] among lots of other inflated items. He looks / is looking [5] furious. The various items show / are showing [6] that he has already spent some time blowing things up. His wife sits / is sitting [7] behind him and she looks / is looking [8] at him. Judging by her expression, she appears / is appearing [9] to be really annoyed. Maybe she was expecting a more romantic holiday. In my opinion, the message of the cartoon is that many people just don't want / aren't wanting [10] to do without the comforts they are used to.

WATCH OUT!

> Grammar summary p. 203

Position of adverbs

Happy people ~~live often~~ in sunny states. → *Happy people often live in sunny states.*
Children ate lots of ice cream ~~last summer at the seaside~~. → *Children ate lots of ice cream at the seaside last summer.*
~~He has been never to London.~~ → *He has never been to London.*

C Put the words in the correct order to make sentences. You may have to change the verb if necessary.

1 look at / at the moment / Mary / some photos
2 happy / money / people / rarely / make
3 in London / find / last year / Nick / happiness
4 some people / in their life / find / never / happiness
5 matter / all over the world / really / friends / to people

2 Travelling the world

FOCUS

QUESTIONNAIRE

What type of traveller are you: an armchair traveller, a luxury tourist or an independent explorer? Answer this questionnaire to find out.

1 If your luggage doesn't arrive on the conveyor belt at the airport, your first reaction is to … .

- **a** cry and book the next flight home
- **b** report the missing bags to the airline and then cry
- **c** report the missing bags and then think how long you can survive without clean clothes and a toothbrush

2 Your idea of a perfect guidebook is … .

- **a** *The Lonely Planet*
- **b** the napkin on which you wrote a hot tip from a local in a restaurant
- **c** a thick volume that contains all the information experts think you should know about your destination

3 Your ideal meal on holiday is … .

- **a** sitting on the floor of a local's house, sharing homemade specialities
- **b** dining in a Michelin-rated restaurant
- **c** enjoying all the comforts of home in an international chain restaurant

4 To get around in a new foreign city you … .

- **a** hire a private driver
- **b** save shoe leather and take a taxi everywhere
- **c** walk yourself to exhaustion

5 You have got lost in a foreign city. You decide to find … .

- **a** the nearest police station
- **b** the nearest bar
- **c** the nearest hotel, check in and wait for daylight

6 When choosing a hotel for your holiday, your most important criterion is … .

- **a** what category it is (one star, two stars, etc.)
- **b** its designer furniture and luxury bath products
- **c** the atmosphere

7 When you are packing, you always include … .

- **a** a good book
- **b** a hair dryer
- **c** an emergency solar-powered radio

8 When you get back from travelling, the first thing you do is … .

- **a** start planning the next trip
- **b** post hundreds of holiday photos on Facebook
- **c** the laundry

Turn to File 2 on page 159 to find out what type of traveller you are.

A Four holiday destinations

BEFORE YOU READ

The following four short texts are about unusual holiday destinations and activities. What exotic or unusual holiday would you like to try?

1

Thailand's coast struggles to balance development with sustainability

The islands that dot Thailand's Andaman coast are renowned for their pristine beaches and turquoise sea. But many of these once untouched shorelines are now littered with garbage and sewage, as the drive to increase tourism has led to rapid and reckless expansion. Now, more locals are hoping to lead the way in preserving unspoiled areas with sustainable development.

Koh Lipe, one of the southernmost islands on the brink of a tourism boom, is currently struggling with questions of how to preserve its delicate ecosystem. Despite being relatively remote, the quiet island has seen a dramatic increase in visitors over the past five years. Anucha Sarthong-in, owner of the eco-friendly Bila Beach Resort, says foreigners are acquiring much of the land to build large resorts with seemingly little concern for the environmental consequences.

Mr Anucha built his resort's bungalows using bamboo he imported from a relative's farm in Malaysia. Completed in 2009, the resort occupies a little under an acre of land with three private bungalows and one dorm-style room. Bila was constructed on a secluded beach and its bungalows are nestled into the jungle's sloping hills. Water conservation is taken seriously; waste-treatment facilities prevent sewage from draining into the ocean. Anucha hopes that more foresight will go into the island's planning so that more locals will be able to hold on to their land and preserve what is left of their natural resources. (234 words)

Adapted from *www.csmonitor.com*

2

CSN: Fiji's Newest Grassroots Voluntourism Program on Garden Island

Community Support Network (CSN) is Fiji's newest non-profit "voluntourism" organization offering a two-week volunteer program on Fiji's untouched Northern Islands. This off-the-beaten-track experience prides itself on being an authentic cultural immersion program and puts a wholesome 80% back into the island communities in the form of training, equipment, infrastructure and education.

Says Jenni, their first volunteer and Assistant Manager in the hospitality industry, from the UK: "Taveuni is a stunning island. CSN really helps to unlock its little secrets whilst you get to relax as everything is organized for you, safe in the knowledge that your money is going back to support the community."

The major priority for CSN is to ensure volunteers are interested in both the conservation element of the program - in this case replanting coral reefs that were destroyed by cyclone Tomas - and the importance of understanding village life, respecting its rules and values and being aware of the difference between western behaviour and traditional island lifestyles. (160 words)

Adapted from *www.muchbetteradventures.com*

3

UNSEEN TOURS: UNCONVENTIONAL SOCIAL ENTERPRISE ON LONDON'S LIVING STREETS

We met Viv, a loud and friendly tour guide, and a little bit rough around the edges, right across from the Temple tube station, just along the River Thames. We handed over our time, trust and £5. And off we went, from our starting point at the park in front of the tube station. To visitors, it is a pretty – if average – park. To Viv, it was home. Literally.

She slept on top of crates under a tarp in the park for over a year. We had gathered, essentially, in her former living room, to begin an Unseen Tour. Unseen Tours was created by Sock Mob, an informal volunteer group that reaches out to London's homeless with friendship and socks.

"We wanted to incorporate our homeless friends' stories as well as offer a way for them to engage with the public, and quickly the idea of a walking tour came about," said Tisha Brown, Temple Tour Coordinator with Unseen Tours. "After all, who knows the streets of London better than the homeless? Homeless people have a wealth of knowledge and stories that they are willing to share with people, and Unseen Tours gives them a chance to do this," said Brown. "The tours are a creative outlet and a source of income for the homeless guides. They are able to engage with other members of society without being stigmatized. They also start to look at themselves differently and begin to take steps to change their lives," explained Brown.

Taking such a tour is a way to give back to the city you are visiting and make a positive impression instead of simply being a tourist. You finish the tour feeling like you have made a new friend. What to do in London with a new friend? Of course, do as the British do and buy them a pint at the pub. (311 words)

Adapted from *http://www.yourtravelchoice.org/2011/05/unseen-tours-londons-living-streets/*

4

Yurt to Yurt Travel with Mongolian Nomads

Yurts are all the rage these days, with posh camping ("glamping") sites springing up all over Europe. You are probably familiar by now with the yurt concept – rounded wooden structures, canvas covered, comfortable, spacious, more like a home than a tent. Mongolian yurts evolved as the home of choice for the nomads of Central Asia. Now you can experience them for yourself. An innovative foundation called Ger to Ger (or "Yurt to Yurt") is working with nomadic families to invite adventurous souls to discover their world.

They work with dozens of Mongolian nomadic herder groups and their communities and have developed a travel network of nomadic trekking, horse riding and 4 × 4 routes through the Mongolian steppe, taking you literally from Ger to Ger, staying with host families and sharing their way of life. It's possibly as close as the modern adventure traveller will get to understanding life as a nomad.

Through tourism incomes, the foundation says that rural nomadic herder groups and their communities are developing an understanding that they are custodians of nomadic culture and heritage, and guardians of the local environment (as it becomes an income asset). The results are certainly tangible. One nomadic herder's testimony mirrors that of many others: "Our household income has increased. So now, I can pay my daughter's tuition." (216 words)

Adapted from *http://www.muchbetteradventures.com/news/view/136/yurt-to-yurt-travel-with-mongolian-nomads*

1 LOOKING AT THE TEXTS

> Skills p. 170

A You are planning your holiday for next year. Skim the four texts on pages 20–21 and decide which one(s) you should choose if you … .

1 don't want to talk to anyone and just want to read a good book
2 don't want to stay in one place but prefer to see as much of the country as possible
3 are travelling with your mother, who likes to combine culture with shopping
4 prefer hands-on holidays helping other people
5 want to get as far away from your normal life as possible
6 are unable to do without a few modern comforts
7 want the money you spend to really be put back into the local community
8 want to get to know a popular tourist destination from an unusual perspective

B Share your choices with a partner. Be prepared to justify your answers.

2 SHORT-ANSWER QUESTIONS / SENTENCE COMPLETION

> Skills p. 178

Answer the questions or complete the sentences with information from text 1.

1 The result of Thailand's efforts to attract more tourists is … . The islands' once pristine shores are now … .
2 Which major issue is Koh Lipe trying to deal with?
3 Mr Anucha's main complaint about foreign investors on his island is that … .
4 What three measures did he take to ensure that his resort is environmentally friendly?

3 MULTIPLE CHOICE

> Skills p. 176

Choose the most suitable option (text 3).

1 Viv, the tour guide … .
  a is an elderly, elegantly-dressed local guide who knows everything about London
  b is an eloquent Londoner who can talk for hours about her city
  c does not have very good manners
  d is a homeless person that calls Temple Park her home

2 Sock Mob is a … .
  a non-government organization that provides socks and food for poor people
  b group of volunteers who want to help people who are down on their luck to improve their lives
  c travel agency that employs homeless people as tour guides
  d charity that provides temporary accommodation for homeless people

4 MEDIATION ENGLISH-GERMAN

> Skills p. 178

Beantworten Sie diese Fragen zu den Texten 2, 3 und 4 stichwortartig auf Deutsch.

1 Erklären Sie, was der Autor mit der Aussage „We handed over our time, trust and £5" meint.
2 Welche Bedeutung hat die Jurte für die mongolischen Nomaden?
3 Welche Gemeinsamkeiten gibt es zwischen den von „Ger to Ger" und „CSN" angebotenen Reisen?
4 Inwiefern glauben beide Veranstalter, dass ihre Angebote der jeweiligen Kultur zu Gute kommen?

5 WORKING WITH WORDS

A Match the words (1–10) from the texts with the correct definitions (a–j).

1 remote
2 concern
3 secluded
4 reckless
5 trust
6 posh
7 tangible
8 rage
9 guardian
10 conservation

a the preservation and careful management of the environment and of natural resources
b ignoring the danger or consequences of an action
c inaccessible and sparsely populated
d sth. that interests you because it is important or affects you
e providing privacy; hidden from general view or use
f capable of being perceived by the senses or the mind
g sth. that is desired intensely
h sb. who watches over or protects sth.
i the trait of believing in the honesty and reliability of others
j elegant and fashionable

B Which of the words in A correspond to these synonyms?

1 foolhardy, heady, rash, heedless
2 real
3 distant, removed
4 fad, craze
5 worry, care
6 preservation
7 reclusive, secret
8 defender, protector

C Write an example sentence for each of the words in A, clearly showing its meaning. Use a dictionary to check.

6 TALKING

Discuss these questions with a partner. Be prepared to justify your answers.

1 What are the good and the bad things about travelling?
2 Is it important for young people to visit other countries?
3 What would make you wiser – travelling around the world for a year or reading 100 books?

B Words in context

1 4

The tourist industry

Tourism is one of the largest business sectors in the world economy. It employs more than 250 million people and is responsible for 8.8% of Gross Domestic Product (GDP) worldwide. In 1950, 25 million people worldwide went abroad on holiday; in 2010, 15 million Britons alone booked a package holiday – and this figure does not include the three or so million individual tourists who didn't use a travel agency and booked their self-catering holiday apartments in the Algarve or in Tuscany by themselves.

Tourism has a long history. Two thousand years ago, rich Romans fled the hot summers in their city and flocked to beachside resorts in the Gulf of Naples. However, it was the advent of affordable transportation that laid the foundation for mass tourism, thus making it possible for the average citizen to book cheap holidays and bring back overpriced souvenirs. Mass tourism, however, has come under heavy criticism. Summer holidays are now associated with crowded beaches, congested airports and heavy traffic jams along Europe's major highways.

Overcrowding, pollution, the loss of genuine culture and unsightly hotel developments that destroy valuable ecosystems are the main criticisms. Many tourists never leave their hotel complexes while they are enjoying their all-inclusive holidays and most of the money they spend doesn't benefit the locals but goes to foreign investors or tour operators. Many tourism jobs are seasonal and held by immigrants working for minimal wages. The fact that tourists need massive amounts of water can add to water shortages for the local population.

On the other hand, tourism can be seen as an engine for economic growth and a means to reduce poverty. For the world's 40 poorest countries, it is the second most important source of foreign exchange earnings, after oil, and one of the few economic sectors able to help them rise above their least-developed country status.

Thus, tourism is a two-edged sword: mass tourism that is ill-conceived has a number of negative consequences, but on the other hand, it can create jobs and encourage the economy in areas that are underdeveloped. Responsible and sustainable tourism, otherwise known as ecotourism, seems to be the answer. But what exactly is ecotourism? The International Ecotourism Society defines it as "responsible travel to natural areas that conserves the environment and improves the well-being of local people". This means that minimizing tourists' impact on the environment (e.g. by saving both water and energy) is an integral part of eco-tourism, as is respect for local cultures.

True eco-travellers, therefore, will look for accommodation in the homes of local inhabitants. They will avoid air transport as, for example, two flights from Frankfurt to South Africa release the equivalent of around six tonnes of CO_2, which is as much as the average German home emits annually. Instead, they will travel on foot, by boat, bicycle or train.

Numerous niche markets have emerged over the years, from adventure travel and backpacking holidays to wildlife tourism or "voluntourism" – there's something for every taste and budget. But no matter what kind of tourist we are, it seems that in the interest of future generations, everyone should be a responsible traveller and help keep the extent of the damage done to our environment as low as possible, regardless of whether we go camping or sightseeing, stay in a luxury hotel or in a youth hostel.

(559 words)

First of all, make sure you understand the meaning of each of the highlighted phrases used in the text on page 24. If you are not sure, look them up in your dictionary. Then complete the tasks below.

1 WORDFIELDS

> Skills p. 176

A **Which different types of tourism are mentioned in the text? Make a list. Add as many more types as you can to the list.**

B **Define "mass tourism" in your own words.**

C **Make a list of all the pros and cons of mass tourism mentioned in the text. Add more arguments to the list.**

Mass tourism	
Pros	*Cons*
...	...

2 COLLOCATIONS

> Skills p. 175

Add nouns to these verbs to make "holiday" collocations:

1 to go ...
2 to travel by ...
3 to travel on ...
4 to book a ...
5 to stay in a ...

> Webcode: FOSEAU0201

3 WORD FORMATION

> Skills p. 173

A **Copy this grid into your exercise book and complete it. Use your dictionary if necessary.**

Noun (person)	*Noun (abstract)*	*Verb*	*Adjective*	*Adverb*
... / ...	... / ...	...	*individual* / ...	...
...	*criticism*	...	...	...
...	...	*associate*	...	———
———	...	*dismiss*	...	...
...	*exploitation*	...	...	———
...	...	...	*economic* / ...	...
———	...	...	*sustainable* / ...	...
———	*definition*	...	... / ...	...

B **Complete this text with words from 3A.**

Mass tourism is seen very ...[1] by many people because of its ...[2] with crowded beaches and congested airports. On the other hand, ...[3] tourism has, by ...[4], fewer of the environmental disadvantages of mass tourism and is therefore more environmentally ...[5]. However, eco-travellers who visit exotic destinations need to be careful that they do not ...[6] the local population.

C Tourism and the environment

BEFORE YOU READ

Long-haul flights to exotic holiday destinations add to global warming. Would you be prepared to give up your holiday to save the planet?

SWEDES WEIGH GLOBAL WARMING VERSUS A BETTER TAN

A GOA, India: Like many other Swedish sun worshippers crowding a white-sand beach here on this morning, Elisabet Brandt considers herself to be a good environmentalist. At home in the south Swedish town of Helsingborg, Ms Brandt waits in the sleet and snow for the bus to take her to work, rather than drive. "I don't even own a car," she says with pride.

B Brandt, a nurse, also sorts and recycles her garbage through a program that has made Sweden a leader for converting household waste into bio energy. And she will, of course, never leave her house without first turning off all lamps. Though half of Sweden's power supply comes from hydroelectric plants, a renewable energy source, many consumers still take care not to waste power to keep bills down. All this has helped Brandt and 9 million other Swedes transform their nation into one of the greenest on earth. […]

C Yet for all their geothermally-heated homes and pricey hybrid cars, Swedes have one dirty habit they refuse to give up: long-distance air travel to warmer and sunnier locales. Like the beaches here in India. The dichotomy is raising moral questions for Swedes and practical problems for the rest of the world. Curbing air travel represents one of the next big frontiers in the crusade against global warming. If green-minded Swedes can't be convinced to curb their wanderlust in pursuit of a tan, what hope is there for the rest of us to change deeply ingrained habits?

D "Yes, I've heard about airplanes and their emissions," Brandt concedes from underneath the sun umbrella where she enjoys a novel and a perfect view of the frothy surf. "It's a tough issue. But I can't say I feel bad about being here. I do so much for the environment at home".

E Swedish travel first reached an all-time high in 2007, when more than 1 million people boarded a plane heading for a non-European destination – nearly twice as many as in 2002, and the numbers continue to increase. Significantly, aviation now accounts for 10 percent of the country's greenhouse-gas emissions – and is growing, one recent study showed. The travel fever comes as the European Union looks for ways to curb emissions from the airline industry, the region's fastest-growing source of greenhouse gases. But even the most environmentally conscious will find excuses for behavior that aggravates the climate crisis. Try convincing Americans to give up their SUVs, or Indians their cows. They will present compelling arguments for keeping up habits that generate greenhouse gases. The Swedes are no different. It shows just how difficult it can be to act locally – even when the Earth's future is at stake. […]

F For light-deprived Scandinavians, escaping for a few weeks during the winter is considered a matter of mental survival – an entitlement fueled by rising incomes and a strong economy. The flights Swedes and other Europeans take to developing countries currently generate half of all aviation-based greenhouse-gas emissions in such nations, according to the European Federation for Transport and Environment. This winter, 300,000 Swedes booked flights to Thailand alone.

G Such facts jolt Katarina Eriksson. The hardware store employee just returned from a three-week trip to north-eastern Brazil and says she knows "we're destroying the world." She and her husband travel abroad every fall and spring – usually to Greece – and plan eventually to retire away from the cold climate of Mora, their home town in the middle of Sweden. […] "You think of your kids and grandchildren – what will life be like for them?" Ms Eriksson says. "But I live for these trips. I used to get depressed every fall and winter, and I think our trips really helped me overcome that."

H Like many people in the industrialized world being asked to sacrifice to cool the planet, Swedes hope technology will preserve their tan lines. Eric Persson is a young Swedish-Brazilian entrepreneur who built the hotel where Eriksson and her husband stayed in South America. He's proud of Sweden's environmental reputation. He's considering installing solar panels on his hotel property, and uses a green ionization technology to clean his pool instead of chlorine. "Of course, no matter how you twist and turn this thing – tourism flights hurt the environment," Mr Persson agrees. "But I don't think you can stop it. You can't expect Swedes to stop traveling to the sun. We just have to trust that aviation technology will develop and get cleaner."

I With Spain's sun coast now so expensive that it is out of economic reach for many middle-class families, many Swedes simply take advantage of low-cost destinations such as India, where they can stay for months in cheap guesthouses without defaulting on bills back home.

J Sussi Oskarson and her partner, Jonnie Cronquist, are spending the winter in Goa […]. At their country home south of Stockholm, they're sticklers for recycling and composting their waste.

"What you take from the earth you should return," Mr Cronquist explains over a drink in a beach bar […]. "That's how we renew our world. And at the same time we travel so much," Oskarson adds with a grimace. "It's a paradox, isn't it?"

(853 words)

Adapted from *Christian Science Monitor*, 23 April 2008

1 MULTIPLE CHOICE

> Skills p. 176

Choose the most suitable option.

1 Which of the following is not mentioned in paragraphs A and B?
- a using public transport
- b buying organic food
- c recycling waste
- d saving energy

2 The "dichotomy" (l. 21) refers to the fact that … .
- a Americans don't want to give up their SUVs even though they are gas-guzzling giants
- b Swedes are sun-deprived and therefore travel to sunny destinations in winter
- c Sweden is an environmental role model for other countries but its citizens are not prepared to go without a holiday in the sun
- d Indians want to protect their holy cows no matter what their environmental impact might be

3 Which of the following demands of the European Union is expressly mentioned in the text?
- a stopping the construction of more airports
- b introducing stricter regulations on the release of CO_2 by aircraft
- c making flights more expensive
- d limiting the number of long-distance holiday flights

4 Eric Persson believes that the answer to the problem is to ... .
 a invent "greener" and more efficient airplanes
 b develop new technologies for getting a sun tan
 c invest in renewable sources of energy
 d reduce the number of flights to tourist destinations

5 In general, Swedes feel that they are entitled to their long-distance air travel because they ... .
 a are unable to change deep-rooted practices
 b meet the Kyoto Protocol obligations, unlike other countries
 c earn enough money and their economy is booming
 d do so much for the environment that they can sin in this one respect

6 What is the author's attitude towards Swedish winter travel? He/She ... .
 a doesn't really have anything against it
 b thinks long-distance holiday flights should be banned completely
 c simply reports the dilemma in a neutral way
 d thinks the Swedes are behaving slightly irresponsibly

2 MEDIATION ENGLISH-GERMAN

> Skills p. 178

Übertragen Sie folgende Sätze und Ausdrücke sinngemäß ins Deutsche.

1 Yet for all their geothermally-heated homes and their pricey hybrid cars, Swedes have one dirty habit they refuse to give up: long-distance air travel to warmer and sunnier locales. (ll. 18-21)
2 If green-minded Swedes can't be convinced to curb their wanderlust in pursuit of a tan, what hope is there for the rest of us to change deeply ingrained habits? (ll. 25-27)
3 ... an entitlement fuelled by rising incomes and a strong economy. (ll. 51-52)
4 ... many Swedes simply take advantage of low-cost destinations such as India, where they can stay for months in cheap guesthouses without defaulting on bills back home. (ll. 82-85)

3 TALKING

In groups, discuss the questions below.

1 Do environmental concerns play a role in your travels? Do you sympathize with the Swedes' desire to escape to sunnier places in winter?
2 The author points out that Swedes increasingly choose developing countries for their holidays as they are cheaper than European destinations. What do you think of this development? What advantages/disadvantages does it have?

4 PROJECT

> Skills p. 190

Work in groups of three or four. Write an article about your region for a new guidebook for young tourists.

First, decide which items you want to include in your article (e.g. important sights / pub scene / hiking tours, etc.) and who is going to write about what. Gather the information and write your part of the article which is then reviewed and edited by the other members of your group. In the end, produce the final draft of your article.

D Further activities

1 DESCRIPTIVE WRITING

> Skills pp. 183–186

A Describing cartoons: Describe what you see and interpret the message the cartoonist is trying to make in about 100 words.

"Can you check your records and see if we've been on a cruise to Africa yet?"

B Describing statistics: Look at the information on backpacking tourists in Australia. Complete the gaps in the text below with words from the box or information from the charts.

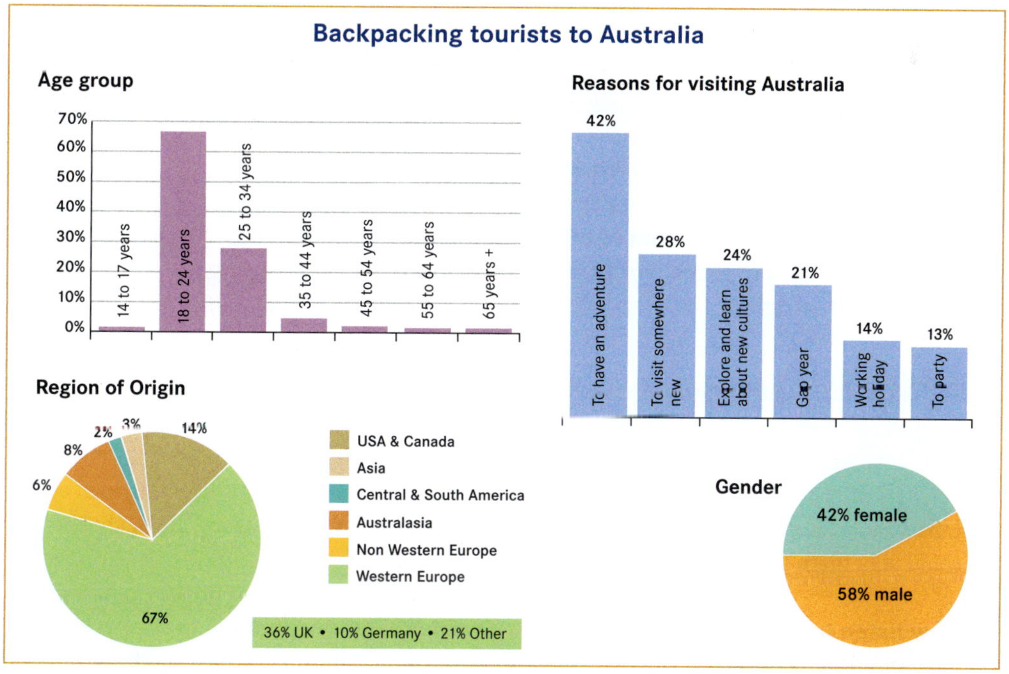

adventure | exploring | largest | majority | minority | more | popular | reasons | roughly | second largest | surprising | visiting

The ...[1] of backpacking tourists in Australia is aged between ...[2] and ...[3] years old as people in the two ...[4] groups make up ...[5] 90% of all the backpacking tourists to Australia. ...[6] backpackers are male (58%) than female. ...%[7] of the tourists come from Western Europe (...%[8] from the UK, ...%[9] from Germany) and the ...[10] group comes from North America (14%). The ...[11] people give for visiting Australia are varied. Having an ...[12] comes in first place (42%), followed by ...[13] somewhere new (...%[14]) and ...[15] new cultures (...%[16]). Only ...%[17] said that they wanted to party. It seems that Australia is a ...[18] destination for many young people, especially from Europe. What I found ...[19] is the fact that they come with such serious goals and that only a ...[20] just wanted a good time.

2 ARGUMENTATIVE WRITING

> Skills p. 181

Choose one of the following topics and write at least 200 words.

1 "Travel helps to promote understanding and communication between countries." Do you agree?
2 Some people like to go on organized trips in a group. Other people prefer to travel alone. Which do you prefer? Give specific reasons and examples to support your choice.

3 LISTENING

> Skills p. 179

A You are going to listen to two friends who want to go on holiday and are leafing through a brochure with some last-minute offers. Complete the gaps with appropriate words or phrases from the box on the right.

Bali ǀ warmer ǀ Nile ǀ almost the same price ǀ Egypt ǀ cruise ǀ golf ǀ bit boring ǀ Sri Lanka ǀ St. Andrews ǀ hot air balloon

The two women don't want to go to ...[1] because they both don't like ...[2] and want to get away from the cold weather to a ...[3] place. The ...[4] from ...[5] to Hobart is out of the question as well, as both don't even know where Hobart is and consider long voyages a ...[6]. So, out of the four offers only two are left: they have to decide between ...[7] and ...[8]. The former includes a ride in a ...[9] over Luxor and a short cruise on the ... [10], the latter has the advantage of being much cheaper - they could stay there for two weeks for ...[11].

B Now listen to the two women again and note down all the phrases that express *agreement, preferences, suggestions* and *rejections*. Compare your results with your partner. Add any to your list that he/she might have found.

4 GROUP DISCUSSION

> Skills p. 187

You are a group of three or four students that want to go on holiday together. Look again at the four destinations on pages 20–21 and allocate one to each student. You have ten minutes in which to prepare a short presentation on "your" destination. You want to persuade the others to join you on "your" trip.

Start with the short presentations, then keep the discussion going for at least 15 minutes or until you come to an agreement. Use the phrases for "agreeing and disagreeing" from exercise 3B.

E Grammar check

FUTURE FORMS

> Grammar summary p. 196

SPOT THE MISTAKES

Spot the mistakes and correct them. Explain why they are wrong.

1 ~~Look at the clouds. It will rain in a minute.~~
2 ~~We buy Viv a pint at the pub after the tour – she's so nice.~~
3 ~~The next ferry to Koh Lipe will leave at 9.25.~~
4 ~~I pack the bags after dinner, so don't bother with them now.~~
5 ~~Tom and Len will leave for Taveuni on Friday.~~

A Read the email and decide if the highlighted verbs have a present or future meaning.

E-MAIL

How are you? I'm[1] fine. Actually, I'm sure that you won't believe[2] me when I tell you that I'm currently waiting[3] in the departure lounge at Ulan-Bator airport, fresh from a Yurt trip in the steppes. I'm heading[4] back home to Bristol in an hour (my plane lands[5] at 6 a.m.) so you'll find[6] me back at my desk the day after tomorrow! I find[7] that somewhat hard to believe at the moment.

Anyway, I'll be[8] back in mobile phone reach again within a few hours. I also wanted to tell you that Karen is coming[9] on Monday. You know, my pen friend from Munich. She's going to do[10] some research at the uni here for a couple of months. When she gets[11] here, I thought we could get together for a ladies' night.

B Look at the various ways of expressing future meaning in the email. Which ones can you find?

C Read this dialogue and say which tense is correct – and why.

JUDITH: I'm really fed up with this winter. I'm starved of sun. I think I'll have / 'm going to have[1] a nervous breakdown. Let's go to Portugal for Christmas!
SIMON: Hold on, dear! Have you forgotten that your cousin comes / is coming[2] in two weeks?
JUDITH: OK, but we could go after that, couldn't we? She leaves / is leaving[3] on the 22nd. I call / 'll call[4] the travel agent now.
SIMON: I think we'll probably get / 're probably going to get[5] cheaper last-minute offers on the Internet ... I don't believe it! The computer has crashed again! I hope the hotline is going to be able / will be able[6] to help me. Sometimes I hate this thing!
JUDITH: Oh, no! That will take / is going to take[7] hours! I'll get / 'm getting[8] my laptop from the office.

WATCH OUT!

Problem words (1)

> False friends p. 267

Ruth was nervous when the plane ~~started off~~. → *Ruth was nervous when the plane took off.*

D Choose the correct word or phrase so that each sentence makes sense.

1 For two days / Two days ago I was really annoyed because I had lost my passport.
2 The latest / last surveys show that some places are being damaged by mass tourism.
3 The travel brochures / prospects always make the hotels sound perfect.
4 Some handys / mobile phones don't work when you are abroad.
5 They were discussing / discussing about where to go on holiday next year.
6 She said she could possibly / eventually go on holiday if she finishes her project on time.

3

Earning a living

FOCUS

The job descriptions below appeared in an American newspaper.

Grooming Salon Associates

As a PetSmart associate, you'll be joining the nation's leading pet retailer. Our vision is to provide Total Lifetime Care for every pet, every parent, every time. We're currently seeking candidates who enjoy working in a team environment.

Our GREAT BENEFITS include:

- Competitive pay
- Comprehensive health plan: medical, dental, vision
- Opportunities for career advancement

Responsibilities include:

- Booking appointments and greeting pets upon check-in
- Answering pet parents' questions and finding solutions for their individual needs
- Bathing, brushing and drying dogs
- Cleaning ears, clipping nails, and performing other necessary services
- Grooming dogs to pet parents' satisfaction
- Being able to work flexible hours (including evenings, weekends, and holidays)

Receptionist / Multiline phone operator – Bilingual (English/Spanish)

Brooklyn-based Ambulatory Surgery Center is seeking a full-time receptionist/switchboard operator for our extremely busy outpatient hospital.

Requirements:

- A minimum of 3 years experience efficiently working in a very high volume front desk, call center, or multi-line telephone system.
- Must be bilingual (English and Spanish).
- Excellent customer service skills, telephone manners/etiquette.
- Fast learner and must be able to work independently as well as in a team environment.
- Must be punctual and reliable.
- Computer skills are a must.
- High school Diploma required; Associate's or Bachelor's degree preferred.

1 **Which of these job descriptions appeals to you? Explain why to a partner.**

2 **Look at the list of requirements for the receptionist's job. Which of them do you consider to be "an absolute must" for every type of job? Explain.**

3 **What other skills do you consider to be important?**

A Going abroad to work

BEFORE YOU READ

Would you like to go abroad to work? What reasons can you think of for going abroad to work? What problems do you think you would face in the new country?

Facing Economic Turmoil at Home, Young Spaniards Flee for Germany

A Even though she's lucky to have a job in Spain, Julia Casado Marco wonders if she should move back to Germany. The young Spaniard studied in Mannheim and worked at a wine merchant's in the southwestern Pfalz region before returning to Spain three years ago. Though she unexpectedly found a job in Murcia in southern Spain, she thinks the real opportunity is in Germany, where the overall economy is much stronger than in her boom-to-bust native country. "Spain and Germany may not be that far apart geographically, but we're very different," she says. "Longer-term, I want to return to Germany." Many Spaniards have stories similar to Marco's. In Spain, even highly-qualified people are having trouble finding jobs. According to Eurostat, Spanish youth unemployment exceeds 40%, the highest on the continent.

B So more and more Spaniards, and other university-educated young people from southern European countries, are seeking jobs abroad. And for them, Germany is a magnet. With a shortage of qualified workers, German economists say that drawing skilled people from other countries is the key to keeping the economy on track. Germany's Federal Employment Agency (BA) expects the number of people of working age in Germany to decrease by 6.5 million by 2025.

C Germany needs 200,000 immigrants a year. By 2030, Germany expects to have a shortfall of more than five million skilled workers, half of them at a university-educated skill level. Even if the country were to succeed in increasing domestic potential, there would still be a gap that can only be filled by skilled workers from abroad. Germany's Federal Employment Agency is thus actively wooing young potential candidates from the European countries hardest hit by the economic crisis: Spain, Greece and Portugal. The German Chamber of Commerce has begun organizing evening informational sessions about emigration in major Spanish cities. Interested Spaniards are told that the average starting salary for an engineer in Germany is 41,000 Euros.

D Some 80% of engineers in Germany have permanent contracts. (In Spain, most people entering the job market are placed by temporary employment agencies and are given six-month contracts). A career start in an engineering firm is recommended in Germany, and candidates don't necessarily have to bring German language skills with them: good English will do. In June, 17,000 Spaniards applied via the European Commission's job exchange program for positions in Germany. In line with that figure, a Goethe Institute spokesperson says demand for German language courses has doubled over the past year.

Job centre in Spain

E Germany is also drawing young applicants from Portugal, Greece, Ireland and some central European countries, but the attraction has been strongest for Spaniards after German Chancellor Angela Merkel, on a visit to Spain in February, extended an invitation to young Spaniards to come and work in Germany because her country had a shortage of highly-qualified, specialized workers.

F Nowadays, in some Berlin neighborhoods, what is striking is how many people can be heard speaking Spanish. Entrepreneur Manuel Wagner noticed that, and, sensing a trend, in March opened a placement agency on Spain's Costa Blanca called World Wide Working that helps prepare for the move to Germany. "A lot of them want to grab a backpack and head north right away. In fact, a lot of them do – and come back, frustrated at not having found a job and not being able to communicate with German people," he says. Proper preparation is key, Wagner says. His agency creates a structured emigration plan for every customer after checking out their CV, professional qualifications, language skills and personal circumstances. Wagner wants to expand his services worldwide, but is presently focusing on Germany because that's where 90% of his customers are going. For the time being, his agency is unique in Spain. He works closely with Eures, the EU Commission's Internet job exchange.

Spanish restaurant in Germany

G For two weeks now, Adrián Lozano Zaplana, 24, has been living in Schömberg, a spa in the Black Forest. Zaplana has a Spanish tourism studies degree, and recently signed a year-long contract with the 3-star Hotel Krone, where he's working in service as his German skills aren't good enough for him to man reception. He's overqualified for the work he's presently doing, but Zaplana takes it in stride. "In Spain, tourism is seasonal. Generally, there are jobs from April to September," he says. The rest of the year, he does temporary work. Whether he'll make it past his three-month trial period on this job, he doesn't yet know. But he's rapidly improving his German skills as he shares an apartment with the hotel's German chef. It helps, he says, that there are "no other Spaniards for miles around." That may be about to change.

(793 words)

Time, 26 July 2011

1 LOOKING AT THE TEXT

Answer these questions with a partner, then report back to the class.

1 Explain what the text is about in four or five sentences.
2 What connection between Spain and Germany is mentioned in the text?
3 How easy/difficult is it for young Spaniards to settle down in Germany?

2 MEDIATION ENGLISH-GERMAN

> Skills p. 178

A Beantworten Sie die folgenden Fragen stichwortartig auf Deutsch.

1 In welchem Dilemma befindet sich Julia Casado Marco?
2 Auf welche Probleme stoßen viele junge Spanier bei der Arbeitsuche in Deutschland und wie könnte man dem entgegen wirken?
3 Warum hätte Adrián Lozano Zaplana eigentlich Grund dazu, mit seiner Beschäftigungssituation unzufrieden zu sein?
4 Warum nimmt er seine Situation dennoch gelassen hin, insbesondere auch, wenn er an die Möglichkeiten, die er in Spanien hätte, denkt?

B Geben Sie den Sinn der folgenden Ausdrücke bzw. Sätze im Textzusammenhang auf Deutsch wieder.

1 boom to bust country (ll. 9–10)
2 Drawing skilled people from other countries is the key to keeping the economy on track. (ll. 23–24)
3 Even if the country were to succeed in increasing domestic potential, ... (ll. 31–33)
4 His German skills aren't good enough for him to man reception. (ll. 90–91)
5 (Zaplana) takes it in stride. (ll. 92–93)
6 That may be about to change. (ll. 100–101)

3 GAPPED SUMMARY

> Skills p. 177

Fill in the missing words from paragraphs B–E. Use one word only for each gap.

These days, many young foreigners are ...[1] employment in Germany which, due to a ...[2] of highly-skilled labour, is concerned about a growing ...[3] between the number of skilled workers available on the German job market and the number needed by German employers. As a result of this worrisome trend, German job centres are now ...[4] qualified applicants from Spain, Portugal and Greece by stressing the fact that the initial ...[5] of a highly-qualified worker in the technical field is considerably higher than that in many other EU countries. A further incentive for young foreigners to look for work in Germany lies in the fact that long-term ...[6] are offered in Germany, whereas in Spain, for example, many of the positions available to young people are only ...[7]. As ...[8] for skilled applicants is currently so great, the German Chancellor recently ...[9] an official invitation to young Spaniards to apply for jobs in Germany.

4 WORKING WITH WORDS

A Find the English equivalents of the following German words in the text.

Heading / paragraphs A & B:
1 ähnlich
2 Chaos
3 konfrontiert sein mit
4 Mangel an
5 sich fragen
6 übersteigen

Paragraphs C, D & E:
1 anwerben
2 Bewerber/in
3 Gehalt
4 inländisch, heimisch, häuslich
5 Kluft, Lücke
6 Nachfrage nach
7 Zeitarbeitsfirma

Paragraphs F & G:
1 (Hochschul-)Abschluss
2 angemessen, richtig, vernünftig
3 einzigartig
4 sich konzentrieren auf
5 (ver)spüren
6 überprüfen

B Which word from the text completes each group of collocations? (They are all from exercise 4A.)

> Skills p. 175

1	... life	... animal	... job market	... flights
2	to be in a ... situation	to have ... tastes in art	students of ... abilities	to attain ... results
3	a high school ...	to be true to a certain ...	the temperature climbed by one ...	the ... to which sb. is responsible
4	a ... experience	to have a ... personality	a ... opportunity	fingerprints are ...
5	the gender ...	to bridge the ...	to close the ...	the generation ...

B Comparing education systems

BEFORE YOU READ

The OECD conducts an international comparison of educational performance every three years, known as PISA (Program for International Student Assessment). Do you know what Germany's current overall ranking is? Do you think tests like this are useful?

Shanghai Surprise: Don't Sweat Global Test Data

A Concern about falling behind internationally is one of America's most popular education anxieties. This week's Washington visit by Chinese President Hu Jintao and all the chatter about Amy Chua's new book on why Chinese-style "tiger moms" raise more successful children than Americans do serve as uncomfortable reminders that the kids in Shanghai did astronomically well on a set of international tests released last month, whereas US kids came in 17th. That makes us sound pretty lame. But the extremists at both ends of the education spectrum – i.e. those telling us international tests are meaningless and those claiming the scores are a sure sign that the sky is falling – are wrong. Here are five reasons you should ignore the hysterical commentary, followed by a commonsense look at what you should care about instead.

B

1. Although the results of international tests are generally presented as an absolute ranking, often the differences between specific countries are not that substantial. For instance, when you look at the scores released last month by the Program for International Student Assessment (PISA), which is conducted by the Organization for Economic Cooperation and Development, the U.S. was in the middle of the pack in science and reading and lagged in math. No, we didn't do as well as we should, but we were ahead of countries like Germany, France and England.

2. It was Shanghai – not all of China – that received top honors on the PISA test. And Shanghai is where the smartest kids in the country go to school. So drawing the breathless conclusions as the media has about China and the PISA data is not unlike taking all the college kids in Cambridge, Mass., home to Harvard and MIT, and declaring them to be a representative sample of higher education across the U.S. When we start testing rural China, we'll get a more accurate picture of what we're really up against.

3. There are differences between countries that international assessments fail to capture. The American educational system is remarkable for the second chances it offers students who struggle in school. If you have to repeat a grade, we don't tell you that you can never go to college. Likewise, if you fail a test, it doesn't automatically put you on a different life path. Even in some industrialized nations, high-stakes tests mean a lot of kids get kicked to the curb. That's not our way.

4. It's worth remembering that during the Cold War, we feared Soviet domination. When I was in school, we were told it was the Japanese who would be our undoing. Yet you don't hear much about Russia anymore, and American policymakers today are scrambling to avoid a "Japanese decade" like the economically anaemic one that country had in the '90s. Past performance in addressing competitive challenges is not a guarantee of future success. So we can't afford to become complacent, but we should maintain some perspective.

5. The 20th century was clearly the American century, but that wasn't necessarily because of the superior quality of our schools. A variety of societal factors such as immigration, a stable government and legal system, respect for property rights and contracts, and openness to trade matter to competitiveness, too. Stanford University economist Eric Hanushek examined international test score data, and what he found should both hearten and worry us. When he crunched the numbers, he concluded that learning – and crucially, not just years in school but how much students actually learned – does matter to a country's economic growth. But the relationship, while quite significant, was not as pronounced when he accounted for some societal factors. In other words, we won't rise or fall on schools alone.

C So what's the takeaway? It's clearly better to do well on these assessments than poorly. (Hanushek also found that improving performance on these tests would be reflected in our national economic performance.) And it is certainly troubling that we are not producing as many students who perform at the top of these assessments as some other countries are. But this is a long-term (and solvable) problem – even as we compete with countries like China that can swamp us in terms of population.

D More immediately, rather than obsessing about international comparisons, we should focus on the data here at home, where there is a genuine educational crisis. Only about 6 in 10 African-American and Hispanic students are graduating from high school. Meanwhile, enormous gaps in achievement exist on state tests as well as our national assessments and other measures, like the SAT. Minority students are also more likely to be in special education and less likely to be in gifted education programs than other students. And remember: America will be a majority-minority country before 2050, according to the U.S. Census Bureau.

E What this means is that if we want to become more competitive internationally, our future engineers and scientists will not come from the students who today are choosing other white-collar professions. Instead, they will have to come from the students who today do not even have that kind of career choice because of poor-quality education in their communities.

F And that's our core education problem. Broken public-school systems constrain social mobility. Although college completion is the most effective social-mobility tool we have, only about 1 in 7 low-income students earn a degree. In other words, what we should really be concerned about is not being outcompeted by other countries but whether we'll start looking like too many of the ones that have static class structures and highly inequitable distributions of wealth. That prospect, much more than what kids in Shanghai or their moms are doing, should alarm us. (947 words)

Time, 20 January 2011

Webcode: FOSEAU0301

1 MULTIPLE CHOICE

> Skills p. 176

Choose the most suitable option.

1 Which of the following ideas is not mentioned in paragraph B?
   a When looking at international rankings, the country as a whole is important, not just one particular region.
   b A school system that allows weak students to get ahead later in life may be better than a school system that scores top test results.
   c Nations can be successful in the future by closely studying the top-ranking countries at the present time.
   d A country can be successful in many fields even if its school system is not highly-competitive in the international rankings.

2 The expression "takeaway" (l. 84) refers to … .
   a food taken home from a restaurant
   b insights gained
   c plans stolen
   d emotions aroused

3 According to paragraph D, the really serious school-related problem that exists in the USA is that … .
   a black and Hispanic high school students are not performing as well as white high school students
   b minority groups will soon constitute the majority of all Americans
   c American high schools simply cannot compete with the best high schools in other countries
   d assessment tests at the national level show even worse results than those administered on the state level

4 Based on information in paragraphs D and E, if the USA is to become truly competitive in the coming decades, the future elite employees will have to be recruited from … .
   a foreign countries
   b the social classes that make up mainstream America
   c underprivileged groups
   d native American groups

5 When the author says in paragraph F that "broken school systems constrain social mobility", he means that young people with a poor education … .
   a are stuck in low-wage jobs
   b can't get around as easily as those with a college degree
   c are down-hearted
   d are less interested in applying for top positions

6 In general, the author's attitude towards the current state of American education is one of … .
   a extreme pessimism about the problem
   b indifference towards the problem
   c anxiety about the problem
   d cautious optimism that the problem can be overcome

2 SHORT-ANSWER QUESTIONS / SENTENCE COMPLETION

> Skills p. 178

Answer the questions or complete the sentences with information from the text.

1 Which phrase in paragraph A indicates that Americans don't feel at ease when the media report large differences in test scores between American and Chinese school children?

2 In paragraph A, the author disagrees with people who are worried about the poor American test results and with people who argue that the scores should not be taken seriously by saying that … .

3 In paragraph A, the metaphorical expression ... refers to the fact that some people are extremely depressed about the poor test scores of American students.

4 ... , mentioned in paragraph B, are exams that are decisive for a student's future.

5 Which phrase in paragraph D describes the fact that some students perform much better than others in tests administered in the USA?

6 With the statement ... in paragraph D, the author refers to the fact that the number of native white Americans will be lower in the future than that of immigrants and their children.

7 According to what the author says in paragraph F, America's education problems may ultimately result in ... and ... .

8 What four concrete reasons mentioned in paragraph B were responsible for making the USA so successful in the last century?

3 WORKING WITH WORDS

A The nouns in the box are all taken from the text. Match them with eight of the explanations/synonyms (1–10).

prospect | concern | degree | property | assessment | gap | sample | distribution

1 the evaluation of a student's performance
2 brochure
3 way in which wealth is shared among members of society
4 building, piece of land or both together
5 chance of future success
6 great difference
7 small amount of something used to show something about the whole
8 worry
9 large company
10 qualification granted for successful completion of one's university studies

B The adjectives in the box are all taken from the text. Match them with eight of the explanations/synonyms (1–10).

lame | substantial | complacent | significant | genuine | gifted | inequitable | competitive

1 talented
2 wanting to keep up with others
3 real, true
4 well-located
5 considerable
6 weak, not very dynamic
7 poisoned
8 satisfied with one's situation/achievements
9 unfair
10 important

4 TALKING

In groups, discuss the questions below.

1 Would you like to work part-time after school? Why? What would be the advantages or disadvantages?
2 What kind of part-time jobs have you had or would you like to have?
3 What would be the ideal job for you? Explain.

C Words in context

Education and the job market

Educating a skilled workforce for the future is one of the main challenges facing governments in the global market place. Because of the strong competition in the field of education, the results of the international PISA tests are often considered to reflect national economic performance. The superior academic performance of high-school students in some Asian and Scandinavian countries, for instance, is a reminder for Americans that academic achievement at high-school level in the USA lags behind many other industrialized nations.

Some observers defend the American education system by saying that it gives weak students who have to repeat a grade a second chance to succeed. The USA also offers excellent educational opportunities at university level – a fact that is illustrated by the high number of foreign students in the United States. However, many experts recognize that there is an educational crisis in the USA demonstrated by the performance gap between African-American and Hispanic students on the one hand, and mainstream white students on the other. If no-one can come up with a solution, upward social mobility for black and Hispanic youngsters will be in jeopardy. Today's minority groups in America will represent the majority of all Americans by the middle of the 21st century, and if the quality of education for minority children is not improved soon, they will not be able to obtain the white-collar jobs, for example in the sciences and engineering, that will guarantee America's ability to compete economically in the coming decades.

Germany faces a different problem on the job market in the future. Forecasts indicate that up to 5 million foreign workers, half of them university-educated, will be needed by 2030 to fill the gap in Germany's workforce. In Germany, the youth unemployment rate is comparatively low and the German Federal Employment Agency is presently wooing highly-qualified job candidates from other EU countries by stressing the fact that starting salaries in Germany, particularly in engineering, are higher than in their own countries. Young Spanish job applicants, for example, whose native boom-to-bust economy has let them down, are attracted by the prospect of permanent labour contracts. In many cases, German language skills are not a prerequisite to finding employment in the Federal Republic.

In order to attract skilled workers from abroad, Germany needs to compete with other countries by offering job opportunities with an attractive working environment, by paying competitive wages and by getting rid of bureaucratic regulations. Both private and government-run placement agencies are thus trying to assist job seekers to secure a German job by helping them perfect their curriculum vitae and find German language courses.

At the moment, many young unemployed people from Spain, Greece or Portugal are so keen to work in Germany that they will make do with jobs for which they are overqualified. For instance, job applicants with academic degrees in the field of tourism studies are often prepared to do manual work or service jobs at German hotels, because this gives them the opportunity to perfect their German language skills, and to thereby find permanent positions in more lucrative jobs, in the long run. If they had stayed in Spain, they may have been forced to take seasonal jobs in the tourism sector – and to do part-time work for the rest of the year.

(556 words)

First of all, make sure you understand the meaning of each of the highlighted phrases used in the text on page 40. If you are not sure, look them up in your dictionary. Then complete the tasks below.

1 WORD FORMATION

> Skills p. 173

A Copy the chart below and add the missing words. Some of the words you need are in the text; you can find the others in a dictionary.

Abstract noun	*Noun: person*	*Verb*	*Adjective*
...	...	...	applicable
...	...	...	competitive
...	...	...	distributive
economy	...	...	... / ...
...	educator	...	...
...	...	...	employable
...	———	...	integrated
...	...	...	performable

B Look up the two adjectives of *economy* in a dictionary and use each of them in a sentence that clearly shows the word's meaning.

C Make sentences with five other words from the chart, but leave a gap for the word. Swap pages with a partner. Can he/she complete your sentences with the correct words?

2 WORDFIELDS

> Skills p. 176

A Find four synonyms for *job* in the text.

B Collect the various "job phrases" highlighted in the text, using these categories. Some phrases can go in more than one category.

job benefits	starting salaries, ...
duration of job	permanent labour contracts, ...
job areas	white-collar jobs, ...
the search for a job	job market, ...
job qualifications	skilled workforce, ...

3 COMPOUND NOUNS

> Skills p. 175

The text contains several compound nouns, i.e. phrases that are made up of a noun which is modified by one or two other nouns.

EXAMPLE > *education system, school system, university level*

Find at least ten examples of compound nouns in the text.

4 VERBAL PHRASES

Verbal phrases consist of a verb and one modifier or a combination of modifiers (e.g. a preposition, noun, adverb, past participle, ...). They are frequently part of an idiomatic expression.

EXAMPLE > let sb. down (l. 31) = *jdn. im Stich lassen*

A Find verbal phrases in the text that correspond to these German expressions.

1 etw. hinterherhinken
2 sich etw. einfallen lassen
3 etw. abschaffen
4 sich mit etw. begnügen

B Now form one sentence with each of the English verbal phrases you have found.

D Further activities

1 LISTENING

> Skills p. 179

Hilmar Schneider

You are going to hear an interview with Hilmar Schneider, spokesman for the Institute for the Study of Labour. The interview is briefly interrupted by a report about the way in which a large international corporation deals with depression in the workplace.

1 7 **A Complete the following text with appropriate information from the first part of the interview. Use one word only for each gap.**

According to Hilmar Schneider, the two basic reasons for the shortage of engineers, researchers and scientists in Germany are ...1 ...2 and the ... 3 ...4, which is not attractive enough. In his view, the fact that young people are leaving Germany as a result of better pay abroad is not ...5. He goes on to say that a total number of ...6 urgently-needed engineers are missing because there is a ...7 between the demand for skilled workers and the supply of graduates turned out by universities. The interviewer then presents a graph which shows that ...8 ...9 might return to those Germany enjoyed back in 1992. The interviewer goes on to talk about people who get depressed on the job and says that depression-related conditions often lead to ...10 ...11. The way one company deals with depression is to offer ...12 and ...13.

1 8 **B Now listen to the report on the problem of depression suffered by workers and the way in which one international company deals with that problem. Make a note of the following information:**

1 preventive measures used by the company to deal with the problem (*3 aspects*)
2 reasons why the company is taking action (*3 aspects*)

1 9 **C Now listen to the rest of the interview with Hilmar Schneider and answer the following questions. Short phrases will do.**

1 What factors have made many employees so unhappy?
2 Why is Mr Schneider optimistic that a solution will be found which is in the interest of the employees?

2 ARGUMENTATIVE WRITING

> Skills p. 181

Choose one of the following topics and write at least 200 words.

1 Under what circumstances would you be willing to apply for a job abroad?
2 Do you think it would make sense to keep students together in a unified school system up to grade 10?
3 Are you worried about Germany being out-performed by emerging countries such as India and China if we leave the school system the way it is right now?

3 DESCRIPTIVE WRITING

> Skills pp. 183–186

A Describing cartoons: Choose one of the cartoons below. Describe what you see and interpret the message the cartoonist is trying to make in about 100 words.

B Interpreting statistics: Look at the bar chart below and interpret it.

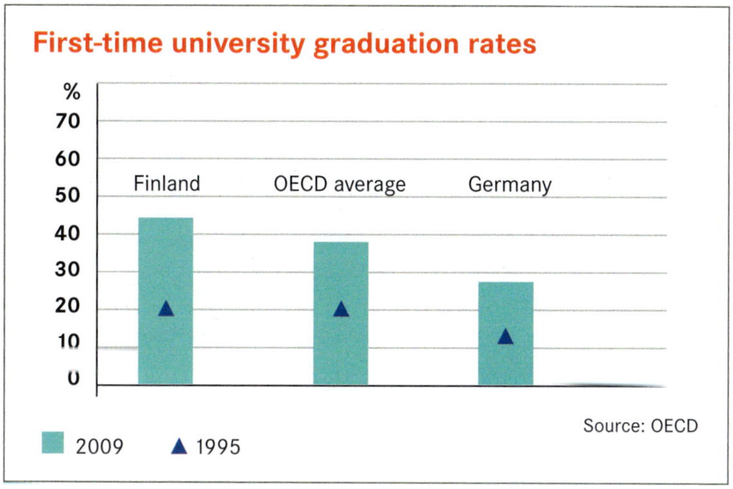

4 GROUP DISCUSSION

> Skills p. 187

Your group has been asked to discuss measures that could be adopted in Germany to increase the number of university graduates fairly quickly. Look at the list of suggestions below, discuss each of them in detail, and then try to reach agreement on which one of them is the most suitable. Keep costs and practicality in mind.

- employ more school teachers and university professors
- lower admissions requirements needed to enrol at a university
- reduce final exam standards, both at high school and college level
- build new college campuses
- eliminate tuition fees at all German universities

E Grammar check

SIMPLE PAST – PRESENT PERFECT

> Grammar summary pp. 194–195

SPOT THE MISTAKES

Spot the mistakes and correct them. Explain why they are wrong.

1 ~~At the beginning of the interview, they have asked me to come in and sit down.~~
2 ~~I work for Smith & Co. for three months now.~~
3 ~~My boss has asked me to start learning Chinese a month ago.~~
4 ~~I didn't go to an interview since several weeks now.~~
5 ~~Jenny only worked for Smith & Co. since the start of the month.~~

A Decide whether to use the *simple past* or *present perfect*.

Less than a decade ago, Germany ...[1] (be) beset by chronic unemployment and pathetic growth. Its more aggressive neighbours, such as Spain, Britain and Ireland ...[2] (look) at Germany as their stodgy old uncle, unable to adapt to a new world. But now, a steady but reformed Germany ...[3] (emerge) as Europe's dominant economic power. According to the OECD, Germany ...[4] (account) for 60% of the GDP growth of the euro zone in 2010, up from only 10% in the early 2000s. Over the last two years, demand for German language courses ...[5] (double) in Spain because Germany ...[6] (become) the "land of opportunity" for many young Spaniards.

B Translate the following sentences into English.

1 Während der Wirtschaftskrise 2009 boten viele deutsche Firmen ihren Vollzeitbeschäftigten eine Arbeitsplatzgarantie bis 2015 an.
2 Kleine Unternehmen spezialisieren sich seit jeher auf die Herstellung von Maschinen.
3 In den letzten Jahren erhoben deutsche Unternehmen dies fast zu einer Kunstform.
4 Die deutschen Exporte stiegen 2010 um satte 18,5% an.
5 Professor Brennan evaluiert seit Beginn der PISA-Studien die Leistung der Schüler in England.

WATCH OUT!

> Skills p. 182

Connectors

~~Despite~~ employers like to train their employees themselves, they don't mind them having previous job experience.
→ *Although employers like to train their employees themselves, they don't mind them having previous job experience.*

C Choose the most appropriate connector so that the text makes sense.

When you go for an interview you should be neat and tidy although / because / due to[1] the first impression you make on a potential employer is extremely important. Otherwise / In other words / For example[2], you might not get the job. Nevertheless / Moreover / In contrast[3], make sure you arrive on time. Despite / However / While[4], you needn't come too early; about ten minutes before the start of the interview is fine. You mustn't be arrogant yet / while / as[5] most employers prefer employees who are modest. In addition, they like employees who are able to work in teams, despite / even though / when[6] it might sometimes be easier for an employee to do the task on their own. If you know a lot about a subject, don't start lecturing. In other words / Nonetheless / On the contrary[7], don't use more than three or four sentences to make it clear that you know what you are talking about. Don't boast about all the wonderful job offers you've had: what / which / that[8] would only indicate that you are not being honest.

4

Individual freedom

FOCUS

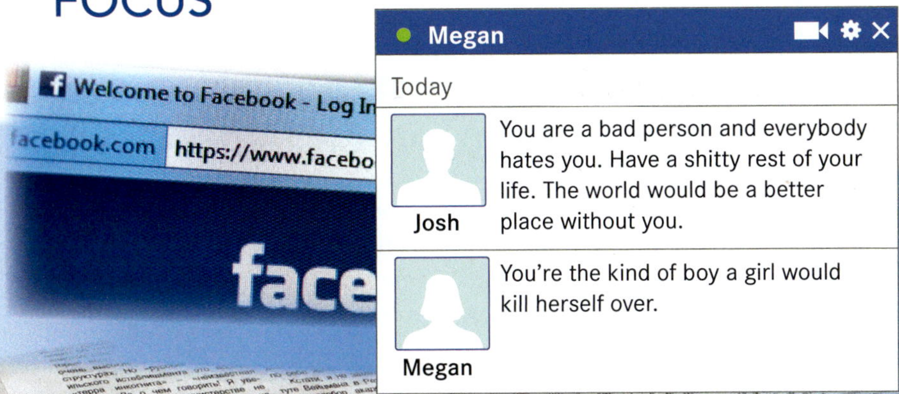

The bullying then exploded with messages and bulletins going out to hundreds of kids.

"The messages were horrendous," Megan's mother said. "They were not just, 'I don't like you anymore.' They called Megan all kinds of horrible names, talking about her weight, the way that she looked, cursing. I mean using things that are unbelievable."

It caused Megan to sob hysterically, and she ran to her room.

A short time later, the 13-year-old committed suicide, hanging herself in her bedroom closet.

"Every single dream, every hope, everything she wanted to be was gone in two hours," her mother said. "Two hours on a computer and that life that was so precious was gone."

www.cbn.com 24 October 2011

Talk about these questions in groups of four or five.

1 Do you worry about cyberbullying? Explain why/why not.
2 What sort of advice would you give to someone who is being bullied?
3 Have you ever been the victim of a crime or are you afraid of becoming one?
4 Does society tackle crime in the right way when it puts criminals behind bars?

A Freedom of speech

BEFORE YOU READ

Have you ever come across any bullying messages on a social networking website? How did you react?

What would you do if you were being cyberbullied?

Facebook Wrestles With Free Speech and Civility

A Dressed in Facebook's quasi-official uniform of jeans, a T-shirt and flip-flops, the 26-year-old Dave Willner hardly looks like a cop on the beat. Yet he and his colleagues on Facebook's "hate and harassment team" are part of a virtual police squad charged with taking down content that is illegal or violates Facebook's terms of service. That puts them on the front line of the debate over free speech on the Internet.

B With Facebook's prominence on the Web – its members upload more than one billion pieces of content a day – the site's role as an arbiter of free speech is likely to become even more pronounced. "Facebook has more power in determining who can speak and who can be heard around the globe than any Supreme Court justice, any king or any president," said Jeffrey Rosen, a law professor who has written about free speech on the Internet. "It is important that Facebook is exercising its power carefully and protecting more speech rather than less."

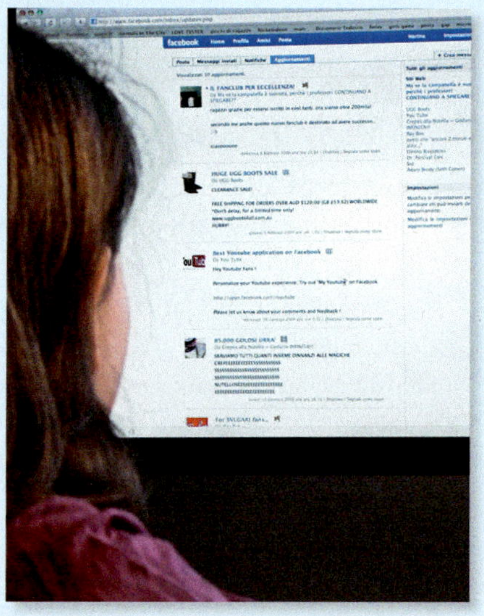

C Some critics say Facebook does not do enough to prevent certain abuses, like bullying, and may put users at risk with lax privacy policies. They also say the company is often too slow to respond to problems. For example, a page threatening violence against an 11-year-old girl from Orlando, Fla., who had appeared in a music video, was still up last week, months after users reported the page to Facebook. The girl's mother, Christa Etheridge, said she had been in touch with law enforcement authorities and was hoping the offenders would be prosecuted. A Facebook spokesman said the company had left the page up because it did not violate its terms of service, which allow criticism of a public figure. The spokesman said that by appearing in a band's video, the girl had become a public figure, and that the threatening comments had not been posted until a few days ago.

D Facebook says it is constantly working to improve its tools [for users] to report abuse and trying to educate users about bullying. And it says it responds as fast as it can to the roughly two million reports of potentially abusive content that its users flag every week. "Our intent is to try to make sure we get to the high-priority, high-risk and high-visibility items most quickly," said

Joe Sullivan, Facebook's chief security officer. In early October, Mr Willner and his colleagues spent more than a week dealing with one high-risk, highly visible case; rogue citizens of Facebook's world had posted antigay messages and threats of violence on a page inviting people to remember Tyler Clementi and other gay teenagers who had committed suicide, on so-called Spirit Day, Oct. 20. Working with colleagues here and in Dublin, they tracked down the accounts of the offenders and shut them down.

E As with schoolyard taunts, most abuse incidents often happen among a small group of people, hidden from casual view. One morning in November, Nick Sullivan, a member of the hate and harassment team, watched as reports of bullying incidents scrolled across his screen, full of mind-numbing meanness. "Emily looks like a brother." (Deleted) "Ronald is the biggest loser." (Deleted) Although the insults are relatively mild, as attacks on specific people who are not public figures, these all violated the terms of service. "There's definitely some crazy stuff out there," Mr Sullivan said. "You can do thousands of these in a day."

F Facebook faces even thornier challenges when policing activity that is considered political by some, and illegal by others. Last spring, for example, the company declined to take down pages related to "Everybody Draw Muhammad Day," an Internetwide protest to defend free speech that surfaced in repudiation of death threats received by two cartoonists who had drawn pictures of Muhammad. A lot of the discussion on Facebook involved people in Islamic countries debating with people in the West about why the images offended. Facebook's team worked to separate the political discussion from the attacks on specific people or Muslims. "There were people on the page that were crossing the line, but the page itself was not crossing the line," James Mitchell, who is Mr Willner's supervisor and leads the "hate and harassment team", said. Facebook's refusal to shut down the debate caused its entire site to be blocked in Pakistan and Bangladesh for several days.

G Facebook has also sought to walk a delicate line on Holocaust denial. The company has generally refused to block Holocaust denial material, but has worked with human rights groups to take down some content linked to organizations or groups, like the government of Iran, for which Holocaust denial is part of a larger campaign against Jews. "Obviously we disagree with them on Holocaust denial," said Rabbi Abraham Cooper, associate dean of the Simon Wiesenthal Center. But Rabbi Cooper said Facebook had done a better job than many other major websites in developing a thoughtful policy on hate and harassment.

H The soft-spoken Mr Willner makes for an unlikely enforcer. An archaeology and anthropology major in college, he said that while he loved his job, he did not love watching so much of the underbelly of Facebook. "I handle it by focusing on the fact that what we do matters," he said.

(868 words)

Adapted from: *The New York Times*, 12 December 2010

1 MULTIPLE MATCHING

> Skills p. 177

Match the statements (a–j) with the corresponding speakers (1–8) mentioned in the text on pages 46–47. Two of the statements don't match.

1 Jeffrey Rosen (paragraph B)
2 Christa Etheridge (paragraph C)
3 Facebook spokesman (paragraph C)
4 Joe Sullivan (paragraph D)
5 Nick Sullivan (paragraph E)
6 James Mitchell (paragraph F)
7 Rabbi Cooper (paragraph G)
8 Dave Willner (paragraph H)

a We may eventually have to close the site down if the abuse gets worse.
b We decided not to take action because it is our policy to permit negative comments about people who have gained a certain degree of prominence.
c I am relatively pleased with the way in which Facebook deals with this very delicate issue.
d The website itself was acceptable - but some of the comments posted on it went too far.
e My team has been really effective in dealing with cyber-bullying so far.
f I hope these criminals will be brought to justice.
g Facebook is so influential that it mustn't take advantage of the position it has.
h We are overwhelmed by masses of weird and offensive messages on our website.
i We are trying to catch the worst offences as fast as possible.
j Even though at times my work can be depressing, I love working here because I know that what I do is important.

2 MEDIATION ENGLISH-GERMAN

> Skills p. 178

A Geben Sie den Inhalt der folgenden Sätze/Phrasen sinngemäß auf Deutsch wieder.

1 ... a virtual police squad charged with taking down content that violates Facebook's terms of service. (ll. 3–4)
2 high-risk and high-visibility items (l. 31)
3 Most abuse incidents are ... hidden from casual view. (ll. 38–40)
4 ... reports ... full of mind-numbing meanness. (ll. 42–43)
5 The soft-spoken Mr Willner makes for an unlikely enforcer. (l. 70)

B Beantworten Sie die folgenden Fragen stichwortartig auf Deutsch.

1 Was werfen Kritiker Facebook vor? (*3 Aspekte*)
2 Wie rechtfertigt sich Facebook gegenüber Kritikern? (*3 Aspekte*)
3 James Mitchell spricht im Zusammenhang mit den Mohammed-Cartoons von einer Trennlinie. Wo genau verläuft diese für Facebook?

3 WORKING WITH WORDS

A Find words and phrases in paragraphs A–C that have the same meaning as the following synonyms or definitions.

1 to break (an agreement)
2 business conditions
3 high visibility
4 given responsibility for
5 rude or offensive things that sb. says to sb. else
6 saying that you will cause sb. pain, unhappiness or trouble
7 seldom
8 tried by a court of law

B Match the phrases (1–6) from paragraphs D–G with the corresponding paraphrase (a–h). Two of the paraphrases don't match.

1 cross the line
2 schoolyard taunts
3 track down the accounts of the offenders
4 thornier challenges
5 walk a delicate line
6 shut down the debate

a end the discussion abruptly
b go further than one should
c confiscate the money of the perpetrators
d be careful not to offend the feelings of any one party
e tougher tests to pass
f method used to persuade another person
g provocations made to make fun of other students
h find out who posted the vicious messages

C Rewrite the following sentences so that their meanings don't change. Use phrases from the text to replace the underlined parts.

1 Facebook's influence on who can speak and who can be heard around the globe will probably become even more apparent.
Facebook's contribution to the promotion of free speech … .
2 The rather careless way in which Facebook acts when it comes to protecting its users from insults may cause harm to them.
Facebook's … may cause harm to its users.
3 Facebook is determined to react as fast as possible to messages which attract the attention of a lot of readers because they are provocative and bullying.
Facebook will take pains to respond to … as fast as possible.
4 The members of the hate and harassment team are regularly confronted with messages that display unimaginably rude behaviour throughout.
The members of the hate and harassment team regularly come across messages that are … .

4 TALKING

Discuss these questions with a partner. Explain your point of view by giving examples.

1 How much of a problem do you think cyber-bullying is? Do you think schools should get involved?
2 What do you think is more important: protecting freedom of speech or protecting individuals' rights to privacy?

5 PROJECT

> Skills p. 190

A Find out more about ways of dealing with bullying if you are a victim. Report back to the class.

Google "cyberbullying" or "stop cyberbullying" to find out more information.

B Find out more about drug prevention tactics. Report back to the class.

Google "mentor foundation" or "time to talk" for more information.

B The war on drugs

BEFORE YOU READ

Look at the title of the following text. What do you think the "change" might be?

Global reformers say it's time for change on drugs

A Forty years after US President Richard Nixon launched his War on Drugs, a conflict that far eclipses the War on Terror, the struggle to contain, let alone end, illicit drug abuse is far from over, spewing violence, corruption and addiction into new markets, brutal capitalism at its most malignant. But, finally, there is a glimmer of hope.

B Yesterday, an extraordinary alliance of the great and good presented their recommendations on how to tackle this worldwide scourge to United Nations Secretary-General Ban Ki Moon in New York. The Global Commission on Drug Policy declared the War on Drugs a resounding failure, and suggested radical measures would have to be taken if the global narco culture was to ever be defeated. Brazil's ex-president, Fernando Henrique Cardoso, who heads the commission, said: "Let's start by treating drug addiction as a health issue, reducing drug demand through proven educational initiatives and legally regulating rather than criminalising cannabis." He and other members of the commission, including former UN Secretary-General Kofi Annan and Virgin tycoon Sir Richard Branson, blasted drug policies, driven by "ideology and political convenience", which have criminalised "tens of millions" of lower-end couriers, dealers or farmers who grow opium, coca or marijuana to escape poverty, because they are addicts. Such policies, said the commission, have not reduced "the availability of illicit drugs or the power of criminal organisations".

C Ban Ki Moon was handed four recommendations. Drug users who "do no harm to others" should be decriminalised. Legal regulation should wrestle control from criminals. Treatment programmes, used in Europe and Canada, should be adopted. And states must respect the rights of people – addicts, dealers and farmers – found at the lower ends of the trade.

D Three factors give the commission's recommendations traction, says Danny Kushlick, external affairs chief for a British lobby group. The global recession makes costly and failed drug policies unsustainable. Unintended consequences, such as the more than 35,000 dead in Mexico's savage

battle with narco-cartels, have taken the War on Drugs to America's doorstep. And President Obama's less "bullish" attitude towards the war makes it politically acceptable for US allies, such as Mexico and Colombia, to publicly raise decriminalisation and legal regulation.

E The War on Drugs has been fed by specious justifications that, despite much evidence to the contrary, "just-say-no" works. Drug warriors emphasise drug seizures, arrests, declining use of specific drugs and so forth. This zero tolerance fantasy is bluntly rejected by commission members. "The War on Drugs has failed to cut drug use, but has filled our jails, cost millions in taxpayer dollars, fuelled organised crime and caused thousands of deaths," said Sir Richard Branson. "We need a new approach, one that takes the power out of the hands of organised crime and treats people with addiction problems like patients, not criminals."

F Given this downside, it is hard to ignore parallels with the failed US experiment on alcohol prohibition in the 1920s, which hugely benefited organised crime. The Associated Press estimated the total cost of the drug war since 1971 at US$ 1 trillion. But, in truth, it is hard to arrive at an accurate figure, especially if "cost" is only measured in terms of money spent by the government to fight crime but ignores the social wreckage, whether from diseases such as HIV/AIDS or hepatitis, or even the cost of home insurance in areas plagued by drug crime. Certainly, the war is fed by huge, arguably unsustainable, budgets.

G Branson urged political and business leaders to consider "alternative, fact-based approaches" to counter illicit drug abuse. "The one thing we cannot do is to go on pretending the War on Drugs is working." Despite claims that prohibition cuts the supply of drugs, world demand has grown. Last year's UN report says illicit drug use has exploded in developing nations – from Africa and Latin America to Southeast Asia and the Middle East. The once Western problem is now a global nightmare.

H Reformers say the state must push aside criminal gangs and regulate the drug trade by taking over the production and supply of drugs. Given the UN estimate that between 155 and 250 million people use illegal drugs (129 to 190 million using cannabis), it indicates a tax bonanza. Relaxing drug laws has been flirted with. Sixteen US states have legalised medical marijuana and five, including California, have ballot initiatives to legalise and regulate the drug. But the test case is Portugal, which decriminalised all illicit drugs in 2001, providing evidence-based analysis to weigh the results. A paper published in the British *Journal of Criminology* last November said: "Portuguese decriminalisation did not lead to major increases in drug use. Indeed, evidence indicates reductions in drug-related harm and criminal justice overcrowding."

I If it really comes to a policy of decriminalisation, politicians will have to step up: something many are loath to do because of fears of being branded "soft on drugs" by opponents. But once drug hysteria is removed from the equation, the cold, hard numbers and public-health benefits of regulating illicit drugs make shattering the old taboos very attractive. Ultimately, says Kushlick, ending prohibition would force governments to face societal issues that contribute to drug abuse. "Criminalisation is a smokescreen. The issue is not whether to legalise or prohibit drugs. But how do you make societies better? That's hard to do if you're being duped by politicians into supporting policies that create harm." (889 words)

Adapted from: *New Zealand Herald*, 4 June 2011

Webcode: FOSEAU0401

1 LOOKING AT THE TEXT

Work with a partner and discuss these questions.

1 Was the change mentioned in the text what you thought it was going to be? Did anything surprise you about the text?
2 What consequences of drug use does the text mention for the consumer and for society?
3 Alcohol is a legal drug. In view of this, do you agree with the measures suggested by the Global Commission on Drug Policy?

2 MULTIPLE CHOICE

> Skills p. 176

Choose the most suitable option.

1 In paragraph A, the author says that compared to the War on Terror, the War on Drugs is … .
- a just as bad
- b harder to win
- c easier to fight
- d useless

2 Which idea is not expressed in paragraph B?
- a A different approach is needed to succeed in the War on Drugs.
- b Preventive steps must be taken.
- c The debate on drugs has to become more matter-of-fact.
- d The financial situation of drug farmers ought to be ignored.

3 One goal of the recommendations mentioned in paragraph C is to … .
- a change the law to allow states to monopolize the drug trade
- b make governments increase the amount of money spent on the War on Drugs
- c deter innocent drug users from becoming addicts
- d find a way to co-operate with the drug cartels

4 In paragraph G, Sir Richard Branson claims that … .
- a the War on Drugs is working because it uses a fact-based approach
- b prohibition and imprisonment deter potential dealers and drug users
- c illicit drug use is now primarily a problem for developing countries
- d people in leading political positions need to adopt more realistic policies

5 According to reformers in paragraph H, governments must decriminalize drug use and assume responsibility for production and supply because this would … .
- a dramatically increase tax revenues for the wealthiest nations
- b lower the amount of drugs crime and prison inmates
- c lead to more convictions of dealers and addicts in court
- d keep the number of addicts stable

6 According to paragraph I, politicians are reluctant to legalize drugs because they … .
- a are afraid voters will think they can't deal with the illicit drug trade and addiction
- b tend to ignore the terrible effects of drug-related crime
- c know rehab facilities are non-existent
- d are sceptical of the health benefits involved with doing so

7 The author's attitude towards the new drugs policy is … .
- a neutral
- b sceptical
- c positive
- d enthusiastic

3 GAPPED SUMMARY

> Skills p. 177

Fill in the gaps with suitable words from paragraphs A, B and C.

It is said that the decade-long effort to fight drugs ...[1] the current campaign to fight terrorism by far. The attempt to ...[2] drug addiction and to prevent it from becoming an even more ...[3] evil may soon shift into a new phase. There is some hope that the global ...[4] can perhaps be ended once and for all. A group of experts on drug policies recently concluded that the War on Drugs had been a total ...[5] and that a radically new approach to deal with the problem was required. They recommended that nations should attempt to decrease the ...[6] for narcotics by concentrating more heavily on new ...[7] ...[8] in the classroom. This group of experts also ...[9] the on-going ...[10] of illicit drugs in a growing number of regions around the world. Furthermore, they stressed the idea that significantly more programmes aimed at helping drug users overcome their addiction should be ...[11] by countries that have so far neglected to introduce them.

4 SHORT-ANSWER QUESTIONS / SENTENCE COMPLETION

> Skills p. 178

Answer the questions or complete the sentences with information from the text.

1 Why do the recommendations of the Global Commission on Drug Reform come at the right time? (*3 aspects*)
2 In paragraph D, the expression ... means the same as bringing up an issue that affects all of society.
3 In paragraph E, the expression ... means that, at first glance, certain explanations used to defend an opinion may appear to be true, but that they are false if you take a closer look.
4 In paragraph E, the phrase ... conveys the idea that politicians tend to favour an attitude of zero tolerance.
5 Why, according to paragraph F, does dealing with the financial aspects of drug abuse alone conceal the true impact of drug abuse? (*2 aspects*)

5 WORKING WITH WORDS

Match the verbs from the text with the nouns on the right to form meaningful phrases. There is always more than one possible answer. Use the phrases to make sentences of your own.

to adopt *to contain* *to raise* *to demand* *to fuel*	a question I the spread of nuclear weapons I a resolution I a child I xenophobia I crops I prices I time and attention I havoc I a pay-raise I protest I five ingredients I a friendlier tone I a vehicle I one's temper I proof I important information I a convincing strategy I an apology I demand for a new product

6 GROUP DISCUSSION

> Skills p. 187

You have been asked to discuss how the problem of drug addiction can best be dealt with. Look at the following list of proposals and discuss the merits of each one and how they could be implemented. Then try to reach an agreement on which of them might be the most effective.

- decriminalize the use of soft drugs only
- decriminalize the use of both soft and hard drugs
- introduce much harsher punishments for drug offences
- intensify anti-drug campaigns in all areas of society
- leave things as they are right now

C Words in context

1 10

Crime and juvenile delinquency

When it's time to sentence convicted criminals, judges are always faced with the task of finding a punishment that fits the crime yet at the same time treats offenders in a fair, just and humane way.

Repeat offenders and violent criminals can expect mandatory prison sentences, sometimes without the possibility of parole, particularly in cases of burglary, robbery, assault, sex-related crimes such as rape or drug-related offences such as drug trafficking and dealing. For these offences, the offenders are generally required to post extremely high bonds if they want to be released on bail pending their trial in a court of law. More lenient punishments may come in the form of suspended sentences, fines or community service for first-time offenders who commit petty crimes or engage in anti-social behaviour such as graffiti-spraying or vandalism. Rehabilitation centres, which prepare prisoners for the time after their release from jail, can help to reintegrate ex-convicts successfully back into society and prevent them from reoffending.

Criminologists are aware of the fact that crime-fighting tools - police, prosecutors, courts, prisons - consume enormous sums of money yet are not very effective as a crime deterrent. For this reason, they have increasingly been turning their attention towards crime prevention. The first step towards this goal is to identify the underlying causes of crime such as broken families, social inequality or economic disadvantage. Although these factors are more common among minority segments of society, one should not ignore the fact that the wealthier members of society may also be tempted to commit "white-collar" crimes such as bribery and tax evasion, for the simple reason of greed. Some people may even consider committing crime to be a game that helps them to overcome boredom. The second measure to prevent crime involves reducing the injustices of a country's social order, for example by improving the education system and providing employment to allow all groups in society a fair chance of getting ahead in life.

Whatever measures governments take to fight or prevent crime, they should definitely focus on juvenile delinquency, as some young offenders under the age of 18 may become the big-time criminals of the future. Many social scientists argue that parents themselves are partly to blame, but in today's world, both fathers and mothers are often obliged to work long hours away from home simply to make ends meet. Thus many kids spend long hours after school without parental supervision. Bored and lacking the maturity needed to make rational decisions, they become increasingly willing to take a risk to get their kicks. Other kids living in similar circumstances may also exert peer pressure on them to do so. The result is familiar: a rising number of cases of shoplifting, drug abuse, cyber-bullying, gang violence, hooliganism, truancy, and binge-drinking - to name but a few of the most offensive activities. Such activities may, of course, also be influenced by the graphic images commonly projected by the media on TV shows, in computer games, in movies or in cyberspace. Some youths may simply be unable to differentiate between fiction and reality and may thus come to see certain objectionable forms of behavior as acceptable.

Some of the measures that have been adopted to get a grip on the problem include placing first-time offenders on probation and/or forcing them to take part in some form of "alternative" punishment. This may include various forms of community work that force them to experience the consequences of their own abusive behaviour first-hand by being confronted with the victims of crime and their individual ordeals. An alternative way to deal with drug offenders is to offer them reduced sentences if they agree to attend drug rehabilitation programmes or counselling sessions. Such offenders may also be eligible for early parole from prison. (623 words)

First of all, make sure you understand the meaning of each of the highlighted phrases used in the text on page 54. If you are not sure, look them up in your dictionary. Then complete the tasks below.

1 WORDFIELDS

> Skills p. 176

A Make a list of words/expressions from the text related to various ...

a	types of crime/delinquency	*burglary, ...*
b	types of punishment	*mandatory prison sentence, ...*
c	people dealing with offenders in the criminal justice system	*judges, ...*
d	alternatives to prison sentences	
e	possible causes of crime	
f	ways in which to tackle crime at its roots	

B Match the crimes you listed in A with the following categories:

a	crimes against people	*(violent) assault, ...*
b	crimes against property	*graffiti spraying, ...*
c	both a and b	*robbery, ...*
d	neither a nor b	*bribery, ...*

C Add any other offences that you can think of to the categories a or b above.

2 MATCHING THE PUNISHMENT TO THE CRIME

Determine the sentence a criminal should get for his/her offence. The following words and phrases will help you.

Criminal	Sentence	Type of offence	Deserves ...
murderer rapist burglar someone who sprays graffiti a criminal who commits assault a first-time offender a repeat offender	a life sentence go to prison/jail for ... years get a prison/jail sentence of ... years be imprisoned for ... years do community service be placed on probation be released on bail take part in a drug rehabilitation programme be eligible for early parole have to pay a fine	violent brutal petty minor drug-related sex-related "white-collar"	a harsh/severe punishment a lenient/light sentence an alternative punishment to be given a second chance

EXAMPLE > *A criminal who commits assault should get a jail sentence of at least two years because it is a violent crime and thus deserves a rather harsh punishment.*

3 PARAPHRASING

Paraphrase the following expressions.

1 a punishment that fits the crime
2 repeat offender
3 crime-fighting tools
4 (they) get their kicks
5 mandatory jail sentences

D Further activities

1 ARGUMENTATIVE WRITING

> Skills p. 181

Choose one of the topics below and write at least 200 words.

1 Would harsher punishments help to fight juvenile delinquency more effectively?
2 How could the problem of binge drinking best be overcome?

2 DESCRIPTIVE WRITING

A Describing cartoons: Describe and interpret the cartoon. Write approximately 100 words.

"Really, Kevin! You'll ruin your teeth!"

B Describing statistics: Describe the statistics below and interpret them with regard to the differences between males and females. Write about 100 words.

> Skills pp. 183–186

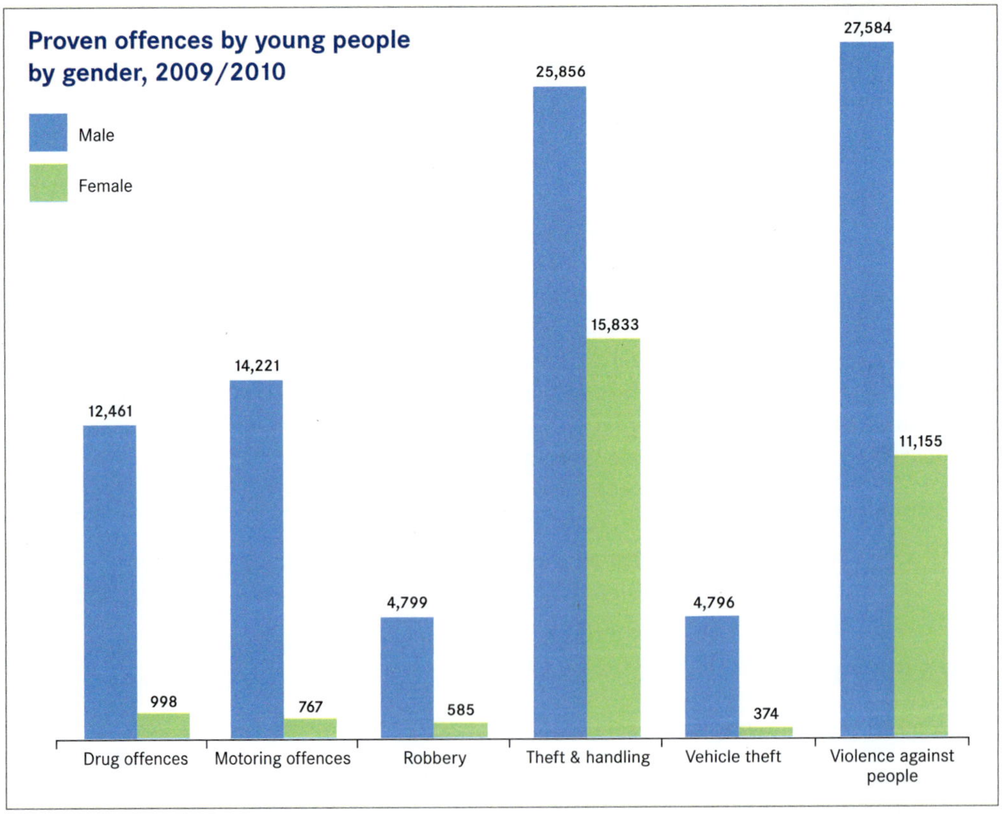

Source: www.justice.gov.uk

3 LISTENING

> Skills p. 179

You are going to hear a radio report about young people and the juvenile justice system in the USA. Listen, take notes and do the exercises below.

1 11

A Fill in the gaps with information from the report.

Experts say girls make up the ...[1] of the juvenile justice system. The jail Jabriera Handy was locked up in was put on lockdown because someone ...[2]. Prosecutor Backstrom and Professor Edelman agree that it makes sense to ...[3].

B Answer the following questions.

1 What personal problems are girls who get in conflict with the law confronted with?
2 What crimes do the majority of girls who end up in jail commit?
3 Why was Jabriera Handy charged with second degree murder?
4 What measures aimed at decreasing the number of offences in America in the long run does prosecutor Backstrom suggest?

C Decide whether these statements are true or false.

1 The new report presented by the Georgetown Center states that the justice system is letting delinquent young girls down.
2 Professor Edelman believes that the future of delinquent girls would look much brighter if they were not sent to jail for what he considers to be minor offences.
3 After the incident in the Baltimore City Detention Center, the girls were given the chance to discuss what had happened with teachers and jail staff.
4 Prosecutor Backstrom thinks that instead of concentrating too much on minor offences committed by young people the justice system should worry more about serious offences.

4 TALKING

> Skills p. 188

A Look at the following list and decide if the actions should be treated as a crime. Give reasons why.

B Rank the offences from most serious (1) to least serious (14).

C Form groups of four to five students and repeat steps A and B as a group.

D Choose a spokesperson to present your ranking and reasons to the class.

- Harold, age 17, robs a petrol station at gunpoint.
- Laurel leaves a shop with change for $10 after she realizes she only gave the cashier a $5 note.
- Dan parks in a handicapped parking space although he is not handicapped.
- Mike is a heroin addict who sells drugs to anyone who wants to buy them.
- Sylvia pickpockets a businessman's wallet containing $150.
- Ed refuses to pay income tax because he does not support government policies.
- Patty is caught with two grammes of marijuana.
- Dorothy is caught with two kilos of marijuana.
- Rob refuses to wear a helmet while riding a motorbike.
- A company pollutes a river with waste from its factory.
- Another company systematically checks the emails of its employees.
- Jake gets drunk and hits a child while speeding near a school entrance.
- Vince sees his best friend shoplifting but does not turn him in.
- Jessie, age 15, steals a lipgloss and comb from a supermarket.

E Grammar check

CONDITIONALS 1, 2 AND 3

> Grammar summary p. 201

SPOT THE MISTAKES

Spot the mistakes and correct them. Explain why they are wrong.

1 ~~If schools and parents made a determined effort to co-operate more closely, there is a chance of getting a grip on binge drinking.~~
2 ~~If juveniles had more useful activities to do in their free time, they had felt less bored.~~
3 ~~If adults would have listened to the boy more, he would not have felt so alienated.~~

A Complete the sentences with the correct form of the verbs in brackets.

1 Social workers claim that if there ... (be) more rehabilitation centres for young criminals, more of these juveniles could be kept from reoffending.
2 If children receive proper guidance, the influence of their peers ... (decrease).
3 If Kevin's parents ... (behave) less violenfly during his childhood, he would definitely not have become as aggressive as he is today.
4 Some people argue that Facebook has done too little to prevent abuse since the company was set up some years ago. They say that if Facebook ... (not/do) more to prevent abuse, it ... (continue) putting some of its users at risk.
5 Facebook officials admit that if the company was able to find ways to respond to abuse even faster, its users ... (be) better protected.
6 If Facebook ... (take) down a site threatening violence against an 11-year-old girl months ago, the girl ... (not/become) a public figure.

B Translate these sentences into English.

1 Es ist keineswegs sicher, dass Gewaltverbrecher von ihren Straftaten abgeschreckt werden könnten, wenn die Strafen härter wären.
2 Die Anhänger der Meinungsfreiheit wären enttäuscht gewesen, wenn Facebook letztes Frühjahr eine Webseite entfernt hätte, in welcher der radikale Islam kritisiert wurde.
3 Wenn noch konsequenter vorbeugende Maßnahmen ergriffen werden, wird die Zahl straftätiger Jugendlicher weiter sinken.

WATCH OUT!

Much – many, (a) little – (a) few, a lot of

~~Much~~ parents worry about their children taking drugs.
→ *Many parents worry about their children taking drugs.*
Martin only has a ~~little~~ friends.
→ *Martin only has a few friends.*

C Complete the gaps with the correct word. Use the comparative form if necessary.

1 He used to drink only ... alcohol, but these days he's drinking too ... of it.
2 Only ... criminals are deterred by harsh punishment.
3 Even though he doesn't have ... money, he considers himself lucky because he has ... friends instead.
4 It's welcome news that ... and ... juveniles are smoking today.
5 ... people are worried about privacy on social networking websites.

5

A changing society?

FOCUS

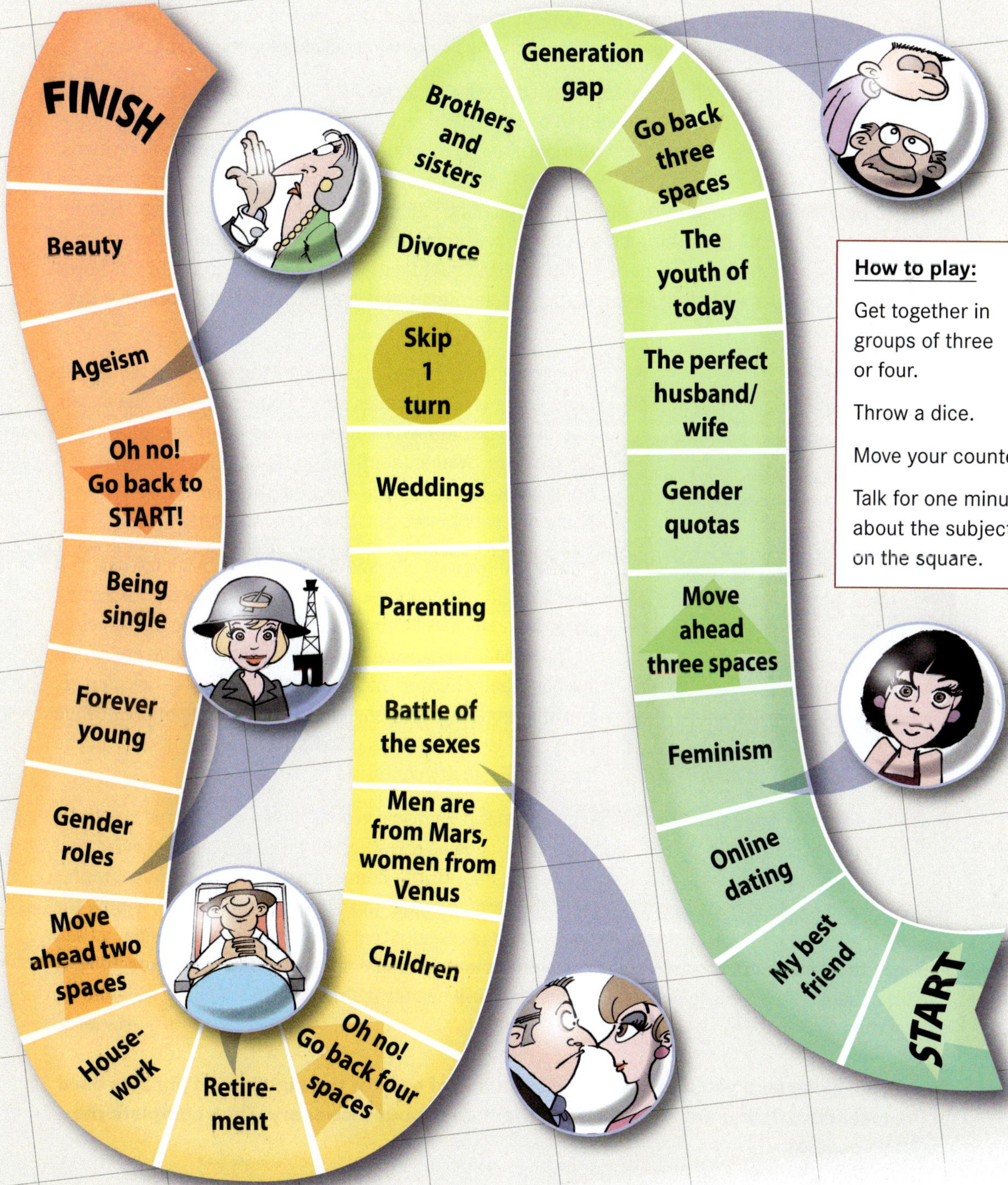

How to play:

Get together in groups of three or four.

Throw a dice.

Move your counter.

Talk for one minute about the subject on the square.

A Words in context

Changes in society

Enormous changes have taken place in our society in the last 50 years. Women in industrialized countries are much better off today in terms of wealth, health and education than they were five decades ago. Even though traditional gender roles have been changing steadily (and more slowly in developing countries), they still play a major role. Despite a long history of women struggling for sexual equality, there are still people (women as well as men) who demand that women should get married, stay at home and raise the children while their husbands or partners go to work and support them. Even though some people claim that the battle of the sexes is over, the emancipation of women has not been fully achieved and the struggle is likely to continue for some time.

Despite the fact that women have entered the job market in large numbers, gender bias continues to be a major factor. The Scandinavians seem to be the only ones taking the idea of equal pay for equal work seriously. In general, a "glass ceiling" continues to exist in many companies and corporations. Employees with young children often experience workplace discrimination, as few employers are willing to provide family-friendly working environments. Paid maternity leave, a hard-won right for women in Europe, is still something most American working women can only dream of. As a recent UN report makes clear: "Women have to have better qualifications, work harder, get by on fewer dollars, show greater negotiating skills, be more determined and put up with more prejudice than their male peers."

Even though the debate about balancing work and family has been going on for decades, most countries, with the exception of the Scandinavian ones, still do not make allowances for mothers. Women continue to do the lion's share of the housework (the infamous "second shift") even as they are being delegated more and more responsibility at work.

In addition, women also shoulder an extra burden which is a direct result of our longer life-expectancy: caring for ageing parents and in-laws. In America, for example, the phenomenon of the so-called sandwich generation – people who are carers for both their children and their ageing parents – is common, but the work is done mostly by women. But how are they supposed to manage this extra responsibility in view of the fact that longevity continues to increase?

These changes in the age structure of the industrialized world's societies have not occurred suddenly. Today's population pyramid is the result of trends, such as lower fertility and greater longevity, that have been apparent for many decades. However, the visible consequences of these demographic changes will become increasingly obvious in the coming years. In the meantime, women will be the ones most affected by these trends and they need to make sure that politicians do everything in their power to make women's lives easier, e.g. by providing more childcare facilities and more full-day schools – though it remains to be seen whether they will be able to find the time to put extra pressure on politicians.

(509 words)

First of all, make sure you understand the meaning of each of the highlighted phrases used in the text above. If you are not sure, look them up in your dictionary. Then complete the tasks on page 61.

1 PARAPHRASING

A Explain the following terms in your own words.

1 sexual equality (l. 5)
2 gender bias (l. 9)
3 maternity leave (l. 13)
4 put up with (l. 16)
5 make allowances for (ll. 20–21)
6 the lion's share (of sth.) (l. 21)

B Find English phrases in the text that have the same meaning as the sentences below.

1 It is very likely that parents will encounter certain prejudices at work.
2 On the whole, it remains a fact that women find it more difficult than men to be appointed to management positions in lots of companies.
3 The fight for women's liberation is still not over.
4 There's yet another task women appear to be solely responsible for.
5 Working women are still being discriminated against, even though their numbers have risen dramatically.

C Find the English equivalents in the text of each of the following German expressions.

1 mit weniger Geld auskommen
2 familienfreundliche Arbeitsbedingungen
3 jemandem geht es besser
4 niedrigere Geburtenrate
5 es bleibt abzuwarten, ob ...

D Now write your own sentences using the English expressions from C.

2 COMPOUND NOUNS

> Skills p. 175

A compound noun is a noun that is made up of two or more words. Most compound nouns in English are formed by nouns modified by other nouns or by adjectives, e.g. *childcare, life-expectancy, industrialized country.*

Find ten more examples of compound nouns in the text.

3 WORD FORMATION

> Skills p. 173

Complete the sentences with the correct form of the word in brackets (they are from the text). Look up both forms in your dictionary and find more words that have the same root.

1 This was no mean ... (achieved) for a woman!
2 Even highly ... (qualifications) nurses earn less than their male counterparts.
3 ... (recently) surveys on gender roles have shown that a lot of German cities do not really feel responsible for the ... (providing) of childcare facilities.
4 Mothers often do not ... (allowance) their daughters to participate in "rough" games for boys.
5 The ... (major) of American husbands do not share in the housework as they do not feel ... (responsibility) for it.

4 MIND MAP

> Skills p. 180

Make your own mind map about the changing role of women in society. Think of appropriate subheadings first (e.g. women at work / family matters / men and women / ...), then add other ideas of your own.

B A gender gap?

BEFORE YOU READ

Who do you think are generally happier: men or women?

He's Happier, She's Less So

By DAVID LEONHARDT

A Last year, a team of researchers added a novel twist to something known as a time-use survey. Instead of simply asking people what they had done over the course of their day, as pollsters have been doing since the 1960s, the researchers also asked how people felt during each activity. Were they happy? Interested? Tired? Stressed?

B Not surprisingly, men and women often gave similar answers about what they liked to do (hanging out with friends) and didn't like (paying bills). But there were also a number of activities that produced very different reactions from the two sexes – and one of them really stands out: Men apparently enjoy being with their parents, while women find time with their mom and dad to be slightly less pleasant than doing laundry.

C Alan Krueger, a Princeton economist working with four psychologists on the time-use research team, figures that there is a simple explanation for the difference. For a woman, time with her parents often resembles work, whether it's helping them pay bills or plan a family gathering. "For men, it tends to be sitting on the sofa and watching football with their dad," said Mr Krueger, who, when not crunching data, enjoys watching the New York Giants with his father.

D This intriguing – if unsettling – finding is part of a larger story: there appears to be a growing happiness gap between men and women.

E Mr Krueger, analyzing time-use studies over the last four decades, has found a stark pattern. Since the 1960s, men have gradually cut back on activities they find unpleasant. They now work less and relax more.

F Over the same timespan, women have replaced housework with paid work – and, as a result, are spending almost as much time doing things they don't enjoy as in the past. Forty years ago, a typical woman spent about 23 hours a week doing an activity considered unpleasant, or 40 more minutes than a typical man. Today, with men working less, the gap is 90 minutes.

G Women are not actually working more than they were 30 or 40 years ago. They are instead doing different kinds of work. They're spending more time on paid work and less on cleaning and cooking.

THE HAPPINESS GAP

A team of researchers has created an index to measure how much people dislike various activities. Based on surveys, the index describes the percentage of time during a given activity when somebody's dominant emotion is negative, whether it be sadness or stress.

Women	Percentage of time women and men find each activity unpleasant	Men
6%	Time at cafe or bar	2%
8	Sports and exercise	9
9	Gardening	17
17	Cooking	12
19	Visiting or hosting friends	7
20	Home repairs	34
25	Laundry and ironing	13
27	Time with parents	7
31	Doing the dishes	23
50	Medical care	59

Source: Research done by Alan Krueger, Daniel Kahneman, Norbert Schwarz, David Schkade and Arthur Stone

H What has changed – and what seems to be the most likely explanation for the happiness trends – is that women now have a much longer to-do list than they once did (including helping their ageing parents). They can't possibly get it all done, and many end up feeling as if they are somehow falling short.

I Mr Krueger's data, for instance, shows that the average time devoted to dusting has fallen significantly in recent decades. There haven't been any dust-related technological breakthroughs, so houses are probably just dirtier than they used to be. I imagine that the new American dustiness affects women's happiness more than men's.

J Betsy Stevenson and Justin Wolfers, economists at the University of Pennsylvania (and a couple) have also looked at the traditional happiness data and have come to the same conclusion as Alan Krueger.

K Ms Stevenson was recently having drinks with a business school graduate who came up with a nice way of summarizing the problem. Her mother's goals in life, the student said, were to have a beautiful garden, a well-kept house and well-adjusted children who did well in school. "I sort of want all those things, too," the student said, as Ms Stevenson recalled, "but I also want to have a great career and have an impact on the broader world."

L A big reason that women reported being happier three decades ago – despite far more discrimination – is probably that they had narrower ambitions, Ms Stevenson says. Many compared themselves only to other women, rather than to men as well. This doesn't mean they were better off back then.

M But it does show just how incomplete the gender revolution has been. Although women have flooded into the work force, American society hasn't fully come to grips with the change. The United States still doesn't have universal preschool, and, in contrast to other industrialized countries, there is no guaranteed paid leave for new parents.

N Government policy isn't the only problem, either. Inside of families, men still haven't figured out how to shoulder their fair share of the household burden. Instead, we're spending more time on the phone and in front of the television.
This weekend, I think I may volunteer to do a little dusting.

(731 words)

Adapted from: *The New York Times*, 26 September 2007

1 GAPPED SUMMARY

> Skills p. 177

Complete the gaps with words and expressions from paragraphs A–H of the text. Use one word only for each gap.

Since the 1960s, a new ...[1] has emerged with regard to women and work: leaving home and joining the workforce has actually resulted in less ...[2]. This was the ...[3] but worrying conclusion of a group of ...[4] who interviewed hundreds of couples last year.
Fifty years ago, women considered themselves, on average, ...[5] than they do today. Whereas men have reduced the number of ...[6] they perceive as ...[7], women are spending more time doing less satisfying things and consequently feel more ...[8]. In addition, the number of things they (theoretically) have to do has increased as well, such as caring for their ...[9] relatives.
It seems that women are now liberated but unhappy because balancing a career and family is still a challenge. There are so many things women feel they should be doing that they fear they are ...[10] ...[11].

2 MEDIATION ENGLISH-GERMAN

> Skills p. 178

Beantworten Sie folgende Fragen zum Text stichwortartig auf Deutsch.

1 Was meint der Autor mit der Aussage: "There haven't been any dust-related technological breakthroughs, so houses are probably just dirtier than they used to be."? (ll. 51-53)
2 Wie unterscheiden sich die Erwartungen der jetzigen Frauengeneration an ihr Leben von denen ihrer Mütter? (*4 Aspekte*)
3 Welche Gründe werden für die Tatsache genannt, dass es in Amerika noch keine wirkliche Gleichberechtigung gibt? (*3 Aspekte*)
4 Erklären Sie im Textzusammenhang den Satz "men still haven't figured out how to shoulder their fair share of the household burden". (ll. 82-83)
5 Warum hat der Autor vor, am Wochenende ein wenig Staub zu wischen?

3 WORKING WITH WORDS

A Which word from the text completes each group of collocations? Use your dictionary if necessary.

> Skills p. 175

1	"All ... and no play makes Jack a dull boy."	The new manager will have her ... cut out for her.	She's not at home, she's still at	Let's get to ... on the laundry right now.
2	The train suddenly stopped for no ... reason.	The ... discrepancy between their wages doesn't bother her.	It was all too ... that the project would fail.	It quickly became ... that they would never finish on time.
3	His wife took a language ... to improve her Italian.	The ship veered off ... and hit a rock.	One ... of action is not to marry at all, I think.	He had soup, followed by fish for the main ... .
4	The car burst into flames on	The financial crisis has had a negative ... on unemployment.	She is already making a real ... in the Labour Party.	This essay explores the ... of poverty on children's health.

B Explain or paraphrase the following expressions from the text. Use a dictionary, if necessary.

1 to stand out (ll. 12-13)
2 to cut back on sth. (l. 30)
3 to replace sth. with sth. (ll. 32-33)
4 to fall short (of sth.) (l. 48)
5 to come to the same conclusion (ll. 58-59)
6 to come to grips with sth. (ll. 76-77)

4 TALKING

Discuss these questions with your partner.

1 Why do women nowadays have longer to-do lists than in the 1960s? Think of the kinds of tasks you would probably find on such lists.
2 Look at the survey results on page 62. Decide which three activities you find most unpleasant and why. Discuss them with your partner and find out whether he/she is of the same opinion. Does the male/female point of view make a difference?

C Age and society

BEFORE YOU READ

What do you think the long-term consequences of an ageing society will be?

A slow-burning fuse

The rich world's population is ageing fast, and the poor world is only a few decades behind. At present just under 11% of the world's 6.9 billion people are over 60. According to a UN forecast, by 2050 that share will have risen to 22% (of a population of over 9 billion), and in the developed countries to 33%. **— A —**

The reasons why

What is making the world so much older? There are two long-term causes and a temporary blip that will continue to show up in the figures for the next few decades. The first of the big causes is that people everywhere are living far longer than they used to. In 1900 average life expectancy at birth for the world as a whole was only around 30 years, and in rich countries under 50. **— B —** For all the talk about the coming old-age crisis, that is surely something to be grateful for – especially since older people these days also seem to remain healthy, fit and active for much longer.

A second, and bigger, cause of the ageing of societies is that people everywhere are having far fewer children, so the younger age groups are much too small to counterbalance the growing number of older people. In the early 1970s women across the world were still, on average, having 4.3 children each. The current global average is 2.6, and in rich countries only 1.6. The UN predicts that by 2050 the global figure will have dropped to just two, so by mid-century the world's population will begin to level out. **— C —** Depending on your point of view, that may or may not be a good thing for the industrialized world, but it will certainly turn the world into a different place.

The temporary blip that has magnified the effects of lower fertility and greater longevity is the baby-boom that arrived in most rich countries after the Second World War. The timing varied slightly from place to place, but in America – where the effect was strongest – it covered roughly the 20 years from 1945, a period when nearly 80m Americans were born. **— D —** For the next 20 years those baby-boomers will be swelling the ranks of pensioners, which will lead to a rapid drop in the working population all over the rich world.

— E — In the richer parts of Asia the populations of Japan, South Korea and Taiwan are already old and will rapidly get even older. Europe is split several ways: Germany, Italy and Spain, for instance, now have tiny families and are therefore ageing fast, whereas France, Britain and most of the Nordic countries have more children to keep them younger. In Eastern Europe, and particularly in Russia, birth rates are low and life expectancy has also taken a knock. America, thanks to a resilient birth rate and high immigration, will still be fairly youthful by mid-century.

Most developing countries do not have to worry about ageing – yet. Although birth rates have dropped, populations are still young and will remain so for a few decades yet, even though HIV/AIDS has killed off many active adults. But in the longer term the same factors as in the rich world – fewer births, longer lives – will cause poorer countries to age too. **— F —** They already have 490m over-60s, and that total is due to more than triple by 2050.

Fewer hands make heavy work

Macroeconomic theory suggests that the economies of ageing populations are likely to grow more slowly than those of younger ones. As more people retire, and fewer younger ones take their place, the labour force will shrink, so output growth will drop unless productivity increases faster. Since the remaining workers will be older, they may actually be less productive.

In most rich countries the ratio of people of working age to those of retirement age will deteriorate dramatically over the next few decades. **— G —** True, there will be fewer young people to maintain, but children cost less than old people and the overall burden will be much heavier than it is now.

For the public finances, an ageing population is a huge headache. In countries where public pensions make up the bulk of retirement income, these will either swallow up a much larger share of the budget or they will have to become a lot less generous, which will meet political resistance (and remember that older people are much more inclined to vote than younger ones). **— H —** And because of a huge increase in the number of over-80s, a lot more money, and careful thought, will be needed to provide long-term care for them as they become frailer. (778 words)

Adapted from: *The Economist*, 25 June 2009

1 MULTIPLE MATCHING

> Skills p. 177

Eight sentences have been removed from the text. Match sentences 1–10 with the correct gaps A–H. Two sentences do not fit.

1. The figures now are 67 and 78 respectively, and still rising.
2. Ageing will almost certainly affect financial markets in a big way, too.
3. In Japan, for instance, which currently has about three workers to every pensioner - already one of the lowest ratios anywhere - the number will halve by 2050.
4. To put it another way, in the rich world one person in three will be a pensioner; nearly one in ten will be over eighty.
5. In some developed countries the numbers have already started shrinking.
6. And even before that happens, the absolute numbers of older people there will swell alarmingly, simply because these countries are so populous.
7. These are the problems of ageing populations, and if they sound comparatively mild, think again.
8. Spending on health, which in most rich countries has been going up relentlessly anyway, is likely to grow even faster as patients get older.
9. As always, the averages mask considerable worldwide diversity.
10. The first of them are now coming up to retirement.

2 MEDIATION ENGLISH-GERMAN

> Skills p. 178

Beantworten Sie folgende Fragen stichwortartig auf Deutsch.

1 Welche beiden langfristigen Gründe für die Überalterung der Welt werden im Text genannt? Wie belegt die Autorin ihre Aussagen?
2 Welche Rolle spielen die Babyboomer in diesem Prozess?
3 Wie sieht die Zukunft Europas aus?
4 Welche Konsequenzen hat eine Überalterung für die Wirtschaft eines Staates?
5 Welche Probleme ergeben sich für die öffentliche Hand?

3 WORKING WITH WORDS

A Match the adjectives on the left to the nouns from the text (on the right) to make collocations. At least three adjectives can be used for each noun and many of them can be used more than once. Use your (online) dictionary if necessary. > Skills p. 175

annual | considerable | disproportionate | dramatic | economic | enormous | equal | false | growing | heavy | major | modest | national | overall | principal | terrible | unknown

average | burden | cause | crisis | diversity | growth | increase | share

EXAMPLE > *annual / national / overall average*

B Copy the table below and find eight expressions from the text that describe an increase or a decrease in numbers.

Increase	Decrease
(that share) will have risen (l. 3)	the numbers have already started shrinking (ex. 1)

C Add as many more words to the list as you can. (Think of verbs and nouns.)

EXAMPLE > *rise steadily / a steady rise; fall quickly / a quick fall*

4 TALKING

Work with a partner and discuss one of the topics below.

1 How and why will Germany's ageing population affect you personally? Make a list. Compare your list with your partner's.
2 Do you feel there is a difference in generational attitudes towards certain issues like the environment, women, same-sex marriage and immigration? How does your generation's view differ from your grandparents' view and in what ways are they similar?

D Further activities

1 DESCRIPTIVE WRITING

A Describing graphs: What will our world look like in the future? Write about 100 words. (Try to use words and phrases from exercise 3B, page 67.)

> Webcode: FOSEAU0501

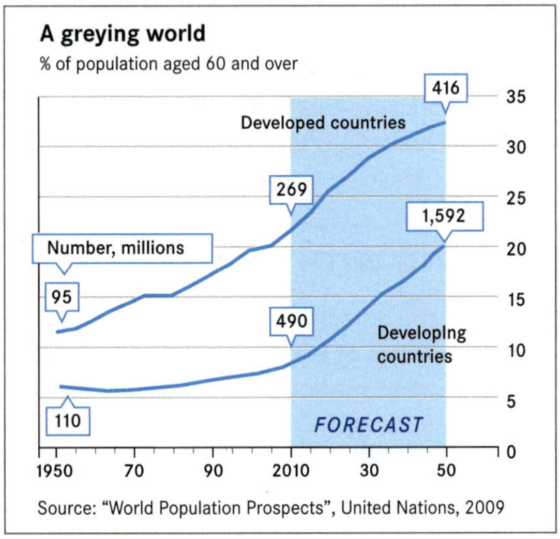

B Describing a cartoon: Describe the cartoon in about 100 words.

"We met, fell madly in love, got engaged, had a lovely wedding and honeymoon. Then things turned sour, we grew bitter, separated and divorced. It was quite a busy weekend!"

> Skills pp. 183–186

2 ARGUMENTATIVE WRITING

> Skills p. 181

Choose one of the following topics and write about 200 words.

1 Do you think there is a "generation gap"? How does it manifest itself?
2 Is your life easier than your parents' or grandparents' lives when they were your age?

3 PROJECT

> Skills p. 190

According to surveys, the wedding day is still the most important day in a couple's life, although divorce rates have been increasing steadily and the vow to stay together "until death us do part" seems to have lost its significance.

In groups, investigate how wedding customs and divorce rates have changed over the years. Pick one of the countries below and compare the year 1920 with the present.

South Africa	England	South Korea	Turkey
USA	India	Russia	China

4 LISTENING

> Skills p. 179

You are going to listen to a reporter interviewing three women at a wedding fair.

1 13 **A Listen once and take short notes on each speaker. Who is she? What is the most interesting thing she says in your opinion?**

1 13 **B Now listen again and complete the texts with appropriate words/expressions from the interviews or answer the questions.**

Interview 1:
The first woman interviewed is a ...[1] by profession. She accompanies the ...[2] and the ...[3] every step along the way from the moment they step through the doors of the hotel. She checks ....[4] for them, invites them to ...[5] and is there for them on the ...[6] as well. She enjoys seeing the couple in their ....[7], she can become ...[8] then.

Interview 2:
The second woman interviewed was ...[1] some of the ....[2] at the fair and felt like a ...[3]. She isn't married but has a boyfriend whom she met ...[4]. She wants to get married ...[5]. At the moment she is living ...[6] but wants to ...[7] with her boyfriend. She thinks that her ...[8] will have to ...[9] double to pay for her and her sister's wedding.

Interview 3:

1 How long has the third woman been married for?
2 How did she and her husband meet?
3 Why does she consider marriage important?
4 She thinks that fewer people marry nowadays. What are the reasons?
5 What advice does she give to younger people?

C Do you think that marriage is important? Write about 100 words.

5 GROUP DISCUSSION

> Skills p. 187

The US magazine *TIME* recently published portraits of people living today whom they considered to have the most influence and the most lasting impact on our times. Only about a quarter of them were women.

Imagine that you are working on an article about influential women for a student magazine. You have to choose two women who you consider important enough to be mentioned in the article. Choose candidates from File 4 (p. 160) or think of your own.

Phase 1: individual (= one-minute speech)
Present your candidate to the group, saying why she should be mentioned in your magazine.

Phase 2: interactive (= group discussion)
As a group, discuss each candidate and the reason why she is important, and make the final choice of the two women whom you consider to be most influential and rank the others in order of their importance.
If there is any time left, discuss possible reasons why only 25% of the most influential people on *TIME*'s list are women and if they really have the same opportunities as men.

E Grammar check

MODAL VERBS

> Grammar summary p. 197

SPOT THE MISTAKES

Spot the mistakes and correct them. Explain why they are wrong.

1 ~~Johanna can Spanish fluently.~~
2 ~~We mustn't run for the train.~~ It doesn't leave for another hour.
3 ~~I will must finish my report this weekend.~~ My boss wants it on her desk by Monday morning.
4 ~~Do I should write to her?~~ I haven't heard from her for a long time.

A Complete the dialogue with the English equivalent of the German verb in brackets. Be careful with the tenses.

JAKE: I've got my first date with Sylvia tomorrow – you know, from the online partner agency. I'm really nervous. You …[1] (*müssen*) be so glad that you've got a proper girlfriend. I wish I had one, too.

TONY: You …[2] (*nicht müssen*) be nervous. This online dating business is completely different. You …[3] (*nicht sollen*) forget that they have already weeded out all the candidates that are unsuitable for you. That's why you …[4] (*müssen*) fill in that questionnaire last month.

JAKE: Yeah, but I'm still nervous. Things simply …[5] (*nicht können*) go wrong like they did last time!

TONY: But that was all your fault. This time you …[6] (*nicht dürfen*) be late, for a start. You …[7] (*sollen*) arrive at least ten minutes early. Oh, and you …[8] (*nicht sollen*) take Fido with you to the restaurant, of course.

JAKE: Are you joking? I …[9] (*nicht können*) leave my dog at home all evening. I …[10] (*müssen*) take him with me. And, according to her online profile, Sylvia really loves dogs. If she doesn't, we …[11] (*nicht müssen*) bother getting together at all.

TONY: Well, you …[12] (*müssen*) be careful with Fido tomorrow evening. If he doesn't behave properly, you …[13] (*können*) have a problem.

JAKE: Maybe you're right. Maybe I …[14] (*sollen*) leave Fido at home. …[15] (you / *können*) dog-sit for me tomorrow night?

WATCH OUT!

Want

~~Some girls want that boys open doors for them, like gentlemen.~~
→ *Some girls want boys to open doors for them, like gentlemen.*
~~Some boys want not to accompany their girlfriends on shopping expeditions.~~
→ *Some boys don't want to accompany their girlfriends on shopping trips.*

B Translate the following sentences into English.

1 Die meisten Leute wünschen sich eine glückliche Beziehung.
2 Sie erwarten nicht unbedingt, dass sie ein ganzes Leben lang hält.
3 Aber sie wollen nur aus Liebe heiraten.
4 Ich möchte nicht, dass du mit ihm ausgehst.
5 Du kannst alles was du willst, wenn du nur willst was du kannst.
6 Warum wollen Mädchen nicht, dass Jungen ständig mit ihren Freunden abhängen?

6

Immigration and diversity

FOCUS

1 14

A Listen to the song and decide if the statements are true or false. Explain your answers by quoting a line from the song.

1 The immigrants come from a neighbouring country.
2 The immigrants are hopeful.
3 The immigrants are penned in during their voyage.
4 The immigrants bring a lot of possessions with them.
5 The immigrants are probably fleeing from oppression.
6 The immigrants see America as the 'Blessed Land'.

B Look at the photos and talk about these questions with your partner.

1 What associations do you have when you see the Statue of Liberty?
2 Have you ever thought of emigrating? Which country would you choose and why?
3 Do you think you would face problems trying to settle in a different culture? Explain.

A Ethnic diversity

BEFORE YOU READ

How multicultural is the place where you live? Have you ever thought of dating or marrying a girl/boy of a different ethnic origin?

Black? White? Asian?

More Young Americans Choose All of the Above

In another time or place, the game of "What Are You?" that was played one night last fall at the University of Maryland might have been mean, or menacing: Laura Wood's peers were picking apart her every feature in an effort to guess her race. "How many mixtures do you have?" a young man asked.

With her tan skin and curly brown hair, Ms. Wood's ancestry could have spanned the globe. "I'm mixed with two things," she said politely. "Are you mulatto?" asked Paul Skym, another student, using a word once tinged with shame that is enjoying a comeback in some young circles. When Ms. Wood confirmed that she is indeed black and white, Mr. Skym, who is Asian and white, boasted, "Now that's what I'm talking about!" in affirmation of their mutual mixed lineage. Then the group of friends – formally, the Multiracial and Biracial Student Association – erupted into laughter and cheers, a routine show of their mixed-race pride.

The crop of students moving through college right now includes the largest group of mixed-race people ever to come of age in the United States, and they are only the vanguard: the country is in the midst of a demographic shift driven by immigration and intermarriage.

...A... Multiracial and multiethnic Americans (usually grouped together as "mixed race") are one of the country's fastest-growing demographic groups. Many young adults of mixed backgrounds are rejecting the color lines that have defined Americans for generations in favor of a much more fluid sense of identity. They are also using the strength in their growing numbers to affirm roots that were once portrayed as tragic or pitiable.

...B... Optimists say the blending of the races is a step toward transcending race, to a place where America is free of bigotry, prejudice and programs like affirmative action. Pessimists say that a more powerful multiracial movement will lead to more stratification and come at the expense of the number and influence of other minority groups, particularly African-Americans. **...C...**

Prof. Rainier Spencer, director of the Afro-American Studies Program at the University of Nevada, Las Vegas says he believes that there is too much "emotional investment" in the notion of multiracialism as a panacea for the nation's age-old divisions. "The mixed-race identity is not a transcendence of race, it's a new tribe," he said. "A new Balkanization of race."

...D...

"All society is trying to tear you apart and make you pick a side," one student said. "I want us to have a say."

The faces of mixed-race America are not just on college campuses. They are in politics, business and sports. And the ethnically ambiguous are especially ubiquitous in movies, television shows and advertising. And student groups like the one at Maryland, offering peer support and activism, are more common. Such a club would not have existed a generation ago – when the question at the center of the "What Are You?" game would have been a provocation rather than an icebreaker.

"The No. 1 reason why we exist is to give people who feel like they don't want to choose a side, that don't want to label themselves based on other people's interpretations of who they are, to give them a place, that safe space," Ms. López-Mullins a group member said. Ms. López-Mullins is Chinese and Peruvian on one side, and white and American Indian on the other.

...E... Though his mother is Japanese and his father is African-American, he had basically one choice when it came to his racial identity. "I was black and proud to be black," Dr. Kelley said. "There was no notion that I might be multiracial. Or that the public discourse on college campuses recognized the multiracial community." Almost 40 years later, Dr. Kelley, the assistant vice president for student affairs at the university, is often in awe of the change on this campus.

"Even if someone had formed a mixed-race group in the '70s, would I have joined?" Dr. Kelley said. " **...F...** "

Not all of the group's 100 or so members consider themselves mixed race, and the club welcomes everyone. At a meeting in the fall, David Banda, who is Hispanic, and Julicia Coleman, who is black, came just to unwind among supportive listeners. **...G...** Mr. Banda and Ms. Coleman are thinking about having children someday. "One of the main reasons I joined is to see the struggles mixed people go through," he said, "so we can be prepared when that time comes." And despite the growth of the mixed-race population, there are struggles.

There is a wider debate among mixed-race people about what the long-term goals of their advocacy should be, both on campus and off. "I don't want a color-blind society at all," Ms. Wood said. "I just want both my races to be acknowledged." Ms. López-Mullins countered, " **...H...** " (943 words)

Adapted from: Susan Saulny, *The New York Times*, 29 January 2011

1 MULTIPLE MATCHING

> Skills p. 177

Match the sentences (1–10) with the gaps (A–H) in the text above. There are two more sentences than you need.

1 That safe space did not exist amid the neo-Classical style buildings of the campus when Warren Kelley enrolled in 1974.
2 One in seven new marriages is between spouses of different races or ethnicities, according to data from 2008 and 2009.
3 There is one common view how the growth of the multiracial population will change the country.
4 They told the other members how liberal people in their hometown, Upper Marlboro, Maryland were.
5 I don't know. My multiracial identity wasn't prominent at the time. I don't think I even conceptualized the idea.
6 But for many of the University of Maryland students, that is not the point. They are asserting their freedom to identify as they choose.
7 They discussed the frustrations of being an interracial couple, even today, especially back in their hometown, Upper Marlboro, Maryland.
8 No one knows quite how the growth of the multiracial population will change the country.
9 And some sociologists say that grouping all multiracial people together glosses over differences in circumstances between someone who is, say, black and Latino, and someone who is Asian and white.
10 I want mine not to matter.

2 MEDIATION ENGLISH-GERMAN

> Skills p. 178

Erklären Sie die folgenden Ausdrücke im Textzusammenhang auf Deutsch.

1 Ms. Wood's ancestry could have spanned the globe (l. 4)
2 they are only the vanguard: (l. 12)
3 a more fluid sense of identity (ll. 16-17)
4 a step toward transcending race (l. 19)
5 will lead to more stratification (l. 22)
6 a new Balkanization of race (l. 29)

3 WORKING WITH WORDS

A Use a member of the word family of the word in brackets to fill the gap. You may have to use the plural of a noun.

> Skills p. 176

It is a great ...[1] (pitiable) that race is still a problem today. There are several racist groups that are still very ...[2] (influence) in politics in many countries. Most of their leaders are ...[3] (bigotry) who pretend to have the well-being of the people at heart but they are full of hatred for people of a different ...[4] (ethnic). Their speeches are usually rife with ...[5] (ambiguous) so that the authorities can't impose a ban on them. They often ...[6] (advocacy) the deportation of illegal immigrants or even asylum seekers as well as harsher punishments for offenders with an ethnic background. They are blind to the ...[7] (society) and political implications of what they preach.

B Match a verb from box 1 with a noun or noun phrase from box 3 to form a collocation or idiomatic expression from the text. You may have to use a particle or article from box 2.

> Skills p. 175

EXAMPLE:

come *at the* *expense (of)*

Box 1	Box 2	Box 3
affirm	a	age
be	a	awe of sth.
come	~~at~~	comeback
~~come~~	in	differences
enjoy	into	~~expense (of)~~
erupt	of	laughter
gloss	over	roots
go	~~the~~	shame
pick	through	side
tinged	with	struggles

C Match these German expressions with words/expressions from the text.

1 demographischer Wandel
2 aktive Förderung von Minderheiten/positive Diskriminierung
3 sind allgegenwärtig in Film und Werbung
4 öffentliche Debatte
5 Allheilmittel/Patentrezept

4 TALKING

Discuss these topics with your partner and share your findings with the class.

1 What does racial identity mean to you?
2 Does race matter to you at all?

B Legislating against racial discrimination

BEFORE YOU READ

Have you ever experienced or witnessed examples of racial discrimination?

FORTY YEARS ON, HOW THE RACE LAWS HAVE FARED

A When the early waves of Commonwealth immigrants landed in Britain in the 1950s and 1960s, racism was instinctive, commonplace and brutal. New arrivals in white communities were routinely abused in the street. Boarding houses infamously carried signs reading: "No blacks, no Irish, no dogs". Black workers were barred from jobs at Euston station and Sikhs could only be hired as bus drivers if they took off their turbans.

Forty years ago today, Britain took its first step against such brazen bias and the first Race Relations Act came into force, outlawing discrimination on the "grounds of colour, race, or ethnic or national origins" in public places. It was a modest piece of legislation covering hotels and restaurants but excluding shops, and failing to tackle prejudice at work or in housing. It also made racial discrimination a civil, rather than a criminal, offence. But the Act remains a landmark moment, the foundation upon which subsequent race relations laws were built. Today, this country has some of the most comprehensive legislation against discrimination in the Western world. Most recently, local authorities have come under a duty to promote racial equality.

Social norms have also altered during the past four decades as any overtly public expression of racist views is widely regarded as unacceptable. However, with the increasing vote for the British National Party and recent clashes between black and Asian youngsters in Birmingham, no one pretends racial prejudice has been obliterated by legislation.

The Home Office Minister recently said that Britain had come a long way in the past 40 years. But he added: "It is very clear to me that racism is still not defeated and none of us should cease our efforts until it is."

B And although blatant bias is banned, many ethnic groups still suffer grave disadvantages compared to their white fellow citizens. Black, Pakistani and Bangladeshi men are three times more likely to be unemployed than whites. They are significantly poorer, live in worse housing and suffer higher infant mortality rates. The ethnic minorities are under-represented at senior levels of business, the civil service and the judiciary and they still only fill 15 of the 646 seats in the House of Commons.

Even where some ethnic groups are successful, there may be invisible barriers to their progress. Danny Sriskandarajah, a migration expert at the Institute for Public Policy Research, said research suggested that Indian doctors as well qualified as their white counterparts still did not achieve such senior posts. But he added: "In the 1960s, 1970s and

1980s, employers felt race relations legislation was an obligation which politically correct forces were forcing down their throats. These days leading businesses are talking about the value of diversity. They are saying that in an ethnically diverse market place they need an ethnically diverse workforce."

Simon Woolley, of Operation Black Vote, said "Pakibashing" by skinheads was routine in the 1960s and 1970s in Leicester where he grew up. Much ethnic minority blood has been spilt in the last 40 years, he added, in the fight against racism. "The fact that people don't live in segregated areas, as they do in Paris or the United States, is testament to how we have moved forward. But there is still much to do - two-thirds of black and ethnic minority people live in the poorest areas of the country.

"The shocking fact that there are so few black and ethnic minority MPs leads many communities up and down the country to feel alienated and frustrated that their concerns aren't being listened to." Sadiq Khan, the Labour MP for Tooting, said: "No one is pretending we are living in a Utopia and much still remains to be done to combat racial prejudice. But when I remember our family's early days in Britain living on a council estate, surrounded by racial abuse and criminal damage, I recognise huge progress has been made in the past four decades."

Half a century after the start of mass immigration, the non-white population stands at about 4.5 million, half of whom were born in this country. That total includes 2.8 million people who describe their background as Asian, 1.1 million who are Black Caribbean or Black African, and nearly 700,000 who are of mixed race. Swaths of the United Kingdom, including the north-east and south-west of England, Wales, Scotland and Northern Ireland, remain virtually all white.

But the ethnic make-up of much of inner London, where whites are now in the minority in some boroughs, and of cities such as Birmingham, Leicester, Bradford and Manchester has been transformed. Even if overt racial prejudice faced by those communities is officially outlawed, combating the inequality and institutional bias they encounter remains among the country's most pressing challenges. (788 words)

Adapted from: *The Independent*, 8 December 2005

> Webcode: FOSEAU0601

1 GAPPED SUMMARY

> Skills p. 177

Complete the text with words from part A. Use only one word for each gap.

Laws to fight racial discrimination in Britain are pretty ...[1] nowadays, covering all fields of life. However, the number of right-wing voters and clashes between ethnic groups are a reminder of the fact that laws haven't ...[2] discrimination completely. Racial discrimination was still ...[3] in Britain in the first decades after the Second World War, as the stories about signs against coloured immigrants show, and so the first Race Relations Act was a ...[4] despite its flaws. Discrimination on the grounds of race was unfortunately only made a ...[5] ...[6] in the Act. Furthermore, not all situations in life were included. ...[7] and discrimination still prevailed when coloured immigrants applied for a job or tried to rent a flat. However, it is not only legislation that has helped to improve the situation of immigrants in Britain over the past forty years, but also the changes in ...[8] ...[9]. Many people nowadays no longer put up with racist opinions, but it would be false to ...[10] the fight against racial bias completely as there is still much more to be done.

2 SHORT-ANSWER QUESTIONS / SENTENCE COMPLETION

> Skills p. 178

Answer the following questions and complete the following sentences with information from part B of the text.

1 What are the drawbacks non-white citizens have still to cope with? (*4 aspects*)
2 What does the migration expert mean when he speaks of "invisible barriers" (l. 48) for ethnic groups, no matter however successful they might be?
3 Most companies agree that workers of different ethnic background are an asset in … .
4 Why does Mr Woolley think that coloured people prefer Britain, in general, and Leicester, in particular, to the French capital or the USA?
5 Why does Mr Woolley think that the British people shouldn't cease their efforts?
6 Despite some improvement in the racial issue, coloured people might … as there is little representation for these people in politics.
7 Some areas of inner London are a good example of the fact that … , although vast regions of the UK are still … .
8 Besides the improvements due to race relations legislation, non-whites in many British cities still face problems. Which problems have to be addressed by British authorities? (*2 aspects*)

3 WORKING WITH WORDS

A Which word from the text completes each group of collocations?

> Skills p. 175

1	… diversity	… minority	… community	… tensions
2	to be in/out of … with sb./sth.	to do sth. … by …	to take …s	to take sth. a … further
3	to be quite an …	a joint …	to put … into one's work	to make a concerted …
4	to mean the … to sb.	to be …s apart	the best of both …s	to do sb./sth. the … of good

B Choose one expression from each list and use it in a sentence of your own.

C Which words collocate with "race" and which ones with "racial" when used in the context of ethnic groups?

abuse | card | course | discrimination | disobedience | equality | hatred | meeting | movement | prejudice | relations | riot | tensions | tracks | winner

D Use words/expressions from the text to complete the following statements.

Racial discrimination was first tackled when the Race Relations Act …[1] (*in Kraft treten*). Since then, the government, local councils and schools …[2] (*sind verpflichtet*) to actively promote racial equality. As a result, the situation in Britain …[3] (*hat sich positiv entwickelt*). However, there is no denying that some ethnic groups still …[4] (*ernste Benachteiligung erfahren*) and the issue of race relations …[5] (*bleibt eine dringliche Herausforderung*) for our generation as well.

4 TALKING

What measures could be taken in your town or city to help to make people of ethnic origins feel more at home? Discuss with a partner and share your findings with the class.

C Words in context

1 15

Immigration and integration

Whether climbing over barbed-wire fences, taking to sea in leaky boats or stowing themselves away in containers, migrants, asylum seekers and refugees throughout the world risk their lives daily in desperate attempts to improve their living conditions.

There is a long history of migration around the world and many reasons that cause the process. Some people abandon their native country due to climatic changes, such as drought or flooding, which leave the land barren or uninhabitable. The thousands of Irish people sailing to America during the Great Famine of the 19th century or the million Dust Bowl migrants of the Great Plains in the USA are just two examples of people in this particular category. Others immigrants flee from religious persecution, political oppression or war in search of safety and liberty. The Pilgrim Fathers of the 17th century are a well-known example of the former while the millions of displaced people in Europe after World War II bear witness to the latter.

A different group, often referred to as economic migrants, are those motivated by economic reasons. One example are the immigrants who cross the "Tortilla Curtain" separating Mexico and the United States. This also applies to the huge number of illegal immigrants from Africa who try to reach Spain or France and who are often the victims of ruthless human traffickers exploiting their desperate situation.

Throughout the centuries, however, some states have actually invited immigrants to come and settle. The United States recruited settlers from Europe in the 19th and 20th centuries and Germany, in the 1950s, invited guest workers from Turkey, Italy and other southern European states to help fuel its booming economy.

However, due to the practically endless number of immigrants, the fear of being swamped by foreigners along with resentment of the immigrants' foreign behaviour and customs ultimately results in xenophobia or racism. This makes settling in a foreign country even more difficult for immigrants than it otherwise should be, but the melting pot ideology of the United States demands that newcomers rapidly assimilate to American culture.

Quotas and citizenship tests are further barriers for immigrants. Even today, so-called "Minutemen" along the Mexican-American border are trying to keep Mexicans out. However, they have so far failed to curb the influx of these undocumented illegal immigrants.

On the other hand, some political initiatives aim to give illegal immigrants the chance to become naturalized citizens, although such initiatives often face opposition, especially in times of economic decline, when immigrants are accused of taking away the jobs of native citizens. Right-wing politicians in many countries have started to speak of a so-called "defining culture", or "Leitkultur", and have demanded that immigrants accept the main political, religious and cultural values of their new host country. However, white supremacy as advocated by radical racist groups such as the Ku-Klux-Klan in the USA or the National Front in Britain, is mainly a thing of the past, both in those two countries and in most other countries, as well.

Many immigrants, however, feel torn between two cultures and feel that they don't really belong to either. Alienation and uncertainty about their identity are often the result, particularly when they still face discrimination. Second- and third-generation immigrants, on the other hand, are more self-assertive, a fact which may sometimes cause outbreaks of racial tension, usually in the ghettos those ethnic minorities are confined to.

Although some European politicians have recently proclaimed that multiculturalism has failed, many other politicians consider cultural and ethnic diversity an asset. They stress the cultural enrichment, the broadening of cultural horizons and the atmosphere of tolerance such pluralism can bring. They also put forward the idea that the diverse ethnic composition of a society can be seen as an advantage in our globalized world. (623 words)

First of all, make sure you understand the meaning of the highlighted phrases used in the text on pages 78–79. If you are not sure, look them up in your dictionary. Then complete the tasks below.

1 WORDFIELDS

> Skills p. 176

A Find words/phrases in the text to describe different groups who come to a country for a variety of different reasons.

EXAMPLE > *migrants, ...*

B Which words/phrases in the text describe negative responses to immigration?

EXAMPLE > *fear of being swamped, ...*

C Which words/phrases in the text describe the positive aspects of immigration?

EXAMPLE > *assets, ...*

2 PARAPHRASES AND SYNONYMS

A Replace the underlined word/phrase by a word/phrase from the text.

1. Many people nowadays have to leave the place they were born in.
2. Ruthless traffickers taking advantage of the deplorable and hopeless circumstances some refugees are in should be punished hard.
3. Some states have introduced even more obstacles for those trying to get political asylum.
4. Fortunately, in many countries, a refugee can become a permanent resident of the state with the same rights as the rest of the people living there.
5. In many states multiculturalism is considered a benefit for society.

B Find the English equivalents of these German expressions.

1. die Menschenhändler
2. Schmelztiegel
3. den Zustrom begrenzen
4. Gastland
5. Staatsbürgerschaftstests
6. ethnische Zusammensetzung

3 ANTONYMS

Find an antonym (= word of opposite meaning) in the text for the following words.

1. tolerance
2. confident
3. oppression
4. jeopardy
5. native/local
6. liking
7. rise
8. shy/timid
9. majority
10. uniformity

D Further activities

1 LISTENING

> Skills p. 179

2 2

You are going to listen to a commentary about immigration. Answer the questions or complete the sentences with information from the text.

1 Europeans and Americans are likely to ... the size of the immigrant population in their home countries.
2 What percentage of the US population was actually born abroad?
3 What percentage of the migrant population in the USA does not have legal residency?
4 Which concerns of the local population make immigration such a difficult problem for policy makers in Europe and the USA? (*3 aspects*)
5 According to the survey, Americans are more worried about the ... of immigration, while Europeans are more concerned about the problem of ... .
6 The author uses the phrase "..." to compare the Americans' attitude to immigrant integratation to the Europeans'.
7 Which group of people is more likely to be concerned about immigration in both Europe and the USA?
8 What phrase does the author use to show that correct information can influence people's attitude towards immigration?

2 DESCRIPTIVE WRITING

A Describing cartoons:
Describe what you see and interpret the message of the cartoon in about 100 words.

B Describing statistics:
Describe and analyse the following line graph.
Write about 100 words.

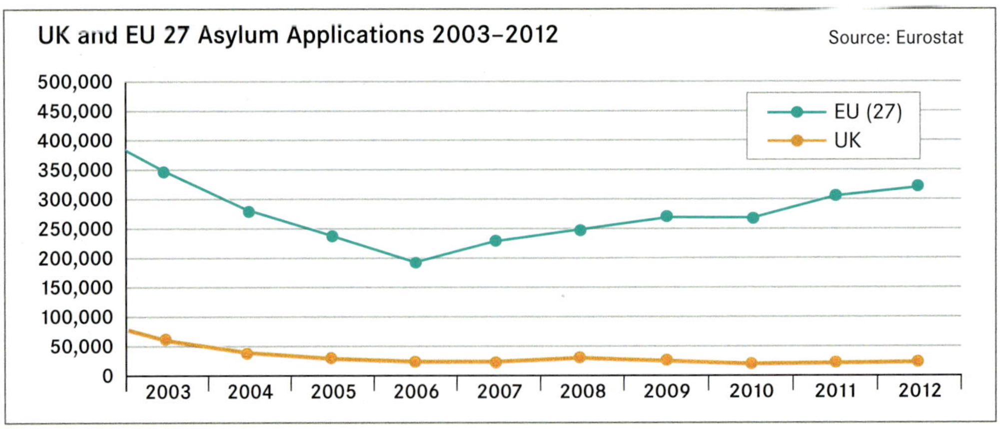

> Skills pp. 183–186

3 ARGUMENTATIVE WRITING

> Skills p. 181

Choose one of the following topics and write at least 200 words.

1. "This multicultural approach, saying that we simply live side by side and live happily with each other has failed. Utterly failed." Discuss this statement made by the German chancellor Angela Merkel in 2010.
2. "There are no benefits to immigration, just problems."
   Do you agree with this statement?

4 PROJECT

> Skills p. 190

You and your classmates want to find out how much racist organizations are still an issue in society today.

Split into groups and collect information on one of the organizations listed below. Prepare a fact sheet on 'your' organization, which gives a comprehensive but not too lengthy overview (who they are, members, activities, successes, etc.). Present your fact sheet as a PowerPoint presentation to the class.

- The Aryan Nation (USA)
- The National Front (UK)
- The Ku-Klux-Klan (USA)
- The Front National (France)
- The NPD (Germany, *optional*)

5 GROUP DISCUSSION

> Skills p. 187

You are a member of a student initiative at your school called "SOS" (= **S**tudents **O**ffer help to **S**chools) which was founded on the belief that young people often have better ideas for solving problems connected with schools than educationalists themselves. You have now been given the task of integrating foreign children better into the German school environment. A British TV team is visiting your school and has asked you to hold your meeting in English.

Phase 1: individual (= one-minute speech)
Present your suggestion to the other members of SOS. Tell them why you think your suggestion is the best one.

Phase 2: interactive (= group discussion)
Discuss the various other suggestions and try to convince the others that your choice is the most effective method to integrate foreigners. If you find that another suggestion is better, be prepared to make a compromise.

Suggestions:

- Foreign schoolchildren should not be allowed to speak their own language in the schoolyard - only German should be permitted.
- There should be compulsory German courses for the parents of all foreign school children if they are unable to speak the language.
- "Information classes" should be held at all schools where there is a higher percentage of migrant children to teach the German pupils more about the ethnic groups in their class.
- Efforts should be made to avoid having a majority of foreign children in any class. This means that migrant children may have to go to schools that are further away from their homes.
- All foreign children - no matter how old they are - should have the opportunity to attend remedial classes in German and other basic subjects on starting school in this country, to enable them to quickly catch up with their German classmates.

E Grammar check

SIMPLE PAST – PAST PERFECT

> Grammar summary pp. 194–196

SPOT THE MISTAKES

Spot the mistakes and correct them. Explain why they are wrong.

1 ~~The president knew about the immigrant problem for a long time when he was sworn into office.~~
2 ~~The police came into the room and arrested the man. He came to the USA illegally.~~
3 ~~If the political situation in his country wasn't so bad, he would have stayed there.~~
4 ~~When his wife had come home, her husband had gone out, but he left a note on the table.~~

A Complete the gaps with the correct verb form. In some cases, you need the passive.

Javier Hernandez …[1] (be) born to Mexican immigrants in the USA. His parents …[2] (leave) Mexico years before. After they …[3] (come) to the "promised land", they soon …[4] (realize) how difficult it was to settle in this new and strange country.
By the time the young boy …[5] (be) four years old, he …[6] (learn) to speak English fluently and even to read the local newspaper. At grammar school he …[7] (take) an interest in languages and by the end of school he …[8] (outdo) his US-born peers completely.
At the age of 16 his parents …[9] (decide) to move back to Mexico. When they …[10] (arrive) at their former hometown, most of the inhabitants there …[11] (move) somewhere else. Javier …[12] (convince) his parents to return to the USA again. After he …[13] (finally/achieve) full legal status in the USA, he …[14] (enroll) at a university in Boston. By the time he …[15] (be) 25, Javier …[16] (find) a well-paid job and …[17] (buy) a nice house for his family. If more illegal immigrants …[18] (have) a fair chance in former years, the USA would have had less trouble with the immigration problem.

B Translate the following sentences

1 Nachdem die Familie aus ihrem Heimatland geflohen war, hofften sie auf ein besseres Leben in ihrem neuen Gastland.
2 Als wir das letzte Mal in den USA waren, erfuhren wir, dass das Einwanderungsgesetz vom Senat abgelehnt worden war.
3 Als der Junge nach Arizona kam, konnte er kein Wort Englisch sprechen.
4 Die Gruppe der Mexikaner wartete schon über 2 Stunden, als die Schleuser kamen.

WATCH OUT!

> False friends p. 267

Problem words (2)

The ~~actual~~ immigration figures published by the Home Office are promising.
→ *The current immigration figures …*

C Choose the correct word so that each sentence makes sense.

1 Immigration policy proves to be too sensible / sensitive an issue for many voters.
2 The cost of monitoring the Mexican-American border has actually / currently turned out be much higher than many politicians expected.
3 During / While the presidency there was no overhaul of the immigration policy.
4 The new measures are the most sensible / sensitive so far with regards to the integration of illegal immigrants.
5 The Prime Minister is actually / currently on holiday and is unable to comment on the situation.
6 During / While many US states have opted for stricter immigration laws, President Obama decided to sign the Dream Act.

7 Spreading the news

FOCUS

Look at the photos above and talk about the following questions in groups.

1. How many hours or minutes per day do you use each of the media above?
2. What are the advantages and disadvantages of each type of media in the pictures?
3. Which media do you think are the most important ones? Put them in order from 1 (most important) to 5 (least important) and explain your choices.
4. Which do you think is most reliable? Explain why.

A The future of journalism

BEFORE YOU READ

Are you interested in the news? Why (not)? What could the news media do to attract more young readers or viewers?

The Technology of Journalism Improves, But Young People Still Ignore the News

A Read up on the *sturm und drang* in the news business and you'll find plenty of pundits predicting the death of print journalism in the next five minutes or so, along with a few (like myself) who think newspapers still have some life left in them. Whichever side you're on, the debate seems to mostly focus on delivery systems and business models – print vs. digital, display ads vs. pay-per-click, and so on. But all the geek-speak loses sight of a more fundamental problem: With each passing year, young people grow less interested in the news, regardless of how it's delivered.

B Statistics bear this out. Both newspaper circulation and network newscast ratings have long been in decline, and the audience that remains grows ever older. Even morning news shows, once thought immune to such trends, are now losing viewers. A Harvard survey found that only one in 20 teens and one in 12 young adults read a newspaper on close to a daily basis.

C Online news fares little better. A recent study found that in 2008, roughly 64 percent of 18-to-24-year-olds said they had viewed a newspaper online within the last year. But by 2009 that had dropped to 54 percent. The figures are even more worrisome when you consider that the study just measured whether a respondent had read online news at all – even once – in the last year.

D I teach journalism at a community college in suburban Philadelphia. At the start of every semester I ask my students how many read a newspaper or news website on a daily basis. Typically, maybe a third to one-half raise their hands. And if this is the response in a journalism class, what might it be in say, an art history course?

E Why don't young people follow the news more closely? In part, it's difficult for them to see how they're affected by current events. We live in a large, powerful and relatively insulated country, and it's easy to feel immune to the boom-and-bust cycles of the global economy if you're still a student delivering pizzas for Dominos and don't yet have a mortgage.

F Yes, we are at war in two countries, but unlike Vietnam there's no draft, and unlike earlier wars no national sense of shared sacrifice, either. And yes, we were attacked on 9/11 in a way that was once unthinkable, but for an 18-year-old college freshman the twin towers fell half a lifetime ago.

G All of this is no excuse. As citizens we have a duty to be informed about the world around us. But if young people don't follow the news, I place the blame mostly with those in the news business, and with newspapers especially.

From a trade to a profession

H For the first half of the 20th century journalism was regarded largely as a trade. Barriers to entry were low – typically just a high school degree was required – and so newsrooms regularly had a healthy influx of young blood.

I Then journalism schools – many of them staffed with theoreticians and academics rather than real reporters – sprang up across the country. Journalism became a middle-class job, then a profession. The pay got better. Newspapers, especially large metro dailies, started taking themselves very seriously. No longer could a talented kid just out of college or even one with a few years' experience land a job at a paper in New York or Chicago, or even Seattle or Denver. Newsrooms grew older.

J By the 1990s and 2000s, newsrooms were increasingly dominated by baby boomers at or approaching middle age. Not surprisingly the tone and content of those papers reflected that mindset, from the news sections to the arts and entertainment pages. If music critics raised on the Beatles and the Rolling Stones struggled to keep up with grunge and hip hop, is it any wonder the news business has been so slow to respond to the Internet revolution going on around it?

K Now the news business faces the toughest time in its history. Thousands of journalists have been axed, dozens of papers large and small have closed and still others are bankrupt. The great recession and the transformation of so-called legacy media in the digital age have shaken the industry to its very core.

L Yet most of the hand-wringing and analysis still focuses on us, the purveyors of news, and not on the consumers of news. To hear some media pundits tell it, if we just shut down the presses, go all-digital and find a workable business model, readers will follow.

M But will they? Will young people suddenly become avid news consumers when the digital transformation is complete? The evidence suggests not. And while solving journalism's logistical problems seems tough but doable, discovering how to capture the attention of a generation that cares little for news in any form is another matter entirely. (805 words)

From: Tony Rogers, *journalism.about.com*, 8 October 2010

> Webcode: FOSEAU0701

1 SHORT-ANSWER QUESTIONS

> Skills p. 178

Answer the following questions by providing the required information from paragraphs A–C of the text.

1 Which expression is used to describe the end of newspapers?
2 Which phrase in paragraph A expresses the author's discontent with the discussion on delivery systems and business models?
3 Which two trends are alarming for the newspaper business?
4 Which word describes the author's concern that young people are not interested in the news?

2 GAPPED SUMMARY

> Skills p. 177

Fill in the missing words from paragraphs D–M of the text. (The missing words are not necessarily in the same order as in the text.)

When young people are asked how many of them read a newspaper or a news website every day, the ...[1] is frustrating. One reason for their lack of interest is that many feel they are not ...[2] by the news directly. It is easy to use this as an ...[3] for this trend, but some of the blame must be put on the profession of journalism itself. The fact is, it is not easy for ...[4] young people to get a job in journalism because most of the positions are already occupied by older journalists. These people, the ...[5] of the news, are one of the reasons why the news business is confronted with the ...[6] period in its history. However, there is also no clear ...[7] that a change from print to digital media will be the answer to the problem. Until the news media can find out how to ...[8] young people's interest in the news again, the figures for readers and listeners will continue to fall.

3 WORKING WITH WORDS

A Match the nouns from the text (1–8) with eight of the explanations/synonyms (a–j).

1 delivery
2 circulation
3 ratings
4 survey
5 respondent
6 freshman
7 newsroom
8 barriers

a person who answers questions, especially in an opinion poll
b a place at a newspaper office where information is received and prepared for printing
c area where people live that is outside the centre of a city
d first-year student
e rules that prevent applicants from entering the job
f a measurement stating how popular something is
g a legal agreement by which a bank lends you money to buy a house
h an investigation into people's opinions
i the number of copies of a newspaper sold each day
j ways of presenting information to customers

B Find the English equivalents in the text of these German phrases.

1 die Daten bestätigen diese Tatsache
2 geschützt gegen solche gesellschaftliche Entwicklungen
3 Zyklen einer ernsten Krise nach einem außergewöhnlichen Aufstieg
4 Sinn für eine gemeinsame Opferbereitschaft
5 eine Blutauffrischung aufgrund eines Zustroms an jungen Menschen
6 spiegelte diese Einstellung wider
7 mussten ihr Bestes geben, um mithalten zu können
8 sind gefeuert worden

4 TALKING

In groups, discuss the questions below. Report your ideas to the class.

1 Do you think that current events at home and abroad have much of an effect on your life? Give examples.
2 Would you like to become a journalist? Why (not)?
3 "Newspapers are old-fashioned and out of date in the digital age." Do you agree?

5 PROJECT: ANALYSING NEWSPAPERS

> Skills p. 190

A In groups, analyse a different newspaper of your own choice. In each paper, look at the following points:

> headlines (size, content, style)
> content (sensational or factual treatment of news)
> language (style, length of articles)
> photographs and layout (use, content, impression on reader)
> sources (stated or not?)

B Use your analysis to give a short presentation on each paper to the class.

B News and social networks

BEFORE YOU READ

Do you think the spread of social networks will increase people's interest in the news? Why (not)?

The people formerly known as the audience

A When a young Tunisian, Mohammed Bouazizi, set himself on fire on December 17th to protest against the police confiscating his fruit stall and the lack of jobs for young people, his action prompted demonstrations by other youths in the town of Sidi Bouzid. A video of one protest, led by Mr Bouazizi's mother, was posted on Facebook, where it was seen by the new-media team at Al Jazeera, a satellite news broadcaster founded in 1996 and based in Qatar that has become the Arab world's most influential media outlet. Al Jazeera showed the video on air, and by the time Bouazizi died of his burns on January 4th, protests had broken out across Tunisia and spread across the Arab world.

B Marc Lynch, an expert on Middle Eastern media at George Washington University, says social media and satellite television worked together to draw attention to the Arab spring. "Social media spread images of protesters in Tunisia that might otherwise have been suppressed by the regime, but it was the airing of these videos on Al Jazeera which brought those images to the mass Arab public and even to many Tunisians who might otherwise not have realised what was happening."

C The staff in Al Jazeera's Arabic and English newsrooms had, as it happened, undergone intense social media training only the month before. Although Al Jazeera had used material from the internet in its coverage before, in Tunisia there was no other choice, because it had no reporters on the ground. With its journalists freshly trained in the use of such material, theory was quickly put into practice.

D The training was the culmination of a two-year initiative to make better use of social media throughout Al Jazeera, prompted by the realisation during the three-week Gaza war of 2008-09 that the channel's audience was swiftly moving online. This meant convincing journalists that social media are not a threat, but "the biggest assets you can have". Instead of flying a reporter somewhere to cover a story, Al Jazeera can draw upon networks of trusted volunteers whose credibility has been established. It also has a website, called Sharek, where photos and videos can be submitted for use – once verified – in Al Jazeera's television and online reports.

E Checking snippets of information posted on Twitter is more difficult. Tweets can be a useful way to gauge the public mood about an issue and are now often incorporated into news coverage as digital "vox pops". Many journalists use Twitter to solicit leads, find sources or ask for information. But Twitter is a public forum where anyone can say anything. Neal Mann, a producer who works for Sky News, a British satellite-news channel, says he thinks it is a journalist's duty to provide reliable information, on Twitter as elsewhere. He works with a network of trusted contacts around the world whose tweets he passes on to his followers. By providing more raw material than ever from which to distil the news, social media have both done away with editors and shown up the need for them.

F Either way, there is clearly a role for people, but not limited to them, to select, filter and analyse the torrent of information being posted on the internet. "And there still is an editorial function that needs to happen – there still needs to be someone who really makes sense of it all," says Jack Dorsey, co-founder of Twitter. This process is known in social-media jargon as "curation", and a growing number of tools is available to do the job.

G Readers and viewers have also become part of the news-distribution system as they share and recommend items of interest via e-mail and social networks. If searching for news was the most important development of the past decade, sharing news may be among the most important of the next. With a single click of a Facebook "Like" button, for example, you can recommend a story or video to your entire network of friends.

H Rather than relying solely on human editors or mindless algorithms to find the best content, it makes sense to use a hybrid approach, analysing contacts and behaviour on social networks to find items of interest, according to John-Paul Schmetz, the co-founder of Cliqz. However, Nick Denton, founder of Gawker Media, a network of popular blogs, is worried that the shift towards social filtering of news is making news organisations too dependent on Facebook. "It's eating their lunch," he says. Facebook's chief technology officer, Bret Taylor, insists that there is no conflict because his firm does not produce content but merely provides "valuable distribution" for it. (762 words)

Adapted from: *The Economist*, 7 July 2011

1 MULTIPLE CHOICE

> Skills p. 176

Choose the most suitable option. The statements relate to paragraphs A–D of the text.

1 People started protesting all over Tunisia after … .
- a Mohammed Bouazizi set himself on fire
- b a video of protesting people was posted on Facebook
- c Al Jazeera showed the video of the protest in a news report
- d Mohammed Bouazizi died of his burns on 4th January

2 According to the text, the fight for democracy in the Arab world was mainly triggered by … .
- a the TV station Al Jazeera
- b social media and digital television
- c the print media
- d the regime in Tunisia

3 Al Jazeera's journalists had to use Internet material in their coverage of the protests because they … .
- a didn't have any reporters on the scene
- b were all young and innovative
- c had just taken part in a social media training course
- d had broadcast information from Internet sources before

4 The expression "theory was quickly put into practice" (paragraph C) means … .
- a putting theoretical knowledge into practice immediately was part of their training
- b theory and practice should always be related
- c they had the chance to use what they had learned about social media in their jobs straight away
- d people forget what they have learned in theory if it's not used in practice quickly

5 Which feature of Al Jazeera's volunteers' contributions is not mentioned in the text? They are … .
- a authentic
- b numerous
- c reliable
- d cheap

2 MEDIATION ENGLISH-GERMAN

> Skills p. 178

Beantworten Sie folgende Fragen zu den Absätzen E–H stichpunktartig auf Deutsch.

1 Wie erleichtert Twitter die Arbeit vieler Journalisten? (*3 Aspekte*)
2 Welche Aufgabe haben die Leser/Zuschauer im digitalen Informations-Zeitalter? (*4 Aspekte*)
3 Wie können Leser die Nachrichten mitgestalten?
4 Welche Gefahr birgt diese Entwicklung?

3 WORKING WITH WORDS

A Complete the gap with a member of the word family of the word in brackets.

> Skills p. 176

1 Al Jazeera is an Arabic and English-language news ... (broadcast) located in Qatar.
2 It has developed into a very ... (influence) source of information in the Arab world.
3 Al Jazeera airs news which may be ... (suppression) by some regimes in the area.
4 Al Jazeera uses Internet sources for its ... (cover) of the news.
5 Its journalists have realized that social media do not pose a ... (threaten) to journalism.
6 Using Internet material was often Al Jazeera's only ... (choose) during the Arab Spring.
7 Of course, it is important to check the ... (credible) of the volunteers providing photos or videos.
8 The material that they ... (submission) for use is only broadcast after it has been verified.

B Find the words in the text which complete the following collocations.

> Skills p. 175

1	up to date ...	reliable ...	a torrent of ...	tourist ...
2	be in a good/bad ...	public ...	in a holiday ...	be in the ... for a party
3	controversial ...	topical ...	to have an ... with sth./sb.	to avoid the ...
4	Internet ...	... of information	to quote your ...	renewable energy ...
5	the latest ...	to bring good/bad ...	a ... story/item/ report	breaking ...
6	the ... manager/ department	a worldwide ... system	the unequal ... of wealth	the geographical ... of a species

C Use phrases from exercise B to complete these sentences.

1 The president was worried about the ... (*Stimmung im Land*) before she made the announcement.
2 According to ... (*die neueste Information*) released by the United Nations, the ... (*ungleiche Verteilung des Wohlstandes*) was still a massive problem.
3 Although it was a ... (*strittiges Thema*), she felt that she had to ... (*der Bevölkerung die schlechte Nachrichten überbringen*).
4 Her advisers wanted her to ... (*das Thema vermeiden*) because their ... (*Informationsquellen*) showed that the president's popularity among the voters was sinking rapidly.

4 TALKING

In groups, discuss the questions below. Report your ideas to the class.

1 What role do you think the new social media play in protest movements in Germany? Give reasons for your answers.
2 Which news sources do you think are the most reliable? Explain your point of view.

C Words in context

Trends in the mass media

Until the 19th century, news used to be spread by the social networks that were already in place because there was no other means available: people chatted at the market place or in taverns and the better-educated classes exchanged letters with gossip and news with their families and friends. The invention of the steam-powered printing press in the early 19th century, along with the growth of the railway network, made it possible for the news to reach a large number of readers. It gave rise to the mass circulation of newspapers that exist today. Britain, for example, still has a large number of national newspapers, classified as either high-quality "broadsheets" or lower-standard "tabloids".

Newspapers developed a monopoly on the news, journalism became a profession and the ownership of newspapers became an important factor in forming public opinion. The same basic model applies to the publicly-owned and privately-owned radio and television stations that have entered the mass market since then. News is gathered and analysed by specialists and disseminated to a mass audience or readership who pays for it either indirectly through advertising or directly at the newsstand or through their licence fees.

Since the turn of the millennium the Internet has fundamentally changed this model and the old social aspect of the media has returned. Skype, blogs, Facebook and Twitter are relatively new media, but they are recreating the ways in which people used to collect, share and exchange information in the past.

As a result, the news is becoming more diverse as new publishing tools have become available. Ordinary people are playing a more active role in the new system as collectors and consumers of news. This makes the news more democratic, but at the same time, more opinionated and partisan and readers have to make more decisions on whether the source of the news is reliable.

Television has undergone serious changes as well in the past two decades. Since the establishment of cable and satellite television channels, there has been concern about the lowering of standards of TV entertainment and news. Daytime talk shows, docusoaps and reality shows are more about humiliation and viewing figures rather than about objective information. This trend can also be seen in the treatment of celebrities, which is often sensationalist and insensitive. The debate about how much privacy celebrities who live in the public eye should expect is still going on.

There has also been growing concern over breaches of privacy caused by social networking websites such as Facebook and MySpace. They have become established forums for keeping in contact with old acquaintances and meeting new ones, but many users feel that their personal details are being circulated far more freely than they would like.

Film piracy and copyright violations are another widely discussed issue. The Internet makes it convenient to illegally copy and distribute movies or printed information on DVD or electronic files, which is online theft of copyright material. Copyright violation can discourage creators such as film makers, musicians or writers from producing more content in the future. The entertainment industry argues that this will have a significant impact on the products offered to consumers in the future. (526 words)

First make sure you understand the meaning of each of the highlighted phrases in the text on page 90. If you are not sure, look them up in your dictionary. Then complete the tasks below.

1 WORD FAMILIES

> Skills p. 176

A Copy the table below and add the missing words.

Abstract noun	*Noun: person*	*Verb*	*Adjective*
reading	...	...	...
...	———	*circulate*	...
specialization / ...	...	...	...
... / ...	...	*advertise*	...
...	...	*inform*	...
consumption	...	...	...
...	———	*decide*	...
...	...	...	*entertaining*
...	...	*produce*	...
...	...	*celebrate*	...

B Make sentences with five words from the table, but leave a gap for the words. Ask your partner to complete the sentences.

2 COMPOUND NOUNS AND COMPOUND ADJECTIVES

> Skills p. 175

Complete this report on media using compound nouns (e.g. *social network*) or compound adjectives (e.g. *better-educated*) from the text.

After the steam-powered ...[1] had been invented, ...[2] newspapers became popular and achieved a huge readership. Many low-quality papers in Britain still have a ...[3] and there are still several ...[4] national newspapers with a smaller readership.
The main competition for the ...[5] television stations comes from private cable and satellite TV channels. Many mass entertainment programmes such as daytime ...[6] have been turned into a successful TV format by embarrassing people to entertain the viewers.
Today new ...[7] such as social networks and weblogs give consumers a more active role in spreading and consuming news. However, one problematic aspect of the new digital media is ...[8] such as film piracy and illegally downloading music from the Internet.

3 WORDS/EXPRESSIONS IN CONTEXT

Complete the sentences with words/expressions from the text that mean the same as the underlined expressions.

1 The innovation of the printing press brought about the newspapers we have today.
The innovation of the printing press ... the newspapers we have today.
2 Stars who face a lot of media attention often complain about intrusion into their private lives.
Stars who ... often complain about ... .
3 Illegal downloads affect the profits of many music labels greatly.
Illegal downloads ... on the profits of many music labels.
4 Producers say that people like watching television programmes that are based on authentic people in authentic situations.
Producers say that people like watching ... .

D Further activities

1 LISTENING

> Skills p. 179

Maggie Wang, a media expert from Shanghai Language Education Press, is talking to Youth Radio about the dangers of the Internet.

2 4 **A Listen to the first part of the interview on Internet addiction and make notes on the following information:**

1 typical symptoms of excessive computer use
2 statistics/figures on Internet dependency

2 5 **B Now listen to the second part of the interview and complete the sentences.**

1 People get addicted to using the Internet because they want to escape from … .
2 Another reason why people access the Internet and social networks so often is because they are looking for … .
3 The Internet cannot provide help for emotional states such as … for very long.
4 One first strategy to break Internet addiction is to do activities such as … .
5 Outside support from experts can help people to find and understand the … that is the cause of their Internet addiction.
6 When they know what their problems are, they develop their … so that they can do without the comfort of the Internet.
7 It is very important for Internet addicts to widen their … .

2 ARGUMENTATIVE WRITING

> Skills p. 181

Choose one of the following topics and write at least 200 words.

1 The number of talk shows in which people reveal private and intimate details of their lives has increased enormously, attracting millions of viewers.
Would you ever consider taking part in such a show? State your reasons.
2 Can you imagine living without the Internet? Give your opinion.
3 "Social networking sites such as Facebook and MySpace enhance people's lives."
Discuss this statement.

3 PROJECT: COPYRIGHT AND DIGITAL PIRACY

> Skills p. 190

**In groups, investigate the copyright laws protecting intellectual property.
Consider the following aspects:**

> a brief history of copyright
> fair use of intellectual property
> the relationship between copyright and innovation
> copyright and the music/film/print media industry
> legal action against "piracy" of songs/films

Present your findings to the class. Suggest a practical solution to the problem of protecting intellectual property on the Internet for both consumers and the copyright holders.

4 GROUP DISCUSSION

> Skills p. 187

You are a member of a local organization that specializes in informing children and young adults about the dangers lurking on the Internet. In order to address as many young people as possible, you are going to put up posters in town. As the posters need to be attractive, you decide to include a cartoon on them.

Phase 1: individual (= one-minute speech)
Introduce yourself and briefly describe your cartoon to the other people at the meeting. Tell them why the problem dealt with in this cartoon is the most important one in your opinion.

Phase 2: interactive (= group discussion)
Discuss the dangers referred to in each of the cartoons and then decide which cartoon is the most relevant for today's younger generation and deserves to be on the poster. Try to come to an agreement and start to plan the campaign.

"The identity I stole was a fake!
Boy, you just can't trust people these days!"

Look at File 3 on page 159 for the remaining cartoons.

5 DESCRIPTIVE WRITING

> Skills pp. 183–186

A Describing a cartoon: Choose one of the cartoons on page 159 (File 3). Describe what you see and interpret the cartoonist's message. Write about 100 words.

B Describing statistics: What do the following statistics tell you about the media habits in the US? Write about 100 words.

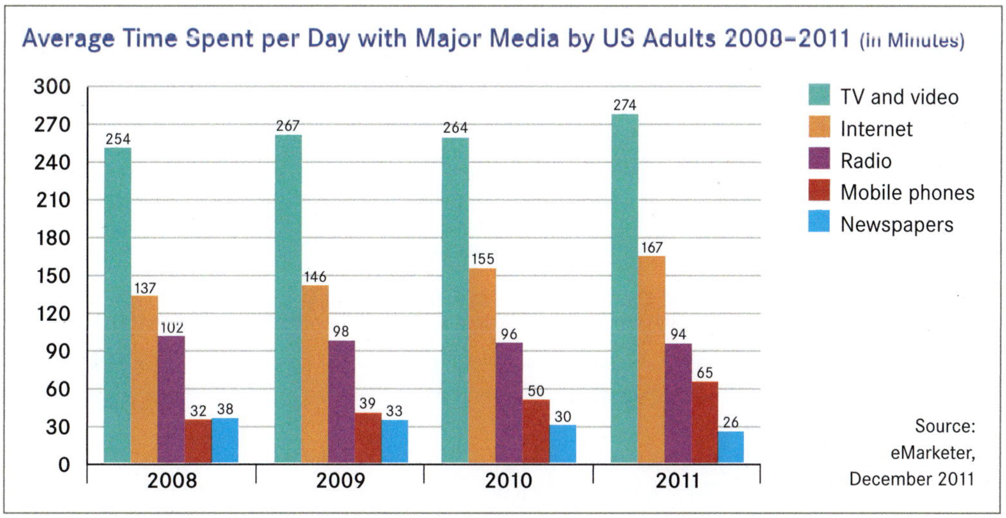

E Grammar check

GERUND / INFINITIVE

> Grammar summary pp. 202–203

SPOT THE MISTAKES

Spot the mistakes and correct them. Explain why they are wrong.

1 ~~He would like surfing the Internet every day if he had enough time.~~
2 ~~He refuses listening to his friend's advice to stop this habit.~~
3 ~~He enjoys to meet his friends online.~~
4 ~~He cannot imagine to do without his computer.~~
5 ~~He's looking forward to buy the new computer game.~~
6 ~~He doesn't mind to sit at the computer playing games most of his spare time.~~

A Complete this report on the dangers of the Internet by using the gerund or the infinitive form of the verb in brackets.

Most young people enjoy ...[1] (surf) the Internet nowadays. But people who are too careless with their security or personal information risk ...[2] (become) the victims of Internet crime. Many people do not mind ...[3] (give) their personal data in social networks when they are asked to do so, and many do this without ...[4] (realize) the dangers involved. This information can be used ...[5] (commit) crimes such as Internet fraud and identity theft. Many employers now also decide ...[6] (check) the Internet ...[7] (get) information on job applicants before offering them a job. Many young people simply refuse ...[8] (listen) to the experts' advice. They recommend ...[9] (be) on the alert when using the world wide web.

B Complete the sentences by using the gerund or the infinitive form of the verb in brackets.

1 The minister thanked the journalists for ... (come) to the press conference and said that he had enjoyed ... (talk) to them.
2 However, one journalist couldn't wait ... (ask) him one final question.
3 The reporter asked the minister ... (explain) why the taxpayers' money had been wasted on unnecessary projects.
4 The minister didn't give any details, but promised ... (inform) him as soon as he had any further information.
5 The journalists considered ... (drop) the matter, but then they decided ... (follow) the story up.
6 After that, the minister refused ... (answer) any more questions and left the meeting.

WATCH OUT!

> False friends p. 267

Problem words (3)

Many young people ~~look~~ TV for hours every day.
→ *Many young people watch TV for hours every day.*

C Choose the correct word to complete the sentences.

1 The computer junkie spent the whole night looking / watching DVDs.
2 He could hardly stand up / get up the next morning.
3 His mother told him that he would disgrace / blame himself if he arrived at work looking so tired.
4 She told him to least / at least get to work on time, otherwise his chef / boss would be really angry.
5 He had to borrow / lend his friend's bicycle so that he could get to work quickly.
6 In the end, he was lucky / happy that his employer wasn't there when he arrived just a little bit late.

8

Energy and the environment

FOCUS

QUESTIONNAIRE

Your carbon footprint is the amount of carbon dioxide that you produce over a period of time by using fossil fuels for energy. Carbon is a key component of the greenhouse gases that pollute our atmosphere and are responsible for global warming.

Find out about your personal carbon footprint by answering the questions below:

	often	some-times	rarely
Do you buy fruit or vegetables from abroad?			
Do you buy meat from abroad?			
Do you travel by car?			
Do you travel by plane?			
Do you leave the lights on when you leave the room?			
Do you leave electrical appliances on standby?			
Do you replace household items rather than repair them? (mobile phones, TVs, etc.)			
Do you buy bath and beauty products?			
Do you keep the room temperature above 20 degrees in winter?			
Do you use a fan to cool down in summer?			
Do you throw away rubbish without recycling it?			

Discuss the following questions in groups:

1 How many times was your answer to the questions in the questionnaire "often" or "sometimes"? What activities do you do that produce a high carbon footprint?

2 Decide on three changes to your lifestyle that would help create a sustainable life and future for you and your children.

A The future of energy

BEFORE YOU READ

What do you think our main sources of energy will be in 20 years' time? Why?

OUR INCREDIBLY DULL ENERGY FUTURE

Even if we make big strides towards clean energy, the future won't look very different from today.

A The future of energy is going to be awesome. Everyone will drive an electric car powered by the sun. We'll completely eliminate our need to burn coal or natural gas, and nuclear power will be a thing of the past.

No, wait. The future of energy is going to be terrible. Peak oil will catch us off guard. Combating climate change will mean abandoning modern conveniences. Within a generation, we'll all be living like it's 1899.

These two predictions couldn't be more different, but they do have one thing in common: they both make the future of energy sound awfully exciting. Whether you're pessimistic or optimistic, you get the feeling that everything is going to change, and fast. But what if it doesn't?

B I think the future of energy is probably going to be a little boring. I don't mean to say that the way we make and use energy now is perfectly safe. Relying so completely on fossil fuels has some mighty big risks, and if we keep on doing what we're doing, we'll eventually pay a stiff price. Changes have to be made. But the way those changes are likely to play out over the next couple of decades is surprisingly underwhelming.

C For instance, in May 2011, the Intergovernmental Panel on Climate Change released a report aimed at detailing the global potential of existing renewable energy technologies and explaining what has to be done to make those technologies work the way we want them to. According to this report, in 2008 all of the countries in the world got 12.9 percent of their energy from renewable sources. By 2030 more than half of the scenarios

showed the world getting about 17 percent of its energy from those sources. That amount of change isn't piddling, but it doesn't represent a massive shift in lifestyle either.

D The truth is that while the optimistic and pessimistic possibilities make for great science fiction, reality is often a lot more messy ... and banal. That's true today, and it was true the last time we totally changed our energy infrastructure.

The first permanent electric grids in the world started operating in 1882. Today, it's tempting to look back and see those events as unequivocal triumphs. But they weren't. It wasn't until the 1920s, following the invention of a multitude of small electric appliances and motors, that electricity became a profitable industry.

E The trouble is that we don't have as much time to transform our energy system today. With a peak in global oil production looming and the effects of climate change already being felt, can we really afford to let the next 20 years go by without something exciting happening? The answer is yes ... and no. Exciting things have to happen, in the sense that we need to set ourselves some energy goals and stick to them. But even if we do that, the world won't be all that different in 2030.

F Integrated Global System Modelling (IGSM) is a computer model designed to make forecasts about issues related to climate change and energy. One of the things it's been used to do is make realistic predictions about how American energy sources might change if we put serious, global limits on atmospheric carbon dioxide concentrations.

G If we limit global carbon dioxide concentrations to 550 parts per million (ppm), we'll be hitting a relatively stringent goal. Carbon dioxide concentrations are already around 390 ppm. And the rise of industrial production in places like China and India is likely to mean that emissions will increase at a faster rate in years to come. A firm 550 ppm limit would be a big deal. But during the next 20 years, the effects of drawing that line in the sand wouldn't be terribly dramatic - at least not in terms of where we get our energy from.

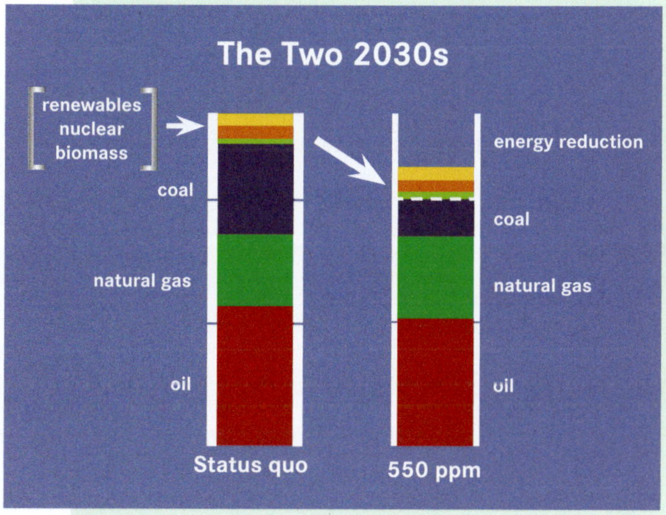

H If we limit carbon dioxide to 550 ppm, IGSM predicts that fossil fuels will still be the United States' biggest energy source in 2030. Our use of renewables will increase, but not by much. By far the biggest changes IGSM expects are a 17 percent decrease in energy use, compared with a 2030 where we've done nothing, and a shift from coal to natural gas. Those are important changes, but they're not necessarily ones you'll notice in your everyday life. New light bulbs will replace old ones. Thermostats and appliances will be a little smarter and more efficient. This 2030 is definitely different from a 2030 where we've done nothing.

I When we look at the future of energy, our goal shouldn't be to create a utopia. Instead, our goal should be to take what we have and make it more sustainable. That's not easy, and it doesn't happen overnight. Like the first utility companies, we're doing a lot of experimentation here and there's no one right answer for how to make all the parts fit together. That's why 2030 is likely to be kind of boring. Boring is the first step in building something amazing. (875 words)

Adapted from: Maggie Koerth-Baker, *Future Tense*, 17 October 2011

1 LOOKING AT THE TEXT

Explain the message of the text in one or two sentences. Why is our energy future going to be "incredibly dull"?

2 SHORT-ANSWER QUESTIONS

> Skills p. 178

Answer the questions with information from the text.

1 What will an optimistic and a pessimistic future of our energy sources and consumption look like?
2 What information does the text give about the development of renewable energy?
3 What does the author use electricity as an example of?
4 What effect would it have to limit the global carbon dioxide concentration to 550 parts per million?

3 GAPPED SUMMARY

> Skills p. 177

Fill in the missing words from paragraphs A–F of the text. Use one word only for each gap.

What does our energy future look like? At the moment, there are two conflicting ...[1]: some experts say it is going to look ...[2], others claim that we will still be ...[3] on fossil fuels in the next few ...[4]. In reality, it looks as if our use of ...[5] energy will rise by only a relatively small ...[6]. History shows that a ...[7] in technology often occurs slowly. It was only after many electric ...[8] had been invented that electricity started to be used widely.
Today the global warming situation is so serious that we can hardly ...[9] to wait until we solve the problem of how to change the way we produce energy. It is high time we set an upper limit to the amount of ...[10] ...[11] in the atmosphere.

4 WORKING WITH WORDS

A Match the words from the text (1–8) with the definitions/paraphrases (a–h).

1 terrible (l. 7)
2 combating (l. 8)
3 conveniences (l. 9)
4 messy (l. 41)
5 electric grid (l. 44)
6 unequivocal (l. 46)
7 utopia (l. 94)
8 amazing (l. 102)

a a perfect but imaginary idea
b very surprising
c things that are useful and can make life easier and more comfortable
d difficult to deal with
e expressing an opinion or intention very clearly
f very unpleasant and frightening
g system of wires for transmitting electricity across a country
h stopping sth. harmful from getting worse

B Find synonyms in the text for the following words.

1 unbelievable
2 boring
3 get rid of
4 giving up
5 at the end
6 for example
7 problem
8 developed
9 substitute

5 INTERPRETING STATISTICS

> Skills p. 185

Describe the graph and say what it tells us about energy trends in the future. Write about 100 words.

6 TALKING

Work in small groups. Which view of our future energy use do you agree with: the optimistic view, the pessimistic view or the author's view?

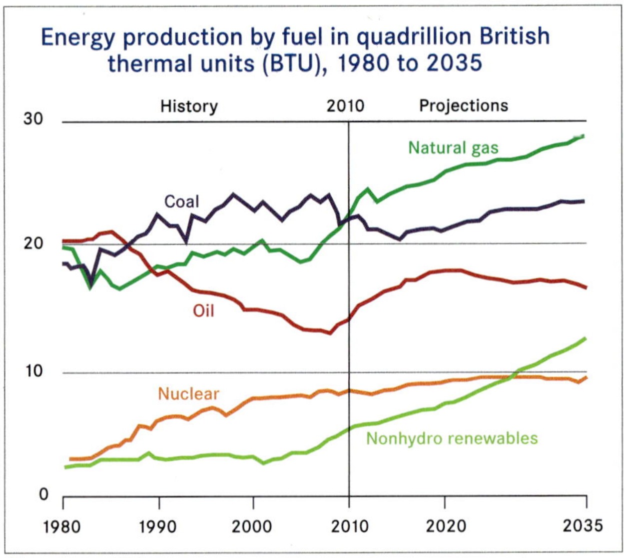

Source: US Energy Information Administration

B Consumer society and waste disposal

BEFORE YOU READ

What do you use to carry your shopping home? What could you do to reduce the amount of waste in your home?

GLOBAL HUNGER for plastic packaging leaves waste solution a long way off

A Five hundred tonnes of Christmas tree lights and at least 25m bags of plastic sweet wrappers, turkey coverings, drinks bottles and broken toys will be thrown away by UK homes this Christmas and new year. But only a tiny proportion of this waste will be recycled. Even at other times of the year, only a little under a quarter of the UK's plastic waste is recycled. Globally, recycling of plastics is even smaller.

Environmental damage caused by plastic waste

B The outcome is a belief that the Earth is being slowly strangled by a gaudy coat of impermeable plastic waste that collects in great floating islands in the world's oceans, clogs up canals and rivers, and is swallowed by animals, birds and sea creatures.

C In many parts of the developing world it acts as a near ubiquitous outdoor decoration, along roads in India, around villages in Africa and fluttering off fences across Latin America. And when it is not piling up, it is often burned in the open, releasing noxious smoke.

D There are no global figures on the true scale of the problem but, according to PlasticsEurope, the European trade association for plastics manufacturers, 265m tonnes of plastic are produced globally each year. In the UK, about two thirds of this is for packaging; globally, this would translate to 170m tonnes of plastic largely created to be disposed of after one use.

E Even at the almost unmatched EU recycling rate of 33%, two thirds of that - or more than 113m tonnes - would end up in landfills, being burned or cluttering up the environment. Such a figure, almost certainly a huge underestimate, would be enough to cover the 48 contiguous states of the US in plastic food wrapping. If the world recycled packaging at the rate the US does, 15%, it would generate more than enough plastic to cover China in plastic wrap. Every year.

F What would a world without plastic look like? In a world where farmers, retailers and consumers use wood, tins, glass bottles and jars, and cardboard to cover their goods, the mass of packaging would increase by 3.6 times, it would take more than double the energy to make and the greenhouse gases generated would be 2.7 times higher.

G To understand this, consider the properties of plastic that make it so attractive: it is durable, flexible, it does not shatter, it can breathe (or not) and it is extremely lightweight. As a result, food and drink are protected from damage and kept for lengths of time previously unimaginable.

H The European Packaging and Films Association (PAFA) says average spoilage of food between harvest and table is 3% in the developed world, compared with 50% in developing countries, where plastic pallets, crates, trays, film and bags are not so widespread. Once the food reaches people's homes, its lifespan is also increased - for a shrinkwrapped cucumber from two to 14 days.

I A less obvious benefit is that, by being much lighter than alternatives, plastic packaging greatly reduces the fuel needed for transport. Because of the huge carbon content of our diets, it is estimated that for every tonne of carbon produced by making plastic, five tonnes are saved, says Barry Turner from PAFA.

Landfill site in Africa

J A more surprising point is made by Friends of the Earth's waste campaigner Julian Kirby, who points out that because it is inert in landfills, plastic waste buried in the ground is a counterintuitive way of "sequestering" carbon and so avoiding it is adding to global warming and climate change.

K This focus on carbon and climate change, however, ignores the very reasons plastic bags and plastic packaging generally first gripped the public imagination - namely that it is such a highly visible result of our throwaway society.

L Many "ethical" products - from sandwiches to nappy bags - have switched to biodegradable plastics, made either from natural products such as cornstarch or by using an additive that helps break down the plastic. However, Turner suggests this will remain a niche, because the process is expensive and - in his words - is "destroying" a resource that could be recycled.

M Recycling plastic is particularly hard because there are so many types and because it is difficult to remove contamination. Increasing recycling is, though, one of the two areas focused on by the plastics industry. It estimates that if every council in the UK operated at the rates achieved by the best local authority for each type of plastic - PET bottles, cartons, trays, bags and so on - the country could raise total plastic recycling from 23% to 45%. "On-the-go" recycling - currently almost nonexistent - also needs to be dramatically improved, said Turner.

N To meet its self-imposed target of zero plastic waste to landfill by 2020, however, the industry is largely looking to incineration, which is highly controversial with environment groups and communities, who worry about how waste ash is disposed of and breathing in emissions from the plants - despite assurances from the Health Protection Agency that modern plants are not damaging to health.

O Environment campaigners want more attention paid to the "waste hierarchy" - reduce, reuse, recycle. To drive this change, the government this month proposed increasing all recycling targets, raising plastics to 50%.

P Globally, 47 industry groups have united to fund research to stop plastic getting into the seas. On land, countries could adopt a system used in several European nations where manufacturers are responsible for recovering a percentage of the plastic they make. "The idea of producer responsibility is one that people are most agreed on, but no one's sure how," said Kirby. (937 words)

Adapted from: *The Guardian*, 29 December 2011

1 MULTIPLE CHOICE

> Skills p. 176

Choose the most suitable option.

1 Britain recycles ... .
  a only a minute percentage of its plastic waste
  b turkey coverings, christmas tree lights and broken toys
  c less than 25 per cent of its plastic waste
  d more than other countries all over the world

2 Which of the following information about plastic is <u>not</u> mentioned in paragraph C?
  a You can see lots of waste plastic material when you travel in India.
  b Plastic waste seems to be everywhere in African villages.
  c Plastic waste is often burnt in the open in America.
  d Plastic waste can be found outside throughout Latin America.

3 Disposing of plastic waste is such a problem because most of the plastic produced is ... .
  a used for packaging
  b thrown away after only one use
  c manufactured globally
  d burnt instead of recycled

4 According to paragraph E, the actual figure for plastic recycling in the EU is ... .
  a correct
  b a secret
  c lower than the recycling rate
  d higher than the rate in the text

5 What would a world without plastic look like?
  a Pollution would be much higher.
  b People would use glass instead.
  c Less packaging material would be needed.
  d Our energy mix would be improved.

6 Which of the following is <u>not</u> mentioned in paragraph G?
  a Plastics can be used and kept for a long time.
  b Plastics will be extremely valuable in the future.
  c Plastics are lightweight.
  d Plastics can conserve food well.

2 MEDIATION ENGLISH-GERMAN

> Skills p. 178

Beantworten Sie folgende Fragen stichpunktartig auf Deutsch. (Absätze H–P)

1 Wie beeinflusst die Plastikverpackung die Haltbarkeit von Nahrungsmitteln?
2 Warum wirkt sich die Plastikverpackung positiv auf die Kohlendioxid-Bilanz aus? (*2 Aspekte*)
3 Warum ist biologisch abbaubarer Plastik keine Lösung des Problems?
4 Warum lässt sich Plastik nur schwer wiederverwerten? (*2 Aspekte*)
5 Wie versucht die Industrie, Plastikabfall auf Müllhalden zu vermeiden?
6 Was verstehen Umweltaktivisten unter „Abfall-Hierarchie"?
7 Wie kann man am Besten verhindern, dass Plastikabfälle das Meer verschmutzen?

3 WORKING WITH WORDS

A Find the English equivalents of the following German words in the text.

1 winzig
2 giftig
3 Eigenschaften
4 Verderb
5 Müllhalde
6 Verschmutzung
7 Verbrennung
8 durchgesetzt

B Use the English words from exercise A to complete this report on waste disposal.

Disposing of waste in a ...[1] without energy recovery is the least sustainable waste management option. An even worse option is ...[2] because burning waste releases ...[3] substances which pollute the air. Laws must be passed and ...[4] to ban the ...[5] of our air and water. One further aspect of our waste problem is food ...[6], which means food which is harmful to eat because it has lost its health-giving ...[7] due to being stored for too long. If each of us took one or two ...[8] measures to reduce, reuse and recycle our waste, it would help the environment enormously.

4 INTERPRETING A CARTOON

> Skills p. 183

Describe the cartoon and interpret the cartoonist's message in about 100 words.

5 PROJECT – SAVING THE EARTH

> Skills p. 190

The earth is suffering from environmental problems which are becoming increasingly dangerous because of humans' irresponsible behaviour.

> Choose one region of the world (e.g. Africa, China, the Arctic, the rain forest, an industrial country) and research information on the environmental problems there. Take issues such as pollution, waste, deforestation, overpopulation, energy and water consumption into account.
> Research possible solutions to these specific problems.

Present your findings to the class with a poster or PowerPoint presentation. > Skills p. 188

C Further activities

1 LISTENING

> Skills p. 179

Christoph Khor, an energy expert, is giving a presentation on energy.

Fukushima nuclear disaster, 2011

A Before you listen: talk about the picture. What was the impact of this incident?

2 6 **B Listen to the presentation on electricity production and take notes. Then answer the following questions.**

1 What fact has changed the energy policies in many countries?
2 Why do many countries still continue to use nuclear power plants?
3 What is the most important disadvantage of fossil fuels?
4 How long does it take to build a hydro power station?
5 What is the benefit of biomass?
6 What are the drawbacks of wind energy?
7 What seems to be the most promising source of energy for the future?
8 What important aspect should we take into consideration when talking about energy production?

2 GROUP DISCUSSION

> Skills p. 187

Work in groups of four or five students.

Phase 1: individual (= one-minute speech)
Introduce yourself briefly and point out what you do personally to save energy.

Phase 2: interactive (= group discussion)
You are members of a European Energy Committee discussing energy concepts for the future. Discuss some of the options below and come to an agreement on which forms of energy you would include in a long-term energy concept for your area (no more than three options).

- energy imported from other countries
- energy from fossil fuels (e.g. coal-fired power stations)
- nuclear energy
- wind power
- solar energy
- hydroelectric power

3 ARGUMENTATIVE WRITING

> Skills p. 181

Choose one of these options and write a composition of at least 200 words.

1 "Our present means of individual transportation will soon be outdated." (Prof. Ferdinand Dudenhöffer, car expert)
Is Germany prepared for this development? Give reasons for your opinion.

2 "Unless the human species manages to slow down the change to the environment, the fate of extinction might be inevitable." (Prof. Yuan Tseh Lee, Nobel Prize winner)
Is Professor Lee right?

Webcode: FOSEAU0801

D Words in context

Energy and the environment

Energy use and supply is of fundamental importance to our society and it is this aspect of human activity that has had the greatest impact on the environment.

Fossil fuels (oil, coal and gas), which represent 80 per cent of total energy consumption, contribute to air, soil, sea and river pollution. Road transport is the main source of toxic gas emissions which result in pollution and contribute to global warming. Greenhouse gases such as carbon dioxide and methane trap heat and light from the sun in the earth's atmosphere so that the temperature rises around the Earth: the so-called greenhouse effect.

Deforestation in the Amazon

Another cause for global warming is the deforestation of tropical rain forests for wood, pulp and farmland. Forests extract carbon dioxide from the atmosphere and store it in trees. Deforestation releases large amounts of carbon, as well as reducing the amount of carbon dioxide capture on the planet. According to research, climate change could lead to the extinction of more than a million species on Earth, and the biodiversity of the rain forests, which are the world's most spectacular ecosystems, will be seriously affected as well. Global warming also causes a rise in sea levels and an increase in the intensity of storms such as hurricanes.

With global warming increasing, the main challenge is how to conserve energy. One alternative is to use advanced technology to reduce our energy consumption. Great hopes rest on the development of non-polluting, renewable energy sources such as solar, wind and biofuels. Encouraging consumers to be more economical with their daily energy consumption is also a key factor in the success of an energy management plan. According to statistics, one person in the USA consumes 30 times more energy than one person in India.

We also have to deal with the problem of waste. Waste production is a reflection of modern consumer society and lifestyle, and developed countries are producing more and more waste, e.g. 900 kg a year per inhabitant in the USA.

Germany has been successful in its fight against growing landfill sites by introducing a sophisticated waste disposal system. The Green Dot system has been one of the most successful recycling initiatives and has led to a reduction in waste. A major part of the success of this programme is the proper sorting of domestic waste.

Any kind of bottle or glass jar that is non-returnable, and on which no deposit has been paid, belongs in the designated glass bin. Other domestic waste, such as paper, cardboard and plastic materials, is collected at scheduled times. Biological waste makes up almost 50 per cent of total waste produced in Germany. It includes leftover food, coffee filters, garden waste, etc. and is put into a brown bin. The rest of the household rubbish is usually incinerated. Hazardous waste, which includes batteries, paint, disinfectants, etc., has to be disposed of in the proper manner.

Educating people to use less energy and to recycle are the best ways to address the environmental problems we face. (500 words)

First of all, make sure you understand the meaning of each of the highlighted phrases used in the text above. If you are not sure, look them up in your dictionary. Then complete the tasks on page 105.

1 DEFINITIONS

Find the highlighted words in the text that match these definitions.

1 a sum of money that is paid when buying a bottle, but which is given back when returning the bottle
2 the existence of a large number of different kinds of animals and plants which make for a balanced environment
3 the act of cutting down or burning the trees in an area
4 the problem resulting from the gradual rise in temperature of the earth's atmosphere, caused by an increase of gases such as carbon dioxide in the air, which trap the heat of the sun
5 the act of getting rid of materials that are no longer needed and that are thrown away
6 the amount of energy, food, or materials used
7 using no more of something than is necessary
8 poisonous
9 burnt until it is completely destroyed
10 thrown-away material, which involves danger to somebody's health and safety

2 WORD FAMILIES

> Skills p. 176

A Copy the chart below and add the missing words. Some of the words you need are in the text, others you will have to find in the dictionary.

Noun (abstract)	*Noun (person)*	*Verb*	*Adjective*
...	...	...	*usable*
...	...	*represent*	...
...	...	*contribute*	...
...	...	...	*manageable*
consumption	...	...	...
...	...	*produce*	...
...	...	*educate*	...

B Make sentences with words from the table, but leave a gap for the words. Ask your partner to complete the sentences with the appropriate words.

3 COMPOUND NOUNS

> Skills p. 175

The text contains several compound nouns. Find ten examples of compound nouns as used in the text.

EXAMPLE > *energy use, energy supply, ...*

4 COLLOCATIONS

> Skills p. 175

Find collocations in the text that correspond to these German expressions.

EXAMPLE > *total energy consumption*

1 große Mengen
2 ernsthaft in Mitleidenschaft gezogen
3 große Hoffnungen
4 großer Teil
5 richtige Mülltrennung
6 nahezu 50 %
7 gefährlicher Abfall

E Grammar check

THE PASSIVE

> Grammar summary p. 200

SPOT THE MISTAKES

Spot the mistakes and correct them. Explain why they are wrong.

1 ~~At the moment a lot of solar cells are being installing on the roofs.~~
2 ~~Will the greenhouse effect reduce by these measures?~~
3 ~~In industrialized countries too much waste is producing by industries and individuals.~~
4 ~~We have to act because our environment has endangered by man-made pollutants for decades.~~

A Complete the text with the correct passive form of the verbs in brackets.

In 2011 a law …[1] (pass) in Germany to shut down nuclear power plants step by step. Environmentalists complain that so far only a few of them …[2] (switch off). It …[3] (not, expect) that many other European countries will do without nuclear power. A lot of effort and money …[4] (need) to find alternatives for energy production. At the moment, solar energy …[5] (finance) heavily by the state. It …[6] (say) that the fossil fuel lobby is not interested in promoting renewable forms of energy. The problem is that the energy market …[7] (control) by some large enterprises. That is why a reliable energy policy …[8] (must, introduce) by the government to ensure a change in our energy mix. And, equally important, these decisions …[9] (should, support) by the population, even if the energy prices do increase at first. But the question of what an energy mix should look like …[10] (not, answered) yet.

B Translate these sentences into English.

1 Das Leben auf der Erde wird durch das Verbrennen fossiler Brennstoffe immer mehr gefährdet.
2 Tatsächlich wird in Industrieländern mehr Energie als je zuvor verbraucht.
3 Auf einem Umweltgipfel sind Maßnahmen zur Verminderung von Treibhausgasen beschlossen worden.
4 Als Folge wurden in einigen Industrieländern Gesetze verabschiedet, die erneuerbare Energien fördern sollen.
5 Man hofft, dass dadurch der Klimawandel gestoppt werden kann.
6 Man kann nicht erwarten, dass die Energiewende innerhalb weniger Jahre erreicht werden kann.

WATCH OUT!

> False friends p. 267

as, how, like, than

~~Consumers are using more renewable energy as in the past.~~
→ *Consumers are using more renewable energy than in the past.*

C Choose the correct option to translate the German "wie" or "als".

1 Martin Jones used to work as / like an engineer in a nuclear power station. (*als*)
2 However, he decided that he wanted to leave the Earth how / than it was for his children. (*wie*)
3 For that reason, he decided to use his experience as / like an engineer to work for renewable energy sources. (*als*)
4 More renewable energy is being produced as / than in previous years, but he thought that was still not enough. (*als*)
5 He aimed to achieve consumption of renewable energy how / like in Germany, where it is as high as / than it has ever been. (*wie; als*)

9 The developing world

FOCUS

Oil field pollution in Nigeria

Village school in South Sudan

Refugee camp in northern Kenya

Mumbai slums, India

Look at the photos and do the following tasks.

1 Describe what you see in the photographs.
2 What do you think are the most urgent problems facing children in these developing countries?
3 In 2010, approximately one billion of the world's inhabitants were forced to get by on less than one Euro per day. What would you be able to buy for one Euro a day here in Germany?

A Words in context

Why is the developing world so poor?

The news is regularly dominated by reports of poverty, famine, starvation, malnutrition or epidemic disease in the developing world. Why do so many of these countries have so much trouble overcoming their difficulties?

First of all, we need to look at the colonial history of the present-day nations in Africa, Asia and Latin America. In the nineteenth and early twentieth centuries, the major European powers turned vast areas of these continents into colonies. Their aim was to exploit the abundant supply of natural resources and thus gain even more wealth. This exploitation prevented the indigenous peoples from controlling their own destinies, developing their own economies or maintaining their own cultural identities. Essential educational and health care services such as schools, universities and health clinics were totally neglected. Moreover, the colonial powers failed to build a sufficient network of roads, rail lines, wells and water lines. In many cases, the European powers divided up their areas of control into new political entities, thereby displacing tribes and clans and forcing these former rivals to live together within newly-drawn political boundaries. These arbitrary policies frequently led to civil wars and, as a result, to waves of refugees – which in turn put further pressure on those regions that had become impoverished by colonial policies. In addition, many of these refugees – unable to make a living out in the inhospitable countryside – eventually migrated to big cities which, in turn, were incapable of coping with so many newcomers. The result was the growth of sprawling slums with abominable living conditions that are a feature of many megacities in developing countries.

After most of the former colonies gained their independence in the mid-twentieth century, the problems described above made it all the more difficult for these newly-formed nations to make social, political or economic progress. In many cases, the most talented people left their native countries to study and work in America or Europe. This development, the so-called "brain drain", makes it virtually impossible for these nations to solve their problems on their own.

The policies of the industrialized countries in the more recent past haven't helped, either. Massive distribution of foreign aid has frequently made Third World nations even more dependent on subsidies, while loans made to them by international financial institutions have led to a massive level of Third World debt, which the developing nations are incapable of repaying. Protective import tariffs on their agricultural produce and other goods exported to America and Europe make it difficult for local producers in the developing world to make a profit and thus improve their standard of living. Their plight is actually made worse by the export of grain and other agricultural products from the EU and the United States to the developing countries. As these exports are subsidized by the EU and the USA, local farmers in developing countries simply can't compete and are forced out of business. As a result, the citizens, and above all the children, of these countries are undernourished or even starve to death.

Long-term solutions will only start to have a real effect when the developed nations start to rethink their aid policies. They could start by offering massive debt relief and by eliminating protective trade policies. In addition, they will have to invest heavily in sewer systems, modern telecommunications technology and alternative forms of energy production connected to modern power grids. (567 words)

First of all, make sure you understand the meaning of each of the highlighted phrases used in the text on page 108. If you are not sure, look them up in your dictionary. Then complete the tasks below.

1 PARAPHRASES AND SYNONYMS

A Paraphrase the following words and/or expressions that appear in the text.

1 natural resources
2 indigenous peoples
3 political entities
4 impoverished
5 foreign aid
6 subsidies

B Find phrases in the text that mean the same as these definitions.

1 difficulty coping with their problems
2 preserving their traditions and customs
3 political positions that are not based on logic and reason
4 an area of land that does not lend itself to human habitation
5 the exit of talented people who seek to live and work abroad
6 the policy of not requiring Third World countries to pay back all of the money they once borrowed

C Find the English equivalents of the following German words or expressions.

1 Ausbeutung
2 Bürgerkriege
3 völlig verarmt
4 Elendsviertel, die sich weit ausdehnen
5 die Notlage
6 Handelsbarrieren

2 WORDFIELDS

> Skills p. 176

A Collect words or phrases from the text that belong to the following general categories.

hunger	*types of infrastructure*
famine, ...	*essential educational and health care services, ...*

B Add any other words that you know to the lists.

3 COLLOCATIONS

> Skills p. 175

Look for the words in the text which complete the following collocations.

1	... and demand	a ... of natural resources	to be in short ...	to cut off ...
2	inner ...	... for learning	to pool one's ...	to be rich in natural ...
3	some watches ... time	... in popularity	to ... control	to ... weight/speed
4	to ... and rule	... a number by two	to ... into different categories	to ... up a cake
5	to be on ...	a bird's eye ...	a room with a ...	a point of ...
6	to provide tax ...	a ... fund for refugees	to show the Earth's surface in ...	a sigh of ...

B A population explosion?

BEFORE YOU READ

More than one billion hectares of agricultural land have already been made infertile by human activity. What consequences will this have for our planet's ability to support 10 billion people?

Can the Planet Support 10 Billion People?

A A United Nations report released on Tuesday projects that world population, instead of stabilizing at above 9 billion by 2050, will keep growing and may hit 10.1 billion by 2100. Growth in Africa remains so high that the population there could more than triple in this century, rising from today's one billion to 3.6 billion, the report said – a sobering forecast for a continent already struggling to provide food and water for its people. Demographers called the new projections a reminder that a problem that helped define global politics in the 20th century, the population explosion, is far from solved in the 21st.

B "Every billion more people makes life more difficult for everybody – it's as simple as that," said John Bongaarts, a demographer at the Population Council, a research group in New York. "Is it the end of the world? No. Can we feed 10 billion people? Probably. But we obviously would be better off with a smaller population."

C Among the factors behind the upward revisions is that fertility is not declining as rapidly as expected in some poor countries, and has shown a slight increase in many wealthier countries, including the United States, Britain and Denmark. Though they were a major focus of development policy in the 1970s and 1980s, programs that encourage family planning have stagnated in many countries, caught up in ideological battles over abortion, sex education and the role of women in society. Conservatives have attacked such programs as government meddling in private decisions, and in some countries, Catholic groups fought widespread availability of birth control. And some feminists called for less focus on population control and more on empowering women.

D Over the past decade, foreign aid to pay for contraceptives – $238 million in 2009 – has barely budged, according to United Nations estimates. The United States has long been the biggest donor, but the budget compromise in Congress last month cut international family planning programs by 5 percent. "The need has grown, but the availability of family planning services has not," said Rachel Nugent, an economist at the Center for Global Development in Washington, a research group.

E The director of the United Nations population division, Hania Zlotnik said in an interview that the revised numbers were based on new forecasting methods and the latest demographic trends. But she cautioned that any forecast looking 90 years into the future comes with many caveats. That is particularly so for some fast-growing countries whose populations are projected to skyrocket over the next century. For instance, Yemen, a country whose population has quintupled since 1950, to 25 million, would see its numbers quadruple again, to 100 million, by century's end, if the projections prove accurate. Yemen already depends on food imports and faces critical water shortages. In Nigeria, the most populous country in Africa, the report projects that population will rise from today's 162 million to 730 million by 2100.

F The implicit, and possibly questionable, assumption behind these numbers is that food and water will be available for the billions yet unborn, and that potential catastrophes including climate change, wars or epidemics will not serve as a brake on population growth. "It is quite possible for several of these countries that are smallish and have fewer resources, these numbers are just not sustainable," Dr. Zlotnik said.

G Well-designed programs can bring down growth rates even in the poorest countries. Provided with information and voluntary access to birth-control methods, women have chosen to have fewer children in societies as diverse as Bangladesh, Iran, Mexico, Sri Lanka and Thailand.

Clinic in Nigeria

H One message from the new report is that the AIDS epidemic, devastating as it has been, has not been the demographic disaster that was once predicted. Prevalence estimates and projections for the human immunodeficiency virus made for Africa in the 1990s turned out to be too high, and in many populations, treatment with new drug regimens has cut the death rate from the disease. But the survival of millions of people with AIDS who would have died without treatment, and falling rates of infant and child mortality – both heartening trends – also mean that fertility rates for women need to fall faster to curb population growth, demographers said.

I Other factors have slowed change in Africa, experts said, including women's lack of power in their relationships with men, traditions like early marriage and polygamy, and a dearth of political leadership. While about three-quarters of married American women use a modern contraceptive, the comparable proportions are a quarter of women in East Africa, one in 10 in West Africa, and a mere 7 per cent in Central Africa, according to United Nations statistics.

J Some studies suggest that providing easy, affordable access to contraceptives is not always sufficient. A trial by Harvard researchers in Lusaka, Zambia, found that only when women had greater autonomy to decide whether to use contraceptives did they have significantly fewer children. Other studies have found that general education for girls plays a critical role, in that literate young women are more likely to understand that family size is a choice. (846 words)

Adapted from: *The New York Times*, 3 May 2011

1 MULTIPLE CHOICE

> Skills p. 176

Choose the most suitable option.

1 The word "sobering" in line 8 means that forecasts are ... .
 a imprecise b self-evident c unanimous d unsettling

2 In paragraph C, the author mentions that efforts to control population growth around the world have failed for several reasons. Which of the following is not mentioned?
 a disagreement over the responsibilities females should have in society
 b influence exerted by religious beliefs
 c unwillingness on the part of some to fund sex education and abortion programmes
 d lack of information about population growth in developing countries

3 When, in paragraph E, Hania Zlotnik says that "any forecast comes with many caveats" (ll. 54–56) she means that … .

a caution must be exercised when making predictions about the future
b the predictions are essentially a foregone conclusion
c predictions of an imminent population explosion are totally unfounded
d a population of 10 billion is a huge problem regardless of the forecasting methods used

4 In paragraph F, the author refers to several assumptions made to support the idea that the population figures in certain countries will rise quite dramatically. Which one is not mentioned?

a Enough water will be available to support millions of future inhabitants.
b More generous foreign aid from industrialized countries will allow developing nations to support rapidly growing populations.
c Military conflict and the spread of disease will not cause birth rates to drop.
d Global warming will not lead to a declining birth rate.

5 According to paragraph H, an even greater effort must now be made to decrease the birth rate in Africa because … .

a fewer people will die of AIDS because new methods of treatment are now available
b progress made in fighting the AIDS epidemic and in securing the survival of babies means that populations will automatically grow
c African women still don't know enough about effective birth-control methods
d African women still haven't gained control over their own lives

6 The most important message conveyed by the author of the text is that … .

a the AIDS epidemic in Africa has killed fewer people than anticipated
b some wealthy countries have reported an increase in their population figures
c supporting up to 10 billion world inhabitants will be a major problem in the future
d rich nations are not keen to supply people in developing countries with contraceptives

2 GAPPED SUMMARY

> Skills p. 177

Fill in the missing words from paragraphs I and J of the text.

In the author's opinion, progress towards reducing population growth in Africa has been slowed down by social …[1] in the region such as people getting married very young and …[2]. This shows how men still have a dominant role in society. The lack of progress is also due to a …[3] of government programmes to provide support for women in the form of low-cost …[4] to birth control. Most experts agree that the …[5] of women to decide whether or not to practise birth control is a prerequisite to achieving a …[6] lower birth rate in Africa. Another aspect that is …[7] to achieving that objective is to make sure that young African women are …[8] so that they can make informed decisions that are in their own interest and which can help them achieve a higher standard of living.

3 WORKING WITH WORDS

A Match these *verbs* from the text (1–6) with the appropriate definition/synonyms (a–f).

1	release	a	forecast
2	project	b	interfere
3	decline	c	enable (sb.) to make progress
4	meddle	d	set free
5	caution	e	fall
6	empower	f	warn of possible dangers

B **Match the *nouns* from the text (1–6) with the correct definition/synonyms (a–f).**

1	demographer	a	someone who is an expert on business and trade systems
2	fertility	b	the state of being common at a particular time or place
3	revision	c	person who gathers statistics on population trends
4	economist	d	means of birth control
5	contraceptive	e	ability of human beings to have offspring
6	prevalence	f	process of changing something in order to improve it

C **Match the *adjectives* from the text (1–6) with the correct definition/synonyms (a–f).**

1	slight	a	capable of existing in its present state over a long period of time
2	critical	b	inhabited by many human beings
3	populous	c	small, hardly noticeable
4	sustainable	d	at the point of being dangerous with regard to possible effects
5	literate	e	available in a quantity that is able to meet the demand
6	sufficient	f	capable of reading and writing

D **Now find the *verb*, *noun* or *adjective* form of all the words listed in parts A, B and C of this exercise. Some of the words do not have all three forms. Start like this:**

	Noun	*Verb*	*Adjective*
A	*release*	*release*	———
B	*demographer*	———	*demographic*
C	*slight*	*slight*	*slight*

4 TALKING

In groups, discuss one of the topics below. Make a list of as many convincing answers as possible. Report your ideas to the class.

1. John Bongaarts (paragraph B) says that “every billion more people makes life more difficult for everybody – it’s as simple as that.” What does he mean? How could this development affect your own life?
2. The text says that some feminists (paragraph C) call for “less focus on population control and more on empowering women”. What do you understand by “empowering women”? What measures might they have in mind and why might these measures be effective?

5 PROJECT

> Skills p. 190

Use the Internet to find out more about one of the following topics. Present your findings to the class.

1. What environmental and/or humanitarian problems affect various African countries, e.g. Nigeria, Sudan, Somalia or the Democratic Republic of Congo? Form groups and choose one country each.
2. Three women were jointly awarded the 2011 Nobel Peace Prize for their non-violent struggles for women’s rights: Liberian President Ellen Johnson Sirleaf, Leymah Gbowee, an activist from Liberia, and Tawakul Karman, a Yemeni rights activist. Wangari Maathai was also awarded the Nobel Peace Prize in 2004. Form groups, choose one woman each and profile her life.

> Webcode: FOSEAU0801

C A much-needed solution

BEFORE YOU READ

Why do you think that baby girls might be welcomed less than baby boys in certain developing countries?

THE WOMEN'S CRUSADE

A In the 19th century, the paramount moral challenge was slavery. In the 20th century, it was totalitarianism. In this century, it is the brutality inflicted on so many women and girls around the globe: sex trafficking, acid attacks, bride burnings and mass rape.

B Yet if the injustices that women in poor countries suffer are of paramount importance, the opportunity females represent in an economic and geopolitical sense is even greater. "Women hold up half the sky," in the words of a Chinese saying, yet that's mostly an aspiration: in a large slice of the world, girls are uneducated and women marginalized, and it's not an accident that those same countries are disproportionately mired in poverty and riven by fundamentalism and chaos. There's a growing recognition that focusing on women and girls is the most effective way to fight global poverty and extremism. The world is awakening to a powerful truth: Women and girls aren't the problem; they're the solution.

C One place to observe this alchemy of gender is in the muddy back alleys of Pakistan. In a slum outside the city of Lahore, a woman named Saima Muhammad used to dissolve into tears every evening. Saima had barely a rupee, and her deadbeat husband was unemployed and not particularly employable. He was frustrated and angry, and he coped by beating Saima each afternoon. Saima's husband accumulated a debt of more than $3,000, and it seemed that these loans would hang over the family for generations. Then when Saima's second child was born and turned out to be a girl as well, her mother-in-law, a harsh, blunt woman named Sharifa Bibi, raised the stakes. "She's not going to have a son," Sharifa told Saima's husband, in front of her. "So you should marry again. Take a second wife." Saima was shattered and ran off sobbing.

D It was at that point that Saima signed up with the Kashf Foundation, a Pakistani microfinance organization that lends tiny amounts of money to poor women to start businesses. Kashf is typical of microfinance institutions, in that it lends almost exclusively to women, in groups of 25. The women guarantee one another's debts and meet every two weeks to make payments and discuss a social issue, like family planning or schooling for girls. A Pakistani woman is often forbidden to leave the house without her husband's permission, but husbands tolerate these meetings because the women return with cash and investment ideas.

E Saima took out a $65 loan and used the money to buy beads and cloth, which she transformed into beautiful embroidery that she then sold to merchants in the markets of Lahore. She used the profit to buy more beads and cloth, and soon she was earning a solid income – the only one in her household to do so. Saima began paying off her husband's debt. Eventually 30 families were working for her, and she put her husband to work as well. Saima was able to pay off her husband's entire debt, keep her daughters in school, renovate the house, connect running water and buy a television.

F What should we make of stories like Saima's? Traditionally, the status of women was seen as a "soft" issue – worthy of mention but of marginal interest. Our awakening as journalists came in China. In 1989, we came across an obscure demographic study that outlined a human rights violation that had claimed tens of thousands more lives. It found that 39,000 baby girls died annually in China because parents didn't give them the same medical care and attention that boys received. Those Chinese girls never received a column inch of news coverage, and we began to wonder if our journalistic priorities were skewed.

G The global statistics on the abuse of girls are indeed numbing. It appears that more girls and women are now missing from the planet, precisely because they are female, than men were killed on the battlefield in all the wars of the 20th century. Surprisingly frequently, we've come across a mother mourning a child who has just died of malaria for want of a $5 mosquito bed net; the mother says that the family couldn't afford a bed net and she means it, but then we find the father at a nearby bar. He goes three evenings a week to the bar, spending $5 each week.

H If poor families spent only as much on educating their children as they do on beer and prostitutes, there would be a breakthrough in the prospects of poor countries. Girls, since they are the ones kept home from school now, would be the biggest beneficiaries. When women hold assets or gain incomes, family money is more likely to be spent on nutrition, medicine and housing, and consequently children are healthier. Yet another reason to educate and empower women is that greater female involvement in society and the economy appears to undermine extremism and terrorism.

I A study in Kenya by Michael Kremer, a Harvard economist, examined six different approaches to improving educational performance, from providing free textbooks to child-sponsorship programs. There are, of course, many examples for the role of intelligent foreign assistance. For our part, we like to think of aid as a kind of lubricant, a few drops of oil in the crankcase of the developing world, so that gears move freely again on their own. That is what the assistance to Samai amounted to: a bit of help where and when it counts most, which often means focusing on women like her. And now Samai is gliding along freely on her own – truly able to hold up half the sky.

(932 words)

Adapted from: *The New York Times*, 23 August 2009

1 MULTIPLE MATCHING

> Skills p. 177

Match these headings with the corresponding paragraphs (C–I) from the text. Two headings do not match.

1 Facing terrible odds
2 Only time will tell
3 A clear case of misguided investment
4 Purely a question of effectiveness
5 Mistaken identity
6 Don't let their resourcefulness go to waste
7 An economic miracle on a small scale
8 Making an exception pays off in this case
9 Not worth a headline

2 SHORT-ANSWER QUESTIONS / SENTENCE COMPLETION

> Skills p. 178

Answer the questions or complete the sentences with information from the text.

1 The phrase ... refers to ethical issues of the highest priority that the world has faced in the course of history.
2 What sort of humiliation are many women confronted with these days? (*4 aspects*)
3 In paragraph B, another word for "torn" is ... .
4 In paragraph C, the fact that women can work wonders if you let them is expressed by the phrase ... .
5 In what ways did Saima's children profit from her newly-found wealth? (*4 aspects*)
6 The author uses two phrases ... to refer to the fact that journalists overlook the plight of women.
7 What example of the plight of women does the author provide?
8 What advantages can be derived from granting social and economic equality to women? (*3 aspects*)

3 MEDIATION ENGLISH-GERMAN

> Skills p. 178

A Geben Sie den Inhalt der folgenden Sätze/Phrasen sinngemäß wieder.

1 Women (are) marginalized. (l. 7)
2 Those same countries are disproportionately mired in poverty. (l. 8)
3 Now Samai is gliding along freely on her own – truly able to hold up half the sky. (ll. 70–71)

B Beantworten Sie folgende Fragen auf Deutsch.

1 Welche Probleme haben Mädchen and Frauen im 21. Jahrhundert? (*6 Aspekte*)
2 Erklären Sie im Textzusammenhang, was der Autor mit dem Satz "We like to think of aid as a kind of lubricant, a few drops in the crankcase of the developing world, so that gears move freely again on their own" (ll. 62–66) meint.

4 WORKING WITH WORDS

Find the English equivalents in the text of the following German words and phrases.

Paragraphs A–D:
1 zufügen
2 Wunschdenken
3 sich konzentrieren auf
4 aufgrund der Ausbildung/Vorkenntnisse für einen Job geeignet
5 (Frustrationen) kompensieren
6 Kredit
7 am Boden zerstört
8 (mit jemandem) einen Vertrag unterzeichnen

Paragraphs E–I:
9 Verstoß
10 Berichterstattung in den Medien
11 erschreckend
12 Aussichten
13 Nutznießer
14 mehr Einfluss verschaffen
15 Beteiligung
16 schwächen, untergraben
17 Ansatz, Vorgehensweise

5 TALKING

Discuss the following questions with a partner.

1 Why is the system of granting microcredits to women so beneficial to families in developing countries?
2 What are some possible reasons why girls have less access to education?
3 The text says that greater female involvement in society and the economy appears to undermine extremism and terrorism. Why might that be the case?

D Further activities

1 ARGUMENTATIVE WRITING

> Skills p. 181

Choose one of the following topics and write at least 200 words.

1 Why is it in the interest of both the industrialized and the developing countries to prevent the population explosion predicted for the developing world?
2 Fatal accidents and spectacular plane crashes generally get more extensive news coverage than the deaths of thousands of children in Africa due to disease and malnutrition. Why is this?

2 GROUP DISCUSSION

> Skills p. 187

Your class has been asked to discuss what young people can do to help overcome poverty in the developing world.

Phase 1: individual (= one-minute speech)
Choose one of the suggestions listed below and briefly say why you favour it.

Step 2: interactive (= group discussion)
Discuss all the suggestions below and try to reach an agreement on which one(s) is/are most suitable.

- sponsor one individual child in the Third World until the child comes of age
- buy Fair Trade coffee and farm produce imported from developing countries
- donate used clothing to organizations that supply people in Third World countries with it
- volunteer to work for organizations, like Oxfam or the Peace Corps, that are active in the developing world
- lend half of your monthly allowance to a micro-credit organization of your choice for a return of 1% interest per year

3 DESCRIPTIVE WRITING

> Skills pp. 183–186

A Describing cartoons: Describe what you see in the cartoon below and interpret the message the cartoonist is trying to make in about 100 words.

B Describing graphs: Describe and interpret the graph below in about 100 words.

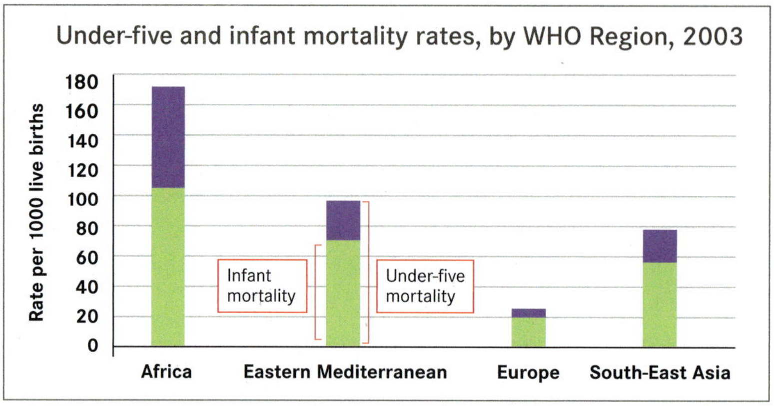

2 9 **4 LISTENING**

> Skills p. 179

You are going to hear an interview with an American congressman. Listen, take notes and complete the following tasks.

A Multiple choice: Choose the most suitable option.

1 The attitude of the interviewer towards the role of the Congressman is one of ...
  a scepticism b sympathy c solidarity d antagonism

2 In order to defend itself, the industry argued that ... .
  a it was cooperating with the government
  b government interference would do more harm than good
  c by sticking to the rules and regulations, their profits would decline

3 Why does the Congressman mention the possibility of a boycott?
  a to make Congressmen aware of the problem
  b to make consumers aware of the problem
  c to force the industry to take action

4 Why should a message be printed on products?
  a to increase consumer awareness of the problem
  b to stop consumers from buying products
  c to encourage consumers to buy more products.

B Short-answer questions / sentence completion: Answer the questions or complete the sentences with information from the interview.

1 At the beginning, the interviewer mentions several parties that signed a certain protocol. Who exactly is he referring to when he speaks of "you" and of certain "powerful people"?
2 How did the industry initially react when accused of misbehaviour?
3 In the Congressman's view, what three approaches are important when working to tackle the problem?
4 For what three reasons is he optimistic that the problem will be solved in the foreseeable future?
5 What does he see as the final alternative if companies don't cooperate with Congress?
6 The interview is about the problem of ... .

E Grammar check

ADJECTIVES AND ADVERBS

> Grammar summary p. 203

SPOT THE MISTAKES

Spot the mistakes and correct them. Explain why they are wrong.

1 ~~Education is viewed critical by many African men.~~
2 ~~When Saima's husband married his second wife, she did not feel happily at all.~~
3 ~~Autonomous women often decide to have significant fewer children.~~
4 ~~Micro-credits function really good.~~

A Complete the sentences with an adjective or an adverb.

Despite Nigeria's huge supply of oil, its economy has ...[1] (hard) moved over the past few decades. Many Nigerians find that ...[2] (hard) to believe and have grown ...[3] (increasing) ...[4] (frustrated). Their situation looks ...[5] (hopeless) indeed. Many areas lack ...[6] (reliable) sources of electricity. There are so many ...[7] (poor) maintained state oil refineries that Africa's biggest crude oil producer has to import most of its fuel. ...[8] (Unfortunate), anger in the dirt-poor southern Delta has ...[9] (recent) turned into a ...[10] (full) fledged insurgency. Many Western journalists report that the local inhabitants are ...[11] (complete) dissatisfied and that the future doesn't look too ...[12] (good). ...[13] (Recent), however, there has been a glimmer of hope as women in the region have achieved ...[14] (considerable) success with ...[15] (non-violent) protest. As they take the ...[16] (main) responsibility for feeding their families, ...[17] (environmental) damage from oil facilities ...[18] (direct) affects their daily struggle to survive.

B Translate these sentences into English.

1 Nigeria könnte erheblich mehr Strom erzeugen, wenn es Erdgas, ein Nebenprodukt der Erdölproduktion, auffangen würde, anstatt es sinnlos abzufackeln.
2 Die korrupte Regierung reagiert unglaublich langsam auf den rasch ansteigenden Zorn der Bevölkerung und kann dadurch die Unruhe nicht mehr eindämmen.
3 Ein Großteil der Bevölkerung wird immer unzufriedener.
4 Im Norden des Landes kommt es inzwischen regelmäßig zu Gräueltaten zwischen militanten Moslems und Christen.
5 Viele Beobachter, die Nigeria äußerst gut kennen, sind der Meinung, dass nur noch drastische Maßnahmen dem Land wirklich helfen können.

WATCH OUT!

> Grammar summary p. 197

mustn't – needn't

You ~~mustn't~~ donate a lot of money – even a small amount can make an effective contribution.
→ *You needn't donate ...* (= *nicht brauchen*; mustn't = *nicht dürfen*)

C Complete each sentence with *mustn't* or *needn't*.

1 Quite frequently, effective aid ... be expensive aid.
2 Access to contraceptives ... only be available to wealthy women.
3 The African people ... be left alone in their fight against AIDS.
4 In view of new medical treatment methods, an AIDS diagnosis ... mean the end of the world any more.

10

The globalized world

FOCUS

1

2

3

4

Look at the cartoons and photos and do the following tasks. > Skills p. 183

1 Match the cartoons/photos (1–4) with the headlines (a–f). There are two more headlines than you need.
   - a Competitiveness restored at the taxpayer's cost
   - b Staying competitive is all that matters any more
   - c No entry!
   - d Access to information in unexpected places
   - e Homogenization of the global market place
   - f Exchange of commodities and ideas

2 What aspects of globalization do the cartoons illustrate? More than one option may apply.
   - a political
   - b economic
   - c cultural
   - d technological
   - e educational

3 How does globalization affect you personally? Talk in groups and make a list.

A Economic aspects of globalization

BEFORE YOU READ

How important do you think countries such as China and India will be for the global economy in the coming years?

Your Next Job: Made in India or China

A There is a chance, and maybe even a good one, that you'll walk into work one Monday morning and find out your job is being moved to China or India. Millions have already seen that happen, from shop-floor machinists to IT specialists, in places as disparate as Italy, the U.S. and South Korea. China is a manufacturing machine, charging into the global market for everything from cars to solar panels. India's highly trained engineers are outdueling Stanford grads for jobs in R&D, software development and other sectors that are supposed to be the West's economic salvation. The harsh realities of the globalization of labor have left much of the world's workforce feeling despondent. Everyone in places like London and Los Angeles is competing with smart applicants from Bangalore or Shanghai who are willing to work long hours for a pittance. When there are 2.5 billion people in those two Asian giants combined, how can anyone's job be safe?

Beijing, capital of China

B Yet there's another way of looking at the great shift of economic power to the East, one that is much less scary and perhaps even inspiring. Those 2.5 billion people are getting richer by the day. This presents an unprecedented opportunity for the workers of the world. Thirty years ago, the average person in China or India could afford almost nothing beyond basic food and other simple necessities of life. That poverty was a problem for all of us. With so little spending power in the developing world, the global economy was dependent on a handful of wealthy nations, especially the U.S. Today, however, China and India have become a new source of growth for the global economy. Hundreds of millions of Chinese and Indians can now splurge on Sony LCD TVs, Australian steaks and Apple iPhones. Last year, Indians and Chinese bought 19.9 million new passenger vehicles, 70% more than Americans did, according to market researcher J.D. Power. This new bonanza for consumer goods increases demand for copper, cotton and other natural resources; the machinery to manufacture those goods; the ships and trucks to transport them; and the people to design and sell them. The result is higher sales and bigger profits for companies such as Boeing and Rio Tinto, as well as more jobs.

C We've already seen the benefits. If not for the continued rapid growth in emerging economies like China and India, the world might easily have descended into a real depression in 2008. China lifted all of East Asia out of the recession by buying capital equipment and consumer goods from Japan, South Korea and the rest of the region. U.S. exports of goods to China reached $92 billion in 2010, a 32% jump. The influence of China and India will only spread and strengthen as the two countries get wealthier and purchase more from the rest of the world. In Western Australia, the local chamber of minerals and energy believes the industry will create 40,000 jobs over the next three to five years in that state alone, in part because of expanding exports to China.

D The newly affluent of China and India are also bringing their money right to your doorstep. Their citizens are becoming active tourists, filling hotel rooms and dining out in Times Square and Tokyo's Ginza. According to the U.N. World Tourism Organization, the number of Chinese traveling outside the country rose to 47.7 million in 2009, 54% more than in 2005, and they spent more than French, Japanese or Canadian travelers. Chinese and Indian companies are expanding overseas in a quest for global presence and markets, creating jobs everywhere. Mumbai-based IT giant Tata Consultancy Services – a firm built on outsourcing from the U.S. and Europe – employs more than 13,000 non-Indians, nine times as many as in 2005. Chinese firms invested $56.5 billion abroad in 2009, up from only $12.3 billion in 2005, and they tend to hire locally as they invest, to absorb talent and know-how. Not one of the 450 people who work in the U.S. for Chinese appliance maker Haier is from China.

E The advance of China and India demands an overhaul in the way we think about jobs. You might just find, for example, that your biggest customers are in Chengdu, not Chicago, or that your boss sits in New Delhi, not New York City. Your paycheck could come in renminbi or rupees instead of in euros or dollars. Sure, in this new economic order, your job may be lost to Chinese or Indian workers. But don't worry. They'll give it right back.

(751 words)

Time, 17 March 2011

1 MULTIPLE CHOICE

> Skills p. 176

Choose the most suitable option.

1 The main purpose of the article is to show that … .
- a the attitude to employment patterns in the Western world is old-fashioned
- b the education systems in the industrialized countries need to produce better-educated job applicants
- c the rise of India and China to economic powers presents more chances than risks for the Western world
- d Western companies benefit from the growing demand for raw materials and commodities

2 The phrase 'China is charging into the global market' (l. 4) means that China is increasingly … .
- a challenging the global market
- b surpassing the global market
- c putting the global market at risk
- d gaining access to the global market

3 In paragraph A the author points out that skilled workers from India and China … .
- a may be able to save the Western world's depressed economies
- b pose a threat to job security in the West
- c are cleverer than those in the industrialized countries
- d should be pitied because they have to work long hours

4 Which of the following ideas is not mentioned in paragraph B?
- a The growing wealth in India and China benefits everybody.
- b Chinese and Indians are buying more and more Western products.
- c Chinese and Indians are quickly becoming more affluent.
- d Consumption in the USA is now less than in India.

5 The phrase 'if not for' (l. 29) could best be replaced by which connector?
a without b despite c beyond d nonetheless

6 Which of the following headings would be most suitable for paragraph C?
a India's and China's political dominance is inevitable.
b Chinese investment helps neighbouring countries escape recession.
c The whole world benefits from India's and China's rise to wealth.
d Level of USA exports depends on Chinese economic growth.

2 GAPPED SUMMARY

> Skills p. 177

Complete the text with suitable words from paragraphs D and E.

As a result of China's and India's economic ...[1], the ...[2] of these two countries are able to enjoy travelling to various other countries. ...[3] business abroad, Chinese and Indian companies seek to ...[4] expertise. Sometimes the workforce they ...[5] when setting up businesses abroad consists exclusively of native people. Even companies whose foundation was ...[6] jobs from industrialized countries are now likely to employ a relatively large share of Europeans and Americans. All these facts show that an ...[7] of the fixed ideas many people in the Western world have about employment is necessary.

3 WORKING WITH WORDS

A Find idiomatic English expressions in the text for the German phrases below.

1 auf den Weltmarkt drängen
2 jemand in einen Zustand der Verzweiflung versetzen
3 im Übermaß Geld ausgeben
4 in einen Wirtschaftsabschwung gleiten
5 Arbeitskräfte, die vor Ort wohnen, einstellen
6 eine Anpassung erfordern

B Complete the following text with the English phrases from exercise A. Take care with the verb constructions and tenses.

With a large number of East Asian countries ...[1] since the 1990s, Western industrialized countries have been facing tough competition, which ...[2] of a large part of their economic structures. Countries like Germany that reacted to the challenge in a suitable way have been able to avoid ...[3], while many other Western nations ...[4]. In Southern European countries, which have been running massive budget deficits for some time, members of the lower middle class, in particular, are becoming deeply frustrated as they can no longer ...[5] commodities in the way they used to do before the euro replaced their national currencies. Some labour experts hope that Chinese firms, which might be interested in ...[6] when investing in Europe, might provide help.

4 TALKING

> Skills p. 188

Discuss the following question with a partner. Present your ideas to the class.

1 Do you think the economic strength of China and India will make it easier or more difficult to find a job after school?
2 Does constant global economic growth worry you in any other way?

Traffic in Beijing

B Words in context

2 10

Globalization – causes and implications

Today, more than ever before, major events impact people not only locally but also nationally or even globally. This is a clear sign of the process known as "globalization". How can this term be best defined? Its main characteristic is global interconnectedness, in which ideas, capital and commodities are shifted across borders and in which people move around the world in search of better opportunities and living conditions.

There is no denying the fact that technological advances are one of the main causes of globalization. In the same way as the invention of the printing press and of the telephone vastly changed communication in the past, today's interconnectedness would be unthinkable without the more recent invention of the microchip.

Globalization has impacted society in various ways, the most relevant ones being political, economic, cultural and environmental. One negative political implication of globalization is the inability of governments to provide traditional welfare services, e.g. education, health and sanitation, to their citizens. In some cases, the former "welfare state" is now being replaced by a rather minimalist state that performs certain core functions such as maintaining law and order for its citizens. As multinational corporations become increasingly influential, the market, not national governments, determines what the true economic and social priorities are to be. As a result, those worried about the erosion of social justice say that globalization benefits only a small percentage of the population while impoverishing the lower classes.

Economic globalization has brought about a greater flow of capital, goods, services and human resources between various regions of the world. To some extent, this development has been caused by powerful countries such as the USA or China and by international institutions like the International Monetary Fund (IMF) and the World Trade Organization (WTO) which tend to dictate economic policies. Globalization also enhances the flow of ideas across borders. A positive outcome of this trend is the spread of the Internet and computer-related services, which provide for more global interconnectedness. However, the potential theft of intellectual property, which disrupts fair competition, poses a real threat. The increasing flow of job seekers across the globe, which has prompted industrialized countries to stave off the newcomers by imposing visa restrictions to ensure that their own citizens are not made unemployed, causes another problem. Some economists, claiming that globalization amounts to recolonization, see grave dangers in forcing it upon the weaker countries.

Globalization also has a profound cultural effect on our lives. Not only does it affect our taste in food, drink and fashion, it also influences the way we think and the types of music and art we enjoy. Critics, however, point out that this poses a threat to the uniqueness of many of the less dominant cultures in the world, i.e. that it results in "cultural homogenization", which will diminish the rich cultural heritage of the whole world. In contrast to this pessimistic view, the proponents of globalization say that it gives us a greater choice without wiping out traditional ways of life.

It is virtually impossible to see any environmental benefits of globalization. Both the flow of goods and the fact that more and more people are travelling lead to pollution and climate change. The rise in consumption resulting from globalization increases the exploitation of our natural resources. (552 words)

First of all, make sure you understand the meaning of each of the highlighted phrases used in the text on page 124. If you are not sure, look them up in your dictionary. Then complete the tasks below.

1 WORKING WITH WORDS

Find the English equivalents of the following German expressions in the text.

1 Migranten (vom eigenen Land) fernhalten
2 sicherstellen, garantieren
3 wechselseitige Verbundenheit
4 eine Regierung, die sich darauf beschränkt, nur das zu tun, was notwendig ist
5 Es lässt sich nicht leugnen, dass ...

2 COLLOCATIONS

> Skills p. 175

A Which word from the text completes each group of collocations?

1	to go with/against the ...	the ... of goods/ services	to be in full ...	an uninterrupted ... of supplies
2	cheese/chocolate ...	a double-page ...	a ... sheet	the ... of ideas
3	to be rotten to the ...	... values of justice and democracy	a nuclear reactor ...	the hard ... of a group of people
4	to ... a family	to ... a piece of property	to ... technical equipment	to ... the peace
5	the latest ...	to go/be out of ...	the ... industry	... -conscious

B Complete the text with English phrases from exercise A which are the equivalents of the German phrases in brackets.

The other day, I noticed ...[1] (*einen zweiseitigen Artikel*) about globalization in my local newspaper in which the author claimed that it was high time for the world's leading nations to work together in order to ...[2] (*den Frieden zu wahren*) on earth. The author also regretted the fact that very few young people in developing countries ...[3] (*sich gegen den Trend stemmen*) of cultural homogenization dictated to them by ...[4] (*modebewusste*) designers in Paris, New York or Milan. Indeed, a number of militant opponents of globalization believe that the values of big multinational corporations ...[5] (*von Grund auf verdorben sind*).

3 SYNONYMS

Replace the underlined parts of the sentences below with synonymous words and expressions from the text. You may have to make minor changes to the verb form.

1 It is indisputable that as a result of globalization the gap between the privileged and the less privileged within a society will gradually increase.
... that globalization will cause the ... .

2 Unlike the welfare state, many a modern government only meets the most basic needs of its citizens.
... the welfare state, a reform-minded government only ... .

3 In general, opponents of globalization fear that, in the end, the vast majority of people around the world will share basically identical values, mindsets and life styles and that, globally, the vast number of unique customs and traditions will be significantly reduced.
One basic argument put forward against globalization is that, ultimately, almost every society will be subjected to ... , a process which will ... that exists globally.

C Cultural effects of globalization

BEFORE YOU READ

Why do you think American fast food might be popular in Russia?

Russia Becomes a Magnet for U.S. Fast Food

A MOSCOW – Earlier in his career, Christopher Wynne put his Russian expertise to work researching arms proliferation for the American government. Now he's engaged in geopolitics of another sort: deploying American fast food for the emerging Russian middle class.

B Russian consumers are increasingly affluent, allowing fast-food chains like Wendy's to charge higher prices than they do in the United States. Mr. Wynne is the top franchisee in Russia for the Papa John's Pizza chain. So far, compared with the largely saturated United States market for fast food, Mr. Wynne says he is finding plenty of demand.

C "I could succeed in my sleep there is so much opportunity here," said Mr. Wynne, who has just opened his 25th Papa John's outlet in Russia, doubling the number in the last year.

American fast food has been going global for years, of course. And China and India continue to be big expansion markets. But lately, the industry is finding a growing appetite for its fare in Russia – not only pizza, but Burger King's Whoppers, Subway's barbecue pulled pork sandwiches, among others.

D "As consumers have more disposable income, they will spend it on fast food," Jack Russo, a fast-food industry analyst at Edward Jones, said in a telephone interview. He compares the market here to the United States half a century ago. For years, McDonald's, which opened its first restaurant on Pushkin Square in 1990 and generated gigantic lines, was the only American fast-food chain in Russia. McDonald's now operates 279 restaurants in Russia.

E Paving the way has been Russia's development in many cities of the modern infrastructure needed for fast food to flourish – including malls with food courts, highways with drive-through locations, and specialty suppliers of frozen foods and packaging.

Moreover, Russian consumers are increasingly affluent, partly because of the trickle down from the nation's lucrative oil exports. And though they still trail far behind the average household income of Americans – $43,539 in the United States versus $7,276 here – Russian consumers tend to have a large portion of their money for discretionary spending.

They are unburdened by the hangover of consumer debt that has curbed American purchasing power. Nor do Russians have high medical bills because the health care system, if flawed, is largely socialized. The income tax is a flat 13 percent. And a majority of Russians own property mortgage-free, as a legacy of the mass privatization of apartments in the 1990s.

As a result, the fast-food chains find they can charge higher prices in Russia than in America. The average check at a Russian fast-food outlet –

$8.92 according to research by a Wendy's franchisee here - is significantly higher than the United States average of $6.50.

F And not all Western food forays have succeeded here, as some companies have stumbled over cultural differences difficult to anticipate. Campbell Soup, for example, left Russia this year because of soft sales on four flavors of soup stock sold in pouches. It had seemed a sure bet because the varieties included a broth that could cut the labor time for making borscht. But as it turned out, Russians prefer to build their borscht from scratch.

G On the other hand, Papa John's hottest-selling pizza this spring was a recipe made especially for the local market but found in no Russian cookbook: a topping of blue cheese, chicken, celery and Tabasco sauce.

(560 words)

The New York Times, 3 August 2011

1 SENTENCE COMPLETION / SHORT-ANSWER QUESTIONS

> Skills p. 178

Answer the questions or complete the sentences with information from the text.

1 The word which is used to describe the situation the fast-food industry in the U.S. finds itself in is ... .
2 The author quotes the fact that Russians have ... to explain why their demand for American fast food has risen recently.
3 What has contributed to the rapid growth of fast food restaurants in Russia? (*3 aspects*)
4 What factors make it easier for Russians than for Americans to spend their earnings? (*4 aspects*)
5 The author attributes the lack of success of several American fast-food companies to ... .

2 MEDIATION ENGLISH-GERMAN

> Skills p. 178

Interpretieren Sie im Textzusammenhang den Inhalt der folgenden Sätze/Phrasen.

1 researching arms proliferation (paragraph A)
2 a growing appetite for its fare (paragraph C)
3 generated gigantic lines (paragraph D)
4 paving the way (paragraph E)
5 the trickle down from (paragraph E)
6 have money ... for discretionary spending (paragraph E)
7 Western food forays (paragraph F)
8 It had seemed a sure bet. (paragraph F)
9 to build ... from scratch (paragraph F)

3 WORKING WITH WORDS

> Skills p. 175

A Match the *verbs* on the left with nouns or phrases on the right to form collocations. Then use the phrases in sentences of your own. Some phrases can be used more than once.

to generate *to operate* *to charge* *to anticipate* *to cut*	sb.'s arrival ׀ a deck of cards ׀ a system ׀ future technological developments ׀ excitement ׀ the cord ׀ a fee ׀ the correct answer ׀ sb. short ׀ a suspect ׀ electricity ׀ on a patient ׀ business ׀ employment ׀ a large crowd ׀ a deal ׀ the enemy ׀ a battery ׀ a machine ׀ a business ׀ sb.'s account ׀ excitement ׀ your own throat ׀ tax revenue

EXAMPLE > *to generate electricity*

B Find the *nouns* in the text that match the following definitions.

1 money borrowed from a bank for the purpose of buying real estate
2 shop through which the products of a big corporation are sold at a discount
3 the particular taste of a certain food or drink
4 rapid increase in or spread of something
5 a situation resulting from things that happened earlier
6 a business person who is given permission to sell a firm's goods or services
7 certain type of food
8 instructions for preparing a particular variety of food

C Match the phrase from the text (1–7) with a phrase that expresses the same idea (a–g).

1 put his expertise to work (paragraph A)
2 consumers are increasingly affluent (paragraph B)
3 continue to be big expansion markets (paragraph C)
4 though they still trail far behind (paragraph E)
5 unburdened by the hangover (paragraph E)
6 a legacy of the mass privatization of apartments (paragraph E)
7 But as it turned out (paragraph F)

a even if they continue to lag considerably
b However, as could be seen later
c a consequence of the large-scale switch to individual ownership of flats
d unaffected by the aftermath of
e took advantage of his broad knowledge to accomplish a goal
f are still business segments that are growing rapidly
g customers are growing richer

4 TALKING

> Skills p. 188

Discuss the following questions with a partner. Present your ideas to the rest of the class.

1 Do you like the fact that globalization has contributed to the spread of exotic dishes to Germany?
2 Why do you think fast food is so popular, both at home and in countries where it was introduced only a short time ago?
3 What potential dangers of consuming too much fast food do you see?

5 ARGUMENTATIVE WRITING

> Skills p. 181

Choose one of the following topics and write at least 200 words.

1 The price of globalization is too high for a nation to pay. Do you agree?
2 A potential shift of the balance of power toward Asia will lead to a decline in the living standard of Western nations. Comment on this point of view.

D Further activities

1 LISTENING

> Skills p. 179

2 11

You are going to hear an extract from a radio report which deals with the impact global media and communications have on culture. Listen, take notes and do the exercises below.

A Fill in the gaps with information from the report.

Some people are afraid that globalization might lead to ...[1]. In this context, A Ramakrishna mentions that there is much discontent which he blames on the ...[2] and the ...[3], in particular. Professor Milner compares globalization to ...[4] and ...[5].

B Answer the following questions.

1 What causes of the pop music culture does A Ramakrishna mention?
2 Which social groups are particularly affected by the discontent mentioned by A Ramakrishna?
3 According to A Ramakrishna, what are the effects of discontent?
4 How are Asian countries regaining some confidence in themselves?

C Decide whether these statements are true or false.

1 All of the main agents of globalization are transnational corporations with well-known brand names.
2 A Ramakrishna fears that young people might develop the illusion that consuming as many things as possible is something worth striving for.
3 An increasing number of young Asians are beginning to hate Western values.
4 Political elites in Asia are ashamed because Asian values have failed in the contest with the West.

2 GROUP DISCUSSION

> Skills p. 187

Many experts consider changes in the field of education to be the key to coping with the growing challenges posed by globalization. Discuss the merits of the following proposals.

Phase 1: individual (= one-minute speech)
Choose one of the suggestions listed below and briefly say why you favour it.

Phase 2: interactive (= group discussion)
Discuss all of the items in the list of suggestions and try to reach some form of agreement as to which one(s) is/are the most valid.

> place more emphasis on teaching foreign languages, sciences and mathematics at the expense of "subordinate" courses like social studies, history or athletics
> make sure that the German school system produces more high-school graduates
> increase the funding for school exchange programmes
> make it obligatory for students to study for one year at a foreign university
> subsidize companies that pay their workers to obtain a university degree while officially employed by them (the so-called "duales Studium")

> Webcode: FOSEAU1001

3 DESCRIPTIVE WRITING

> Skills pp. 183–186

A Interpreting cartoons: Describe the cartoon and interpret its message in about 100 words.

B Interpreting statistics: Interpret the bar chart below in about 100 words. Explain how it relates to globalization.

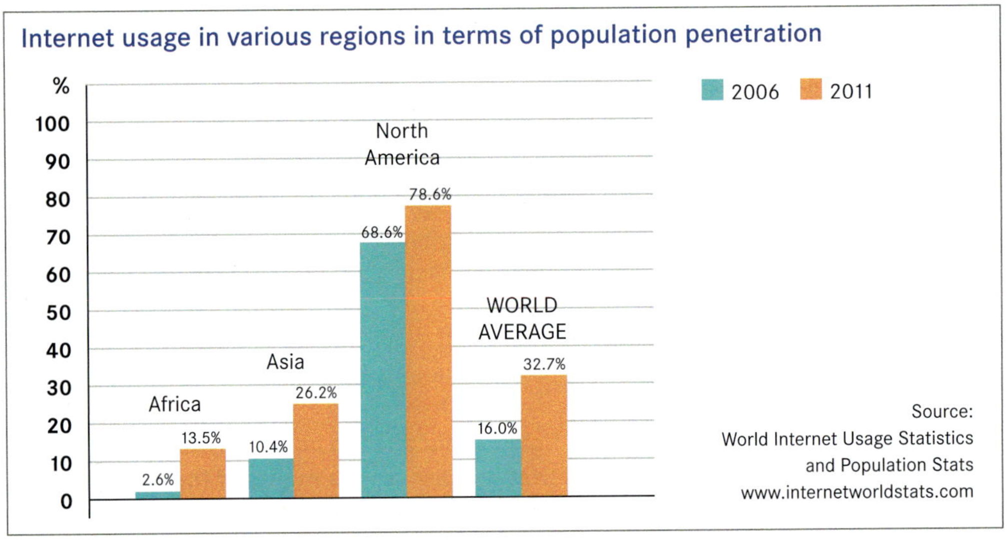

4 PROJECT

> Skills p. 190

Some critics of globalization claim that it is a modern form of imperialism. Investigate to what extent this claim might be true.

> Split up into six groups. The first three groups should investigate the ways in which imperialism functioned and the consequences it had on Congo, India and China respectively. The second three groups should concentrate on the way in which globalization operates and on the consequences it has had on these countries.

> After completing these tasks, the two groups dealing with the same country should compare their findings and establish whether or not there are parallels.

> Present your findings to the class.

E Grammar check

PARTICIPLE CONSTRUCTIONS

> Grammar summary p. 205

SPOT THE MISTAKES

Spot the mistakes and correct them. Explain why they are wrong.

(You may have to add a conjunction or preposition, e.g. *though*, *despite*, *with or while*)

1 ~~Being weak for several centuries, Asian nations are now regaining confidence in their values.~~
2 ~~Chinese and Indian companies are expanding overseas in a quest for global presence, created jobs everywhere.~~
3 ~~Reducing its United States work force over the past five years, G.M. increased the number of workers in its Mexican plants.~~
4 ~~Global competition and its pressure on American wages intensifying, American workers deserve a more focused approach from Washington.~~
5 ~~Many of the foods considering to be local are results of a globalization process that has been in operation for more than five centuries.~~
6 ~~Marveling at the speed and flexibility of Chinese companies, experts warn that economic growth in China comes at the expense of human rights.~~

A Match the sentence beginnings (1–6) with the most appropriate endings (a–f) below.

1 With globalization and the IT revolution advancing at a tremendous speed,
2 Mr Wynne has just opened his 25th Papa John's outlet in Russia,
3 Pressed by high unemployment and eager to keep jobs in the USA,
4 In the past, workers with average skills, doing an average job,
5 New technology and globalization are eliminating more and more "routine" jobs done by semi-skilled workers,
6 After restructuring the country's economy within two decades,

a the Auto Workers union agreed that companies could hire some workers at $14 an hour, with lower benefits.
b thus widening income gaps and fueling resentment even more.
c the best jobs will require workers to have a better education.
d China's leaders should now make sure that they apply democratic principles.
e doubling the number in the last year.
f could afford an average lifestyle.

WATCH OUT!

"bei"

Mr Chen lives ~~by~~ his parents because he can't afford a flat of his own.

→ *Mr Chen lives with his parents because he can't afford a flat of his own.*

B Translate the following sentences into English, using the correct translation for *bei*.

1 Sarah Samson arbeitet als Kassiererin bei der Firma Wal-Mart.
2 Wenn die Firma sie entlässt, muss sie bei ihren Eltern wohnen.
3 Bei der augenblicklich hohen Arbeitslosigkeit in Deutschland sollten es die Unternehmen vermeiden, Arbeitsplätze ins Ausland zu verlagern.
4 Bei der Abfahrt des Zuges mit der IBM-Delegation versammelte sich eine riesige Menschenmenge am Bahnhof in Shanghai.

11

Clashes of interest

FOCUS

Look at the photos and cartoons and do the following tasks.

1 How do the photos and cartoons above relate to the topic of this unit?
2 What other current examples of clashes of interest in today's world can you think of?

A Differing political systems

BEFORE YOU READ

From the Western point of view, what advice might China need?
Do you consider it to be politically wise to offer advice to China?

Advice for China

From: Ministry of State Security
To: President Hu Jintao
Subject: The Arab Spring

Demonstration in Cairo

A Dear President Hu: You asked for our assessment of the Arab Spring. Our conclusion is that the revolutions in the Arab world contain some important lessons for the rule of the Chinese Communist Party, because what this contagion reveals is something very new about how revolutions unfold in the 21st century and something very old about why they explode.

B Let's start with the new. Sometime around the year 2000, the world achieved a very high level of connectivity, virtually flattening the global economic playing field. This web of connectivity was built on the diffusion of personal computers, fiber-optic cable, the Internet and Web servers. What this platform did was to make Boston and Beijing or Detroit and Damascus next-door neighbors. It brought some two billion people into a global conversation.

C Well, sir, while we were focused on the U.S. recession, we went from a connected world to a "hyperconnected world." It has connected Boston, Beijing and now Baotou in inner Mongolia. This deeper penetration of connectivity is built on smarter cellphones, wireless bandwidth and social networks. This new platform for connectivity, being so cheap and mobile, is bringing another two billion people into the conversation from more and more remote areas.

D To put it in Middle Eastern terms, sir, this new platform has connected Detroit and Damascus and Dara'a. Where is Dara'a, you ask? Dara'a is the small Syrian border town where the uprising in Syria began and whose residents have been pumping out video, Twitter feeds and Facebook postings of regime atrocities ever since.

E The point, sir, is the world is now hyperconnected, and there is no such thing as "local" anymore. Everything now flows instantly from the most remote corners of any country onto this global platform where it gets shared. What the laptop plus the Internet plus the search engine did for Web pages was enable anyone with connectivity to find *anything* that interests them and what the cellphone plus the Internet plus Facebook are doing is enabling *anyone* to find anyone who interests them – and then coordinate with them and share grievances and aspirations. The days when Arab dictators could take over the state-run TV and radio and shut off all information to their people are over. The Syrians can't shut off their cell-phone networks now any more than they can shut off their electricity grids.

F Sir, think about this: Syria has banned all foreign networks, like CNN and the BBC, but if you go to YouTube and type in "Dara'a" you will see the most vivid up-to-date video of the Syrian regime's crackdown – all shot with cellphones or flip-cams by Syrians and then uploaded to YouTube or to newly created Web sites like Sham News Network. Nothing stays hidden anymore.

G The second trend we see in the Arab Spring is a manifestation of "Carlson's Law," posited by Curtis Carlson, the C.E.O. of SRI International, in Silicon Valley, which states that: "In a world where so many people now have access to education and cheap tools of innovation, innovation that happens from the bottom up tends to be chaotic but smart. Innovation that happens from the top down tends to be orderly but dumb." As a result, says Carlson, the sweet spot for innovation today is "moving down," closer to the people, not up, because all the people together are smarter than anyone alone and all the people now have the tools to invent and collaborate.

H The regime of Hosni Mubarak of Egypt was just too dumb and slow to manage the unrest. The Tahrir revolutionaries were smart but chaotic, and without leadership. Therefore, the role of leaders today – of companies and countries – is to inspire, empower, enable and then edit and meld all that innovation coming from the bottom up. But that requires more freedom for the bottom. Do you see what I mean, sir?

I But this is not about technology alone. As the Russian historian Leon Aron has noted, the Arab uprisings closely resemble the Russian democratic revolution of 1991 in one key respect: They were both not so much about freedom or food as about "dignity." They each grew out of a deep desire by people to run their own lives and to be treated as "citizens" – with both obligations and rights that the state cannot just give and take by whim.
If you want to know what brings about revolutions, it is not G.D.P. rising or falling, says Aron, "it is the quest for dignity." We always exaggerate people's quest for G.D.P. and undervalue their quest for ideals. "Dignity before bread" was the slogan of the Tunisian revolution. "The spark that lights the fuse is always the quest for dignity," said Aron. "Today's technology just makes the fire much more difficult to put out."

J We need to keep that in mind in China, sir. We should be proud of the rising standard of living that we have delivered for our people. Many of them appreciate that. But it is not the only thing in their lives – and at some point it won't be the most important thing. Do you see what I mean, sir?

(866 words)

By Thomas L. Friedman, *The New York Times*, 4 June 2011

1 GAPPED SUMMARY

> Skills p. 177

Fill in the missing words from the text. Use one word only for each gap.

One thing that increasingly helps rebellions around the world ...[1] is the growing degree of ...[2] among the peoples of the world which, of course, is the result of the availability of many relatively new fields of technology worldwide. This broader ...[3] of high-tech into ever more ...[4] regions on earth has had a dramatic effect in the recent past, most importantly the popular ...[5] of the masses in many parts of the Arab world, where people decided to vent their personal ...[6] on the streets. Naturally, many an oppressive regime has reacted to this outpouring of emotions by resorting to a ...[7] on public dissent - not a clever way of responding but rather ...[8]. In the view of many experts, the media tend to ...[9] the role that improving economic conditions plays in many revolutions. Although the demonstrators ...[10] a better life style, what they want more than anything else is the ability to attain greater self-respect.

2 MULTIPLE CHOICE

> Skills p. 176

Choose the most suitable option.

1 The main intention of the author is to ... .
   a make fun of China's government by creating a totally unrealistic situation
   b make China recognize the need for greater political freedom
   c inform the reader about recent innovations in communications technology
   d inform the reader about the revolutions in various Arab nations

2 When the author speaks of "virtually flattening the global economic playing field" (l. 9), he means that ... .
   a practically every nation now has the chance to dominate its competitors on the world market
   b many countries have been all but squashed by the economic predominance of a few trading nations
   c almost every nation on earth now has access to top international sports venues
   d every country has the chance of competing in the global market under practically equal conditions

3 When the author speaks of "regime atrocities" (l. 22), he is referring to ... .
   a acts of barbarity committed by those in power
   b a programme of strict law enforcement
   c a crackdown on lawlessness by a legitimate government
   d certain questionable activities encouraged by a rogue government

4 What effect of an increasingly "hyperconnected" world (l. 23) is not mentioned by the author?
   a People in the most remote areas of the world can gain access to information about events taking place around the globe.
   b Tyrants can still cut off the supply of vital information to their citizens, thereby keeping them ignorant.
   c Virtually any act of political violence or suppression can be uncovered by the users of new technologies.
   d More information and education at the grass roots level usually lead to more innovative, albeit chaotic societies.

5 According to the information provided in paragraph I, one of the main functions of today's government leaders should be to ... .
   a press for better educational and vocational opportunities for their citizens
   b encourage their citizens to perfect their skills at using the Internet, including social networking sites such as Facebook and Twitter
   c promote economic growth and prosperity, above all else
   d motivate their citizens to be innovative and enable them to use their ingenuity for the common good of society

6 According to one political commentator, the leading motive for social revolution around the world is the attempt to gain ... .
   a more self-respect
   b more political and religious freedom
   c better living standards even at the expense of political liberty
   d the freedom to choose one's own lifestyle

3 WORKING WITH WORDS

A Paraphrase the following expressions from the text.

1 It brought people into a global conversation (paragraph B)
2 innovation that happens from the bottom up (paragraph G)
3 manage the unrest (paragraph H)
4 smart but chaotic (paragraph H)
5 give and take by whim (paragraph I)
6 undervalue their quest for ideals (paragraph I)

B Find the words in the text which complete the following collocations.

> Skills p. 175

1	the ... of law	an unwritten ...	majority ...	as a ...
2	an advanced course ...	the ... of CO_2 in the air	a rising sea ...	at the local/ national ...
3	to adopt a new party ...	to provide a ... for expressing one's opinion	an oil exploration ...	a railway station ...
4	to put somebody on the ...	to purchase oil/ gas on the ... market	a weak ...	a nice vacation ...
5	to ... into debt/ difficulties	to ... according to plan	to ... dry	to ... a business/ country

C Complete the text with English phrases from exercise B which are the equivalents of the German phrases in brackets.

...[1] (*in der Regel*), many Chinese are becoming increasingly dissatisfied with the political situation in their country because they are now better informed by the Internet about other countries. This relatively new development ...[2] (*hat die führenden Politiker in eine peinliche Situation hineinmanövriert*) as many Chinese citizens feel they are not adequately protected by ...[3] (*ein verbindliches Rechtssystem*). In the future, the government may thus ...[4] (*in Schwierigkeiten geraten*). So far, protest in China has only been staged ...[5] (*auf örtlicher Ebene*), but this may soon change. For the Chinese Communist party, the challenge will be ...[6] (*ein politisches Programm zu beschließen*) so that ...[7] (*das Land geführt werden kann*) with social unrest.

4 TALKING

In groups, discuss the following questions and report back to the class.

1 Have you ever been to a demonstration? What was it about?
2 Do you think that demonstrations or protest marches can ever achieve real change?

5 ARGUMENTATIVE WRITING

> Skills p. 181

Choose one of the topics below and write at least 200 words.

1 Many political regimes have a long history of civil rights violations, including violence directed against their own citizens. Should other countries or international organizations intervene more quickly to help save the lives of the civilians affected?
2 Do you think a trade boycott or a boycott of sporting events is an adequate response when it comes to dealing with countries that use violent means to suppress their own citizens?

B Terrorism and the rule of law

BEFORE YOU READ

Do you think that any means are justified to deter terrorist attacks?

CONFRONTING TERRORISM

Jan Egeland *is Europe director at Human Rights Watch and the former U.N. under-secretary general for humanitarian affairs and Norwegian secretary of state for foreign affairs.*

A Only those who have stood close to the devastating impact of terror will know how deep the immediate shock and fear runs. I saw the horrendous effects in Norway – just as Americans saw them in New York and Washington 10 years ago. Traveling the world for the United Nations and the Red Cross, I witnessed the way massive on-going terror affects society, from Iraq to Afghanistan and from Colombia to Israel, the West Bank and Gaza. In the aftermath of a deadly terror attack, a shocked and confused public will always turn to its leaders for answers.

B We know what the right answer is. The effective way to confront terror is to reaffirm the values that terrorists want to tear down. The wrong answer is to go over to the "dark side" and fight terror in ways that violate our most basic human rights. The recent discovery by Human Rights Watch in archives in Tripoli of documents that appear to detail how the United States and Britain handed over suspects to Muammar el-Qaddafi's torturers again underscores the folly of sacrificing our principles in the name of security. The consequences of the American and European breakdown in principled leadership after the 9/11 atrocities will not go away until there has been accountability for the torture and the abuse of detainees.

Mourners in Oslo, July 2011

C Confronting terrorism means rigorous, well-resourced and global efforts by police and intelligence services to prevent attacks and bring to justice criminals of the worst kind. It should never mean arbitrary arrests, secret detention and rendition of detainees to tyrants and torture. But this is exactly what happened when American and European leaders willingly left the moral high ground and the legitimacy of lawful response, and instead bent and broke the same international laws that previous leaders had worked for generations to enshrine. There still has been no real accountability anywhere for the criminal acts that sent terrorism suspects, some certainly guilty and some innocent, from one torture chamber to the next in Europe and the Middle East.

D It does not have to be like this. After the massive terrorist attacks in Oslo, the Norwegian leadership, the victims and the general public were remarkably unanimous in declaring that the best response was a vigorous rally around democratic values and the rule of law. After a mass murderer massacred youth leaders and smashed central government buildings – unleashing terror that had not been seen since the Nazi occupation in the 1940s – Norwegians looked for guidance and got it. From the king and the prime minister, down through the ranks of government and political opposition, the mantra has been that the liberal values of freedom of expression and tolerance are the way to confront terror. There is consensus that this is not a contest to see which side can better break the other – it is a question of proving to everyone that we offer a better alternative – and thus can prevent the recruitment of new terrorists.

E Will the Norwegian model trump the many previous examples of terror being met with unlawful and counterproductive methods? The threat from an international group like Al Qaeda is different from that of a domestic terrorist – and no one will know how Norwegians would have reacted had the attack been the work of Islamist extremism instead of home-grown, right-wing extremism. But the lessons of a decade of terror remain the same: it was a betrayal of our deepest values when our leaders agreed to hand over secret prisoners to the likes of Qaddafi, Bashar al-Assad and Hosni Mubarak, and when some of our countries' top lawyers bent the law to see how our intelligence services could get away with torture.

F This stain will not go away unless there is a criminal investigation of the top Bush administration officials who authorized these crimes. It is equally important for European officials who actively participated in the C.I.A. programs of rendition, secret detention and abusive interrogation techniques to be fully investigated and prosecuted. Until that happens, the issue will haunt successive U.S. and European governments each time the archives of a tyrant is uncovered and the hypocrisy is exposed.

G The best way to honor the victims of terrorism is to prove that we represent a better alternative. It is all a question of leadership. The moral high ground means never opening the torture chamber. (726 words)

Jan Egeland, *The New York Times*, 11 September 2011

1 SHORT-ANSWER QUESTIONS / SENTENCE COMPLETION

> Skills p. 178

Answer the questions or complete the sentences with information from the text.

1 As they felt extremely threatened by terrorism, the USA and Britain made the mistake of confronting it by ... . (*2 aspects*)
2 What ways of dealing with terrorism have to be avoided under any circumstances? (*3 aspects*)
3 The author uses the phrase ... to express the fact that governments in the Western world no longer abided by the ethical principles that had once been valid in their countries.
4 The author uses the phrase ... to express the fact that governments in the Western world that fought terrorism by resorting to illegal methods have not been held responsible for that behaviour yet.
5 What do practically all Norwegians agree on? (*3 aspects*)

2 MEDIATION ENGLISH-GERMAN

> Skills p. 178

A Beantworten Sie die folgenden Fragen stichpunktartig auf Deutsch.

1 Wie reagierten die Norweger auf die terroristischen Anschläge in ihrem Land? (*2 Aspekte*)
2 In welchem Punkt ist sich der Autor bezüglich dieser Reaktion nicht sicher?
3 Was ist in den Augen des Autors das einzige Mittel, mit dem das im Text erwähnte Unrecht wieder gut gemacht werden kann?
4 Welches Problem sieht der Autor für den Fall, dass dies nicht geschieht?
5 Gegen Ende des Textes schreibt der Autor: „we represent a better alternative“. Fassen Sie, davon ausgehend, den Textinhalt zusammen.

B Geben Sie die folgenden Ausdrücke bzw. Sätze sinngemäß auf Deutsch wieder.

1 to reaffirm the values that the terrorists want to tear down (ll. 17–18)
2 principled leadership (l. 27)
3 well-resourced efforts by police (ll. 30–31)
4 enshrine (laws) (l. 40)
5 our intelligence services could get away with torture (ll. 76–77)

3 WORKING WITH WORDS

A Find the words in the text that match the following synonyms/explanations.

Paragraphs A & B:

1 responsibility
2 extremely cruel and violent action
3 state a belief again
4 disobey a principle

Paragraphs C & D:

5 preserve (a principle) in written form so that people will remember and respect it
6 act of handing over
7 suddenly let a strong feeling have its full effect

Paragraphs E, F & G:

8 act of being disloyal to a friend or of giving up a moral principle firmly stuck to in the past
9 a way of pretending that you have better moral principles than you really have
10 act of questioning sb. intensively in order to obtain information
11 charge and judge sb. for a crime in a court of law

B Rewrite the following sentences so that their meaning does not change. Use phrases from the text to replace the underlined parts. You may have to adapt them to fit the context.

1 People who <u>have eye-witnessed</u> terror attacks <u>are aware of the tremendous amount of pain and horror instantly inflicted by them</u>.
People who ... terror attacks ... .

2 However, governments must never be tempted <u>to turn to absolutely inappropriate ways</u> of combating terrorism.
But it would make no sense if governments ... of fighting terrorism.

3 Using illegal measures would <u>definitely prove that they are ill-advised</u> to assume that they can <u>forget about their ethical principles</u>.
Doing so would ... of assuming that they must ever ... .

4 <u>Practically all Norwegians agree</u> that the proper reaction to terrorism is to stick to democratic principles instead of resorting to <u>means which might achieve the opposite of what is intended</u>.
... among Norwegians that in their fight against terrorism they must never sway from the path of democracy instead of applying ... .

5 Not only do we need to prosecute terrorists, but we must also make sure that secret services officials do not <u>escape punishment for deliberately hurting human beings</u>, even if politicians <u>officially permitted these illegal acts</u>.
Apart from bringing terrorists to justice, we must also make sure that secret service officials don't ..., either, though politicians may have ... .

4 TALKING

In groups, discuss the following questions and report back to the class.

1 Name as many basic freedoms guaranteed by the German Constitution as you can think of.
2 Can you imagine any circumstances in which it would be acceptable for the German government to declare a state of emergency and subsequently curtail basic freedoms? List them.
3 Do you agree with Jan Egeland's view that the human rights of suspected terrorists should be protected at all costs. Why (not)?

C Words in context

Why resolution of conflicts is in our interest

2 12

In an age of globalization and at a time when many societies are becoming increasingly heterogeneous, new conflicts of interest are becoming ever more apparent, both at the national and international level. These conflicts will require our urgent attention if we are to maintain world peace and prosperity in the coming decades.

First, there is growing rivalry over a limited number of natural resources worldwide. If an equitable distribution of these resources cannot be found, the result could easily be armed conflict in many of the world's already volatile regions. This threat is compounded by ideological divisions over what economic and political systems are to be trusted. Are capitalist economies the key to achieving global growth and prosperity – or does capitalism inherently lead to the exploitation of both resources and human labour? Is the Social Democratic model of Western Europe a good compromise or is the cost of financing generous social programmes too high for it to be able to compete with unregulated, free-market economies? Finally, can dictatorships, Stalinist regimes and radical theocracies that suppress their peoples and preach hate be overcome for good?

Israeli-Palestinian border, Jerusalem

Another stark contrast is the one between rich and poor, which leads to calls for a more equal distribution of wealth. It is also an important reason for the emergence of political and religious extremism and religiously-motivated terrorist movements, particularly in Islamist-dominated societies. These terrorists believe that Western society is fundamentally corrupt and oppressive and that Christians must be combatted. More troubling is the potential ability of terrorists and rogue governments to attain weapons of mass destruction, such as chemical, biological or nuclear weapons.

This realistic possibility makes the question of fighting nuclear proliferation all the more pressing and raises the question of whether nations should continue to export weapons, especially to regions that are rife with conflict. The question of whether military force should be used to prevent Iran from developing an atomic bomb is one that is hotly debated. There is also a fundamental debate over whether it makes sense for Western democracies to rely primarily on massive military might to combat their enemies. Do they achieve convincing results by waging war or would it perhaps make more sense for them to try to set a positive example by living out their true ideals, both at home and around the world. Would such a policy – one based on justice, universal human rights and constitutional law – be a more persuasive means of swaying international opinion and policy and fighting extremism?

Fighting terrorism also raises other important questions for the Western democracies. Should suspected terrorists be granted the due process of law instead of being denied those fundamental legal rights enjoyed by American or Western European citizens? Protecting individual liberties at home is, of course, an equally important issue. Should, for example, freedom of speech on the Internet be unlimited or should the government have the right to monitor and censor messages in the name of national security, as some countries already do? Should citizens be able to gain unlimited access to the secrets of their governments in order to promote accountability or should such information remain confidential so that these governments can protect their sovereignty?

Eventually, all of these questions will have to be addressed if we are to defuse national and international conflicts before they explode.

(552 words)

First of all, make sure you understand the meaning of each of the highlighted phrases used in the text on page 140. If you are not sure, look them up in your dictionary. Then complete the tasks below.

1 PARAPHRASING

A Paraphrase the following expressions that appear in the text.

1 (they) will require our urgent attention (l. 3)
2 a limited number of natural resources worldwide (ll. 5–6)
3 this threat is compounded (l. 8)
4 nuclear proliferation (l. 24)
5 persuasive means of swaying international opinion (l. 32)
6 to monitor and censor messages (l. 37)
7 defuse ... conflicts before they explode (ll. 41–42)

B Find phrases in the text that mean the same as the following.

1 allowing the court system to determine guilt or innocence
2 In the course of time, each of these issues will have to be dealt with.
3 prosperity which is spread equally among the social classes
4 unveil any amount of clandestine information
5 having an ample number of armed struggles

C Find the equivalents of the following German expressions in the text.

1 Krieg führen
2 instabile Teile der Welt
3 wichtige Fragen aufwerfen
4 mit gutem Beispiel vorangehen
5 Schurkenstaaten
6 für mehr Transparenz sorgen
7 ein für alle Mal überwunden werden
8 Gesetze, die mit der Verfassung im Einklang stehen
9 seine wahren Ideale vorleben

2 WORD FAMILIES

> Skills p. 176

Use a member of the word family of the words in brackets to fill the gaps. Make sure you get the verb forms right and, if necessary, add a preposition.

In Western societies, a growing number of disillusioned voters are no longer ...[1] (confidence) that democratically elected governments are interested ...[2] (distribution) wealth in a fair way. That's why more and more ...[3] (extremism) parties ...[4] (emergent). Their members feel ...[5] (exploitative) by the banking system and think it is a matter of utmost ...[6] (urgent) to inject a larger degree of ...[7] (idealistic) into the political process. Despite their dissatisfaction, the situation is, of course, much better than that in ...[8] (oppress) regimes, where citizens seeking ...[9] (attainable) democracy ...[10] (combatant) brutally.
It is the ...[11] (convince) of political observers in the West that the ...[12] (proliferate) of all kinds of weapons must be stopped. Of course, it would be ...[13] (preference) if these rogue governments could be overcome once and for all. They say that ...[14] (generous) with them is out of the question and that ...[15] (compromise) them is something inconceivable.

D Further activities

1 DESCRIPTIVE WRITING

A Describing a cartoon: Describe the cartoon and interpret its message in about 100 words.

> Skills pp. 183–186

B Interpreting statistics: Interpret the bar chart below in about 100 words.

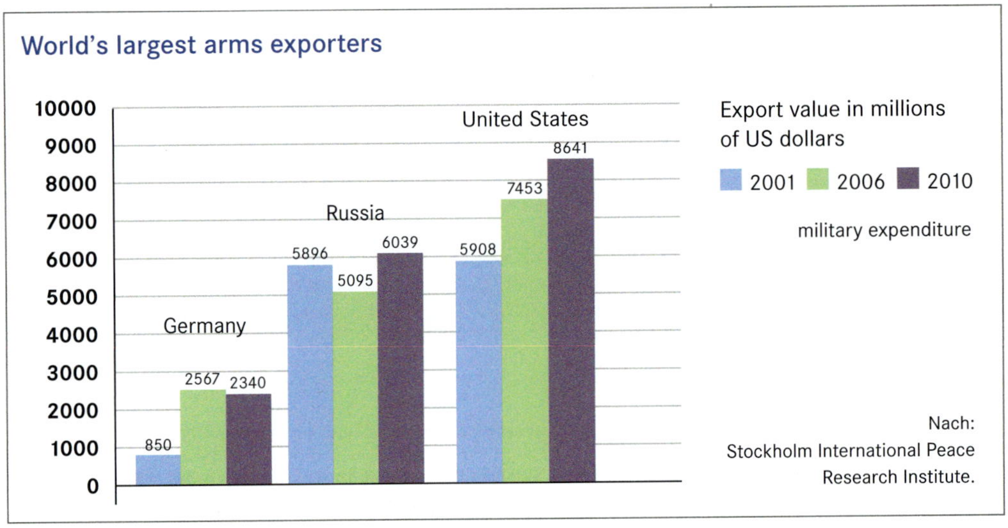

2 PROJECT

> Skills p. 190

Using the Internet or library reference books, find out more about <u>one</u> of the following topics. Present your findings to the class.

1 The fight over water will be one of the major issues of the future. Find examples of regions where this trend can already be observed and examine how both individual citizens and the political stability of the region as a whole will be affected.

2 How does the Chinese government deal with opposition to official Communist party policies? Find recent examples of ways in which either well-known Chinese dissidents or ethnic minority groups have been treated in order to illustrate your findings.

3 What sparked uprisings during the "Arab Spring"? Focus your research on one particular country in the region.

3 LISTENING

> Skills p. 179

2 13 **You are going to hear a radio report which deals with the "Arab Spring" and America's changing relationship to the Arab world. Listen, take notes and complete the following task assignments.**

A Answer the following questions.

1 What lessons become evident when one looks at the outcome of the first free elections in Tunisia and Egypt?
2 What makes Deborah Amos think that the Arab Spring "has hardly run its course"?
3 What, in Khaled Fahmy's view, is the difference between the Arab uprisings of the 20th century and those of the early 21st century?
4 According to various observers, why may America have more difficulty in exerting influence on the Arab world?

B Decide whether these statements are true or false.

1 Greg Gause thinks that the Arab uprisings constitute a natural disaster.
2 Americans are afraid that the Muslim Brotherhood may not be as cooperative as the Mubarak regime was.
3 Khaled Fahmy is of the opinion that Arab uprisings were directed against influential American politicians.
4 It's hard to imagine the Arab Spring happening without the use of American networking sites.

C Fill in the gaps in the text below with information from the report.

The first chapter of the history the Arab world is now writing deals with …[1]. People now simply want to have …[2] and the university professor Greg Gause thinks that …[3] is bound to be very important. This spells trouble for the USA because at the moment …[4] are high. It's interesting to note here that American values played a major role in the revolution because they …[5] of the demonstrators.

4 GROUP DISCUSSION

> Skills p. 187

There are a number of issues that pose a grave threat to global peace and stability. Look at the list below and discuss them.

Phase 1: individual (= one-minute speech)
Choose one of the suggestions listed and briefly say why it poses a threat.

Phase 2: interactive (= group discussion)
Discuss all of the items in the list of suggestions and try to reach some form of agreement as to which one(s) need(s) to be tackled most urgently.

- arms exports by rich countries to (poor) regions rife with conflict
- exploitation of both domestic and foreign workers/consumers as a result of unregulated capitalism
- trade barriers imposed by rich countries, which adversely affect the poor countries
- lack of access to natural resources (fossil fuels, water, etc.)
- the hypocrisy of the West championing basic human rights in principle but often ignoring them in practice

E Grammar check

REPORTED SPEECH

> Grammar summary p. 198

SPOT THE MISTAKES

Spot the mistakes and correct them. Explain why they are wrong.

1 ~~Mr Egeland told the press that he saw the horrendous effects of terrorism in Norway some time ago.~~
2 ~~He added that the violation of human rights is the wrong way to fight terrorism.~~
3 ~~The press reported that the attack was committed by a home-grown terrorist.~~
4 ~~My friend asked me if I think a terrorist attack may happen in Germany in the near future.~~
5 ~~The newspaper article stated that the motives of today's terrorists have changed.~~

A Put the following statements into reported speech.

1 The IT revolution will increasingly cause political upheaval in authoritarian states in the near future.
→ *The media expert stated that ...*
2 The world has had a very high level of connectivity for more than one decade.
→ *He added that ...*
3 The cheap new platform for connectivity is bringing another two billion people into the conversation from more and more remote areas.
→ *The journalist voiced his opinion that ...*
4 The quest for dignity has been one key factor driving the Arab uprisings.
→ *He added that ...*
5 I'm sure that the consequences of the breakdown in principled leadership after the 9/11 atrocities will not go away very soon.
→ *The terrorism expert said ...*
6 The most fundamental clash of interest is that between the world's *haves* and its *have-nots*.
→ *An African leader said that ...*
7 Will it ever be possible to achieve a fairer world?
→ *The author of the article raised the question ...*
8 Why do you think that the Arab Spring is irreversible?
→ *The reporter asked the Middle East expert ...*

> Webcode: FOSEAU1101

WATCH OUT!

Problem words (4)

> False friends p. 267

Levels of political violence may well ~~raise~~ if the problem of poverty is not solved.
→ *Levels of political violence my well rise if the problem of poverty is not solved.*

B Choose the correct highlighted word or phrase to complete each sentence.

1 The windows of the President's car are made out from/in/of bullet-proof glass.
2 The bomb went off right next/nearly/besides/beside a busy street café.
3 In my meaning/opinion/belief, the president is following the right policy/politic/politics.
4 The terrorists escaped and are being looked after/looked for/searched after by the police.
5 The negotiators hope to reach a settlement in the next day/in the next time/in the next future/in the near future.
6 Officials found it necessary to check/control/proof/prove the packages.
7 Rescue agencies stood/stayed/kept/further kept working until they had freed all the survivors.
8 The terrorist suspect got/became a 15-year prison sentence for planting the bomb.

12 Looking ahead

FOCUS

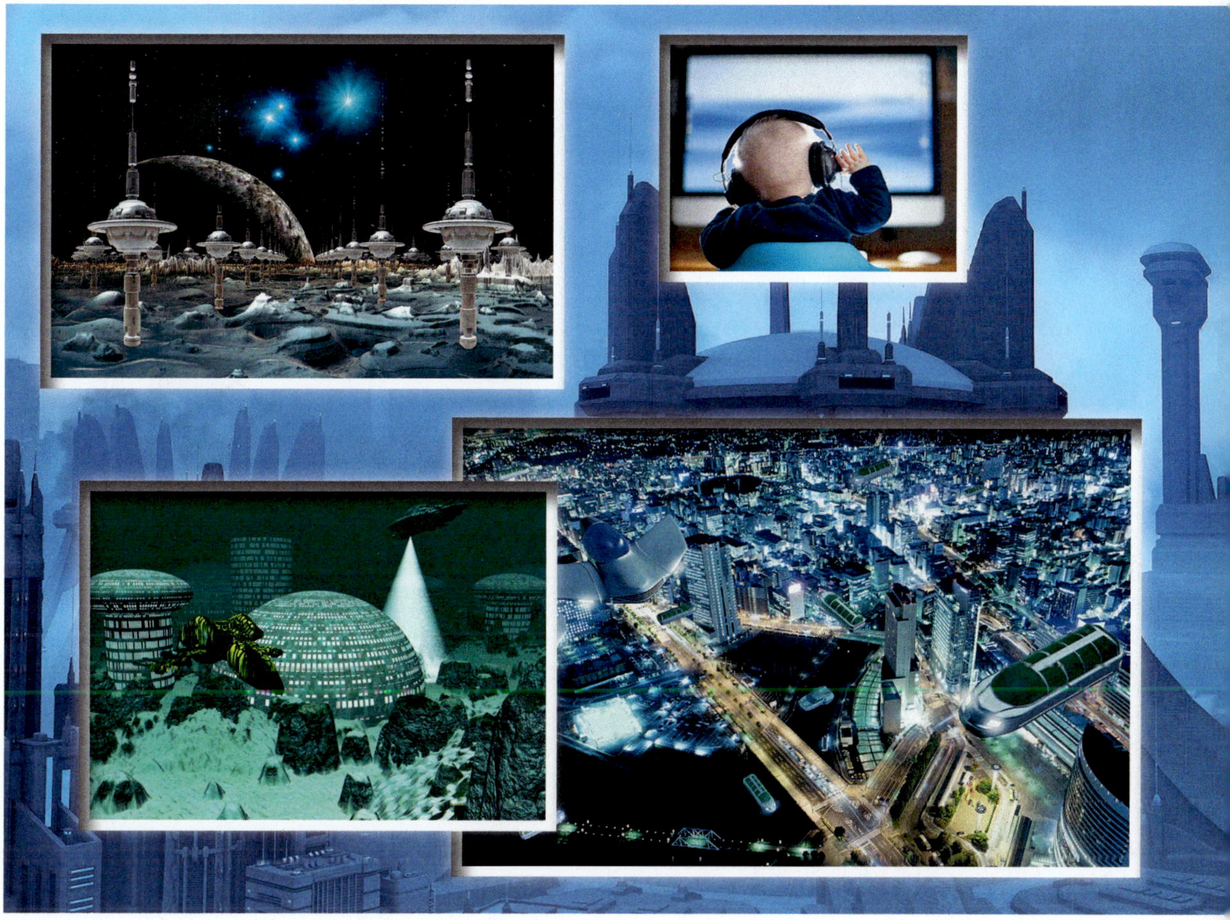

Look at the photos and do the following tasks.

1 Imagine that you can travel through time into the future ... to the year 2035, perhaps. Think about the following questions:
- Where will you live? What will your home look like?
- What job will you have?
- What means of transport will you use?
- Will you have children? Where will they go to school?
- What will you do in your free time?
- Where will you spend your holidays?

2 Talk to your partner about your ideas and report back to the class.

A The future of technology and mankind

BEFORE YOU READ

Which technological issues might mankind have to deal with in the future?
Which questions about the future would you like to ask a leading scientist?

Ten Questions for Ray Kurzweil

Entrepreneur, inventor and philosopher Ray Kurzweil, born 1948 in Queens (New York City), is one of the leading scientists of our time. A pioneer of flat-bed scanning and the optical character recognition (OCR), Ray Kurzweil often speculates on the future of technology and mankind. The following questions were put to him by TIME magazine.

Q: 1 … ?

A: Our intuition about the future is linear. But the reality of information technology is exponential, and that makes a profound difference. If I take 30 steps linearly, I get to 30. If I take 30 steps exponentially, I get to a billion.

Q: 2 … ?

A: By the time we get to the 2040s, we'll be able to multiply human intelligence a billionfold. That will be a profound change that's singular in nature. Computers are going to keep getting smaller and smaller. Ultimately, they will go inside our bodies and brains and make us healthier, make us smarter. We'll be online all the time. Search engines won't wait to be asked.

Q: 3 … ?

A: We've always been responsible for the triage of our time. I actually think these technologies enable us to focus better. My father was a musician, and he had to hire an orchestra and raise money just to hear his compositions. Now a kid in her dorm room can do that with her synthesizer and computer.

Q: 4 … ?

A: We will reprogram our biology. My cellphone's probably updating itself as we speak, but I'm walking around with 1,000-year-old software that was for a different era. One gene, the fat insulin receptor gene, says, "Hold on to every calorie, because the next hunting season may not work out so well." I'd like to be able to tell my fat insulin receptor gene, "You don't need to do that. I'm confident I'll have food tomorrow."

Q: 5 … ?

A: We'll grow *in vitro* cloned meats in factories that are computerized and run by artificial intelligence. You can just grow the part of the animal that you're eating. Some people say, "Oh, that sounds yucky." I say, "Well, why don't you go visit a factory-farming installation? You'll find that getting meat from living animals is yucky." But we'll need a marketing genius to sell the idea.

Q: 6 … ?

A: People are most resistant to the idea of dramatic extensions to life expectancy, because it affects every decision they make. They have this cycle of life in mind. People sort of wax philosophical – "Oh, I don't want to live past 100." I'd like to see them say that when they're 100.

Q: 7 … ?

A: The consensus in the field is that there's somewhere between a thousand and a million technologically advanced civilizations just in our own galaxy. But once you get to a point where we are, within a few centuries at most, these civilizations would be doing galaxy-wide engineering. It's impossible we wouldn't be noticing that. So my conclusion is that we may be the first.

Q: 8 … ?

A: Technology is a double-edged sword. New technologies can be used for destructive purposes. The answer is to develop rapid-response systems for new dangers like a bioterrorist creating a new biological virus. We don't have to just sit back and wait.

Q: 9 … ?

A: I think we are evolving rapidly into one world culture. It's certainly one world economy. With billions of people online, I think we'll appreciate the wisdom in many different traditions as we learn more about them. People were very isolated and didn't know anything about other religions 100 years ago.

Q: 10 … ?

A: I believe our civilization is going to be vastly more intelligent and more spiritual in the decades ahead. You can argue how we got here, but we are the species that goes beyond our limitations. We didn't stay on the ground. We didn't stay on the planet. Our species always transcends.

(673 words)

> Webcode: FOSEAU1201

Adapted from: *Time*, 6 December 2010

1 MULTIPLE MATCHING

> Skills p. 177

Match the questions (A–L) with the gaps (1–10) in the text. There are two more questions than you need.

A Do you think we'll find intelligent life elsewhere in the universe?
B How exactly will technology make us healthier?
C How will our technological progress make us feel about God?
D How will science affect the religious and ethnic differences in the world?
E Is it a mistake to use the events of the recent past as a method of predicting the future?
F Speaking of marketing, what idea about the future do you have the hardest time selling?
G What are the dangers of technological innovation?
H Will economic progress go hand in hand with technological progress?
I Will this make it more difficult for us to focus?
J Will we be able to do without food?
K Will we be eating differently?
L You predict we'll reach a point with artificial intelligence that you call the singularity. How will that affect us?

2 MULTIPLE CHOICE

> Skills p. 176

Choose the most suitable option.

1 In answer 2 Kurzweil predicts the emergence of ... .
a nanobots b androids c humanoids d medibots

2 The story about his father ... .
a shows the difficulties involved with being a musician in the past
b illustrates the point that technology makes things easier
c proves that young people have become smarter
d shows that musical talent is not a question of age

3 The comparison with the cellphone shows that, in future, technology will ... .
a enable us to prevent diabetes
b help us to live healthier lives
c fail to make our lives more worthwhile
d end our hunter-gatherer mentality

4 Food production in the future will ... .
a be less disgusting than its present form
b be sterile but very healthy
c lack taste but be highly efficient
d have to be made more attractive to people

5 The idea of living past the age of 100 is ... .
a welcomed by most people
b absolutely inconceivable for most people
c rejected by most people
d a philosophical issue

6 Which statement best sums up answer 7?
a Although there are numerous advanced societies in our galaxy, we are in the lead.
b Other advanced societies in our galaxy are either non-existent or disinterested.
c Our society might not be the most advanced but it will be in the centuries to come.
d The numerous advanced societies in our galaxy are ignoring our presence.

7 Technological progress ... .
a will mean the end of world religions
b has fostered isolationism
c just serves business interests
d can help bridge divides

8 In answer 10 Kurzweil depicts mankind as ... .
a ignorant of its true potential
b always maintaining the status quo
c taking up new challenges
d having lost faith in God

3 WORKING WITH WORDS

A Use a member of the word family of the word in brackets to fill the gap.

> Skills p. 176

1 The anti-age drugs currently on ... (sell) all over the USA are not really reliable.
2 Predictions made by some scientists lack ... (profound) and analytical precision.
3 There is no reason why people should lack ... (confident) in what Ray Kurzweil predicts.
4 One might even call Kurzweil ... (wisdom) although some of his views certainly ... (destruction) the long-held beliefs of many people.
5 He believes that technology can help to ... (extension) the human life span beyond 100 years.

B Find the English equivalents of the following German expressions in the text.

1 einzigartig in der Natur
2 Fleisch im Reagenzglas erzeugen
3 philosophieren
4 zweischneidiges Schwert
5 in der Wissenschaft / unter Wissenschaftlern herrscht breiter Konsens
6 über die Grenzen hinaus gehen

B The future of learning?

BEFORE YOU READ

Can you imagine staying at home and studying online instead of going to school every morning? What would be the advantages or disadvantages?

Can Computers Replace Classrooms?

A K12 Inc. of Herndon has become the country's largest provider of full-time public virtual schools, upending the traditional American notion that learning occurs in a schoolhouse where students share the experience. In K12's virtual schools, learning is largely solitary, with lessons delivered online to a child who progresses at her own pace. Conceived as a way to teach a small segment of the home-schooled and others who need flexible schooling, virtual education has evolved into an alternative to traditional public schools for an increasingly wide range of students – high achievers, strugglers, dropouts, teenage parents and victims of bullying among them. "For many kids, the local school doesn't work," said Ronald J. Packard, chief executive and founder of K12. "And now, technology allows us to give that child a choice. It's about educational liberty. We are harnessing technology to deliver quality education to any child, regardless of Zip code."

B It's an appealing proposition, and one that has attracted support in state legislatures, including Virginia's. But a rising chorus of critics argues that full-time virtual learning doesn't effectively educate children. "Virtual schooling would appear to make it possible to go from kindergarten through eighth grade without ever stepping into a real classroom," David M. Foster said, a member of the state Board of Education of Virginia. "I'm not sure I want to encourage that. ... Collaborative problem solving, socialization, working with other people is key not just to the global economy but to getting along in life."

C Yet despite criticism, full-time virtual schools are proliferating. About 250,000 students are enrolled in full-time public virtual schools in 30 states, according to Susan Patrick of the International Association for K-12 Online Learning, a trade association. Although that's just a fraction of the country's 50 million schoolchildren, their number is growing fast, Patrick said.

D In the past two years, more than a dozen states have passed laws and removed obstacles to encourage virtual schools. And providers of virtual education have been making their case in statehouses around the country. K12 has hired lobbyists from Boise to Boston and backed political candidates who support school choice in general and virtual education in particular. This year, K12 gave about $500,000 in direct contributions to state politicians across the country.
"We understand the politics of education pretty well," Packard told investors recently.

E If K12 were a school district, it would rank among the 30 largest of the nation's 1,500 districts. The company, which began in two states a decade ago, now teaches about 95,000 students in virtual schools in 29 states. It sells a variety of ways to learn online, ranging from hybrid schools – in which students meet in a classroom but take courses via computer – to à la carte courses purchased by traditional schools. But K12's core business - and the one proving most controversial – is full-time virtual public schools.

F For Tyler Hirata, going to school used to mean waking up at 6 a.m. and clambering aboard a yellow bus. Now he snoozes until midmorning and pads downstairs to the computer in his Dumfries home. "This is fantastic!" said Tyler, 8, who had attended a Prince William County school but was enrolled this fall in the Virginia Virtual Academy – a public institution run by K12 and open to any student in the commonwealth. Tyler said the best thing about taking third grade online is that it requires less than three hours a day.

G There are drawbacks, though. Tyler said he misses some of the best parts of school, such as lunchtime. And recess. And friends. "Believe me," he said, "if you are home-schooled, you will want friends."

H Virtual class sizes tend to be larger than at traditional schools – the Virginia academy averages 60 students per teacher, according to a school document. So in the primary grades, the model relies on the intensive work of a parent "learning coach," who provides most lessons away from the computer, using books and 90 pounds of other educational materials shipped to families by K12. In the older grades, the bulk of learning is online, with software that sometimes aims to mimic real-life experiences for students, such as a high school biology lab featuring an animated frog dissection.

I While virtual schools continue to expand, their effectiveness is unclear. "We have no real evidence one way or another," said Tom Loveless, a Brookings Institution scholar who served as a paid consultant to K12 in its early years. On measures widely used to judge all public schools, such as state test scores and graduation rates, virtual schools tend to perform worse than their brick-and-mortar counterparts. At the Colorado Virtual Academy, which is managed by K12 and has more than 5,000 students, the on-time graduation rate was 12 percent in 2010, compared with 72 percent statewide. K12 officials say the weak test results are related to the program often attracting students who struggled in regular schools.

J One of K12's oldest and biggest schools is the Agora Cyber Charter, a statewide virtual school that began in Pennsylvania in 2005. The school markets itself as an option for at-risk students who are failing at their neighborhood school. Last year, about two-thirds of its students came from low-income families. Many lived in unstable homes, said Aimée Saunders, who taught history at K12's Pennsylvania schools for four years. Some of those children didn't have an adult who could serve as the learning coach. Instead, they were left home alone and did little or no schoolwork, she said. "You take students who normally would struggle because of their home environment and then you put them in their home to learn," Saunders said. "It doesn't work that well."

K Rapid student turnover can compound the problem. Of the 8,700 students who enrolled in 2010-11, more than a quarter withdrew during the year, according to school records. "New students were always coming in," Saunders said, which "made it difficult to be able to focus on the students I already had."

L Yet Saunders says that despite all the problems, virtual schools provide an important new option for families and should be forgiven for missteps. After all, many traditional public schools have failed to help the neediest children. Maybe virtual ones won't ...

(1025 words)

Adapted from: *www.thefiscaltimes.com*

1 SHORT-ANSWER QUESTIONS / SENTENCE COMPLETION

> Skills p. 178

Answer the questions or complete the sentences with information from paragraphs A–D of the text.

1 K12 is in the process of turning the ... upside-down that studying takes place in ..., because it offers comprehensive schooling online.
2 Originally, online lessons were developed for ... .
3 What type of students may profit from a virtual school? (*5 aspects*)
4 A lot of people, though, question this method, because in their opinion it ... .
5 What evidence does the author supply to support the claim that virtual schools are becoming ever more popular? (*2 aspects*)

2 MEDIATION ENGLISH-GERMAN

> Skills p. 178

Beantworten Sie die folgenden Aufgaben auf Deutsch.

1 Erklären Sie aus dem Textzusammenhang, was Packard meint, wenn er sagt: „We understand the politics of education pretty well." (Absatz D)
2 Was ist ein „à la carte course"? (Absatz E)
3 Kopieren Sie nachstehende Tabelle über die Vor- und Nachteile der Online-Schulen und vervollständigen Sie sie.

Vorteile (*4 Aspekte*)	Nachteile (*7 Aspekte*)
> Schüler bestimmen ihr Lerntempo selbst > ...	> Kinder werden nicht effektiv unterrichtet/erzogen/ausgebildet > ...

4 Welche Gründe geben die K12-Betreiber als Erklärung für das schlechte Abschneiden ihrer Schüler bei landesweiten Vergleichen an? (*4 Aspekte*)

3 WORKING WITH WORDS

A Match the words/expressions from the text with their definitions below.

1 to compound
2 conceived as
3 to proliferate
4 to make one's case
5 to rank
6 be enrolled in
7 counterpart
8 recess

a to have a position relative to others
b to be officially registered
c to make more intense, stronger or more marked
d sb./sth. that has the same function as another
e to grow rapidly
f envisioned as
g to provide reasons and facts to support one's argument
h a break between lessons

B Match these German expressions with expressions from the text.

1 ein reizvoller Vorschlag (paragraph B)
2 Gesetze verabschieden und Hindernisse aus dem Weg räumen (paragraph D)
3 politische Kandidaten unterstützen (paragraph D)
4 Erfahrungen aus dem „echten" Leben nachahmen (paragraph H)
5 keine richtigen Beweise haben, weder dafür noch dagegen (paragraph I)
6 Anzahl der Schüler, die termingerecht ihren Abschluss gemacht haben (paragraph I)
7 eine Alternative für gefährdete Schüler (paragraph J)
8 öffentlichen Schulen ist es nicht gelungen, den bedürftigsten Kindern zu helfen (paragraph L)

C Find all the words in the text that have to do with 'school' and develop a mind map together with your partner. Check Unit 3 as well for words that you might find useful. Compare your mind maps in class. > Skills p. 180

4 TALKING

Discuss the following questions with a partner and report your ideas to the class.

1 In your opinion, what role will teachers have in the future? Can they be replaced by computers?
2 What do you think your school will look like in 2035?

C Words in context

Science and technology

The world today is threatened by climate change and overpopulation; the planet has to support seven billion people (and the figure is constantly rising) who are competing for resources such as water and energy as well as land and jobs. How are we going to deal with all these problems?

For those people who are optimistic about the future, the main asset we have is our own inventiveness. According to them, the answers will come from pure scientific research, which will provide new technologies for us to apply in our daily life. A watershed invention such as the Internet, for example, was just one scientist's vision not much longer than a generation ago; now it is as common as electricity and there is no end in sight to the possibilities for its future development.

Scientists often find themselves at the centre of controversy because of their research. One highly controversial field of study is the science of genetics. In theory, scientists are able to produce so-called "designer babies" according to the wishes of their parents. They could, for example, ask for a baby with blue eyes, blond hair and a high IQ. Scientists could also theoretically produce embryonic or adult stem cells in the laboratory which could be used to reproduce human tissues and organs. Tailor-made organisms could enable doctors to ensure the survival of patients suffering from previously incurable diseases. Scientific achievements now affect our lives profoundly and the possibilities for genetic engineering are undoubtedly going to increase in the future.

"I GUESS THERE'LL ALWAYS BE A GAP BETWEEN SCIENCE AND TECHNOLOGY"

Another source of controversy within the scientific community are genetically-modified (GM) plants. On the one hand, genetic engineering allows farmers to grow crops in places where standard crops don't grow easily and therefore they could produce food in parts of the world where it is desperately needed. Genetically modified plants could also reduce farmers' reliance on dangerous pesticides or help to eradicate diseases that affect crops in the developing world. On the other hand, there is much that is still unknown about the long-term effects of such foods on human and animal health, the environment or biodiversity in general. Studies have shown, for example, that some pests are now "super-resistant" to pesticides as a result of coming into contact with GM plants. It is no wonder that many people are suspicious of this tinkering with nature and are concerned that the results will be unpredictable.

Scientific progress seems, therefore, to be a double-edged sword. Ray Kurzweil prophesies that within a couple of decades, we will have 'nanobots' in our blood stream. These are basically small robots the size of blood cells, that will keep us healthy at the cellular and molecular level and will prolong the human life span. The fact that a greater life expectancy will add to our population crisis is just one of the negative consequences that can result from new scientific breakthroughs. Likewise, the futurist Thomas Frey predicts a future with driverless vehicles (drones) or robots that can build houses from material produced by a 3D-printer. However, he is quick to point out that there would also be a downside to these developments: drones can drop bombs just as easily as they can deliver a pizza, and robots that can build houses can also be used to destroy them. Thus it is wise, perhaps, to maintain a healthy scepticism towards the idea that scientific research and technological progress will automatically provide a panacea for every problem we face.

(574 words)

First of all, make sure you understand the meaning of each of the highlighted phrases used in the text on page 152. If you are not sure, look them up in your dictionary. Then complete the tasks below.

1 SYNONYMS

Rewrite the sentences, replacing the underlined parts of the sentences with a synonymous expression from the text.

1 What can we do to guarantee that the human race doesn't die out?
What can we do to ... of the human race?
2 Science has always provided solutions to our problems and this will be the case in future, too.
There is ... the solutions science will provide for our problems.
3 It is often difficult to wipe out dangerous illnesses.
It is often difficult ... .
4 Public attention is again focusing on stem-cell researchers at the moment.
Currently, stem-cell researchers ... public attention.
5 Research can have a great impact on our lives.
Research can ... .
6 Some farmers still count on chemicals every day.
Some farmers' ... chemicals is still a day-to-day reality.

2 COLLOCATIONS

> Skills p. 175

A Find the English equivalents of the following German expressions in the text.

1 um Rohstoffe konkurrieren
2 ein gesundes Maß an Skepsis beibehalten
3 in so großem Maßstab
4 Langzeitfolgen für
5 maßgeschneiderte Organismen
6 genetisch veränderte Pflanzen
7 Krankheiten ausmerzen
8 an der Natur herumpfuschen/herumbasteln

B Use collocations or expressions from the box to complete the sentences.

double-edged sword | in the scientific community | adds to our crisis | watershed | breakthrough | main asset | panacea

You want to say ...
1 In the end, scientific innovations can have both a positive and negative outcome.
Some scientific innovations can be a ... .
2 Inventions like the computer chip marked an important change.
The invention of the computer chip was a ... in the development of technology.
3 Patience is most useful and valuable thing researchers can possess.
Patience is the ... of researchers.
4 Fellow researchers always examine the results of tests closely.
Test results are always examined closely ... .
5 Scientists found a solution to the problem last month.
Scientists had a ... last month.
6 Only with the help of research will we be able to solve all the problems that might face us in the future.
Research is the ... for all our future problems.
7 A further problem for our difficult situation is that many states are in dire straits.
The fact that many states are short of money ... .

D Further activities

1 DESCRIPTIVE WRITING

> Skills pp. 183–186

A Describing cartoons: Describe the cartoon and interpret the message the cartoonist is trying to make in about 100 words.

B Interpreting statistics: Look at the chart below and interpret it.

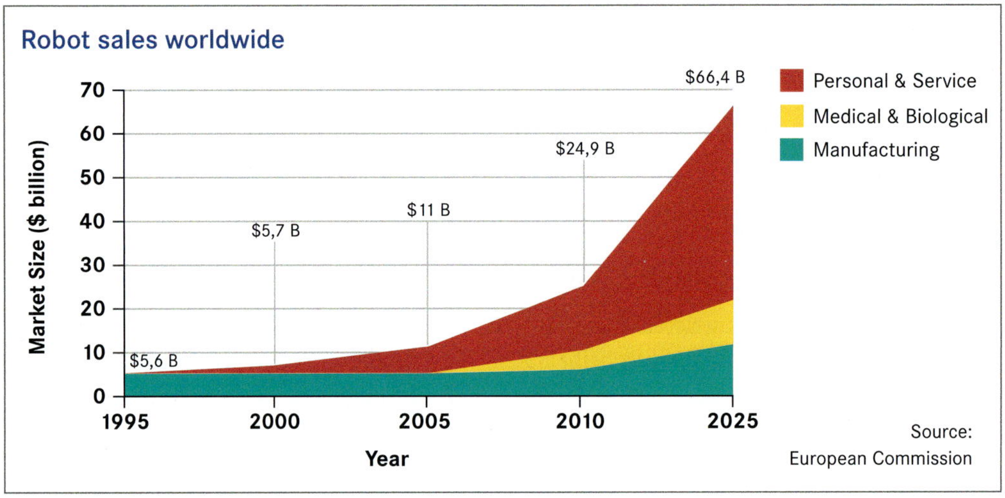

2 LISTENING

> Skills p. 179

2 15 **You are going to hear a radio report about new developments in the use of human skin cells. Listen and complete the sentences.**

1 Both teams did … .
2 The main idea was … skin cells and turn them into embryonic stem cells.
3 The latter are so called … cells which means they can grow into any cell in the body.
4 The argument about the pros and cons of stem cells started roughly … .
5 Why might the new approach end the controversy about stem cells? In the long run, laboratories will stop … .
6 Most criticism of the use of embryonic stem-cell research comes from the fact that … .
7 Japanese researchers can by now produce … such as heart and nerve cells.
8 The use of stem cells is aimed at creating … for a particular person.
9 The main problem scientists face is … the … ; without this knowledge even stem cells can't really do the trick.
10 There is one worry left. Researchers are worried that such new cells could cause … .
11 Among scientists it is believed that this problem … .

3 ARGUMENTATIVE WRITING

> Skills p. 181

Choose one of the following topics and write at least 200 words.

1 The worldwide spread of genetically-modified food seems to be unstoppable. In Europe, GM food has to be marked, but there are still many people who want GM products to be banned from the EU altogether. Do you agree with this view?

2 Do you think that it is right to spend immense sums on exploring space, as long as so many problems remain unsolved on earth?

4 GROUP DISCUSSION

> Skills p. 187

You are a member of a committee that is choosing the winner of this year's Best Invention award. Today you are in a meeting with the other members of the committee to decide which of the finalists will be the winner and receive the $50,000 prize.

Phase 1: individual (= one-minute speech)
Present 'your' invention to the group and briefly tell them why you think it deserves to be awarded the prize.

Phase 2: interactive (= group discussion)
Next, the group should decide on the winner and the first runner-up - who will receive a consolation prize of $10,000. Try to persuade the others to vote for your 'invention', but be prepared to compromise if you think someone else's invention deserves to win the prize more than yours.

Look at File 5 on pages 161–162 for descriptions of the finalists.

5 PROJECT: A WEB-QUEST

> Skills p. 190

Throughout the course of history, mankind has always faced life-threatening challenges. In the last few decades, these challenges have become more daunting than ever. Population explosion, climate change and the threat of terrorism are just some of the issues that are likely to accompany us in the coming decades.

Task

You are a team of students doing research on which global issues are relevant today and are likely to remain so in the future. Each team deals with one issue from the list below (the list can be changed by the teacher).

- Social issues, e.g. development of mega-cities, family, living together, discrimination against disabled persons and the elderly ("ageism")
- Economic issues, e.g. lack of employment opportunities, minimum wage, starvation, trade issues
- Political issues, e.g. terrorism, human rights
- Technological issues, e.g. Mars mission, hydrogen age

How to proceed

Prepare a PowerPoint presentation on your topic for your class, in which an introductory movie-clip, cartoon or graph gives your classmates an idea of what your presentation is about. The main part should present some particular aspects of the topic to give your fellow students an insight into the problem and possible solutions. Finally you should create a worksheet for them so that they can fill in information on the topic.

E Grammar check

MIXED GRAMMAR

> Grammar summary pp. 193–208

Complete the email by filling in the correct form of the words in brackets. Sometimes you may need to add more words, e.g. a preposition.

E-MAIL

Dear Mike,

I ...[1] (read) an article in the paper the other day. It was on technological trends to watch out for in the next few decades. Though I'd rather ...[2] (concentrate) on other matters, I had to read it in preparation for a lesson. But it ...[3] (turn/be) quite interesting reading.

The article, although mostly ...[4] (deal) with energy matters, was written by a well-known futurologist. After I ...[5] (look) up some of the technical words, I ...[6] (write) down the key statements of the text. In general the article was pretty ...[7] (optimistic). At least it gave a ...[8] (positive) outlook than the one I ...[9] (read) before. And you know what I think of people who are always pessimistic!

It mentioned that researchers ...[10] (currently/work) on a promising project in the field of nuclear fusion. But not even this (in)famous futurologist dared to predict when this revolutionary technology ...[11] (put) into practice. But I am looking forward ...[12] (such a reactor/build).

I wonder if people ...[13] (think) about the far-reaching consequences of such a technology: energy in abundance without any negative side effects. Since the beginning of the Industrial Revolution, a clean energy supply ...[14] (be) a major issue. This article wants ...[15] (convince) its readers that energy in the future ...[16] (supply) without ...[17] (affect) the environment.

This futurologist also objected ...[18] (focus) only on this source of energy. He wanted energy ...[19] (be) affordable to Third World countries as well. He was in favour of small-scale energy solutions ...[20] (take) advantage of renewable energy sources.

But he also dealt with the ethics of technological progress. Only last year, he ...[21] (point out), we ...[22] (all/confront) with the downside of genetic engineering again. This is ...[23] (hard) surprising. The scenarios of designer babies and genetically-modified ...[24] (make) the headlines again and again.

The article mentioned the work that ...[25] (already/do) to decipher the human genome and highlighted some of the dreadful consequences that might bring with it. If the futurologist ...[26] (be) in a science fiction film, I ...[27] (not/surprise). But in the end the author stressed the benefits of such ...[28] (high/sophisticated) technology. If technology ...[29] (continue) at that pace, our world ...[30] (bare/be) recognizable in a few years.

But, who ...[31] (remember) the breakthroughs in the first decades of the 21st century in 2125? By then all this ...[32] (probably/become/outdate). The technological innovations ...[33] (consider) breakthroughs in the 19th century are mostly on display in museums today.

But enough of the future for tonight, though I ...[34] (strong/recommend) that you read that article – it really provides food for thought!

Goodnight
Tony

Appendix

Files

FILE 1 Unit 1, part D, exercise 4

Ideas / Possibilities

1 Seek positive emotion as a path to success

Happiness can lead to success, rather than just the other way around. Happy individuals are predisposed to seek out new opportunities and set new goals. After reviewing data of 225 studies gathered from more than 275,000 individuals, a team of psychologists concluded that while previous research assumed that happiness stemmed from success and accomplishment, success is often a result of positive emotions. Success is the result of many factors, including physical health, intelligence, family and expertise.

2 Do something nice for someone else

Hold a door open for someone at the bank, give someone directions if they look lost, or make a point to compliment three people on your way to work. Small or big, directed at friends or strangers, random acts of kindness make the person performing the kind act happier when they're grouped together, according to Sonja Lyubomirsky, an experimental psychologist at UC Riverside. Doing a considerate thing for another person five times in one day made the doer happier than if they had spread out those five acts over one week. Lyubomirsky explains that because we all perform acts of kindness naturally, it seems to please us more when we're more conscious of it. There are social rewards, too, when people respond positively.

3 Count your blessings

Count your blessings - but not everyday. Sonja Lyubomirsky, an experimental psychologist at UC Riverside, found that people who wrote down five things they were grateful for once a week were happier than those who did it three times a week. "It's an issue of timing or frequency," says Lyubomirsky, "When people do anything too often it loses the freshness and meaning. You need to have optimal timing." Another exercise is to think of a person who has been kind to you that you've wanted to thank - a teacher, mentor or parent - and write a letter, once a week to different individuals over two months. You don't even have to send it to feel happier.

4 Make time

Society is plagued by time bankruptcy. But what if people asserted more control over their time to optimize their use of it? Psychologists will say prioritize, set realistic daily goals that fit into the bigger picture and some time might be recovered. Maybe set aside two nights in your calendar to focus on those things that you'd like to spend more time on.

FILE 2 Unit 2, FOCUS

What type of traveller are you?

You are an independent traveller if you chose these answers:

1c	Lost luggage is no fun, but a positive attitude helps a lot. You can't do anything anyway.
2b	Who knows the place better?
3a	Where else could you get an authentic 'taste' of the country? That's food for thought!
4c	You'll get around just fine!
5b	Have a drink on me while asking for directions ...
6c	Designer furniture isn't comfortable anyway!
7a	In case you lack good company!
8a	If your holiday was good, you might want to go there again; if not, you need alternatives ...

<u>If your choice of options corresponds to at least six of the above</u>, you are an independent explorer, more likely to be found on a bus full of locals and chickens than on a tour bus with a guide holding a microphone.

<u>If your choice of options corresponds to four or five of the above</u>, you definitely like to get away from it all from time to time but you appreciate the comforts of home when you are on the road. Not that we're saying there's anything wrong with that.

<u>If your choice of options corresponds to three or fewer of the above</u>, you are a probably an armchair traveller. You are more comfortable around your own neighbourhood than the Quartier Latin in Paris. Rent a good travel DVD and curl up for the night.

FILE 3 Unit 7, part D, exercise 4

Signs of the social networking times.

FILE 4 Unit 5, part D, exercise 5

Candidates

Robin Chase

The culture of the Internet, at its best, involves people working together to make life better. Sometimes called cooperative capitalism or social entrepreneurship, it is practiced every day by millions of individuals and a small but growing number of for-profit companies. For years, Robin Chase, a co-founder of Zipcar, has run such a business, in which people share a community-based pool of vehicles. Customers use Zipcar, which rents cars by the day or hour (when public transportation won't quite do the job) and makes smart use of technology like GPS to connect people with cars and trucks that are parked near them.

Robin's work illustrates what's best about people using the Internet: not well-intentioned yet futile do-goodism, but business that's also a community service. It's about people using the Internet to work together in the service of one another.

Oprah Winfrey

Oprah's always moving forward, seeking, changing – like the great explorers who reset the horizon every time they sailed. Her curiosity is undiminished. So is her passion for healing the bruised parts of the world and wielding truth against the bruisers.

She readied the launch of her new cable channel, powered up on radio, supervised her magazine and learned how to tweet. She flew tens of thousands of miles back and forth to the school in Africa whose 300 students remain the closest thing to her heart. She gets exhausted, she rallies, maybe because she knows what can happen when a brilliant little girl born into poverty gets it in her head that anything is possible.

How on earth can you sum up Oprah? If she were a destination, it would be the place where joy serves the world's greatest need.

Hadizatou Mani

Facing power with truth, demanding justice and making change possible are things that are easier said than done. It takes courage, resilience and a belief in one's own voice and truth – qualities that Hadizatou Mani, a woman who was sold as a slave at the age of 12, possesses, not out of her wealth or education, but out of her simple and most essential belief in human dignity and women's rights to equality and justice.

Mani, now in her mid-20s, was sold into slavery for $500 in 1996. Her home country, Niger, outlawed slavery in 2003, but the practice still continues and manifests itself through the trafficking of mostly women and children – not just in Niger but in many other parts of the world as well.

It is not easy to know you are worth more than what you are being told, to know you have the right to stand up against injustice, to know the world is still beautiful and safe despite its horrors. Mani had the courage to take her country to a West African court for failing to enforce its own laws and denying her her right to freedom. "I knew that this was the only way to protect my child from suffering the same fate as myself. Nobody deserves to be enslaved," she said. And she proved it when she won her case in 2008.

Sister Mary Scullion

In 1976, a young Philadelphia nun named Sister Mary Scullion began her work as an advocate for the homeless, driven by a personal conviction that "none of us are home until all of us are home". By 2000, there were fewer than 200 people living on the streets of the City of Brotherly Love. That's in large part thanks to an extraordinarily well-run program, founded by Sister Mary and Joan McConnon. More than 95% of those who cycle through their Project H.O.M.E. (the acronym stands for Housing, Opportunities for Employment, Medical Care, Education) have never again returned to life on the streets - a success rate that has made the program a model for dozens of other U.S. cities. Meanwhile, Sister Mary, 55, has become the darling of luminaries like Bill Clinton, though that hasn't impacted her humility or her famously ribald sense of humor. When Jon Bon Jovi (a loyal Project supporter) described Mary to the press as a nun "who swears and spits," the good sister merely replied, "I do not spit" - and then returned to her work of tirelessly saving her city, one desperate citizen at a time.

FILE 5 Unit 12, part D, exercise 4

Best Invention Finalists

Deep Green Underwater Kite

Swedish company Minesto's underwater kite resembles a child's toy as it swoops and dives in ocean currents. But since seawater is 800 times as dense as air, the small turbine attached to the kite - which is tethered to the ocean floor - can generate 800 times more energy than if it were in the sky. Minesto calls the technology Deep Green and says it can generate 500 kilowatts of power even in calm waters; the design could increase the market for tidal power by 80%, the company says. The first scale model will be unveiled next year off the coast of Northern Ireland.

The Plastic-Bottle Boat

In the four months it took British adventurer and banking heir David de Rothschild and crew to sail a boat made of discarded soft-drink bottles from San Francisco to Australia, Americans used some 8.7 billion plastic bottles. Drawing attention to that waste was the point of Rothschild's voyage aboard the Plastiki, a 60-ft. catamaran built with 12,500 recycled plastic bottles and a fully recyclable plastic material called Seretex and held together with organic glue made from cashew-nut husks and sugarcane. The bottles were packed into the Plastiki's pontoons in a pomegranate-like structure, giving the boat 68% of its buoyancy. Rothschild's mission to change the public's perception of plastic continues as his team brainstorms new ways to reuse the commonly discarded material in everything from surfboards to wind turbines. "Every year in the U.S., we are throwing away a billion dollars' worth of building material," he says.

The Almost Waterless Washing Machine

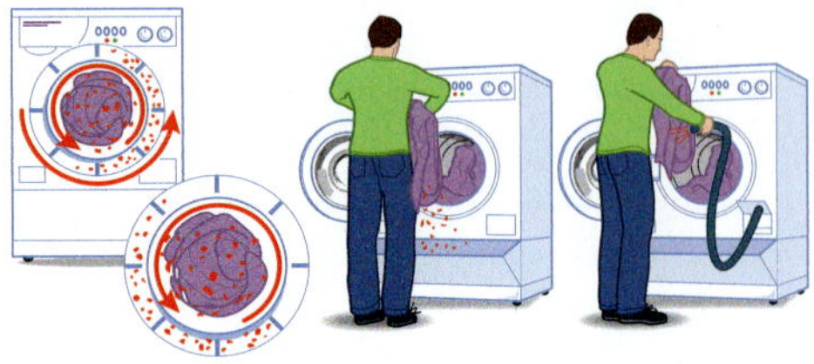

You probably don't think about this every time you separate your whites, but the U.S. uses more than 330 billion gallons of water on laundry each year, according to the British firm Xeros Ltd. The company is developing a machine that draws cleaning power from reusable, stain-absorbing nylon beads, requiring much less water - as much as 90% less - than a normal washing machine. A commercial version is due out next year: good news for conservation and your monthly water bill.

Woolfiller

Not many solutions to moth holes have inspired fan pages on Facebook. But Woolfiller provides a surprisingly easy solution to the age-old problem of holey sweaters. Take the special wool and felting needle and poke the needle - which has small hooks along the point - through the wool and your moth-eaten garment. The repeated action binds the fibers together, making a felt patch on your cardigan, sock or rug. Heleen Klopper from the Netherlands created Woolfiller as part of an interactive museum exhibition on sustainability, and so many visitors wanted to buy it that she started making kits. Klopper has come to see moths as design collaborators. Their damage is her opportunity to add a twist - a red square, say, on a blue turtleneck. "When something is broken," says Klopper, "people dare to do new things". Moths, eat your hearts out.

The English-Teaching Robot

Call it the job terminator. South Korea, which employs some 30,000 foreigners to teach English, has plans for a new addition to its language classrooms: the English-speaking robot. Students in a few schools started learning English from the robo-teachers late last year; by the end of this year, the government hopes to have them in 18 more schools. The brightly coloured, squat androids are part of an effort to keep South Korean students competitive in English. Not surprisingly, the proposal has worried a few human teachers - and with good reason. Experts say the bots could eventually phase out flesh-and-blood foreign English teachers altogether.

Exam practice

READING COMPREHENSION TEXTS

Reading text I

Green and Greener in Suburban Towns

A For two years, Valerie Williams had been considering making the five-bedroom home she grew up in more energy efficient - hoping to shrink her $350-monthly utility bill - but more pressing expenses always came first. Then the town of Babylon came up with an offer she couldn't refuse: if she and her husband, Carlos, paid $250 for an energy audit, the town would finance the recommended upgrades. The couple would repay the town at a monthly rate below the savings on their utility bill. The audit, done this month, found that by insulating walls, basement and attic, at a cost of $6,879, the Williamses could save about $1,300 a year.

B New York City and other major urban centers have ambitious, high-profile environmental programs. But it turns out that throughout the suburbs, towns like Babylon, on Long Island, are exploring and adopting a wide variety of innovative ways to save energy, protect their residents' health and reduce pollution. Some of these towns are offering energy retrofits; others are limiting or banning the use of fertilizers to avoid chemicals leaching into the groundwater. In a bold action, the Town of Islip changed its zoning ordinance last month to allow windmills up to 156 feet high in industrial zones, for warehouses and other businesses that may want to produce their own electricity and sell any excess energy to the local utility. "There's a very strong environmental sensibility among suburbanites," said Lawrence C. Levy, executive director of the National Center for Suburban Studies at Hofstra University in Hempstead, N.Y. "One of the reasons that people move to the suburbs is for the cleaner air and open spaces. They guard this zealously and with their votes."

C Buildings are a major target of local environmental action because, through their heating, cooling and other uses of energy, they are among the biggest emitters of carbon dioxide, the main gas linked to global warming. Representatives from some Long Island towns and villages came together five years ago with their eye on building-related pollution. Since then, 10 of 13 towns in the area have set new energy efficiency standards in their building codes for new construction. Among these towns is Southampton, which decided to tailor its energy conservation to building size, so that homes that use the most energy are required to become the most energy efficient. Southampton is a wealthy resort town with many houses of more than 10,000 square feet; its law, passed last year, creates a tier system that calls for stricter energy-saving measures, like higher levels of insulation and more window glazing, for bigger homes. The assumption is that if you can afford a house that's 10,000 square feet, you can also make sure it's highly energy efficient. Besides its attractiveness as a money saver, the code appeals to residents who realize that the alternative may be more smokestacks on the local horizon. "People don't want a big power plant out here, so what do we have? We have conservation," said Robert S. DeLuca, president of Group for the East End, an environmental group, and a member of the committee that produced the new code.

D Green features can make a home more valuable, but in the short term add to building costs, so one question to consider is, "Is the consumer willing to pay for that?" Sometimes the municipality, in its desire to do good, would mandate changes when incentives tend to work better. And there is only so much change the towns can impose. Requiring that homes be built smaller would greatly shrink the carbon footprint of buildings, but even environmentalists agree this is not realistic. There are other obstacles to going green. Villages, wary of changing their character, often resist increasing building density even if that means forcing development to go elsewhere and contributing to suburban sprawl. And poor suburbs are less likely than affluent ones to join the movement. There are no real resources, and it's unlikely that you'd have the kind of galvanizing leadership in these communities to take on climate issues. Leaders usually advocate for affordable housing and things like that."

E But even wealthier areas need financial incentives in order to draw participants like Mrs. Williams. So far more than 200 homes have been audited, with potential savings of close to $1,000 a year each on average. The town pays for the program, now a pilot, with $2 million from its solid waste reserve fund. New state and federal laws, and millions of dollars in federal stimulus grants, have also helped spur such initiatives. "This is a program that helps the environment, helps homeowners save money, creates local jobs, reduces our reliance on fossil fuels and it's at no cost to taxpayers," said Steve Bellone, Babylon's town supervisor.

F The fragmented government on Long Island, with its many towns and special districts, often means competition for development projects or government grants - and that the quest to go green has created healthier rivalries. "All the town supervisors want to be known as the leanest and greenest," Mr. Bellone said and added that he strongly believed sustainability was a matter of survival. "Over time, residents are going to demand it, and housing stock and commercial stock that are green are going to be more valuable," he said. "This positions Babylon to be a prosperous community for the long term." (891 words)

Adapted from: Mireya Navarro, *The New York Times*, October 2009

Reading text II

News from everywhere

A "This is London." For decades the *BBC World Service* has been a reliable and respected voice in distant lands. Like other international outfits such as America's *Radio Liberty* and Germany's *Deutsche Welle*, it does not provide propaganda. But it does give a reassuring and reasonable take on the world, valuable especially for those audiences whose local media are too cash-strapped, or too bullied, to give the full picture.

B Now technology is cutting costs and stoking competition, eroding the Westerners' advantages. Big transmitters were costly; podcasts and webcams, FM radio and cable television are cheap and often open to all. As the old signals fade, rival outfits are crowding the airwaves. Iran and Russia have both launched 24-hour English television-news channels. China added a second one last month. The newcomers may start off with unappealingly wooden presenters and nakedly biased reporting. But they can improve, as Al Jazeera [...] has done. China plans to outspend America hugely in coming years. Western budgets are flat or shrinking: Britain's Foreign Office, which pays for some of the BBC's external services, faces a 25%-cut.

C The right response to such challenges is not for Western countries to bin their broadcasts, but to target them better. Compared with other forms of foreign aid (or defence spending) they are cheap. The *BBC World Service* cost £281m ($442m) last year. The broadcasts not only rile dictators, but comfort their beleaguered opponents. In places like Myanmar, Somalia or Iran, too poor or too dictatorial to attract independent commercial media companies, providing solid news may be the best that the West can do. They also counter the propaganda from state media machines in places such as Russia and China. Without its own voice, the West's case risks failing by default.

D The dilemma is what to do in places where local media are stronger and more varied. The answer for the different international broadcasters will vary from country to country. The case is strong for providing core global English-language programming, aimed at urban, well-educated audiences that make trade and investment decisions (or are thinking about where to send their children to university). Leaving that solely to commercial stations such as CNN would be a mistake. For outfits like the BBC, repackaging existing news-gathering for this international audience is a minor cost, with decent returns (especially if the programmes carry advertising, as they should). The old broadcasters need to learn new tricks too. For modern-minded viewers and listeners, the days of loyalty to a particular channel may be waning. But if the content is good and well-presented, it will flourish on the internet: for some, it will be better to invest in packaging material for YouTube, rather than renting satellite frequencies.

E Television broadcasting in local languages, however, is costly and tricky. An American television service in Arabic has been a flop. Heavy-handed efforts in vernacular services also risk crowding out promising locals, by pinching good journalists. The international broadcasters should remember that one aim is to make themselves redundant.

F International broadcasters should therefore devote resources sparingly to countries where reliable news is already plentiful. They should concentrate on offering material that such markets fail to provide. In India, for example, it makes little sense to match local stations' vernacular-language coverage of local news. Better to offer a view from outside, such as foreign and business news from faraway places that local broadcasters may lack the budget or the confidence to cover. And, to save money, they should buy more programming from outside, rather than trying to make it all in-house. As well as preaching pluralism, the old state-backed outfits should practise it too.

G Even if the glory days are gone, voices like the *World Service* are still needed - and worth paying for. Just make sure that they are directed towards the places that need them most.

(642 words)

Adapted from: *The Economist*, 14 October 2010

Reading text III

Slum Visits: Tourism or Voyeurism?

MICHAEL CRONIN's job as a college admissions officer took him to India two or three times a year, so he had already seen the usual sites - temples, monuments, markets - when one day he happened across a flier advertising "slum tours". "It just resonated with me immediately," said Mr. Cronin, who was staying at a posh Taj Hotel in Mumbai. "But I didn't know what to expect." Soon he found himself skirting open sewers and ducking to avoid exposed electrical wires as he toured the sprawling Dharavi slum, home to more than a million. — **A** — "Nothing is considered garbage there," he said. "Everything is used again."

Slum tourism, or "poorism", as some call it, is catching on. From the favelas of Rio de Janeiro to the townships of Johannesburg to the garbage dumps of Mexico, tourists are forsaking, at least for a while, beaches and museums for crowded, dirty slums. When a British man named Chris Way founded *Reality Tours and Travel* in Mumbai two years ago, he could barely muster enough customers for one tour a day. Now, he's running two or three a day and recently expanded to rural areas.

Slum tourism isn't for everyone. Critics charge that ogling the poorest of the poor isn't tourism at all. It's voyeurism. The tours are exploitative, these critics say, and have no place on an ethical traveler's itinerary. Slum tourism [according to Professor David Fennel] is just another example of tourism's finding a new niche to exploit. **— B —** "It affirms in my mind how lucky I am - or how unlucky they are," he said.

Not so fast, proponents of slum tourism say. Ignoring poverty won't make it go away. "Tourism is one of the few ways that you or I are ever going to understand what poverty means," said Harold Goodwin from the International Center for Responsible Tourism in Leeds. "To just kind of turn a blind eye and pretend the poverty doesn't exist seems to me a very denial of our humanity." The crucial question, Mr. Goodwin and other experts say, is not whether slum tours should exist but how they are conducted. **— C —**

Many tour organizers are sensitive to charges of exploitation. Some encourage participants to play an active role in helping residents. A church group in Mazatlán, Mexico, runs tours of the local garbage dump, where scavengers earn a living picking through trash, some of it from nearby luxury resorts. **— D —** The tours have proven so popular that during high season the church group has to turn people away.

By most accounts, slum tourism began in Brazil 16 years ago, when a young man named Marcelo Armstrong took a few tourists into Rocinha, Rio de Janeiro's largest favela, or shantytown. His company, *Favela Tour*, grew and spawned half a dozen imitators. Today, on any given day in Rio, dozens of tourists venture into places even Brazil's police dare not tread. Organizers insist the tours are safe, though they routinely check security conditions. Luiz Fantozzi, founder of the Rio-based *Be a Local Tours*, says that about once a year he cancels a tour for security reasons.

— E — Rajika Bhasin, a lawyer from New York, recalls how, at one point during a favela tour, the guide told everyone to stop taking pictures. A young man approached the group, smiling and holding a cocked gun. Ms. Bhasin said she didn't exactly feel threatened, "just very aware of my surroundings, and aware of the fact that I was on this guy's turf." Still, she said, the experience, which included visiting galleries featuring the work of local artists, was positive. "Honestly, I would say it was a life-changing experience," Ms. Bhasin said.

Proponents of slum tourism say that's the point: to change the reputation of the slums one tourist at a time. Tour organizers say they provide employment for local guides and a chance to sell souvenirs. Chris Way has vowed to put 80 per cent of his profits back into the Dharavi slum. The catch, though, is that Mr. Way's company has yet to earn a profit on the tours, for which he charges 300 rupees (around $7.50). After receiving flak from the Indian press ("a fair criticism," Mr. Way concedes), he used his own money to open a community center in the slum. **— F —**

But slum tourism isn't just about charity, its proponents say; it also fosters an entrepreneurial spirit. Even critics of slum tourism concede it allows a few dollars to trickle into the shantytowns, but say that's no substitute for development programs. (847 words)

Adapted from: Eric Weiner, *The New York Times*, 9 March 2008

READING COMPREHENSION TASKS

Task I: Mixed reading tasks

A MULTIPLE CHOICE QUESTIONS (6)

Choose the most suitable answer according to the information given in Text I.

1 The Williams family invested in energy efficiency ... .
- a when their energy supplier announced an increase in energy prices
- b because they had high hopes for a tax return after a successful audit
- c as the cost-benefit ratio was rather tempting, even in the short term
- d since the costs for insulation and other measures were pretty low at that time

2 Which statement best sums up paragraph C?
- a Houses affect global warming and thus building regulations must be changed.
- b The energy efficiency of houses has both a global and an individual impact.
- c Global warming and housing are linked and people should not doubt that.
- d Well-built houses positively affect the owners' financial budget.

3 When the author calls the Southampton system a "tier system" (line 28) he means that ... .
- a different standards apply to different types of homes
- b the energy-conservation measures are well-funded
- c a mass reduction of greenhouse gases is intended
- d measures are ranked according to their effectiveness

4 Which reason for not making suburbs greener is not mentioned in paragraph D?
- a Many communities simply lack the necessary funds for it.
- b Communities fear crowdedness irrespective of the consequences elsewhere.
- c Conservationists doubt that build-small-initiatives can really be enforced.
- d There is doubt about the positive effect of homes on the carbon footprint.

5 According to the information given in paragraph E, Steve Bellone's statement at the end of the paragraph ... .
- a can fully be supported
- b should be questioned
- c is too doom-and-gloom
- d disregards the environment

6 According to paragraph F, in most Long Island communities green features in housing projects ... .
- a are certainly there to stay, develop and increase in number
- b are of a passing interest to town supervisors
- c depend only on the availability of grants
- d are on the up, but will be ended by all the rivalries

B MEDIATION ENGLISH–GERMAN (6)

Beantworten Sie folgende Fragen zu Text I auf Deutsch.

1 Städte und Gemeinden auf Long Island, wie etwa Southhampton, ergreifen unterschiedliche Maßnahmen, um Umwelt und Bevölkerung zu schützen. Stellen Sie die im Text genannten Maßnahmen mit Ausnahme derer von Southhampton dar.

2 Vorstädter gelten als umweltbewusst. Welche zusätzlichen Gründe haben die dort ansässigen Hauseigentümer – etwa die von Southampton – bei ihren Häusern auf Energieeffizienz zu achten?

Task II: Mixed reading tasks

A SHORT-ANSWER QUESTIONS / SENTENCE COMPLETION (7)

Answer the following questions or complete the sentences by providing the required information with words from paragraphs A–C of Text II.

1 The text claims that internationally operating broadcasting companies such as the *BBC World Service* can be relied on, as such a company … but rather tries to … .
2 Which developments have ended the domination of Western broadcasting companies such as the *BBC World Service* on other continents?
3 Asian competitors of the *BBC World Service* have to improve on the following two aspects: … and … - which can be done as an example shows.
4 Why is the work of the *BBC World Service* and/or the *Deutsche Welle* not welcome in dictatorships?
5 Which term used in the text means "to lose due to lack of effort (to change something)"?

B GAPPED SUMMARY (5)

Fill in the gaps with the most suitable words taken from paragraphs D–G of Text II. Use one word only for each gap.

The challenges for the *BBC World Service* and similar Western broadcasters are varied. The answers, therefore, have to be tailored to the specific needs of each country. One answer could be to focus on English-language programs on different topics. The target group are listeners and viewers from …[1] areas. On the other hand broadcasters can no longer can count on the …[2] of their audience. Quality programs, however, will succeed on the Internet. Western broadcasters should avoid services in local languages as an American example shows. These programs often entice journalists away from local services. International broadcasters should focus on …[3] and services local broadcasters can't offer due to a tight …[4]. As international broadcasters advocate …[5], they should take this to heart and therefore not only broadcast in-house programs.

Task III

MULTIPLE MATCHING (6)

Match sentences (1–8) with gaps (A–F) in Text III. Two sentences do not fit.

Gap	A	B	C	D	E	F
Sentence	…	…	…	…	…	…

1 The tours may be safe, but they can be tense.
2 The real purpose, he believes, is to make Westerners feel better about their station in life.
3 The group doesn't charge anything but asks participants to help make sandwiches and fill bottles with filtered water.
4 The center offers free medical treatment for females only.
5 Many tour participants were shocked by the danger of those tours and sued the tour operators.
6 It offers English classes and a chess club.
7 He joined a cricket game and saw the small-scale industry, from embroidery to tannery, that quietly thrives in the slum.
8 Do they limit the excursions to small groups, interacting respectfully with residents? Or do they travel in buses, snapping photos from the windows as if on safari?

WRITING

Task IV: Descriptive writing

A DESCRIBING A PICTURE

Describe the situation in the picture and state what point is being made. Write about 100 words.

B DESCRIBING STATISTICS

What does the following graph tell you about the situation in the USA? Write about 100 words.

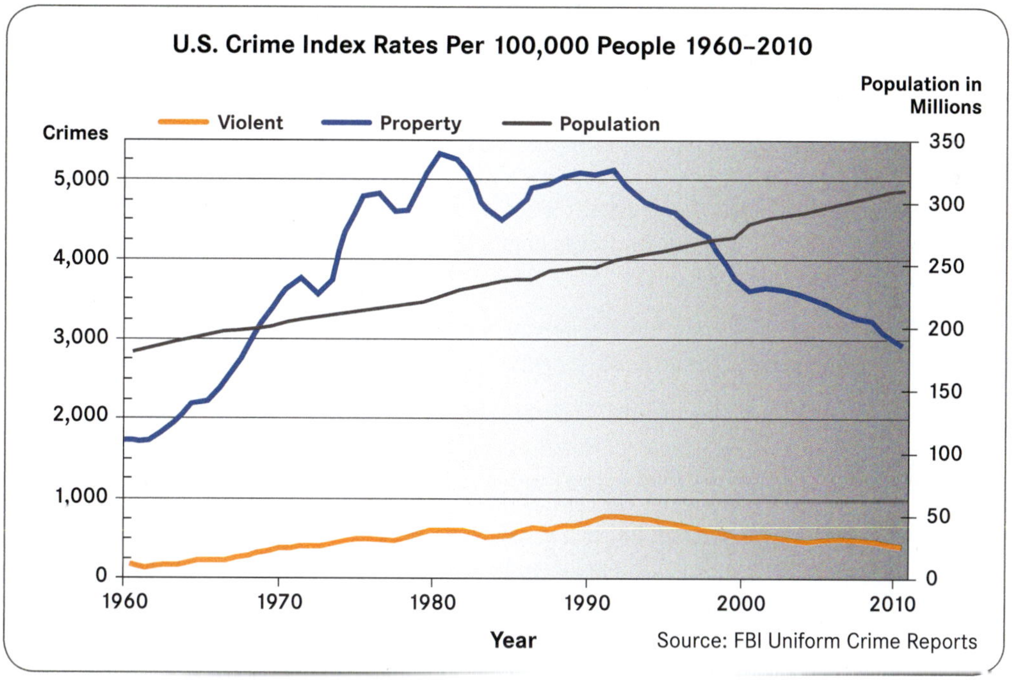

Task V: Argumentative Writing

Choose one of the following topics and write at least 200 words.

Composition topic 1:

Nuclear energy
"No nation in the world should be allowed to continue producing nuclear energy." Do you agree with this statement?

Composition topic 2:

Chinese as a foreign language
"Students should learn Chinese rather than any other foreign language in Germany, as China is our future." Discuss this statement made by a German politician.

Language study skills

RECEPTION: READING

A Approaching a text

We often have different reasons for reading a text. Sometimes, for instance, when we read a newspaper in our mother tongue, we often just need to skim over the text to get a rough idea of what the article is about. In other situations, for example, when we are studying for exams, we need to take a closer look at the text, paying attention to every word or at least to the key words in it. If you have to answer questions on a text, then you should read the text extremely carefully, and not just once, but twice.

1 Skimming for gist

Skimming for gist means reading a text quickly for its general sense without worrying about every word.

In practice, however, skimming is not as easy as it sounds. The problem is that some people worry too much, and may start skimming, but soon panic and reach for their dictionary.

Follow these steps.

Step 1 Read the title and, if there is one, the introduction to the text to find out what the topic is. Also pay attention to words highlighted in bold, pictures and captions (*Bildunterschriften*).

Step 2 Study the exercises carefully before you begin reading and learn to recognize skimming exercises, e.g. *Read the text and say what the writer's opinion on career women is.*

Step 3 Concentrate on the key words. These are sense transmitters like nouns, verbs and maybe adjectives/adverbs that qualify them. Use word recognition skills wherever possible. > Word recognition p. 172

Step 4 If you can't understand an important key word, read on. Many such words become clear from the context or are even explained by a synonym just a few lines further on.

As a rule, texts used for skimming have a clear structure. Arguments and evidence are presented logically and the most important points are often repeated for emphasis or in the conclusion.

2 Finding specific pieces of information in the text

Many text comprehension tasks, e.g. multiple choice, require you to find specific pieces of information in the text very quickly, so that you don't have to read the whole text over again.

Follow these steps.

Step 1 Look for key words in the text that refer to the question. If the question asks for the author's opinion on a certain topic, look for words such as *think*, *believe*, *opinion*, etc. Try to keep a clear vision of the word or phrase you are looking for in your head so that it's easier to find when you are reading the text.

Step 2 If you need to, follow the text with your finger until you find the key word that you are searching for. If you have a clear vision of the word in your head, it will jump out at you as soon as you see it.

3 Close reading for detail

All the units in this book contain three long English texts with detailed work on content and vocabulary. Close reading for detail is an essential skill that you cannot do without.

Don't just dive straight into the text; follow these short steps to help you understand the text better without getting lost in the details.

Step 1 Read the title and ask yourself what the text could be about. If there is an introduction to the text, read this too. It is generally in simpler language and is intended to help you. You might also want to look at any photos or illustrations accompanying the text to get a better idea of the contents.

Step 2 Try to get an overview of the structure of the text. Which part contains the main information in the text? How is the text structured? (Does it have subtitles? Is it split into paragraphs?) Pay attention to words that the author uses to structure their argument, such as *only, but while, that's why, while, however*, etc.

Step 3 Read the text through to get the general sense. Concentrate on the key words (nouns and verbs, sometimes qualified by adjectives and adverbs).

Step 4 Look at the content questions. These will give you an idea of what the examiner thinks is important and what to look for.

Step 5 Now read the text in detail, sentence by sentence. If you have borrowed your coursebook from your school, don't mark texts. Make a list of words in an exercise book. Otherwise mark any words you don't understand with a highlighter or by underlining them. If there is a sentence that you can't understand at all, don't panic. Ignore it for the moment and return to it later. If there are a lot of unknown words, don't panic, either. You will often be able to work out the meaning of some of them from the context, and you might not need to know their meaning at all. > Word recognition p. 172

Use your dictionary to find out the meaning of those words that you can't understand by other means. Only look up a word in the dictionary the first time you read the text if the meaning of the whole sentence depends on that one word. > Using a dictionary p. 173

Step 6 When you have dealt with the unknown words, read through the text a third time as a continuous piece of prose. Then answer the questions.

4 Working with key words and expressions

As you know, words fall into a number of groups or 'classes' according to what function they have. Some words are 'structural', such as 'am' in the sentence, *I am writing this now* and 'have been' in *You have been warned!* Similarly, prepositions and many adverbs express time, place and relationship between people and things. Articles and connectors (*and, but, because*, etc.), pronouns and devices such as question tags (..., *have you?* ..., *isn't it?*) are also 'structural' words and phrases.

Structural words and phrases do not have much to do with the basic or 'core' sense of a text.

Core sense is expressed by nouns, verbs and verb groups (*can come, ought not to go*) and sometimes by qualifiers (adjectives and adverbs). These word classes are often called 'sense transmitters'.

Look at this paragraph from a letter to the editor. The letter is about an article dealing with single parents. Copy out the 'sense transmitters'.

I'd like to object most strongly to the one-sided articles on lone parents that have appeared in your paper in recent months. Just because a man or woman is bringing up children alone, this does not mean that he or she is a bad parent. Most single parents are as conscientious as two-parent families.

You will find that focusing on key words and expressions will not only help you to work faster and more effectively, it will also make reading less wearisome and more enjoyable.

B Dealing with unknown words

In the *Oberstufe* you will meet quite a lot of new words, particularly towards the end of the course when texts become longer and more demanding. Looking words up in the dictionary requires time and effort and doesn't always help you to understand the most important information in the text. For this reason, knowing how to deal with new words is a key skill that you can't do without.

1 Word recognition: Don't use a dictionary, use your head!

When you come across a new word, don't use your dictionary until you have tried quicker and easier ways of finding out what the word means.

Ask yourself these three key questions:

1. Is the word given in an annotation?
2. Do I really need to know what this word means, or can I understand the sentence without it?
3. Can I work out what the word means by thinking about ... ?
   a international words
   b similarities between English and German
   c what I know about word formation
   d the context

Also look out for synonyms used elsewhere in the text.

a International words

A large number of words - for example *computer*, *jeans* and *steak* - are international words that are the same in many languages.

b Similarities between English and German

In addition to these international words, there are two other big groups of words that are very similar in English and German.

The first and biggest group contains words such as *to bring*, *to come*, *friend*, *garden*, *house*, *mother*, *street*, *winter*, and so on, that come from an old form of German. It is, of course, usually easy for German speakers to recognize the meanings of such words.

Watch out for 'false friends', though!

The second group of very similar words is made up of vocabulary based on words from other languages, usually Latin or Greek (German, *Fremdwörter*).

> False friends p. 267

aggressive | biology | combined | conflict | democracy | depressive | formality | hurricane | paragraph | poetic | politics | risk | socialism | traditional

c Word formation

If you come across a word that you think you don't know, then look again – it might just be related to a word that you do know, or it might be a root word that you are familiar with, with a prefix or suffix added to it, which can help you to work out the meaning, e.g. *formal – informal, clockwise – anticlockwise, change – changeable, stupid – stupidity.*

d Looking at the context

You can often guess the probable or approximate meaning of a word by looking at its context, i.e. by thinking about the topic, the meaning of the sentence it appears in and by working out whether the word you're looking for is a verb, a noun or an adjective.

Read the sentences below and try to work out the meaning of the words in bold from the context.

Business is bad at the moment and we don't expect it to **rally** for at least a year. All the signals are very **inauspicious**, I'm afraid.

Even if you don't understand *rally* and *inauspicious*, you can work out from the context that *rally* is a verb which describes a positive development and *inauspicious* is an adjective with a negative meaning.

2 Using a dictionary

You are allowed to use an English-English or monolingual dictionary both in class and in exams. If you can't work out the meaning of a word by other means, dictionaries are an essential tool. Like any other tool, however, you have to learn how to use a dictionary effectively and efficiently. What follows is a guide, but only *you* can get familiar with your dictionary and only *you* can do the necessary practice.

To get started, make sure you look at the key to your dictionary's entries. The key gives you an overview of what your dictionary has to offer.

a Key to dictionary entries

Wörterbucheintrag

uncountable = unzählbares Nomen

North American English = Aussprachevariante

Wortart

Erste Bedeutung

Verweis auf einen anderen Eintrag

verb/noun + 'to' infinitive = zusammengesetzter Ausdruck, in dem das Verb von *to* + Infinitiv gefolgt wird

Zweite Bedeutung

countable = zählbares Nomen

idiom = Redewendung

Synonym

verb/noun = zusammengesetzter Ausdruck aus Verb und Nomen

alarm /ə'lɑːm; *NAmE* ə'lɑːrm/ *noun, verb*
■ *noun* **1** [U] fear and anxiety that sb feels when sth dangerous or unpleasant might happen: *'What have you done?' Ellie cried in alarm.* ◇ *I felt a growing sense of alarm when he did not return that night.* ◇ *The doctor said there was no cause for alarm.* ⇨ note at FEAR **2** [C, usually sing.] a loud noise or a signal that warns people of danger or of a problem: *She decided to* ***sound the alarm*** (= warn people that the situation was dangerous). ◇ *I hammered on all the doors to* ***raise the alarm.*** – see also FALSE ALARM **3** [C] a device that warns people of a particular danger: *a* ***burglar/fire/smoke alarm.*** ◇ *The cat* ***set off the alarm*** (= made it start ringing). ◇ *A car* ***alarm went off*** *in the middle of the night* (= started ringing). **4** = ALARM CLOCK: *The* ***alarm went off*** *at 7 o'clock.* IDM **a'larm bells ring / start ringing** if you say that **alarm bells are ringing**, you mean that people are starting to feel worried and suspicious
■ *verb* **1** to make sb anxious or afraid SYN WORRY: [VN] *The captain knew there was an engine fault but didn't want to alarm the passengers.* [also VN **to** inf] ⇨ note at FRIGHTEN **2** [VN] to fit sth such as a door with a device that warns people when sb is trying to enter illegally

b What dictionaries tell you

As well as telling you the meaning of the headword in various contexts (often in sample sentences) all monolingual dictionaries approved for use in the *Oberstufe* also give you information on:

- spelling and splitting (hyphenating) rules
- the word class or part of speech (adjective, verb, noun, etc.)
- pronunciation and stress
- forms and derivatives (plurals, formation of past tense, related words and expressions)
- register (colloquial, formal, etc.)
- differences between British English (BE) and American English (AE), and perhaps notes on other forms of English, such as Australian, as well.

In addition to the above, dictionaries also provide you with valuable information on such things as whether a verb takes an object or whether a noun is countable or uncountable. Please don't ignore this information. It will help you to avoid mistakes.

c How to use a dictionary efficiently

- Only use them when you must.
- Read through the list of abbreviations used in your dictionary and make sure you understand what they mean.
- Note all the words you want to look up before turning to your dictionary. Look up the words in alphabetical or reverse alphabetical order.
- You may find unknown words in the definitions or context sentences given in the dictionary. If you do, don't panic or give up. Use your word recognition skills before looking further in the dictionary.
- Note the part of speech of the word you want to look up - e.g. noun - and ignore all the other entries for that word.
- When you have found the meaning, write it down immediately. If you don't, you may have to look it up again.

If you get into these good dictionary habits now, you won't waste any time in exams!

Read the following text then use your dictionary to do the exercises below.

The world's last mammoth rain forest

The green tangle that is the Amazon rainforest is among the most complex environments in the world. But the threat to this massive expanse is as simple as a mathematical equation. The Amazon forest holds about one-third of the world's remaining tropical woods, but Brazil accounts for only four per cent of the tropical timber market. So, as expected, Brazilian and international timber companies have set their sights on where most of the tropical wood remains - the Amazon.

1. Which part of speech is "mammoth" (headline)? Replace it with another word without changing the meaning.
2. Which part of speech is "tangle" (line.1)? Which meaning of 'tangle' applies here? Give the dictionary entry (number/letter) and a possible German translation.
3. Which part of speech is "expanse" (line.2)? Which dictionary entry applies here (number/letter)? Name two adjectives that are often used with this word.
4. Which part of speech is "holds" (line.3)? Give the dictionary entry (number/letter) and a possible German translation. Give an English expression for "ich vertrete die Ansicht / bin der Ansicht, dass ..." using the word 'hold'.
5. What kind of expression is "(have) set their sights on" (line.5)? Give a possible German translation.

3 Collocations and compounds

a Collocations

A collocation is a combination of words that make up a generally accepted fixed expression.

For example, the noun *team* collates with another noun, *captain* to make the expression *team captain*. It does not, however, collate with *head* or with other possible alternatives like *boss, chief* or *commander*.

Similarly, *head* collates with *teacher* to make *head teacher*, but it does not collate with, say, *executive*. If you were to say, 'Jane Brown is the *head executive* of our firm', you would be understood. The correct collocation, however, is *chief executive*.

In the same way, the noun *photo* collates with the verbs *take* and *shoot* to form the collocations *to take a photo* and *to shoot a photo*. It does not collate with *make*, though, as it does in German.

For this reason, it is essential to learn collocations as complete units. In other words, don't learn just *love*, learn *to fall in love*.

b Compounds

Some words go together so often that they become a compound. They may be written with or without a hyphen, or they may become one word:

daughter-in-law | car park | airport

The more frequently words are used together, the closer they become. For example, in the last 60 years, we have seen *air port* change to *air-port* and then to *airport*. Because of changes like these, you may see compounds written in different ways. If in doubt, check them in a good, up-to-date dictionary such as the Oxford Advanced Learner's Dictionary.

4 Learning new vocabulary

There are different ways of learning new vocabulary. Try to find out which one suits you best. One thing, however, applies to every method – we learn words better when we not only write down the key word, but also any expressions, synonyms, antonyms, related words, sample sentences and possibly phonetics that that belong to it. Collocations and compounds are especially important, but pay attention also to any phrasal verbs you might find.

A dictionary entry for the word *pay* could look something like this:

pay (noun) – *Bezahlung, Gehalt, Lohn*
payslip – *Gehaltsabrechnung*
pay day – *Zahltag*
pay-off – *Abfindung*
pay (verb) – *zahlen*
pay for sth – *etw bezahlen*
pay off – *auszahlen*
pay as you go (phone) – *Prepaid(-Handy)*

Obviously you do not need to write down everything that you find in the dictionary, but do consider which derivatives (*abgeleitete Wörter*) of the new word that you were already familiar with and in which context you came across them. Leave some space for future updates so that your vocabulary grows and grows.

a **Memory cards / Index cards (*Karteikarten*):** Try to find memory/index cards and boxes with a few compartments. Write down the English word (and any other words or information that belongs to it) on one side of the card and the German meaning on the other. As soon as you know a word, move it from the first to the second compartment of the box. You could revise the words in the second compartment perhaps once a week and move them into the third compartment whenever you think they have definitely been added to your long-term memory. If you find that you have forgotten any words, move them back to the first compartment again to be revised and practised more often, e.g. every other day.

b **Vocabulary book:** If you want to write down any words that you learn in class, then you should keep a vocabulary book. Look for one with two (or three) columns on each page for the English word, German word (and sample sentences, idioms or collocations) so that you can cover up one of the columns when you are practising your vocabulary. If you are the type of person that is easily bored by vocabulary learning, try to make it less systematic by choosing a page at random and practising those words, sometimes English-German and sometimes German-English. Variety is the spice of life!

c **Word families:** In order to try to learn the derivatives of a word, make a list of word families (*approve - approval - approving - disapprove - disapproval*).

d **Wordfields:** The best way to learn thematic word fields is to make a mind map. This is also a good visual method of learning vocabulary for a class test. Write the key word or topic in the middle of the page and all of the major terms belonging to it in a circle around it. Then write any important words belonging to the major term around it too.

> Mind mapping p. 180

e **Vocabulary trainer:** If you are the type of person that learns better using a computer, then look for suitable vocabulary trainer software in bookshops or online. This type of software contains many vocabulary exercises which make vocabulary learning more exciting and fun. Make sure you buy the correct type of software for your grade in school. Otherwise, you can find many free vocabulary trainers online.

C Mixed reading tasks

1 Multiple choice

The multiple choice section is made up of a number of questions or incomplete statements followed by four answers or options for answering the question or completing the statement. Only one answer or option is correct.

Three of the answers or options for finishing the statement are so-called "distracters" which seem to be correct at first glance but which, on closer inspection, prove to be wrong. Never mark more than one answer/option on your exam paper. If you do, you will lose points.

Multiple choice tasks are designed to test both overall and detailed comprehension of an authentic English-language text.

You may be asked to answer questions regarding

- the general theme of the text,
- specific information in a certain paragraph,
- the author's personal attitude,
- the meaning of idiomatic phrases.

You may also be required to specify what information is not mentioned in the text.

Follow these steps.

Step 1 Skim the text, reading for gist. > Skimming for gist p. 170

Step 2 Read the questions that deal with asking for the gist of the text (often the first or the last question). Do this by looking at the options given and eliminating those that seem particularly improbable or illogical.

Step 3 Find the line(s) in which specific information is referred to. Take a closer look at this/these particular passage(s) and choose the correct option.

If asked to identify information not provided in the text, read all of the options and eliminate the ones which relate to information which is mentioned in the text. One option should be left over. This is the answer.

If asked to identify the author's attitude or intention, look for passages that reveal the author's opinions and/or emotions.

2 Multiple matching

In this type of exercise, you are asked to make correlations between ideas which are related to one another in some way. The aim of the exercise is for the student to demonstrate that he/she has understood specific information contained in either a longer text or several short paragraphs. The items are offered in two separate lists.

You may be asked to match
a questions and answers,
b headings and paragraphs,
c speakers and statements.

You may also be asked to complete a paragraph by matching the correct sentence to the letter in the gap.

Each of these multiple matching tasks needs to be dealt with individually.

a Matching questions and answers

Read the answers for gist, then make the appropriate matches.

b Matching headings and paragraphs

Read the relevant paragraphs for gist, then make the appropriate matches.

c Matching speakers and statements

Find each speaker in the text and read carefully what he/she says. Choose a statement which expresses similar or identical ideas. You may find that details such as age, profession, ethnic background, etc. can help you match speaker and statement.

3 Gapped summary

In this type of exercise, you are presented with the summary of either a short text or individual paragraphs of a longer text. This summary contains gaps which you are to complete with appropriate words contained in the original text or paragraphs. The aim of the exercise is to test text comprehension rather than knowledge of vocabulary.

Follow the steps on page 178.

Step 1 Find the passage in the original text which corresponds to the gapped sentence in the summarized text.

Step 2 Find a word in the original text which completes the gapped sentence in a way that reflects the meaning of the original text (one word per gap only). Looking for the appropriate form of the missing word (noun, verb, adjective, adverb) will prove helpful, but do not change the word.

4 Short-answer questions / Sentence completion

This type of exercise consists of either

- questions that have to be answered using appropriate statements provided in the text or
- incomplete sentences that have to be completed with information contained in the text.

Follow these steps.

Step 1 Read the question / incomplete sentence carefully.

Step 2 Look for key words or phrases in the text that also appear in the question / incomplete sentence or which are very similar to them.

As soon as you have found one aspect, look for others in the same paragraph. In most cases, they are grouped together.

You will normally be informed about the number of aspects needed to answer the question. Make sure you provide the required number of aspects. Do not give more aspects than asked for as examiners will deduct points if you do.

5 Mediation: English–German

In this type of exercise, you are expected to

- relate information or
- explain the meaning of a difficult sentence or idiomatic phrase from an English-language text in German.

In doing so, you must not translate literally. The aim of the exercise is to prove that you have understood the meaning of the relevant text passage(s), sentence(s) or phrase(s).

Follows these steps.

Step 1 The question will be in German. Read it carefully.

Step 2 Look for key words or phrases in the text which are the same as, or similar to, words and phrases in the question.

Step 3 Check your dictionary to see if the phrase to be mediated is explained. Make sure you use the explanation in the context used in the text.

Step 4 Make notes.

Step 5 As soon as you have found one aspect, look for others in the same paragraph. In most cases, they are grouped together.

Step 6 Relate in German what you have found out. Make sure you provide the number of aspects asked for.

RECEPTION: LISTENING

In order to understand spoken English, e.g. on TV, in telephone conversations, in job interviews, etc. you should prepare yourself well for the situation in hand. Often listeners have problems understanding accents or they get distracted by background noises and have to really concentrate to hear the most important information. Use the method described below when you are dealing with listening exercises in *Focus on Success Erweiterte Ausgabe 3rd edition* to help you to overcome those difficulties more easily.

1 Preparing to listen

Before listening, activate what you already know about the topic you are going to hear. Look at any photos, illustrations or statistics. Most importantly, read the listening comprehension question thoroughly. Doing all of this will help you to predict what you will probably hear. Take notes if you need to.

2 Listening for gist

> When listening for gist, try to understand the important ideas of the text and, especially, the ideas you need to fulfil the task.
> Don't concentrate on single words or specific text passages. Try to understand the main "message(s)" in the text.
> You don't need to write down any notes when listening for gist, but you can if you wish.

3 Listening for detail

> The second time you listen to the text, listen out for any information that is important to the task and note it down.
> Pay attention to easy to understand words, e.g. names of people and places, numbers, words and expressions which are similar to German words and expressions.
> In spoken language, people often repeat themselves, so listen for repetitions and signal words.
e.g. *In other words ...* (i.e. something will be explained more carefully),
I'm afraid that ... (something negative will follow),
Why don't you ... ? (a piece of advice will be given)
> Listen out for any words or phrases that show the structure of the text so that you don't lose track of what's happening, e.g. *however, in my view, in conclusion*, etc.
> Note down key words, not complete sentences. A grid like the one below can be quite helpful. This example relates to a question on the changing roles of women and men in society:

	changed role	*reasons*	*consequences*
men			
women			

> Use abbreviations and symbols to save time:

Symbols	
=	*the same as*
≠	*not the same as*
+	*and*

Abbreviations	
e.g.	*for example*
km	*kilometres*
w., w/o	*with, without*

Shortened words	
govt	*government*
impt	*important*
kids	*children*

- Do not try to translate specific words.
- If you don't understand something, let it pass. After the listening exercise is over, try to guess the bits you did not understand completely. Above all, don't panic!

4 After listening

- Convert your key words and notes into clear sentences as quickly as possible - you might not be able to understand your notes or handwriting later!
- Try to answer the question(s) in as much detail as possible. If you didn't understand something completely, write down what you think the answer might be and give a reason for your answer - you don't get any marks for leaving a blank space!

WRITING

A Mind mapping

A mind map is a sensible way of organising your ideas and is also a good method for learning vocabulary, brainstorming, collecting ideas and for preparing a composition or a presentation.

> Dealing with unknown words p. 172

What you need: A large sheet of paper (A3) and coloured markers.

Step 1 Write the main topic clearly in a large circle in the centre of the page.

Step 2 Write down the most important terms related to the topic around the main topic and link them to the topic word with thick lines.

Step 3 According to the same principle, add more words and ideas to each of the sub-topics.

Step 4 Highlight important terms using colours, highlighters, symbols, etc.

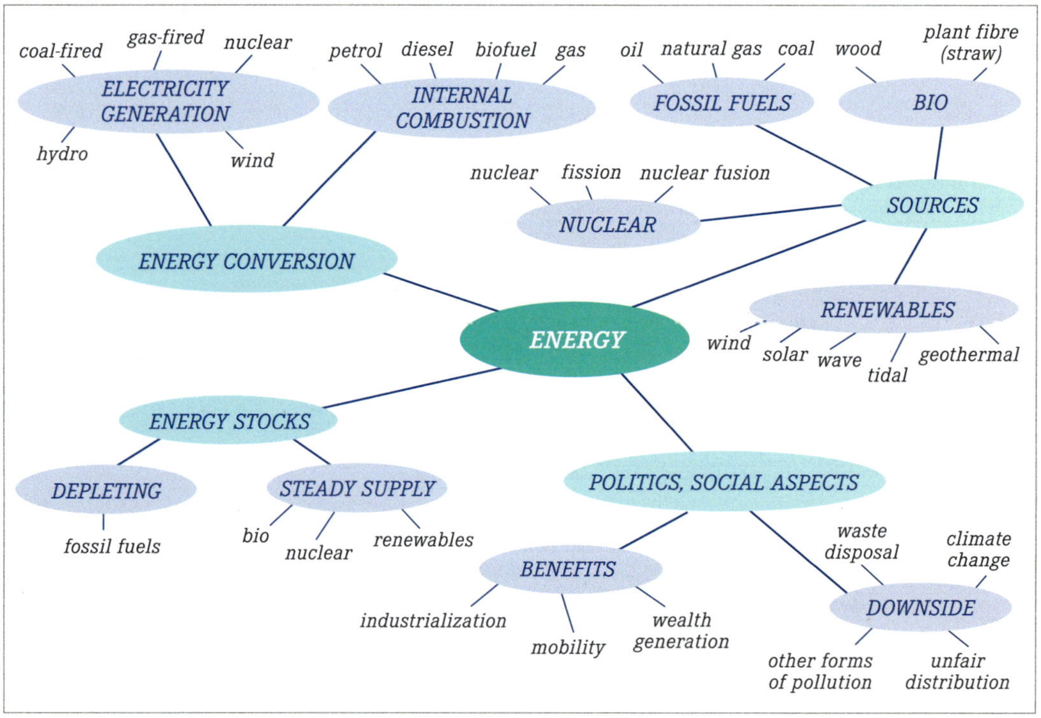

B Compositions

1 How to deal with a composition

Step 1 Gain an overview of your topic. What aspects need to be included and what could be left out?

Step 2 Brainstorm ideas relating to your topic. Lists or mind maps are best suited to brainstorming. > Mind mapping p. 180

Step 3 Think of a structure for your text. Structure your ideas as clearly as possible when drawing your mind maps or writing your lists.

Step 4 Write your text. Leave room for corrections, changes and additions. Important: structure your argument more clearly by using structural words or connectors (use the flap on the back cover *Language for writing* for help).

Step 5 Check your draft for:
- spelling mistakes: words that sound the same, e.g. *there/their*, *meet/meat*, etc.
- grammar mistakes: use of tenses; -ly endings on adjectives
- false friends: "aktuell" is not the same as *actual*, "spenden" does not mean *spend*
- word order
- clarity of ideas: use of structural words / connectors such as *however*, *on the other hand*, *as a result*, etc.

2 Structuring a composition

There are basically two ways of approaching this writing task, depending on the topic itself. You may decide that it is appropriate to approach the topic from a "dialectic" point of view, i.e. by dealing with both the positive and negative sides of the problem and then coming to a solution. In many cases, this is advisable - particularly when no simple and clear-cut solutions seem to be at hand. On the other hand, you may feel compelled to argue either for or against a certain course of action because you have strong opinions on the matter.

If you are asked to present reasons for acting in a particular way or to explore the background of a problem, it is necessary to provide a logical sequence of arguments that build upon one another. Always build up to a climax, with your most convincing argument appearing last.

When writing an essay, it is vital that you first of all organise your thoughts into a logical structure so that the reader can follow the train of thought easily. Making a mind map is a good way of doing this. > Mind mapping p. 180

A composition consists of an introduction, the main part and a conclusion (see example composition on page 183). Remember that your arguments must always be illustrated by appropriate examples or explanations. You are usually expected to provide three arguments. > Sample composition p. 183

a Introduction

In your opening paragraph, the reader needs to be led up to the topic you plan to write about. This can be done in various ways, depending on the topic and your own personal preferences. You may, for example, make a reference to
- a historical development and how things are different now,
- a current topic of debate that needs to be dealt with at the moment,
- some shocking event that requires immediate attention,
- stagnation in society, meaning that change is desperately needed now,
- a quotation from a well-known figure in public life,
- the latest statistics/figures published by a well-known source.

Your next step is to directly pose a question regarding how to deal with the state of affairs you have just described.

Avoid expressing your own personal opinion in the introduction; reserve this for the conclusion.

b Main part

In the main part you have to develop three arguments on one and the same topic. It is sufficient to provide either an explanation or an example to back up your argument.

c Conclusion

The concluding paragraph of your composition should contain a very brief summary of the most important arguments and/or your personal opinion. In the ideal case, you should try to expand on the topic, i.e. try to put it in a larger context. However, you should avoid presenting and developing a new argument here. Remember that arguments should clearly be reserved for the main part of your composition.

d Useful connectors for essay writing

It can be very helpful to keep a list of useful connectors that you can learn off by heart and use to structure every essay so that the reader doesn't lose their train of thought. You should try to include them in every essay. That way, you'll get used to expressing your thoughts in an exact, clear and logical way. When you are reading a text, pay attention to any connectors that you see (and try to note down any that you don't already know!).

Here is a list of connectors to help you structure your essay clearly.

Structuring your arguments

> *In his text 'The world's changing energy supplies' Knapp discusses many aspects of energy and the environment. Firstly, he states that ... Secondly / Then he goes on to say that ... Another point he makes is that ... Finally, ...*

Backing up your argument

> *Due to / Because of / As a result of all the discussions about renewable sources of energy ...*

> *Renewable energy has been talked about a lot. Therefore, the public ...*

> *Renewable energy has been talked about a lot, so the public ...*

Making additional points

> *In addition, / Moreover, Knapp points out that these energy forms ...*

> *In addition to / Besides / As well as mentioning the high development costs of many renewable forms of energy, Knapp points out that ...*

Expressing an opposing argument

> *Although the demand for cheap energy is continuing to rise ...*

> *In spite of the rising demand for cheap energy ...*

> *While/Whereas the demand for cheap energy is continuing to rise ...*

> *Our current main sources of energy are running out. However, / But nevertheless ...*

> *On the one hand, our current main sources of energy are running out; on the other hand, the demand for cheap energy is continuing to rise.*

Giving examples

> *The writer is of the opinion that nuclear fusion is a safe energy source compared with other energy sources, for example / for instance / such as / e.g. ...*

Summing up

> *As a consequence, / All in all, / Consequently, Brian Knapp thinks that ...*

> *To sum up, / To conclude, I would like to say that ...*

3 Sample composition

Tackling youth unemployment

At the moment, one of the heated debates taking place in German society is that of how to deal with youth unemployment in an increasingly globalized economy. What options do we have to deal with this potentially threatening situation?

Introduction
- reference to topic
- direct question
- no personal opinion(s)

Sentence connectors

It is easy to see that companies will simply not be willing to hire juveniles unless there is enough overall demand for the company's products and the prospect of being able to make a reasonable return on their investment. No one can seriously doubt that companies need to be given more incentives to offer high-quality job training programmes. One such incentive, for instance, could consist of a tax break for companies that offer such programmes to school leavers. Such programmes would enable young people to acquire the skills necessary to survive in today's economic climate, which, because of globalization, is intensely competitive. Similarly, it can be argued that the unemployment rate among juveniles will only drop if growth in *all* sectors of the economy is stimulated by the government. Therefore, if the rules regulating hiring and firing were relaxed, companies would be less reluctant to hire new workers.

Moreover, another way to improve the situation is for the government to invest more heavily in education. Providing the financial means to employ more teachers would surely enable schools to improve the performance of weak students who haven't been making the grade. The Scandinavian countries have demonstrated that by improving their school systems, the unemployment rate among young people can be kept very low. This is necessary due to the fact that the more recent PISA studies have shown that German schools are no longer among the best in the world. German school-leavers thus have a slim chance of competing successfully in the job market.

Main body
- two-three arguments on the same topic
- argument = topical sentence + supporting reason + example

In conclusion, I would like to say that it is primarily up to the government to change the current state of affairs. Leaving things as they are not only involves the danger of young people falling victim to radical political ideas presented by right or left-wing demagogues, it is also unethical to rob young people of the chance of getting ahead in life.

Conclusion
- summary of most important arguments
- personal opinion
- no new arguments

C Describing/Interpreting cartoons and pictures

After briefly describing what you see and relating what any captions or speech bubbles say, your task is to interpret the message the cartoonist or photographer is trying to convey. You should neither interpret the cartoon or picture superficially nor over-interpret it.

Step 1 Give an overview of what the picture/cartoon is about: Describe what you see. Take a good look at the people and the objects and consider their size. Also look carefully at facial features that may reveal emotions and/or character.

Step 2 Interpret the message: Take the details and their relevance into account. Consider whether the message of the cartoon/picture is serious or trivial, humorous or sad. Mention any references to current events or political controversies.

Sample photo description

In the foreground of this photo, on the right-hand side, you can see a very young girl, apparently alone, working on a building site. She is kneeling down and is laying large, heavy bricks in long rows on the ground. Her clothes and shoes look dirty, and her hair is tied back which suggests that she has been working hard for a long period of time and that she does it often. On the one hand, her facial expression shows concentration, but it is almost expressionless, suggesting that she is used to doing this. I feel that by showing the long rows of bricks fading into the background and the lone child, the photographer wants to portray exactly how hard children in third world countries have to work, and at the same time, they want to highlight the shocking normality of child labour in these countries. (147 words)

Useful expressions for describing pictures/cartoons

> *in the photo* NOT ~~on the photo~~
> *in the foreground/background*
> *on the right-hand side / left-hand side*
> *at the top/bottom*

Useful verbs for describing pictures/cartoons

> *The photo shows ...*
> *The photographer wants to portray ... / suggests that ...*
> *I feel / It seems that ...*
> *The photo makes you think that ...*
> *The person/place appears to be / is / looks / seems ... (+ adjective)*

⚠

> We use the **present progressive** to say what is happening in a photo/cartoon.
 - *She **is kneeling down** and **is laying** large, heavy bricks in long rows on the ground.*
> We often use verbs like *to appear to be, to be, to look, to seem* + adjective to describe the state of things in photos, i.e. to describe what things are like. In this case, these verbs are always used in the **simple present**. - *Her clothes and shoes **look dirty**.*

Now use the highlighted words and expressions in the example description, as well as the tips above to help you to write your photo description on page 16.

D Describing statistics and graphs

When dealing with statistics and graphs, you are required to interpret numbers.

Graphs, charts and tables show how two or more sets of information are related.

Types of diagram

Table

	USA	UK
1995	*495*	*105*
2005	*718*	*85*

Graph, line graph

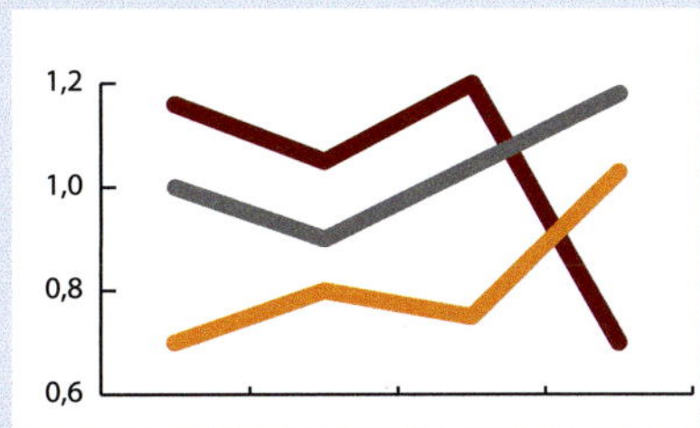

Bar chart

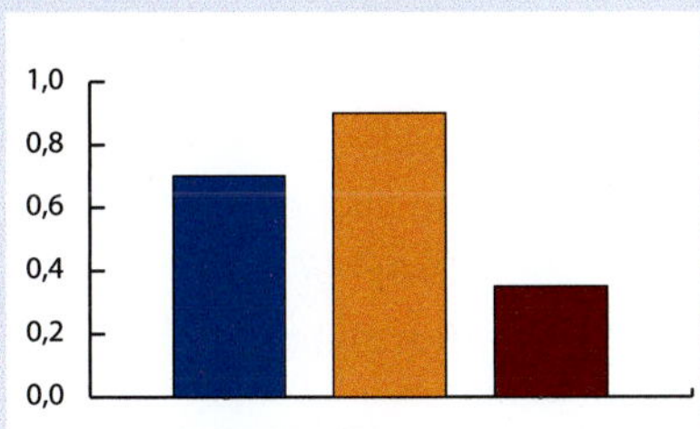

Pie chart

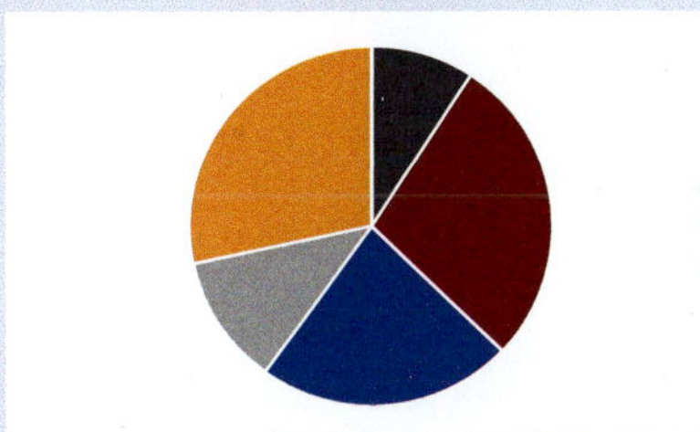

1 Structuring your description

Follow these steps to structure your description properly:

Step 1 Describing what you see: Don't just list all of the details, but give an overview of the situation, describing what the statistics are about and why they have been compiled.

Step 2 Analysing trends, developments and sizes: What conclusions can we draw from the data? Can we show any results from it?

2 Useful phrases for describing statistics

Just like with cartoons, it is sensible to have a list of phrases at hand for describing charts, graphs and tables.

Talking about values and amounts

> *more / less than ...*
> *no less than ...*
> *eighty-five per cent (said that ...)*
> *On the other hand, almost ...*

Talking about proportions, shares and percentages

> *(over) half of ...*
> *more / less than one third / quarter of ...*
> *the (vast) majority of ...*
> *a mere third of ...*

Talking about developments and trends

> *a huge / sharp increase / decrease*
> *a small / slight raise / dip*
> *levels out, remains constant*
> *drastically, gradually, sharply, steadily*
> *rises / increases / hits a maximum*
> *drops / decreases / falls / plunges*
> *over a period of ...*
> *between 2000 and 2012*

Verbs and nouns help you to describe growth and decline in a diagram.

Direction	Verb	Noun
up	climb	climb
	increase	increase
	rise	rise
	go up	
	soar	
	reach a peak	
	flatten off	
	recover	
	decline	decline
	decrease	decrease
	dip	dip
	drop	drop
	fall	fall
	slide	slide
down	bottom out	
level	remain constant	
	not change	no change
	stabilize	stabilization
fluctuation	fluctuate	fluctuation

Adjectives and **adverbs** can be used to express the **quality** or **rate** of changes in a graph.

Adjective	Adverb
slight	slightly
gradual	gradually
steady	steadily
steep	steeply
sharp	sharply
sudden	suddenly
slow	slowly
dramatic	dramatically
fast	fast

EXAMPLES

Sales of MP3 players increased steadily.
There was a sharp fall in the sales of CDs.
Sales of mobile phones remained constant.

In your interpretation of the graph, only include information which is needed to explain the overall trend or to compare and contrast information.

Don't forget that there is a limited number of words available for this task.

ORAL GROUP DISCUSSIONS

Whether you are taking part in a group discussion structured as a role-play or as a consensus-finding activity, keeping the following points in mind can help you to perform well.

The criteria teachers use to assess your performance are as follows:
- language competence
- contribution to task achievement
- strategic competence

1 Preparing for a discussion
- Learn and use the *Language for discussions* phrases from the flap on the inside back cover of the book. You can also use it in class to help you to express your ideas clearly and logically.
- Think carefully about your ideas on the topic when preparing for the discussion. Make a mental note of the most important items or write down some key words in English and try to bring them in during the discussion. Make sure your arguments are based on facts. You may even wish to note down some questions and answers on the topic.
- Anticipate what other participants may say and be prepared to react appropriately.

2 During the discussion
- During the discussion, structure your arguments logically.
- Speak clearly, distinctly and not too fast. Try to remain confident and calm. Taking some deep breaths right before the discussion may help you. Always think before you speak.
- Try to stick to the topic at all times.
- Maintain eye contact with the other participants.
- Bear in mind that a group discussion is a team performance. It is essential that all participants get an equal chance to speak, so neither monopolize the discussion nor be too quiet. Try to involve quiet and shy participants by asking them what they think.
- Several times during the discussion, give partial summaries of what has been said so far.
- All members of the group should come up with a summary together at the end of the discussion.

Here are some words and phrases to help you have a more natural discussion:

Joining in the discussion	
> *Can I just say that ... ?*	> *Well, if you ask me ...*
Involving others in the discussion	
> *What do you think, Sven / Svenja?*	
Expressing understanding, amazement, etc.	
Ach so. / Ah ja.	*I see. / Right. / Oh, right.*
Oh je!	*Oh dear!*
Echt?	*Really?*
Gut. / Okay.	*Fine.*
Alles klar.	*OK then.*
Das ist doch wohl nicht dein Ernst!	*You're kidding!*

PRESENTATION AND PROJECT SKILLS

A Searching for information on the internet

The internet offers us a world of resources that can be valuable for writing essays and presentations, but it is important to know how and where to look.

Step 1 Make a note of what it is exactly that you are looking for and have some specific terms at hand that you want to search for. Without a specific plan, you risk getting lost in the depths of the internet.

Step 2 Think for a moment about where you should start your research. It is a good idea to keep a list of English sources and websites which could be helpful in any situation, e.g. online encyclopaedias, online dictionaries (e.g. *Leo*) facts and figures about different countries (*World factbook*), news sites (e.g. *BBC / CNN*), science and technology sites, etc.

Step 3 Use a reliable search engine and enter the most specific terms possible to speed up your search. Only choose English websites from the search results.

Step 4 Be sure to only choose reliable sources. In general, the internet is not always reliable because every user can upload websites. Always check who is responsible for the content and don't just take any information that you find.

Step 5 Before reading an article word for word, just skim it, pick out paragraphs or information that is relevant to your topic and ignore the rest. > Skimming for gist p. 170

Step 6 Avoid copying whole paragraphs from websites. Instead, make notes on the most important information and save the website under "Favourites". That way you can always come back to it later should you require further information, e.g. quotes or statistics.

B Giving a presentation or a talk

The ability to speak in front of a audience is an important skill not only for school, but also for your working life. A successful presentation doesn't just depend on the quality of the content, but also on the structure and presentation of the content.

1 Preparation

Step 1 Collect ideas and information on the topic by brainstorming, looking in books, checking the internet, etc. Select the ideas which are most useful in supporting your topic.

Step 2 Group these ideas into logical units and put these units into a sequence which makes up a clear train of thought.

Step 3 When giving talks on non-controversial subjects, e.g. global warming, measures against unemployment, divide your talk into three sections:

1. Introduction: statement of topic and your opinion/ideas (about 15% of the whole talk or presentation)
2. Development: evidence to support your opinion/ideas (about 75%)
3. Conclusion: repetition of your opinion/ideas and a very brief summary of most important reasons (about 10%).

If you are talking about controversial topics such as euthanasia or the legalization of drugs, then you can divide your talk up like this:

1. Introduction: proposal on the solution to a controversial problem, e.g. "Hash should be legalized". Do not give your own opinion yet. (about 10% of the whole talk or presentation)
2. Development I: arguments against the proposal ("cons") (about 40%)
3. Development II: arguments for the proposal ("pros") (about 40%)
4. Conclusion: your own opinion with brief summary of reasons. (about 10%)

Step 4 Consider how you can make your presentation livelier and more interesting (by using visuals, audios, anecdotes, etc.).

Step 5 Read through your presentation or talk several times and prepare postcard-sized prompt cards with brief notes and key words which will help you to remember important aspects during your presentation or talk. Make sure that you can pronounce every word on your prompt cards (using the phonetic translation in your dictionary or an online dictionary).

Step 6 Find out about the venue, and order and organize and test any equipment you are going to use. If you are using visual aids for your presentation or talk, it is always important to practise using them in this preparation phase.

2 Using visual aids

- Use visual aids to show how things look, work or relate to each other.
- Choose a visual aid which is suited to your material and the situation.
- Use a flip chart or the board for recording audience feedback or for collecting ideas.

10 Golden rules for giving a presentation

1. **Before you start**, lay out your materials (script, prompt cards, etc.) and set up your equipment.
2. **Begin** by greeting the audience with a smile and thanking them for coming. Then move on quickly to an attention-grabber to establish positive contact with the audience, e.g. a quotation, a provocative statement or an interesting question. 'Visuals', e.g. a photo or an object connected with the topic, are also good attention-catchers.
3. **Avoid jokes.** These can fall flat, particularly in a foreign language, and then your talk will start with an embarrassed silence.
4. Pay attention to **body language**. Turn to face your audience, maintain eye-contact with them, speak slowly and clearly (only reading from prompt cards) and use gestures to help you explain what you are talking about. Vary the volume of your voice in accordance with the points you want to get across.
5. **During the talk or presentation**, use **signalling language** (*first, to sum up*, etc.) to help the audience understand more easily what you are talking about.
6. Encourage **questions** to involve the audience. If you don't want your audience to ask spontaneous questions during your presentation or talk, however, say that there will be time for questions at the end.
7. Use **language** which your audience will understand easily. Try not to use a lot of technical words if your audience might not be too familiar with them.

8 Keep your audience interested by introducing different elements to your presentation such as **visuals**, **handouts**, etc. If you decide to use PowerPoint, make sure that your slides are clearly structured and not too packed with text or photos.

9 Stick to the **KISS** (keep it short and simple) rule to give an effective presentation or talk.

10 **In the conclusion**, summarize the main points you made during your presentation. Finish with a short, memorable sentence.

3 Dealing with the question phase

> Try to anticipate questions you might be asked and prepare answers.
> Never say 'I don't know', but offer to find the answer.
> Never start a debate with one person.
> Thank the audience for their attention when all the questions have been answered.

Useful phrases and expressions for giving presentations and talks

Introducing your topic

> *Good morning/afternoon/evening. My name is ...*
> *The topic of my presentation/talk is ...*
> *I'm going to talk about ...*
> *First, I'll talk about ... Second, ...*

Dealing with questions

(At the beginning)

> *If you have any questions, please feel free to interrupt me.*
> *I'd prefer to take any questions at the end.*

(At the end)

> *So, if there are any questions, I'd be happy to answer them.*
> *Are there any more / any final questions?*

Structuring your presentation

> *To begin, I'd like to look at ...*
> *I'd like to focus on ...*

Giving examples / Referring to visuals

> *Let me give you an example.*
> *OK. Now I'd like to show you ...*
> *As you can see, this graph/column/picture shows ...*
> *Can everybody see that?*

Summing up

> *Before I finish, I'd like to summarize the key points.*
> *In conclusion ...*

C Doing projects

A project is a longer piece of individual or pair work that is produced largely outside the classroom and generally without the direct help of a teacher – though he or she will, of course, advise you. You will usually work on your project in a group.

Projects fall into four stages, which you should work through systematically:

1 Planning the project
2 Collecting information
3 Compiling information
4 Presenting the finished project

1 Planning

One hour invested in planning your project can save hours of unnecessary work later on. Good planning will also help you to produce a more interesting and understandable project file.

Divide your topic into logical sub-sections. Make a mind map or notes about anything and everything that has to do with the topic. Then organize this material into a manageable form.

> Mind mapping p. 180

The mind map below has to do with environmental protection in the home. Complete the gaps a–e using the words in the box below.

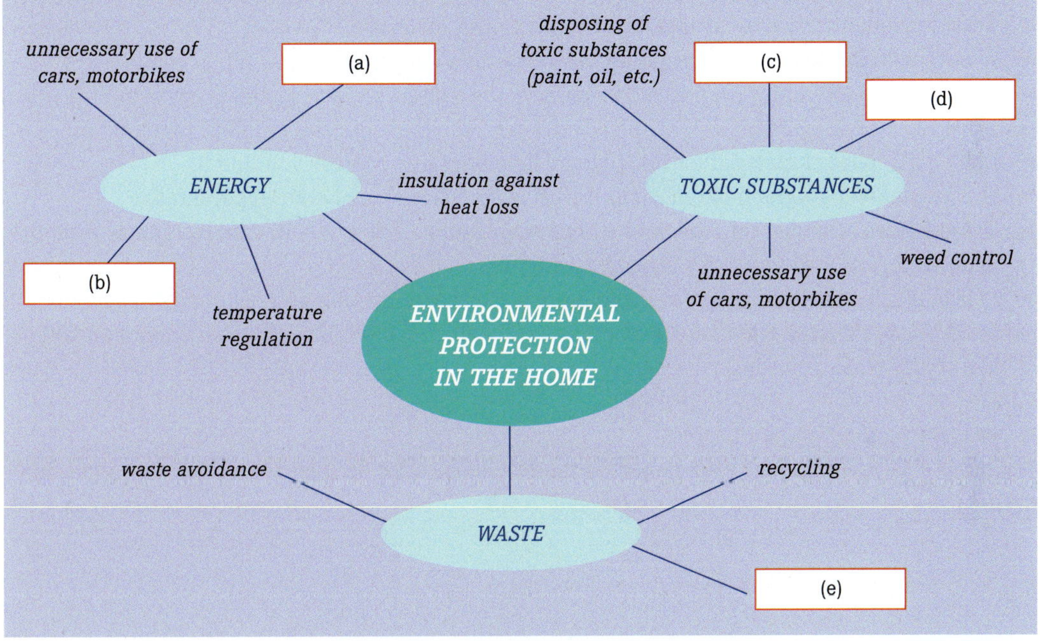

cleaning agents | controlling consumption | pest control | stand-by switches | unnecessary electric gadgets

Once you have a clear and practicable list of topics and sub-topics, go on to the next stage. Don't forget, though, that the project plan can be revised in accordance with the information you collect.

2 Collecting information

According to topic, you can get information from some or all of these sources:

- your family, friends and neighbours; other pupils; teachers of other subjects
- encyclopaedias; yearbooks; reference books (school and public library)
- the press, particularly weekly news magazines and specialist magazines
- TV, particularly the third programmes and the English-language channels *CNN*, *NBC* and *BBC World*

- radio, particularly *Voice of America, BBC World Service, Deutschlandfunk, Daily Motion*
- local banks: firms and utilities working in your topic area
- local charities; pressure groups, e.g. *Greenpeace*
- information services of government departments; chambers of commerce (*Industrie- und Handelskammer*)
- information agencies such as the *British Council, America House*, das *Deutsch-Amerikanische Institut, United States Information Service* (USIS)
- the internet

When collecting material, try to select an English-language source whenever possible. If you have to use German sources, don't try to translate this material into English. It is much better to make brief English notes from the German information and then compose your own English text.

3 Compiling information

Here are some useful tips. They sound obvious but are frequently ignored.

- Organize your project file with dividers between each section and sub-section. Keep your file tidy!
- Keep a detailed and an up-to-date list of contents and materials.
- Always note the source of information, with date, as soon as you find it. When you use oral information from family, friends and so on, give the source, e.g. Anecdotal, Ebersbach, 23.08.12.
- Don't make piles of material for filing later. File material as soon as you find it.
- Use a separate paragraph for each point with generous spacing between paragraphs.
- Use sub-titles or paragraph headings whenever possible. This will help you to organize your material logically and to give a clear presentation.
- Collect illustrations and graphics - line graphs, pie charts, column and bar charts to support texts. Visual material will make your presentation much more interesting and understandable. Use colour when you can.

4 Presenting the finished project

You may be asked to present your project to the rest of the class or even at an open day or parents' evening. See the tips on *Giving a presentation or a talk.*

> Giving a presentation or talk p. 188

Grammar summary

THE SIMPLE PRESENT

1 I **play** tennis twice a week.
2 We **live** in Bavaria.
3 Mr Brown **teaches** us English every day.
4 I **don't like** conference calls.
5 **Does** he **like** travelling?

> Man gebraucht das **simple present** für regelmäßige, sich wiederholende Ereignisse oder Handlungen (1, 3) und für Dauerzustände (2, 4, 5).
> Mit Ausnahme der 3. Person Singular (*he, she, it*) hat das **simple present** dieselbe Form wie der Infinitiv (1, 2).
⚠ Die **3. Person Singular** endet auf *-(e)s* (3).
> Ist **kein Hilfsverb** im Satz vorhanden, werden **Verneinung** und **Fragen** mit der entsprechenden Form von *to do* gebildet (4, 5).

Das **simple present** wird häufig mit den folgenden **Zeitangaben** benutzt:

> *always, never, often, rarely, seldom, sometimes*
> *generally, mostly, normally, regularly, usually*
> *every day/week/month/..., every morning/afternoon/...*
> *on Mondays/Tuesdays/..., on weekdays*
> *in (the) summer/winter/...*
> *at Christmas/Easter, at weekends*

THE PRESENT PROGRESSIVE

1 **I'm calling** to say that Ben's ill.
2 He'**s staying** in bed today.
3 The computer **isn't working**.
4 **Are** you **eating** lunch?

> Man benutzt das **present progressive** (auch **present continuous** genannt) für Vorgänge oder Handlungen, die im Moment des Sprechens oder Schreibens passieren und noch nicht abgeschlossen sind (1, 3, 4).
> Es wird auch für vorübergehende Situationen gebraucht (2).
> Das **present progressive** wird mit dem Präsens von *to be* und der *-ing*-Form des Vollverbs gebildet.
> Da beim **present progressive** immer ein Hilfsverb vorhanden ist, wird die **Verneinung** mit *not/n't* gebildet (3).
> Fragen werden durch Umstellung gebildet (4).

Das **present progressive** wird oft mit den folgenden **Zeitangaben** benutzt:

at the moment, at present, now, this week/month, currently

⚠ Diese Verben bilden normalerweise **keine progressive-Form**:

be, believe, doubt, feel (meinen), *hate, hear, imagine, know, like/dislike, love, mean, notice, prefer, realize, recognize, remember, see* (begreifen), *seem, suppose, think* (meinen), *understand, want, wish*

THE SIMPLE PAST

1 We **wanted** to go to the USA two years ago.
2 She **went** on a school trip to London.
3 Jasmin **did not enjoy** her holiday in Rimini last summer.
4 Where **did** you **go** last year?

> Man benutzt das **simple past**, um über Vergangenes zu berichten.
> Das **simple past** wird auch gebraucht, wenn man sagen will, **wann** etwas geschehen ist (1, 3, 4).
> Bei **regelmäßigen** Verben wird das **simple past** durch das Anhängen von *-ed* an den Infinitiv gebildet (1).
⚠ Die unregelmäßigen Verben haben eine Sonderform (2), die man sich merken – auswendig lernen! – muss. > Irregular verbs p. 265
> Ist **kein Hilfsverb** im Satz vorhanden, bildet man die **Verneinung** und **Fragen** mit *did/didn't* (3, 4).

Das **simple past** wird häufig mit den folgenden **Zeitangaben** benutzt:

> *yesterday, the day before yesterday, the week/month/... before last*
> *last night/week/month/summer/December/Easter/...*
> *two/three/... hours/days/years/... ago*
> *in 2005 / in the 20th century ...*
> *at that time, in those days*

THE PAST PROGRESSIVE

1 The teacher **was talking** to Heather **during the break**.
2 The students **were eating** lunch when the fire alarm (suddenly) **rang**.
3 I **wasn't doing** anything particular when he **arrived**.
4 **Were** you **having** breakfast when I **phoned**?

> Wenn man ausdrücken möchte, dass eine Handlung zu einem bestimmten Zeitpunkt oder während eines bestimmten Zeitraumes in der Vergangenheit **im Gange** war, benutzt man das **past progressive** (auch **past continuous** genannt) (1).
> Das **past progressive** wird auch benutzt, um zu verdeutlichen, dass eine Handlung im Gange war, als ein neues Ereignis (plötzlich) eintrat (2–4).
> Man bildet das **past progressive** mit *was/were* und der *-ing*-Form des Vollverbs (1).
> Die **Verneinung** wird mit *was not / wasn't* bzw. *were not / weren't* gebildet (3).
> **Fragen** bildet man durch Umstellung (4).
⚠ Einige Verben haben normalerweise **keine progressive-Form** (siehe die Liste unter **present progressive** S. 193).

THE PRESENT PERFECT

1 I**'ve bought** a new computer.
2 I **haven't seen** the new film yet.
3 How long **have** you **had** a laptop?
4 We**'ve had** snow **for** two weeks.
5 She**'s had** a cold **since** December.

> Wenn man ausdrücken will, dass etwas geschehen ist, ohne dass der genaue Zeitpunkt des Ereignisses wichtig ist, wird das **present perfect** benutzt (1, 2).
> Man gebraucht das **present perfect** auch, um zu sagen, seit wann oder wie lange ein Zustand oder eine Handlung schon andauert (3–5). Dafür wird sehr oft *for* bzw. *since* verwendet. (Im Deutschen steht dafür „seit" plus Gegenwart.)
> Das **present perfect** wird mit *have/has* und der 3. Form des Vollverbs gebildet.
⚠ Die unregelmäßigen Verben haben eine Sonderform (1, 2), die man auswendig lernen muss.

> Irregular verbs p. 265

> Die **Verneinung** wird durch das Einfügen von *not/n't* nach *have/has* gebildet (2).
> **Fragen** bildet man durch Umstellung (3).

Das **present perfect** wird oft mit den folgenden Zeitangaben benutzt:

> *already, still (not), (not) yet*
> *(not) ever, just, lately, never, recently*
> *so far this week/month/..., till/until now*

THE PRESENT PERFECT PROGRESSIVE

1 I**'ve been learning** English since I was ten.
2 They**'ve not been speaking** to each other lately.
3 **Has** he **been planning** the presentation for long?

> Das **present perfect progressive** (auch **present perfect continuous** genannt) benutzt man für Handlungen und Vorgänge, die in der Vergangenheit begonnen haben und zum Zeitpunkt des Sprechens bzw. Schreibens noch nicht beendet sind.
> Das **present perfect progressive** wird mit *have/has been* und der *-ing*-Form des Vollverbs gebildet (1).
> Die **Verneinung** bildet man durch das Einfügen von *not/n't* unmittelbar nach *have/has* (2).
> **Fragen** werden durch Umstellung gebildet (3).
⚠ Einige Verben haben normalerweise **keine progressive-Form** (siehe die Liste unter **present progressive**, S. 193).

THE PAST PERFECT

1 Laura couldn't pay. She **had forgotten** her purse.
2 Nina **had** already **left** the coffee bar by the time I arrived.
3 When I visited John in hospital, he **had been** there for ten days.

> Mit Hilfe des **past perfect** drückt man aus, dass zwei Handlungen oder Vorgänge in der Vergangenheit aufeinander folgten (1, 2). Die Handlung, die zeitlich voranging, steht im **past perfect**.
> Das **past perfect** wird auch verwendet, um auszudrücken, dass ein Zustand vor einem Zeitpunkt der Vergangenheit begann und zu diesem Zeitpunkt noch andauerte (3).

⚠ Wenn zwei oder mehrere kurze Handlungen in der Vergangenheit direkt aufeinander folgen, wird für alle Handlungen das **simple past** verwendet:
*The cat **ran** out when Joanne **opened** the door.*

THE PAST PERFECT PROGRESSIVE

1 Rod **had been preparing** for his interview for three weeks when he got another job offer.
2 When I found Mary, I could see that she **had been crying**.

> Das **past perfect progressive** (auch **past perfect continuous** genannt) wird verwendet, wenn man ausdrücken will, dass eine Handlung oder ein Vorgang vor einem Zeitpunkt in der Vergangenheit begonnen hatte und bis (oder fast bis) zu diesem Zeitpunkt andauerte.

THE FUTURE

A will

1 In the future people **will use** public transport more often.
2 We can only hope that everyone **will accept** this shift in attitudes.
3 You've forgotten your purse? Don't worry. **I'll lend** you some money.
4 Ms Smith **will not be** at the meeting this afternoon.
5 I **won't come** either.
6 **Will** he **get** the job?

> Das **will future** benutzt man, um Vorhersagen zu machen (1) oder Vermutungen über die Zukunft zu äußern (2).
> Man benutzt es auch, wenn man sich spontan zu etwas entschließt, Angebote oder Versprechen macht (3).
> Das **will future** wird mit *will* + Infinitiv des Vollverbs gebildet. Es hat für alle Personen die gleiche Form (1-3).
> Die **Verneinung** bildet man durch das Einfügen von *not* unmittelbar nach *will* (4). Im gesprochenen Englisch sagt man häufig *won't* (5).
> **Fragen** werden durch Umstellung gebildet (6).

Das **will future** kommt häufig mit den folgenden einleitenden Verben und Ausdrücken vor:

> *believe, expect, forecast, hope, imagine, suppose, think*
> *It's clear/obvious that ..., There's no doubt that ...*

B going to

1 Look at these clouds. It'**s going to rain** soon.
2 This time I'**m going to get** good marks in the class test.
3 Tom **isn't going to work** at the club any more.
4 When **are** you **going to take** your driving test?

> Das **going to future** benutzt man für Ereignisse und Situationen, die nach Meinung des Sprechers bald eintreten werden (weil es bereits Anzeichen dafür gibt) (1).
> Es wird auch für Pläne und Absichten gebraucht (2).
> Das **going to future** wird mit *am/is/are* + *going to* + Infinitiv gebildet (1, 2).
> Die **Verneinung** bildet man durch das Einfügen von *not/n't* unmittelbar nach *am/is/are* (3).
> **Fragen** werden durch Umstellung gebildet (4).

⚠ Der **Gebrauch des Futurs** hängt in gewissem Maße von der Absicht oder Sichtweise des Sprechers ab. Dies gilt insbesondere für das **going to future** und für zukünftige Ereignisse. Daher ist es im Zweifelsfall ratsam, das neutralere **will future** zu benutzen.

C The present progressive / The simple present

1 We'**re leaving** the house at 10.30.
2 The bus **goes** at 11 o'clock.

> Man kann das **present progressive** auch **mit einer Zeitbestimmung der Zukunft** (*at 10.30, this afternoon, on Sunday*) für bereits feststehende Pläne und Verabredungen verwenden (1).

> Genau wie im Deutschen wird auch im Englischen das **simple present mit einer Zeitangabe** benutzt, um fest terminierte Vorgänge (Fahrpläne, Stundenpläne, Programme usw.) anzugeben (2).

MODAL AUXILIARY VERBS

1 He **can speak** several languages.
2 You **must accept** your new situation.
3 We **needn't go** to work today.
4 **May** I **interrupt** you?

> Um zu sagen, was geschehen kann, muss, darf, soll usw., benutzt man ein modales Hilfsverb in Verbindung mit einem Vollverb (1-4).

⚠ Im Englischen steht ein Hilfsverb - anders als im Deutschen - nie ohne Vollverb:
- Lena kann Spanisch. ⟶ *Lena can **speak** Spanish.* NICHT: ~~Lena can Spanish.~~

> Modale Hilfsverben - nicht jedoch die Ersatzverben (siehe unten) - haben bei allen Personen immer die gleiche Form, einschließlich der 3. Person Singular (keine *-s*-Endung) (1, 2).

> Die **Verneinung** wird durch das Einfügen von *not/n't* unmittelbar nach dem Hilfsverb gebildet (3).

> **Fragen** bildet man durch Umstellung (4).

> Abgesehen von *could* (wenn damit eine Fähigkeit ausgedrückt werden soll) kann man modale Hilfsverben nur im Präsens und - mit einer geeigneten Zeitangabe - mit zukünftiger Bedeutung benutzen, zum Beispiel:
- *You **can go** home now.* (Präsens)
  *You **can go** home an hour early tomorrow.* (Futur)
- *I **must write** these letters now.* (Präsens)
  *I **must write** a long report next week.* (Futur)

⚠ Um andere Zeitformen bei modalen Hilfsverben zu bilden, z. B. die Vergangenheit, muss ein geeignetes Ersatzverb gebraucht werden:

must *The provider **had to block** access to the internet last December.*
can *I **couldn't start** the car yesterday.* (Fähigkeit)
*We **weren't allowed to go** home early last Friday.* (Erlaubnis)

Übersicht der modalen Hilfsverben nach Funktion

Funktion	Modale(s) Hilfsverb(en)	
Fähigkeit	*He **can** speak several languages.* *The first satellites **could** only transmit sound.*	
Möglichkeit	*With your qualifications you **could** work abroad.* *The boss **may** come in at any moment.* *He **might** ask you what you are doing.*	
Bitte	***Can** I have a word with Ms Sims, please?* ***Could** I speak to Ms Sims, please?* ***May** I interrupt you?* ***Might** I ask you a personal question?*	(neutral) (höflich) (betont höflich) (äußerst höflich)
Erlaubnis	*You **can** go in now.* *The boss is free. You **may** go in now.*	(neutral) (gefällig)
Verbot	*We **mustn't** be late for work tomorrow.*	
Pflicht	*You **must** wear a hard hat in the factory.*	
Wahl	*Most shop workers **needn't** work on Sundays.*	
Empfehlung	*You **should** get better qualifications.* *You **ought to** get better qualifications.* *You **must** get better qualifications.*	(neutral) (betont) (streng)

REPORTED SPEECH

A Aussagesätze

1 Some people **claim** that 'servant' robots **are putting** people out of work.
2 The speaker **reminded** his audience that there **were** some jobs robots **couldn't do**.

> Wenn man einem Dritten berichten möchte, was während eines Gespräches gesagt wurde, benutzt man die **indirekte Rede**.

> Bei Verwendung der indirekten Rede benutzt man ein einleitendes Verb wie *claim, say, remind, answer, think, mention* usw., um zu verdeutlichen, dass eine Äußerung wiedergegeben wird.

> Steht das einleitende Verb in der Vergangenheit - also *said, answered, mentioned* usw. -, dann verschieben sich die Zeiten wie folgt:

direkte Rede		indirekte Rede
simple present *she works hard*	→	simple past *she worked hard*
present progressive *she is working hard*	→	past progressive *she was working hard*
simple past *she worked hard*	→	past perfect *she had worked hard*
past progressive *she was working hard*	→	past perfect progressive *she had been working hard*
present perfect *she has worked hard*	→	past perfect *she had worked hard*

present perfect progressive *she has been working hard*	⟶	**past perfect progressive** *she had been working hard*
past perfect *she had worked hard*		(keine Verschiebung) –
past perfect progressive *she had been working hard*		(keine Verschiebung) –
will *she will work hard*	⟶	**would** *she would work hard*
am/is/are going to *she is going to work hard*	⟶	**was/were going to** *she was going to work hard*
would/might etc. *she would work hard*		(keine Verschiebung) –
would have/might have etc. *she would have worked hard*		(keine Verschiebung) –

⚠ Die modalen Hilfsverben werden folgendermaßen verschoben:

Modalverb	Bedeutung	indirekte Rede
can	Fähigkeit	*could, was/were able to*
can	Erlaubnis	*was/were allowed to*
may	Möglichkeit	*might*
may	Erlaubnis	*was/were allowed to*
must	Pflicht	*had to*
mustn't	Verbot	*was/were not allowed to*
needn't	freie Wahl	*did not / didn't have to*

> Außer wenn man über ein Gespräch berichtet, das am selben Tag stattgefunden hat, müssen fast alle **Zeit**- und einige **Ortsangaben** entsprechend der folgenden Tabelle geändert werden. (Angaben, die nicht aufgeführt sind, bleiben unverändert.)

direkte Rede		indirekte Rede
today	⟶	*on that day*
tomorrow	⟶	*the next day*
yesterday	⟶	*the day before*
the day after tomorrow	⟶	*two days later*
the day before yesterday	⟶	*two days before*
next day/Friday/week/Christmas/...	⟶	*the following day/Friday/week/Christmas/...*
last Friday/week/summer/...	⟶	*the Friday/week/summer/... before*
two years/months/weeks/... ago	⟶	*two years/months/weeks/... before*
now, at present	⟶	*then*
at the moment	⟶	*at that moment*
at this time	⟶	*at that time*
here	⟶	*there*
in this place	⟶	*at that place*
this	⟶	*that*
these	⟶	*those*

B Fragesätze

1 A member of the audience **asked what had led** to the widespread use of robots in factories.
2 She **wanted to know if/whether** her job **was endangered**.

> Bei indirekten **Fragen** unterscheidet man zwischen Fragen mit Fragewort (1) und Fragen ohne Fragewort (2).
> Bei Fragen **mit Fragewort** wird das Fragewort übernommen (1).
> Bei Fragen **ohne Fragewort** benutzt man *if* bzw. *whether* (= ob), um zu verdeutlichen, dass es sich um eine Frage handelt (2).
> Alle anderen Änderungen erfolgen wie bei den Aussagesätzen (siehe **Aussagesätze** S. 198).

C Bitten, Aufforderungen und Befehle

1 Lucy **asked the engineer to show her** the robot.
2 He **told her not to go** too close to it.

> **Bitten** werden meist durch *asked* (= bitten) (1), **Aufforderungen** und **Befehle** durch *told* (= sagen) (2) eingeleitet.
> Bei **positiven Sätzen** erscheint das Verb als *to* + Infinitiv (1).
> Bei **negativen Sätzen** wird *not* unmittelbar vor *to* gesetzt (2).

⚠ Die beiden Verben *to ask* und *to tell* stehen immer mit einem Objekt, das die angesprochene Person erwähnt (1, 2). Ist dies vom Kontext her nicht erkennbar, wird einfach ein passender Begriff eingesetzt:

> *Ben said, 'Don't enter the studio when the red light is on.'*
> *Ben* ***told everybody*** *not to enter the studio when the red light was on.*

THE PASSIVE

1 Measures **are being introduced** to reduce traffic pollution.
2 Pollution **is caused by** some thoughtless people.

> Ist der Verursacher einer Handlung unbekannt oder zweitrangig, benutzt man das Passiv. Im Vordergrund steht also das Ergebnis des Vorgangs (1).
> Möchte man den Verursacher doch angeben, benutzt man einen *by agent* (2).
⚠ Der Verursacher wird mit *by* – auf keinen Fall mit *from* – eingeleitet.
> Das Passiv wird mit einer Zeitform von *to be* und der 3. Form des Vollverbs gebildet:

Zeit	Zeitform von *to be*	3. Form
simple present	*am/is/are*	*affected*
present progressive	*am/is/are being*	*introduced*
simple past	*was/were*	*buried*
past progressive	*was/were being*	*built*
present perfect	*has/have been*	*installed*
will-Futur	*will be*	*blocked*
going to-Futur	*am/is/are going to be*	*sacked*

> Beim Gebrauch von modalen Hilfsverben wird nach folgendem Muster verfahren:

bei Aussagen	Hilfsverb + *to be* + 3. Form	*must be displayed*
bei Fragen	Hilfsverb + Subjekt + *to be* + 3. Form	*Can ... be persuaded?*

⚠ Das Verb *to be* bleibt im Infinitiv immer unverändert.

THE IMPERSONAL PASSIVE

1 **It is said that** petrol will soon cost more.
2 He **is thought** to have completed the training course.

> Das **impersonal passive** wird vor allem dann benutzt, wenn man sich objektiv bzw. unbeteiligt ausdrücken möchte. Daher kommt diese Struktur oft in Polizeiberichten, seriösen Zeitungsartikeln usw. vor.

> Bei Verben des Berichtens, Denkens usw. benutzt man häufig das Satzmuster:
It is/was/... + 3. Form des einleitenden Verbs + *that*-Satz (1).
Hier sind weitere Beispiele dieses Musters:
Aktiv *Some **say** that companies which cause pollution should be heavily fined.*
Passiv ***It is said that** companies which cause pollution should be heavily fined.*
Aktiv *Experts **recommended** that more be spent on public transport.*
Passiv ***It was recommended** that more be spent on public transport.*

> Um das Subjekt des *that*-Satzes zu betonen, kann man folgendes Muster benutzen:
Subjekt + *is/was/...* + 3. Form + *to be* + andere Satzteile (2):
Aktiv *Many **believe** that the minister is thinking of raising fuel taxes.*
Passiv *The minister **is believed to be** thinking of raising fuel taxes.*

⚠ Der *by agent* wird in solchen Passivsätzen folgendermaßen verwendet:
Aktiv *The speaker felt that the idea was too radical.*
Passiv *The idea was felt to be too radical **by** the speaker.*

IF-SENTENCES

1 If we **invest** in new technology, a lot of people **will lose** their jobs.
2 A lot of people **will lose** their jobs if we **invest** in new technology.
3 If more people **took part** in re-training schemes, they **wouldn't have to worry** about finding new employment.
4 We **won't have** political censorship if we **don't start** to censor the internet.
5 **Will** we soon **have** political censorship if we **start** to censor the internet?

> Ein **Konditionalsatz** besteht aus zwei Teilen: dem ***if*-Teil** und dem **Hauptteil**.
Der ***if*-Teil** drückt eine **Bedingung** aus, der **Hauptteil** eine **Folge**.
> Bei **Konditionalsätzen** kommen folgende **Zeitmuster** am häufigsten vor:

Typ I	*If + simple present*	+	*will*-Futur
Typ II	*If + simple past*	+	*would* + Infinitiv
Typ III	*If + past perfect*	+	*would have* + 3. Form des Verbs

> Der *if*-Teil kann hinter dem Hauptteil stehen. In diesem Fall steht kein Komma dazwischen (2, 4, 5).
> Je nach Sinn kann der *if*-Teil, der Hauptteil oder beide Teile des Satzes **verneint** werden (3, 4).
> Bei **Fragen** kann nur der **Hauptteil** zu einer Frage geformt werden. Dann steht dieser Teil **an erster Stelle** (5).

> *if*-Sätze werden gemäß der **Wahrscheinlichkeit** der zu erwartenden Folge eingesetzt:
Typ I: Folge (fast) sicher.
*If we **invest in** new technology, a lot of people **will lose** their jobs.*
D.h. viele Leute werden (vermutlich) ihre Stellen verlieren, da wir (sehr wahrscheinlich) in die neue Technologie investieren werden.
Typ II: Folge theoretisch möglich, aber kaum wahrscheinlich.
*If we **invested in** new technology, a lot of people **would lose** their jobs.*
D.h. es ist kaum zu erwarten, dass viele Leute ihre Stellen verlieren werden, da wir (wahrscheinlich) nicht in die neue Technologie investieren werden.
Typ III: Folge unmöglich, da die Bedingung nicht erfüllt wurde und bereits in der Vergangenheit liegt.
*If we **had invested in** new technology, a lot of people **would have lost** their jobs.*
D.h. der Sprecher weiß schon, dass keiner den Job verloren hat, da wir in die neue Technologie nicht investiert haben.

GERUND/INFINITIVE

1 Max **enjoys reading** in the park.
2 Can you **afford to buy** that new computer software?
3 Cem and Julie **continued to meet** even though they had split up.
4 Cem and Julie **continued meeting** even though they had split up.
5 Alison **normally likes going to** parties, but **today** she would **prefer to stay** at home.

> Nach einigen Verben folgt immer die *-ing*-Form **(gerund)** (1).
Am wichtigsten sind:

admit, avoid, consider, deny, enjoy, finish, give up, imagine, mention, (not) mind (etwas/nichts dagegen haben), *miss, practise, recommend, risk, stop, suggest*

> **Nach einigen Verben** folgt immer der Infinitiv **(infinitive)** (2).
Die **wichtigsten** Verben dieser Gruppe sind:

afford, choose, decide, expect, hope, manage, mean, plan, promise, refuse, want

⚠ Nach den Verben *begin, continue, intend* und *start* kann der **Infinitiv** oder die ***-ing*-Form beliebig benutzt werden** (3, 4).

> Einige Verben werden **je nach Bedeutung** entweder mit dem **Infinitiv** oder mit der ***-ing*-Form** benutzt. Die **wichtigsten** Verben dieser Gruppe sind:

like, dislike, love, hate, prefer

> Wenn von einer **allgemeingültigen Situation** die Rede ist, folgt auf diese Verben die ***-ing*-Form**. Handelt es sich aber um eine **Ausnahmesituation**, dann verwendet man den **Infinitiv** (5).

advise, allow, encourage, forbid, permit, recommend
Handelt es sich um einen **konkreten Einzelfall**, wird mit diesen Verben ein **Objekt + Infinitiv** verwendet.
*I strongly **advise you to** be more polite to people.*
Wenn es sich aber um eine **allgemeine Situation** handelt, dann steht das nachfolgende Verb in der ***-ing*-Form**.
*Most firms don't **allow smoking** in their offices.*

forget/remember

Die Struktur ***forget/remember* + *-ing*-Form** bezieht sich auf die Vergangenheit. Sie drückt etwa die Idee „Ich werde nie vergessen ..." aus.

⚠ „Vergangenheit" bezieht sich hier nicht auf *forget/remember*, sondern auf das nachfolgende Verb.

*I still **remember getting** my first job.*

*I'll never **forget going** to the Japanese headquarters last year.*

Die Struktur ***forget/remember* + Infinitiv** dagegen bezieht sich auf die Zukunft. Sie drückt etwa die Idee aus „Ich darf nicht vergessen, etwas zu tun" bzw. „Ich habe noch etwas zu tun, weil ich es bis jetzt vergessen habe".

*Dad, please **remember / don't forget to pick me up** from the station.*

*Oh dear. I **forgot / didn't remember to pick Sally up** from the station.*

regret

Die Struktur ***regret* + *-ing*-Form** drückt Bedauern über eine vergangene Situation bzw. einen vergangenen Vorfall aus. Häufig geht es dabei um verpasste Chancen.

*I really **regret leaving** school without any qualifications.*

*I know they will **regret buying** such a big, expensive car.*

Die Struktur ***regret* + Infinitiv** – fast immer mit einem Verb des Mitteilens wie *inform, say, tell* kombiniert – drückt eine schlechte Nachricht aus.

*I **regret to say** that I can't attend the meeting tomorrow.*

*We **regret to inform** you that the vacancy has now been filled.*

stop

Bedeutet ***stop*** „aufhören, etwas zu tun", steht das nachfolgende Verb in der ***-ing*-Form**.
Bedeutet ***stop*** aber „kurz anhalten, um etwas anderes zu tun", folgt ein Verb im **Infinitiv**.

*For heaven's sake **stop shouting** at me.*

*I'm a little late because I **stopped to give** somebody a lift.*

try

Bedeutet ***try*** „etwas ausprobieren", steht das nachfolgende Verb in der ***-ing*-Form**.
Bedeutet ***try*** aber „sich anstrengen, etwas zu tun", folgt ein Verb im **Infinitiv**.

*I **tried phoning** Ellie, but she wasn't at home.*

*We'll **try to repair** your computer by the weekend.*

ADJECTIVES AND ADVERBS

1 John has a **new** printer.
2 He always buys **expensive** equipment.
3 My computer has become **very slow**.
4 That CD sounds **terrible**.
5 We can make printouts **quickly** and **cheaply**.

> Um **Personen** oder **Sachen** näher zu beschreiben, benutzt man **Adjektive** (1–4).
> Adjektive stehen **unmittelbar** vor Substantiven oder **unmittelbar nach** einer Form von *be* (bzw. *become* oder *seem*, die *be* ersetzen können) (3).
> **Adjektive** können mit Verben wie *feel, look* (aussehen), *sound, smell* und *taste* eine **sinnliche Wahrnehmung** ausdrücken (4).
> Um einen **Tätigkeitsverb** näher zu beschreiben, setzt man ein **Adverb unmittelbar hinter das Verb** bzw. Verb + Objekt (5).

⚠ Im Englischen können ein Verb und sein Objekt - anders als im Deutschen - nicht durch ein Adverb getrennt werden. Also NICHT: ~~We can make quickly printouts~~. (siehe **word order** unten)

> Adverbien werden auch benutzt, um **Adjektive, andere Adverbien** und **ganze Sätze** näher zu bestimmen:
*MP3 players have become **surprisingly cheap**.* (Adverb + Adjektiv)
*My fax machine prints out **terribly slowly**.* (Adverb + Adverb)
***Luckily** Gerd left a message on my mailbox.* (Satzadverb)

> Die meisten Adverbien werden durch Anhängen von *-ly* an das Adjektiv gebildet (5). Eine kleine Anzahl von Adverbien hat dieselbe Form wie Adjektive; die häufigsten sind:

fast, hard, early late, long, daily

COMPARISON OF ADJECTIVES AND ADVERBS

1 A hundred years ago life was **slower** and people may have been **happier**.
2 Which technological innovation is the **most/least important**?
3 Today you can copy data **more easily than** ever before.

> **Einsilbige** und **zweisilbige Adjektive**, die auf *-y* enden - zum Beispiel *easy, happy* und *lucky* -, werden mit *-(i)er/-(i)est* gesteigert (1).

> **Mehrsilbige Adjektive** und **Adverbien**, die auf *-ly* enden, werden mit *more/most* gesteigert (2, 3).
⚠ Die Adverbien, die dieselbe Form wie das entsprechende Adjektiv haben (*fast, hard, early* usw.), werden mit *-er/-est* gesteigert.

> Um Personen oder Sachen im Satz miteinander zu vergleichen, gibt es folgende Möglichkeiten:

Kein Unterschied	*as good as*	genau so gut wie
Unterschied	*not as good as*	nicht so gut wie
Unterschied	*better than*	besser als

WORD ORDER

positions of adverbs of time, place and frequency

1 She goes shopping **every week**.
2 Their school is located in a small town **outside of Frankfurt**.
3 **Last year** we went to Italy for our holidays.
4 Paul and Emily went to **the USA last year**.
5 She **always finishes** school early on Fridays.
6 He **is never** at home when I call.
7 I like to stay at home **now and then**.
8 Gina acted **strangely during the presentation last week**.

> Zeitangaben (Wann?) und Ortsangaben (Wo?, Wohin?) stehen in der Regel am Satzende (1, 2).

> Um die Zeit eines bestimmten Ereignisses hervorzuheben, kann man die Zeitangabe an die erste Stelle setzen (3).

> Stehen eine Zeitangabe und eine Ortsangabe zusammen am Satzende, dann gilt die Reihenfolge Ort vor Zeit (alphabetisch merken: O vor Z!) (4).

> Besteht eine Häufigkeitsangabe aus einem Wort, z.B. *always, often, sometimes*, steht sie unmittelbar vor dem Vollverb (5).

> Lautet das Vollverb *to be*, steht das Adverb direkt dahinter (6).

> Besteht die Häufigkeitsangabe aus mehreren Wörtern, z.B. *every day, now and then*, steht sie wie eine Zeitangabe am Satzende (7).
> Adverbien der Art und Weise stehen in der Regel am Satzende. Kommen noch Zeit- oder Ortsadverbien hinzu, lautet die Reihenfolge: Art und Weise - Ort - Zeit (AOZ) (8).

RELATIVE CLAUSES AND CONTACT CLAUSES

1 Car manufacturers are designing cars **which/that** can use hydrogen fuel cells.
2 Wildernesses are being spoiled by tourists **who/that** want to go to 'unspoiled' places.
3 Tony filled in a job satisfaction questionnaire **(which/that)** he found on the internet.
4 Fred Foley is an artist **whose** fortune amounts to over €400 million.
5 Call centre employees, most **of whom** come from India, work long hours.
6 Some non-GM crops are attacked by pests **against which** they have no resistance.

> Relativsätze werden benutzt, um den Hauptsatz durch zusätzliche Informationen genauer zu bestimmen.
> Für **Sachen** benutzt man das Relativpronomen *which* bzw. *that* (1) und für Personen *who* bzw. *that* (2).
> Steht das Relativpronomen für das **Objekt des Hauptsatzes**, dann kann man es weglassen (3). Solche Relativsätze heißen **contact clauses**.
> Um **Besitz** bzw. **Zugehörigkeit** anzuzeigen, gebraucht man *whose* unmittelbar vor dem **Substantiv** bei Personen und Sachen (4).
> Steht eine **Präposition** vor dem **Relativpronomen**, wird *whom* für Personen und *which* für Sachen benutzt (5, 6). In solchen Fällen ist der Gebrauch von *that* nicht möglich.

DEFINING AND NON-DEFINING RELATIVE CLAUSES

1 The first Europeans **who** settled in Australia came from Britain.
2 Sydney, **which** is famous for its unusually designed opera house, is situated on the south-eastern coast of Australia.

> Im **ersten Beispielsatz** ist der Sinn des Hauptsatzes *The first Europeans came from Britain* ohne den Relativsatz *who settled in Australia* offensichtlich falsch bzw. unvollständig. Relativsätze dieser Art - die wesentlich für das Verständnis des gesamten Satzes sind - nennt man **defining relative clauses** (notwendige oder bestimmende Relativsätze).
> Im **zweiten Beispielsatz** ist die Aussage des Hauptsatzes *Sydney is situated on the south-eastern coast of Australia* ohne den Relativsatz völlig verständlich, weil der Relativsatz *which is famous for its unusually designed opera house* eine zusätzliche, also nebensächliche, Information enthält. Daher werden solche Relativsätze ***non-defining relative clauses*** (nicht notwendige oder nicht bestimmende Relativsätze) genannt.
⚠ Notwendige Relativsätze werden immer **ohne** trennende **Kommas** benutzt. Dies signalisiert, dass sie fester Bestandteil der Hauptaussage sind.

PARTICIPLE CONSTRUCTIONS

1 Malaria, preventable with a treated bed net **costing** less than one pound, is endemic.
2 Many men believe that any work **involved** with cooking is a woman's chore.
3 **Losing** more and more people to AIDS, Africa now needs effective help more urgently than ever before.

4 **Burdened** with declining life expectancy, large parts of Africa are caught in a poverty trap.
5 **Having fetched** water from a river for many years, some women in developing countries are now happy to be able to use the Hippo Roller.
6 **Despite facing** extreme destitution, many rural residents haven't given up hope.
7 Donors should invest in projects that help local inhabitants become self-supporting, **thereby making** sure that the money isn't wasted.
8 Poor infrastructure is a key barrier to economic growth in Nepal, **thus causing** huge additional costs to the transport of commercial goods.
9 Life is becoming hard in the developing countries, **with** many small farmers **going** out of business.
10 AIDS represents a major challenge to sub-Saharan Africa, currently **killing** more than two million people every year.

Die englische Sprache ist geprägt durch die häufige Verwendung von Partizipialkonstruktionen. Diese ermöglichen einen eleganteren Sprachfluss.

> Partizipialkonstruktionen verkürzen Relativsätze; dabei kann entweder das **present participle** (1) oder das **past participle** (2) verwendet werden.
> Sie werden auch verwendet, um adverbiale Nebensätze zu vekürzen. In diesen Fällen unterscheidet man zwischen Partizipialkonstruktionen ohne Konjunktion (3–5) und solchen mit Konjunktion (6–9). In Sätzen ohne Konjunktion ist der Inhalt des Satzes auch ohne eine solche klar. Dagegen sind Konjunktionen nötig, um zu verhindern, dass der logische Zusammenhang des Satzes verloren geht. Zum Beispiel wird der Inhalt von Satz 6 unklar, wenn die Konjunktion *despite* ausgelassen wird.
> Wie bei der Verkürzung von Relativsätzen kommen auch bei der Verkürzung von adverbialen Nebensätzen das **present participle** (3, 6–9) und das **past participle** (4) zur Anwendung. Darüber hinaus wird hier auch noch das **perfect participle** verwendet (5), und zwar um die Vorzeitigkeit der Handlung im Nebensatz auszudrücken. *(Nachdem sie jahrelang Wasser aus dem Fluss geholt hatten, ...)*
> Schließlich verknüpft man mit einer Partizipialkonstruktion zwei Hauptsätze zu einem einzigen Satz, und zwar ausnahmslos mittels **present participle** (10).

COUNTABLE AND UNCOUNTABLE NOUNS

1 Visit our website for more **information** on our firm. NICHT ~~informations~~
2 Have you read the paper today? The political **news** is interesting. NICHT ~~news are~~
3 Where can I get some **advice**? NICHT ~~an advice~~

> Einige wichtige **Substantive** sind **zählbar im Deutschen, nicht jedoch im Englischen**. Diese Substantive können also nicht ohne weiteres mit dem unbestimmten Artikel *a/an* oder mit einem Zahlwort benutzt werden.
Hier ist eine Liste solcher Wörter, die Sie auswendig lernen sollten:

advice, baggage, damage, data, equipment, evidence, furniture, information, knowledge, luck, luggage, machinery, news, progress, research, rubbish, work (housework, homework)

> Um diese Substantive im Plural zu verwenden, muss *some, a bit of* bzw. *a piece of* hinzugefügt werden (3).

SOME AND *ANY*

1 **Some** head teachers prefer to hold regular weekly meetings with their staff.
2 They haven't got **any** women working in their company.
3 Have you got **any** information about arrival times?
4 Can I have **some** more coffee, please?
5 Would you like **some** mineral water?
6 There's **something** I need to do but I can't remember what it is.
7 He can't find that letter **anywhere**. Maybe **somebody** took it.

> Wir verwenden *some* in **bejahten Aussagen** (1) und *any* in **verneinten Aussagen** (2) und **„echten" Fragen** (3).

> Drückt die Frage eine höfliche **Bitte** (4) bzw. ein **Angebot** (5) aus, worauf eine positive Antwort erwartet wird, verwenden wir ebenfalls *some*.

> Wir verwenden die Zusammensetzungen von *some* and *any* - also *somebody/someone, something, somewhere, anybody/anyone, anything* und *anywhere* - in genau derselben Art und Weise (6-7).

THE DEFINITE ARTICLE

1 **Sociologists** say that **violence** is increasing among young people.
2 Is **the current trend** partly caused by **the violent films** they watch?
3 **Most sentences** are not tough enough.
4 Nearly **half the prisoners** in **British prisons** are under 25.
5 **Spring** is my favourite season but **the spring** we're having this year is more like **winter**.
6 We had **breakfast** late this morning so we came to work **by car** instead of **by bus**.
7 They are thinking of legalizing soft drugs in **the Netherlands**.

> Hat ein Substantiv eine allgemeine, uneingeschränkte Bedeutung - also „alle ohne Ausnahme" - dann steht es ohne Artikel (1, 5).

> Ist die Bedeutung eines Substantives auf bestimmte Fälle eingeschränkt, benutzt man den Artikel (2, 5).

> Ferner wird der Artikel in den folgenden Fällen und Wendungen im Englischen - z.T. anders als im Deutschen - nicht gebraucht:
> - bei *most* in der Bedeutung „die meisten" (3),
> - bei öffentlichen Gebäuden im allgemeinen Sinn (4),
> - bei Mahlzeiten (6),
> - bei Verkehrsmitteln (6),
> - bei Straßennamen,
> - bei Tageszeiten, Wochentagen, Monaten und Jahreszeiten im allgemeinen Sinn (5).

> Der Artikel wird verwendet nach *all* und *half* (4) und mit den Pluralnamen von Staaten (7).
> ⚠ Der bestimmte Artikel steht im Englischen (viel) seltener als im Deutschen. Daher: *When in doubt, leave it out!*

THE INDEFINITE ARTICLE

1 Yesterday I met **a woman** who works for **a friend** of my father's.
2 We'll have to buy **a** new **computer**.
3 That's **an** interesting **idea**.
4 Jane's **an accountant**? I thought she was **a sales rep**.
5 My father has been **a non-smoker** all his life.
6 How much does petrol cost **a liter**?
7 We give presentations twice **a month**.

> Der unbestimmten Artikel a/an steht bei einer einzelnen, nicht näher bestimmten Person (1), einer Sache (2), oder einem Begriff (3).

> Anders als im Deutschen verwenden wir im Englischen den unbestimmten Artikel in folgenden Fällen:
- bei Berufsangaben (4),
- bei Angaben über Nationalität, Religion, Politik oder Gruppenzugehörigkeit (5)
- bei Maß- (6), Verpackungs-, und Zeitangaben (7)
- bei den folgenden Wendungen:

to be in a hurry	in Eile sein, es eilig haben
to come to an end	enden
to have a bath/shower/...	sich baden/duschen/...
to have a go	es ausprobieren
to have a turn at (+ -ing-Form)	an der Reihe sein, etwas zu tun
to make a noise	Lärm machen
to take a seat	Platz nehmen
for a change	zur Abwechslung
for a long/short time	lange/kurze Zeit
in a loud/quiet voice	mit lauter/ruhiger Stimme
What a pity!	Wie schade!
without a break	ohne Pause

⚠ Bei *half, quite, rather* und *such* wird der unbestimmte Artikel nachgestellt:

> The meeting starts in half **an** hour.

> We had quite **a** successful year in 2005.

> Jack can be rather **an** idiot sometimes.

> We've never had such **a** big order.

Unit word list

Dieses Wörterverzeichnis enthält alle Wörter in **Focus on Success Erweiterte Ausgabe 3rd edition** in der Reihenfolge ihres Auftretens. Nicht aufgeführt sind internationale Wörter wie *hotel*, *e-mail* usw.

Wörter, die in den Hörverständnisübungen vorkommen, sind mit einem orangefarbenen Balken, und Wörter, die in den *Files* vorkommen, mit einem blauen Balken gekennzeichnet.

UNIT 1

page 6

achievement [ə'tʃi:vmənt]	Leistung, Errungenschaft, Erfolg
thrill [θrɪl]	Begeisterung, überwältigendes Gefühl
effort ['efət]	Bemühung, Anstrengung, Leistung
gratitude ['grætɪtju:d]	Dankbarkeit
to **consist of sth.** [kən'sɪst əv]	aus/in etw bestehen
quote [kwəʊt]	Zitat
to **justify** ['dʒʌstɪfaɪ]	rechtfertigen, begründen
to **express** [ɪk'spres]	ausdrücken

page 7

contribution [ˌkɒntrɪ'bju:ʃn]	Beitrag
glider ['glaɪdə]	Segelflugzeug
climate change ['klaɪmət tʃeɪndʒ]	Klimawandel
campaigner [kæm'peɪnə]	Aktivist/in
gliding ['glaɪdɪŋ]	Segelfliegen
to **lack sth.** [læk]	(zu) wenig von etw haben
confidence ['kɒnfɪdəns]	Selbstvertrauen, Zuversicht
smooth [smu:ð]	glatt, ruhig, sanft
to **overuse sth.** [ˌəʊvə'ju:z]	etw zu viel/oft gebrauchen
to **attempt sth.** [ə'tempt]	etw versuchen, etw wagen
current ['kʌrənt]	Strömung
rising air [ˌraɪzɪŋ 'eə]	aufsteigende Luft(strömung)
potty ['pɒti]	verrückt, plemplem
compelling [kəm'pelɪŋ]	spannend, mitreißend
to **yell out** [ˌjel 'aʊt]	(laut) ausrufen, herausschreien
to **suit sth.** [su:t]	zu etw passen
independent streak [ɪndɪˌpendənt 'stri:k]	Unabhängigkeitsdrang
throughout my life [θru:ˌaʊt maɪ 'laɪf]	in meinen ganzen Leben, mein ganzes Leben lang
to **make a living out of sth.** [ˌmeɪk ə 'lɪvɪŋ aʊt əv]	mit etw seinen Lebensunterhalt bestreiten
to **deal with sb.** ['di:l wɪð]	mit jdm zu tun haben, mit jdm zurechtkommen
completion [kəm'pli:ʃn]	Vervollständigung, Ergänzung
to **be a good match for sb./sth.** [bi ə ˌgʊd 'mætʃ fə]	gut zu jdm/etw passen
apparent [ə'pærənt]	offensichtlich, klar
to **do without sb./sth.** [ˌdu: wɪ'ðaʊt]	ohne jdn/etw auskommen
according to [ə'kɔ:dɪŋ tə]	nach, gemäß
rather ['rɑ:ðə]	ziemlich
pretty ['prɪti]	ziemlich
gripping ['grɪpɪŋ]	fesselnd
vein [veɪn]	Ader, Art

page 8

thrill [θrɪl]	*hier:* Nervenkitzel
of a lifetime [əv ə 'laɪftaɪm]	einmalig
to **prove one's worth** [ˌpru:v wʌnz 'wɜ:θ]	sich beweisen, seine Stärke unter Beweis stellen
promotion [prə'məʊʃn]	Beförderung
to **deserve** [dɪ'zɜ:v]	verdienen
nerve-wrecking ['nɜ:v rekɪŋ]	nervenaufreibend
patient ['peɪʃnt]	geduldig
impatient [ɪm'peɪʃnt]	ungeduldig
to **mind** [maɪnd]	etw dagegen haben
not necessarily [ˌnɒt nesə'serəli]	nicht unbedingt
rumour ['ru:mə]	Gerücht
ambition [æm'bɪʃn]	Ehrgeiz
to **quit** [kwɪt]	kündigen, aufgeben
prom [prɒm]	Promenade
plain [pleɪn]	einfach, schlicht
appeal [ə'pi:l]	Anziehungskraft, Reiz
seaside ['si:saɪd]	(am) Meer
godson ['gɒdsʌn]	Patensohn
transaction [træn'zækʃn]	(Geschäfts-)Vorgang
frantically ['fræntɪkli]	wie wild, wie verrückt
topping ['tɒpɪŋ]	Garnierung *(z. B. Schokosoße, Nussstreusel)*
to **charge sth. for sth.** [tʃɑ:dʒ]	etw *(Preis, Gebühr)* für etw verlangen
to **charge extra** [ˌtʃɑ:dʒ 'ekstrə]	einen Aufpreis verlangen
to **be in a sorry state of affairs** [bi ɪn ə ˌsɒrɪ ˌsteɪt əv ə'feəz]	in einem jämmerlichen Zustand sein, ganz schön heruntergekommen sein
indicator ['ɪndɪkeɪtə]	Gradmesser, Indikator
to **dribble** ['drɪbl]	sabbern, tropfen
to **replace** [rɪ'pleɪs]	ersetzen, austauschen

in sb.'s view [ɪn ˌvjuː]	nach jds Ansicht/Meinung
to **contribute** [kən'trɪbjuːt]	beitragen

page 9

to **bother** ['bɒðə]	stören, belästigen
to **train as sth.** ['treɪn əz]	eine Ausbildung zum/in etw machen
ecologist [i'kɒlədʒɪst]	Umweltforscher/in, Ökologe/-in
scarlet macaw [ˌskɑːlət mə'kɔː]	der Hellrote Ara *(südamerik. Papageienart)*
conservation [ˌkɒnsə'veɪʃn]	Schutz, Naturschutz
to **affect** [ə'fekt]	beeinträchtigen
to **breed** [briːd]	brüten
incentive [ɪn'sentɪv]	Anreiz
fare [feə]	Fahrpreis
wicked ['wɪkɪd]	böse, schlecht, schlimm
to **get one's way** [ˌget wʌnz 'weɪ]	seinen Willen bekommen, (mit etw) durchkommen
hopelessness ['həʊpləsnəs]	Aussichtslosigkeit, Hoffnungslosigkeit
to **balance** ['bæləns]	ausgleichen
GDP, Gross Domestic Product [ˌdʒiː diː 'piː, ˌgrəʊs dəˌmestɪk 'prɒdʌkt]	BIP, Bruttoinlandsprodukt
to **get on with sth.** [ˌget 'ɒn wɪð]	mit etw weiterkommen
to **surround** [sə'raʊnd]	umgeben
to **let go of sth.** [ˌlet 'gəʊ əv]	sich von etw lösen, etw vernachlässigen
impact ['ɪmpækt]	Auswirkung(en), Einfluss, Folgen
unless [ən'les]	außer wenn, es sei denn
defeat [dɪ'fiːt]	Niederlage(n)
to **stick to sth.** ['stɪk tə]	an etw festhalten
concerned [kən'sɜːnd]	besorgt
living creature [ˌlɪvɪŋ 'kriːtʃə]	Lebewesen

page 10

bliss [blɪs]	Glück, Glückseligkeit
crammed ['kræmd]	vollgestopft
paraphernalia [ˌpærəfə'neɪliə]	Zubehör, Utensilien
affluence ['æfluəns]	Wohlstand, Überfluss
consumption [kən'sʌmpʃn]	Konsum, Verbrauch
to **mute** [mjuːt]	dämpfen
welfare ['welfeə]	Wohl
to **strive for sth.** ['straɪv fə]	nach etw streben
elaborate [ɪ'læbərət]	ausgefeilt, aufwändig
adage ['ædɪdʒ]	Sprichwort
well-being ['wel biːɪŋ]	Wohl, Wohlergehen
to **subdue** [səb'djuː]	unterdrücken
saying ['seɪɪŋ]	Sprichwort, Redensart
prosperity [prɒ'sperəti]	Wohlstand
possessions [pə'zeʃnz]	Besitztümer
equipment [ɪ'kwɪpmənt]	Ausrüstung, Geräte
economist [ɪ'kɒnəmɪst]	Wirtschaftswissenschaftler/in
to **point out** [ˌpɔɪnt 'aʊt]	darauf hinweisen
beyond [bɪ'jɒnd]	jenseits
presumably [prɪ'zjuːməbli]	vermutlich
shelter ['ʃeltə]	Behausung, Unterkunft
public order [ˌpʌblɪk 'ɔːdə]	öffentliche Ordnung
to **meet a need** [ˌmiːt ə 'niːd]	ein Bedürfnis befriedigen
wealth [welθ]	Reichtum, Wohlstand
to **generate** ['dʒenəreɪt]	erzeugen
life expectancy ['laɪf ɪkspektənsi]	Lebenserwartung
to **be stuck** [bi 'stʌk]	festsitzen
to **rate** [reɪt]	einschätzen, bewerten, einstufen
similar ['sɪmələ]	ähnlich
likewise ['laɪkwaɪz]	ebenso, gleichermaßen
flat [flæt]	*hier:* auf gleichem Niveau
scholar ['skɒlə]	Gelehrte/r, Wissenschaftler/in
to **condemn** [kən'dem]	verurteilen
self-defeating [ˌself dɪ'fiːtɪŋ]	das Gegenteil bewirkend, kontraproduktiv
contest ['kɒntest]	Wettbewerb, Wettstreit
pleasure ['pleʒə]	Vergnügen
grand [grænd]	prachtvoll, imposant
debt [det]	Schuld(en)
anxious ['æŋkʃəs]	besorgt, beunruhigt, bang
to **regret** [rɪ'gret]	bereuen
to **sacrifice** ['sækrɪfaɪs]	opfern
leisure ['leʒə]	Freizeit
suburbia [sə'bɜːbiə]	Vorstädte, Wohnsiedlungen am Stadtrand
traffic congestion ['træfɪk kəndʒestʃən]	Verkehrsstau
commute [kə'mjuːt]	Arbeitsweg, Pendelstrecke/-zeit
to **clog** [klɒg]	verstopfen
to **worsen** ['wɜːsn]	sich verschlimmern
to **engage in a behaviour** [ɪnˌgeɪdʒ ɪn ə bɪ'heɪvjə]	ein Verhalten an den Tag legen
to **claim** [kleɪm]	behaupten, erklären, verkünden
to **feed on sth.** ['fiːd ɒn]	sich von etw ernähren, *hier:* von etw gespeist werden
insecurity [ˌɪnsɪ'kjʊərəti]	Verunsicherung, Unsicherheit
insane [ɪn'seɪn]	wahnsinnig, verrückt
rat race ['ræt reɪs]	erbarmungsloser Überlebenskampf
over time [ˌəʊvə 'taɪm]	mit der Zeit
gain [geɪn]	Gewinn
elsewhere [ˌels'weə]	anderswo
surely ['ʃʊəli]	sicherlich, mit Sicherheit

page 11

disconnect [ˌdɪskə'nekt]	Diskrepanz, Bruch
despite [dɪ'spaɪt]	trotz
subdued [səb'djuːd]	gedämpft
culprit ['kʌlprɪt]	Schuldige/r, Übeltäter, *hier auch:* Sündenbock
gasoline *AE* ['gæsəliːn]	Benzin, Sprit
housing ['haʊzɪŋ]	Wohnungen, Wohnungsbau, Wohnungsmarkt

slump [slʌmp] – starker Rückgang, Krise
to cite [saɪt] – anführen, zitieren
underlying [,ʌndə'laɪɪŋ] – zugrunde liegend
to fire ['faɪə] – (Personal) entlassen
median ['mi:diən] – mittlere/r/s
job tenure ['dʒɒb tenjə] – Anstellungsdauer
cause [kɔ:z] – Anlass
immediate [ɪ'mi:diət] – unmittelbar
to condition [kən'dɪʃn] – konditionieren
blissful ['blɪsfl] – glückselig, glücklich
to match sth. [mætʃ] – mit etw übereinstimmen
to budge [bʌdʒ] – sich bewegen, sich von der Stelle rühren
income ['ɪnkʌm] – Einkommen
inequality [,ɪnɪ'kwɒləti] – Ungleichheit
to involve [ɪn'vɒlv] – mit sich bringen, zur Folge haben
modest ['mɒdɪst] – klein, unerheblich
ultimately ['ʌltɪmətli] – letztlich, letztendlich
finding ['faɪndɪŋ] – Ergebnis
particularly [pə'tɪkjələli] – insbesondere
widower ['wɪdəʊə] – Witwer, *hier:* Verwitweter
divorcee [dɪ,vɔ:'si:] – Geschiedene/r
to estimate ['estɪmət] – schätzen
to suggest [sə'dʒest] – darauf hindeuten
to devise [dɪ'vaɪz] – ausarbeiten, erfinden
policies *pl.* ['pɒləsiz] – Strategien, Programme
to elevate ['elɪveɪt] – anheben
feelgood quotient ['fi:lgʊd kwəʊʃnt] – *etwa:* Wohlfühlquotient
to depend heavily on sth. [dɪ,pend 'hevɪli ɒn] – sehr von etw abhängen
no matter [nəʊ 'mætə] – ungeachtet, ganz egal
to rank [ræŋk] – einen Platz *(in einer Rangliste)* einnehmen
paternalistic [pə,tɜ:nə'lɪstɪk] – bevormundend, paternalistisch
welfare state [,welfeə 'steɪt] – Wohlfahrtsstaat, Sozialstaat
to provide [prə'vaɪd] – bieten, zur Verfügung stellen, liefern
health care ['helθ keə] – Gesundheitsfürsorge, Gesundheitswesen
to outlaw ['aʊtlɔ:] – (gesetzlich) verbieten
despair [dɪ'speə] – Verzweiflung, Hoffnungslosigkeit
to mandate ['mændeɪt] – (gesetzlich) vorschreiben
novelist ['nɒvəlɪst] – Romanautor/in
to re-engineer [,ri: endʒɪ'nɪə] – umarbeiten, umorganisieren
spirit ['spɪrɪt] – Geist
the bare necessities [ðə ,beə nə'sesətiz] – die absolut lebensnotwendigen Dinge
prosperous ['prɒspərəs] – wohlhabend
level ['levl] – Niveau, Grad
majority [mə'dʒɒrəti] – Mehrheit
purchasing power ['pɜ:tʃəsɪŋ paʊə] – Kaufkraft

page 12

to refer to sth. [rɪ'fɜ: tə] – sich auf etw beziehen, auf etw verweisen
survival of the fittest [sə,vaɪvl əv ðə 'fɪtɪst] – Überleben der bestangepassten Individuen
educated ['edʒukeɪtɪd] – gebildet, ausgebildet
to disapprove of sth. [,dɪsə'pru:v əv] – etw ablehnen
tough [tʌf] – hart
competitive [kəm'petətɪv] – wettbewerbsorientiert, leistungsorientiert
to gamble ['gæmbl] – spielen, wetten
discrepancy [dɪs'krepənsi] – Diskrepanz
to keep up with the Joneses [ki:p ,ʌp wɪð ðə 'dʒəʊnzɪz] – *etwa:* mit den Nachbarn mithalten
to decline [dɪ'klaɪn] – zurückgehen, abnehmen
bank account ['bæŋk əkaʊnt] – Bankkonto
to plummet ['plʌmɪt] – (drastisch) fallen, abstürzen
real estate ['rɪəl ɪsteɪt] – Immobilien
to be made redundant [bi ,meɪd rɪ'dʌndənt] – (betriebsbedingt) entlassen werden
unproven [ʌn'pru:vn] – unbewiesen
doubtful ['daʊtfl] – zweifelhaft
closely related to [,kləʊsli rɪ'leɪtɪd tə] – eng verbunden mit
marital status [,mærɪtl 'steɪtəs] – Familienstand
belief [bɪ'li:f] – Überzeugung
to boost [bu:st] – steigern, fördern
inspiring [ɪn'spaɪrɪŋ] – anregend, inspirierend
misleading [,mɪs'li:dɪŋ] – irreführend
promising ['prɒmɪsɪŋ] – vielversprechend
with regard to [wɪð rɪ'gɑ:d tə] – hinsichtlich, bezüglich
to elect [ɪ'lekt] – wählen
to pass a law [,pɑ:s ə 'lɔ:] – ein Gesetz verabschieden/erlassen
leadership ['li:dəʃɪp] – Führung

page 13

to adapt [ə'dæpt] – anpassen
mood [mu:d] – Stimmung, Laune
to desire sth. [dɪ'zaɪə] – sich etw wünschen
desire (for sth.) [dɪ'zaɪə] – Wunsch (nach etw), Verlangen (nach etw)
to be in high spirits [bi ɪn ,haɪ 'spɪrɪts] – bei bester Laune sein
to join [dʒɔɪn] – beitreten
convincing [kən'vɪnsɪŋ] – überzeugend
to split [splɪt] – (sich) aufteilen
comprehensive [,kɒmprɪ'hensɪv] – umfassend
properly ['prɒpəli] – richtig, angemessen
to win sb. over [,wɪn 'əʊvə] – jdn umstimmen, jdn überzeugen
runner-up [,rʌnər 'ʌp] – Zweitplatzierte/r

page 14

to make your heart sing [,meɪk jɔ: ,hɑ:t 'sɪŋ] – das Herz höher schlagen lassen, jdn von Herzen glücklich machen
in scientific terms [ɪn saɪən,tɪfɪk 'tɜ:mz] – wissenschaftlich ausgedrückt
common denominator [,kɒmən dɪ'nɒmɪneɪtə] – gemeinsamer Nenner
to shine [ʃaɪn] – glänzen
short-term [,ʃɔ:t 'tɜ:m] – kurzfristig
state [steɪt] – Zustand, Verfassung
to measure ['meʒə] – messen

fundamental [ˌfʌndəˈmentl]	grundlegend
temporary [ˈtemprəri]	vorübergehend
high [haɪ]	Hochstimmung
pendulum [ˈpendjələm]	Pendel
ecstasy [ˈekstəsi]	Begeisterung, Ekstase
stage [steɪdʒ]	Phase
default setting [dɪˌfɔːlt ˈsetɪŋ]	Standardeinstellung
as it were [əz ɪt ˈwɜː]	sozusagen, gewissermaßen
contentment [kənˈtentmənt]	Zufriedenheit
common [ˈkɒmən]	*hier:* gemeinsam
fulfilling [fʊlˈfɪlɪŋ]	erfüllend
equation [ɪˈkweɪʒn]	Gleichung
to **enhance** [ɪnˈhɑːns]	fördern, steigern
cheerful [ˈtʃɪəfl]	vergnügt, gut gelaunt
light-hearted [ˌlaɪt ˈhɑːtɪd]	heiter, unbekümmert
blue [bluː]	deprimiert
downcast [ˈdaʊnkɑːst]	niedergeschlagen
miserable [ˈmɪzrəbl]	elend
at times [ət ˈtaɪmz]	manchmal, bisweilen
a loved one [ə ˈlʌvd wʌn]	nahestehender Mensch
loss [lɒs]	Verlust
contented [kənˈtentɪd]	zufrieden, wunschlos glücklich
gloom [gluːm]	Trübsinn, düstere Stimmung
peace of mind [ˌpiːs əv ˈmaɪnd]	innerer Friede, Seelenfrieden
interviewee [ˌɪntəvjuːˈiː]	Befragte/r
content [kənˈtent]	zufrieden
discontent [ˌdɪskənˈtent]	Unzufriedenheit
to **occur** [əˈkɜː]	vorkommen, sich ereignen
to **be at odds with oneself** [bi ˌət ˈɒdz wɪð]	mit sich hadern, mit sich selbst uneins sein
to **affect** [əˈfekt]	beeinflussen
spirits *pl.* [ˈspɪrɪts]	Stimmung
proof [pruːf]	Beweis(e)
dispirited [dɪˈspɪrɪtɪd]	entmutigt
wisdom [ˈwɪzdəm]	Weisheit, Klugheit

page 15

down in the dumps [ˌdaʊn ɪn ðə ˈdʌmps]	niedergeschlagen, deprimiert
on top of the world [ɒn ˌtɒp əv ðə ˈwɜːld]	überglücklich
over the moon [ˌəʊvə ðə ˈmuːn]	(vor Freude) ganz aus dem Häuschen
sb.'s heart sinks [ˌhɑːt ˈsɪŋks]	jdm wird bang, jdm wird das Herz schwer
on cloud nine [ɒn ˌklaʊd ˈnaɪn]	auf Wolke sieben
to **feel let down** [fiːl ˌlet ˈdaʊn]	(von jdm/etw) enttäuscht sein
thrilled to bits [ˌθrɪld tə ˈbɪts]	(vor Freude) ganz aus dem Häuschen
to **be considered sth.** [bi kənˈsɪdəd]	als etw gelten
succession [səkˈseʃn]	Abfolge, Folge

page 16

primarily [praɪˈmerəli]	hauptsächlich
roughly [ˈrʌfli]	ungefähr
outcome [ˈaʊtkʌm]	Ergebnis
trust (of sb.) [trʌst]	Vertrauen (in jdn)
party official [ˌpɑːti əˈfɪʃl]	Parteifunktionär/in
to **be tempted to do sth.** [bi ˈtemptɪd tə]	versucht sein, etw zu tun
to **skimp on sth.** [ˈskɪmp ɒn]	an etw sparen, mit etw knausern
earthquake-proof [ˈɜːθkweɪk pruːf]	erdbebensicher
baby formula [ˈbeɪbi fɔːmjələ]	Babynahrung
to **embrace** [ɪmˈbreɪs]	annehmen
failure [ˈfeɪljə]	Scheitern, Versagen
to **fail** [feɪl]	scheitern, versagen
volcanic [vɒlˈkænɪk]	vulkanisch, Vulkan-
variety [vəˈraɪəti]	Art, Sorte
to **weather** [ˈweðə]	überstehen
calamity [kəˈlæməti]	Unheil, Katastrophe
unredeemable [ˌʌnrɪˈdiːməbl]	*hier:* unverzeihlich
policy [ˈpɒləsi]	Politik, Vorgehensweise
entire [ɪnˈtaɪə]	gesamt, ganz
gross [grəʊs]	brutto
to **precede** [prɪˈsiːd]	vorausgehen, vorangehen
by-product [ˈbaɪprɒdʌkt]	Nebenprodukt
to **tackle sth.** [ˈtækl]	etw angehen, etw in Angriff nehmen
covertly [ˈkʌvətli]	verdeckt, insgeheim
to **counsel** [ˈkaʊnsl]	raten
to **approach sth.** [əˈprəʊtʃ]	sich einer Sache nähern
crab [kræb]	Krebs
to **criticize** [ˈkrɪtɪsaɪz]	kritisieren
recommendation [ˌrekəmenˈdeɪʃn]	Empfehlung

page 17

grand [grænd]	groß, großartig
the essentials *pl.* [ði ɪˈsenʃlz]	die wesentlichen Dinge
editorial staff [edɪˌtɔːriəl ˈstɑːf]	Redaktion
to **publish** [ˈpʌblɪʃ]	veröffentlichen, herausbringen
special issue [ˌspeʃl ˈɪʃuː]	Sonderausgabe, Sonderheft
to **notice** [ˈnəʊtɪs]	feststellen
preoccupied [ˌprɪˈɒkjupaɪd]	besorgt
preparation [ˌprepəˈreɪʃn]	Vorbereitung
staff meeting [ˌstɑːf ˈmiːtɪŋ]	*hier:* Redaktionssitzung
to **seek** [siːk]	suchen
path [pɑːθ]	Weg
to **seek sth. out** [ˌsiːk ˈaʊt]	etw ausfindig machen
goal [gəʊl]	Ziel
to **review** [rɪˈvjuː]	überprüfen, begutachten, durcharbeiten
to **gather sth.** [ˈgæðə]	etw sammeln

to **conclude** [kən'klu:d]	folgern, den Schluss ziehen, zu dem Schluss kommen
to **assume** [ə'sju:m]	davon ausgehen, annehmen
to **stem from sth.** ['stem frəm]	auf etw zurückzuführen sein, von etw herrühren
accomplishment [ə'kʌmplɪʃmənt]	Leistung
physical ['fɪzɪkl]	körperlich, physisch
health [helθ]	Gesundheit
expertise [ˌekspɜ:'ti:z]	Kompetenz, Sachverstand, Fachwissen
to **make a point to do sth.** [ˌmeɪk ə 'pɔɪnt tə du]	es sich zur Aufgabe machen, etw zu tun; darauf Wert legen, etw zu tun
directed at sb. [də'rektɪd ət]	an/auf jdn gerichtet
random ['rændəm]	willkürlich, beliebig
kindness ['kaɪndnəs]	Freundlichkeit, Liebenswürdigkeit
to **perform sth.** [pə'fɔ:m]	etw ausführen
considerate [kən'sɪdərət]	aufmerksam, rücksichtsvoll
doer ['du:ə]	Handelnde/r
to **spread sth. out** [ˌspred 'aʊt]	etw verteilen
to **please sb.** [pli:z]	jdm gefallen, jdn zufrieden stellen
to **be conscious of sth.** [bi 'kɒnʃəs əv]	sich einer Sache bewusst sein
reward [rɪ'wɔ:d]	Belohnung, Gewinn
to **count one's blessings** [ˌkaʊnt wʌnz 'blesɪŋz]	dankbar sein (für das, was man hat)
grateful ['greɪtfl]	dankbar
frequency ['fri:kwənsi]	Häufigkeit
freshness ['freʃnəs]	Originalität, Frische
to **plague** [pleɪg]	plagen, heimsuchen
bankruptcy ['bæŋkrʌpsi]	Bankrott
to **assert** [ə'sɜ:t]	geltend machen
the big picture [ðə 'bɪg pɪktʃə]	das große Ganze
to **recover sth.** [rɪ'kʌvə]	etw wiedererlangen
to **set sth. aside (for sth.)** [ˌset ə'saɪd]	etw vorsehen (für etw)

page 18

to **spot** [spɒt]	erkennen
wilderness ['wɪldənəs]	Wildnis
valley ['væli]	Tal
to **frame** [freɪm]	einrahmen
mountain range ['maʊntən reɪndʒ]	Gebirgszug
to **inflate** [ɪn'fleɪt]	aufblasen
to **judge** [dʒʌdʒ]	urteilen
to **appear** [ə'pɪə]	scheinen
annoyed [ə'nɔɪd]	genervt, verärgert
comforts *pl.* ['kʌmfəts]	Annehmlichkeiten
to **be accustomed to sth.** [bi ə'kʌstəmd tə]	an etw gewohnt sein
rarely ['reəli]	selten
to **matter** ['mætə]	wichtig sein

UNIT 2

page 19

to **go places** [ˌgəʊ 'pleɪsɪz]	herumkommen, reisen
explorer [ɪk'splɔ:rə]	Entdecker/in
conveyor belt [kən'veɪə belt]	Förderband
guidebook ['gaɪdbʊk]	Reiseführer
napkin ['næpkɪn]	Serviette
local ['ləʊkl]	Einheimische/r
volume ['vɒlju:m]	Band, Buch
speciality [ˌspeʃi'æləti]	Spezialität
to **dine** [daɪn]	speisen, dinieren, essen
chain [tʃeɪn]	Kette
to **hire sb.** ['haɪə]	jdn engagieren
exhaustion [ɪg'zɔ:stʃən]	Erschöpfung
daylight ['deɪlaɪt]	Tageslicht, *hier:* Tagesanbruch
criterion (*pl.* **-a**) [kraɪ'tɪəriən, -iə]	Kriterium
hair dryer ['heə draɪə]	Fön
emergency [ɪ'mɜ:dʒənsi]	Notfall
solar-powered [ˌsəʊlə'paʊəd]	solarbetrieben
laundry ['lɔ:ndri]	Wäsche
food for thought [ˌfʊd fə 'θɔ:t]	ein Denkanstoß
to **lack sth.** [læk]	etw nicht haben
to **appreciate** [ə'pri:ʃieɪt]	zu schätzen wissen
to **curl up** [ˌkɜ:l 'ʌp]	sich zusammenrollen

page 20

to **struggle** ['strʌgl]	kämpfen, sich abmühen
to **balance sth. with sth.** ['bæləns wɪð]	etw mit etw vereinbaren, etw mit etw auf einen Nenner bringen
sustainability [səˌsteɪnə'bɪləti]	Nachhaltigkeit
to **dot the coast** [ˌdɒt ðə 'kəʊst]	entlang der Küste verstreut sein
renowned for sth. [rɪ'naʊnd fə]	für etw berühmt, für etw bekannt
pristine ['prɪsti:n]	makellos, unberührt
turquoise ['tɜ:kwɔɪz]	türkis(farben)
untouched [ʌn'tʌtʃt]	unberührt
shoreline ['ʃɔ:laɪn]	Küsten(linie)
to **be littered with sth.** [bi 'lɪtəd wɪð]	mit etw übersät sein
sewage ['su:ɪdʒ]	Abwasser
drive [draɪv]	Schub, Aktion, Antrieb, Schwung
reckless ['rekləs]	leichtsinnig, unbesonnen, rücksichtslos
to **lead the way** [ˌli:d ðə 'weɪ]	die Richtung weisen, es vormachen
to **preserve** [prɪ'zɜ:v]	erhalten, bewahren, schützen
unspoiled [ˌʌn'spɔɪld]	unberührt, unversehrt
sustainable [sə'steɪnə'bl]	nachhaltig
southernmost ['sʌðənməʊst]	südlichste/r/s
on the brink of sth. [ɒn ðə 'brɪŋk əv]	kurz vor etw
currently ['kʌrəntli]	im Moment, aktuell

delicate ['delɪkət]	empfindlich
ecosystem ['i:kəʊsɪstəm]	Ökosystem
remote [rɪ'məʊt]	entlegen
eco-friendly ['i:kəʊ frendli]	umweltfreundlich
resort [rɪ'zɔ:t]	Ferienanlage
to **acquire** [ə'kwaɪə]	kaufen
seemingly ['si:mɪŋli]	anscheinend
concern for sth. [kən'sɜ:n fə]	Sorge um etw, Rücksicht auf etw
bamboo [ˌbæm'bu:]	Bambus
to **occupy** ['ɒkjupaɪ]	*(Raum)* einnehmen
acre ['eɪkə]	Morgen *(ca. 4047qm)*
dorm (room) [dɔ:m]	Schlafsaal
secluded [sɪ'klu:dɪd]	abgeschieden
to **nestle** ['nesl]	sich schmiegen, eingebettet sein
sloping hill [ˌsləʊpɪŋ 'hɪl]	sanft ansteigender Hügel
water conservation ['wɔ:tə kɒnsəveɪʃn]	Wassersparen
waste-treatment facility ['weɪst tri:tmənt fəsɪləti]	Kläranlage
to **drain** [dreɪn]	abfließen
foresight ['fɔ:saɪt]	Voraussicht, Weitblick
to **hold on to sth.** [ˌhəʊld 'ɒn tə]	*hier:* etw behalten
resources [rɪ'sɔ:sɪz]	Ressourcen, Schätze
grassroots ['grɑ:sru:ts]	Basis-
volunteer [ˌvɒlən'tɪə]	Freiwillige/r, ehrenamtlich Tätige/r
off the beaten track [ɒf ðə ˌbi:tn 'træk]	abseits ausgetretener Pfade
to **pride oneself on sth.** ['praɪd əv]	auf etw stolz sein, sich etw auf etw zugute halten
cultural immersion programme [ˌkʌltʃərəl ɪ'mɜ:ʃn prəʊgræm]	*Programm zum Kennenlernen einer Kultur vor Ort*
wholesome ['həʊlsəm]	gesund, positiv
hospitality industry [ˌhɒspɪ'tæləti ɪndəstri]	Gastgewerbe
stunning ['stʌnɪŋ]	fantastisch, umwerfend
to **unlock** [ˌʌn'lɒk]	entschlüsseln, erschließen
to **ensure** [ɪn'ʃʊə]	sicherstellen, gewährleisten
to **replant** [ˌri:'plɑ:nt]	neu anpflanzen
coral reef [ˌkɒrəl 'ri:f]	Korallenriff
cyclone ['saɪkləʊn]	Wirbelsturm, Zyklon
value ['vælju:]	Wert
to **be aware of sth.** [bi ə'weə əv]	sich einer Sache bewusst sein

page 21

unconventional [ˌʌnkən'venʃənl]	unkonventionell
social enterprise [ˌsəʊʃl 'entəpraɪz]	soziales Unternehmen
living ['lɪvɪŋ]	lebendig
rough around the edges [ˌrʌf əraʊnd ði 'edʒɪz]	kantig, ungeschliffen
to **hand sth. over** [ˌhænd 'əʊvə]	etw (über-)geben
literally ['lɪtərəli]	buchstäblich
crate [kreɪt]	Kiste
tarp [tɑ:p]	Plane
to **gather** ['gæðə]	sich versammeln
to **reach out to sb.** [ˌri:tʃ 'aʊt tə]	jdn zu erreichen versuchen
the homeless [ðə 'həʊmləs]	Obdachlose
to **incorporate** [ɪn'kɔ:pəreɪt]	aufnehmen, einbauen, einbeziehen
homeless ['həʊmləs]	obdachlos
to **engage with sb.** [ɪn'geɪdʒ wɪð]	mit jdm in Dialog treten, mit jdm ins Gespräch kommen
walking tour ['wɔ:kɪŋ tʊə]	Führung, Rundgang
to **come about** [ˌkʌm ə'baʊt]	entstehen
wealth of sth. ['welθ əv]	Fülle von etw
outlet ['aʊtlet]	Ventil, Betätigungsfeld
source of income [ˌsɔ:s əv 'ɪnkʌm]	Einkommensquelle
society [sə'saɪəti]	Gesellschaft
yurt [jɜ:t]	Jurte
to **be all the rage** [bi ˌɔ:l ðə 'reɪdʒ]	der letzte Schrei sein
posh [pɒʃ]	schick, vornehm
to **spring up** [ˌsprɪŋ 'ʌp]	aus dem Boden sprießen
familiar [fə'mɪliə]	vertraut
structure ['strʌktʃə]	Gerüst, Rahmen
canvas ['kænvəs]	Leinwand
spacious ['speɪʃəs]	geräumig
to **evolve** [ɪ'vɒlv]	entstehen, sich entwickeln
nomad ['nəʊmæd]	Nomade/-in
foundation [faʊn'deɪʃn]	Stiftung
nomadic [nəʊ'mædɪk]	Nomaden-
adventurous [əd'ventʃərəs]	abenteuerlustig
herder ['hɜ:də]	Hirte/-in
4 × 4 [ˌfɔ: baɪ 'fɔ:]	Allradfahrzeug
steppe [step]	Steppe
host family [ˌhəʊst 'fæməli]	Gastfamilie
rural ['rʊərəl]	ländlich
custodian [kʌ'stəʊdiən]	Hüter/in, Wächter/in
heritage ['herɪtɪdʒ]	Erbe
guardian ['gɑ:diən]	Hüter/in
income asset ['ɪnkʌm æset]	*etwa:* Aktivposten, der Einkommen ermöglicht
tangible ['tændʒəbl]	spürbar, greifbar
testimony ['testɪməni]	Aussage
tuition [tju'ɪʃn]	Unterricht

page 22

to **skim** [skɪm]	*(Text)* überfliegen
hands-on [ˌhændz 'ɒn]	praktisch, praxisnah
modern comforts *pl.* [ˌmɒdn 'kʌmfəts]	moderne Annehmlichkeiten
shore [ʃɔ:]	Küste
measure ['meʒə]	Maßnahme
to **take measures** [ˌteɪk 'meʒəz]	Maßnahmen ergreifen
elderly ['eldəli]	älter, betagt
manners *pl.* ['mænəz]	Manieren, Umgangsformen
non-government(al) organization [nɒn gʌvən,mənt ɔ:gənaɪ'zeɪʃn]	Nichtregierungs-organisation
mediation [ˌmi:di'eɪʃn]	Vermittlung

page 23

inaccessible [ˌɪnək'sesəbl] unzugänglich
sparsely populated [ˌspɑːsli 'pɔpjuleɪtɪd] dünn besiedelt
privacy ['prɪvəsi] Privatsphäre
to **perceive** [pə'siːv] wahrnehmen
mind [maɪnd] Bewusstsein
intense(ly) [ɪn'tens] intensiv, stark
to **watch over sb./sth.** ['wɒtʃ əʊvə] sich um jdn/etw kümmern, über jdn/etw wachen
trait [treɪt] Charakterzug
honesty ['ɒnəsti] Ehrlichkeit
reliability [rɪˌlaɪə'bɪləti] Zuverlässigkeit
foolhardy ['fuːlhɑːdi] tollkühn, verwegen
heady ['hedi] berauscht
rash [ræʃ] impulsiv, unbesonnen
heedless ['hiːdləs] achtlos, unachtsam
distant ['dɪstənt] entfernt
fad [fæd] Modeerscheinung, kurzlebiger Trend
craze [kreɪz] Wahn, Modeerscheinung
reclusive [rɪ'kluːsɪv] zurückgezogen
defender [dɪ'fendə] Verteidiger
wise [waɪz] klug

page 24

package holiday ['pækɪdʒ hɒlədeɪ] Pauschalurlaub
self-catering holiday apartment [self ˌkeɪtərɪŋ 'hɒlədeɪ əpɑːtmənt] Ferienwohnung für Selbstversorger
to **flee sth.** [fliː] vor etw flüchten
to **flock** [flɒk] strömen
resort [rɪ'zɔːt] Urlaubsort, Ferienort
gulf [gʌlf] Golf
advent ['ædvent] Aufkommen, Beginn
affordable [ə'fɔːdəbl] erschwinglich, bezahlbar
to **lay the foundation** [ˌleɪ ðə faʊn'deɪʃn] den Grundstein legen
citizen ['sɪtɪzn] Bürger/in
overpriced [ˌəʊvə'praɪst] überteuert
to **associate** [ə'səʊʃieɪt] in Verbindung bringen, assoziieren
congested [kən'dʒestɪd] verstopft
traffic jam ['træfɪk dʒæm] Stau
overcrowding [ˌəʊvə'kraʊdɪŋ] Überfüllung
genuine ['dʒenjuɪn] echt, authentisch, wahr
unsightly [ˌʌn'saɪtli] unansehnlich
development [dɪ'veləpmənt] Bau, Bauprojekt
valuable ['væljuəbl] wertvoll
to **benefit sb.** ['benɪfɪt] jdm zugute kommen, jdm nutzen
tour operator ['tʊər ɒpəreɪtə] Reiseveranstalter
seasonal ['siːzənl] saisonal, saisonabhängig
wage [weɪdʒ] Lohn
massive ['mæsɪv] riesig, gewaltig, enorm
to **add to sth.** ['æd tə] zu etw beitragen, etw vergrößern
water shortage ['wɔːtə ʃɔːtɪdʒ] Wassermangel
engine ['endʒɪn] Lokomotive, Motor
economic growth [iːkəˌnɒmɪk 'grəʊθ] Wirtschaftswachstum
means [miːnz] Mittel, Möglichkeit
poverty ['pɒvəti] Armut
foreign exchange earnings *pl.* [ˌfɒrən ɪks'tʃeɪndʒ ɜːnɪŋz] Deviseneinnahmen
two-edged sword [ˌtuː edʒd 'sɔːd] zweischneidiges Schwert
ill-conceived [ˌɪl kən'siːvd] schlecht durchdacht, schlecht geplant
to **encourage** [ɪn'kʌrɪdʒ] fördern, anregen
otherwise ['ʌðəwaɪz] auch
ecotourism ['iːkəʊ tʊərɪzəm] Ökotourismus
to **conserve** [kən'sɜːv] schützen, bewahren
integral part [ˌɪntɪgrəl 'pɑːt] wesentlicher Bestandteil
eco-traveler *AE* ['iːkəʊ trævələ] Ökotourist/in
to **release** [rɪ'liːs] freisetzen
equivalent [ɪ'kwɪvələnt] Gegenwert, Entsprechung
to **emit** [ɪ'mɪt] ausstoßen, emittieren
numerous ['njuːmərəs] zahlreich
niche market ['niːʃ mɑːkɪt] Nischenmarkt
to **emerge** [ɪ'mɜːdʒ] aufkommen, entstehen
wildlife tourism ['waɪldlaɪf tʊərɪzəm] Safari-Tourismus
extent [ɪk'stent] Ausmaß
regardless of [rɪ'gɑːdləs əv] ganz gleich, egal

page 25

to **dismiss** [dɪs'mɪs] abtun, wegschicken, entlassen
crowded ['kraʊdɪd] überfüllt

page 26

long-haul flight [ˌlɒŋ hɔːl 'flaɪt] Langstreckenflug
to **weigh** [weɪ] gegeneinander abwägen
tan [tæn] Sonnenbräune
sun worshipper ['sʌn wɜːʃɪpə] Sonnenanbeter/in
to **crowd** [kraʊd] füllen, sich drängen
environmentalist [ɪnˌvaɪrən'mentəlɪst] Umweltschützer/in
sleet [sliːt] Schneeregen
household waste [ˌhaʊshəʊld 'weɪst] Haushaltsmüll
power supply ['paʊə səplaɪ] Stromversorgung
hydroelectric plant [haɪdrəʊɪˌlektrɪk 'plɑːnt] Wasserkraftwerk
renewable [rɪ'njuːəbl] erneuerbar
power ['paʊə] Strom
to **transform** [træns'fɔːm] verwandeln, umgestalten
geothermally-heated [dʒiəˌθɜːməli 'hiːtɪd] mit Erdwärmeheizung
pricey ['praɪsi] teuer
to **refuse** [rɪ'fjuːz] sich weigern
locale [ləʊ'kɑːl] Ort, Örtlichkeit, Region

dichotomy [daɪ'kɒtəmi]	Zwiespalt, Gegensatz
to **raise** [reɪz]	*(Frage, etc.)* aufwerfen
to **curb** [kɜ:b]	eindämmen, beschränken
frontier ['frʌntɪə]	Grenze
crusade [kru:'seɪd]	Kreuzzug, Feldzug
green-minded [ˌgri:n 'maɪndɪd]	umwelt(schutz)orientiert
wanderlust ['wɒndəlʌst]	Reiselust
pursuit (of sth.) [pə'sju:t]	Jagd (nach etw)
deeply ingrained [ˌdi:pli 'ɪngreɪnd]	tief verwurzelt
to **concede** [kən'si:d]	zugestehen
underneath [ˌʌndə'ni:θ]	unter
frothy ['frɒθi]	schäumend
surf [sɜ:f]	Brandung
all-time high [ˌɔ:l taɪm 'haɪ]	historischer Höchststand
to **board** [bɔ:d]	*(Flugzeug)* besteigen
significantly [sɪg'nɪfɪkəntli]	bezeichnenderweise
aviation [ˌeɪvi'eɪʃn]	Luftfahrt, Flugverkehr
to **account for sth.** [ə'kaʊnt fə]	etw ausmachen
conscious ['kɒnʃəs]	bewusst
excuse [ɪk'skju:s]	Ausrede
to **aggravate** ['ægrəveɪt]	verschlimmern
compelling [kəm'pelɪŋ]	zwingend, überzeugend
to **keep sth. up** [ˌki:p 'ʌp]	etw beibehalten
to **generate** ['dʒenəreɪt]	erzeugen
to **be at stake** [bi ət 'steɪk]	auf dem Spiel stehen
light-deprived ['laɪt dɪpraɪvd]	von Lichtmangel betroffen
entitlement [ɪn'taɪtlmənt]	Anspruch
to **fuel** ['fju:əl]	anheizen, anfachen
federation [ˌfedə'reɪʃn]	Verband

page 27

to **jolt** [dʒəʊlt]	aufrütteln, schockieren
hardware store ['hɑ:dweə stɔ:]	Eisenwarenhandlung, Baumarkt
eventually [ɪ'ventʃuəli]	irgendwann (einmal)
to **retire** [rɪ'taɪə]	sich zur Ruhe setzen
to **overcome** [ˌəʊvə'kʌm]	überwinden, hinwegkommen über
tan line ['tæn laɪn]	Bräunungsstreifen
entrepreneur [ˌɒntrəprə'nɜ:]	Unternehmer/in
solar panel [ˌsəʊlə 'pænl]	Solarmodul
property ['prɒpəti]	Grundstück
chlorine ['klɔ:ri:n]	Chlor
no matter how you twist and turn this thing [nəʊ ˌmætə haʊ jə 'twɪst ən 'tɜ:n ðɪs θɪŋ]	wie man es (auch) dreht und wendet
to **default on sth.** [dɪ'fɔ:lt ɒn]	mit etw *(Zahlung)* im Verzug sein
to **be a stickler for sth.** [bi ə 'stɪklə fə]	es mit etw sehr genau nehmen
grimace [grɪ'məs]	Grimasse
gas-guzzling ['gæs gʌzlɪŋ]	spritfressend
to **be sun-deprived** [bi 'sʌn dɪpraɪvd]	mit wenig Sonne auskommen müssen
role model ['rəʊl mɒdl]	Vorbild
demand [dɪ'mɑ:nd]	Forderung
expressly [ɪk'spresli]	ausdrücklich
construction [kən'strʌkʃn]	Bau
regulations *pl.* [ˌregju'leɪʃnz]	Vorschriften, Bestimmungen
release [rɪ'li:s]	Freisetzung
aircraft ['eəkrɑ:ft]	Flugzeug

page 28

to **invent** [ɪn'vent]	erfinden
to **be entitled to sth.** [bi ɪn'taɪtld tə]	zu etw berechtigt sein, auf etw einen Anspruch haben
deep-rooted ['di:p ru:tɪd]	tief verwurzelt
practice ['præktɪs]	Praktik
obligation [ˌɒblɪ'geɪʃn]	Verpflichtung
to **sin** [sɪn]	sündigen
in this respect [ɪn ðɪs rɪ'spekt]	in dieser Hinsicht
to **ban** [bæn]	verbieten, abschaffen
concern [kən'sɜ:n]	Anliegen, Angelegenheit
to **sympathize with sth.** ['sɪmpəθaɪz wɪð]	Verständnis für etw haben
to **edit** ['edɪt]	redigieren
final draft [ˌfaɪnl 'drɑ:ft]	endgültige Fassung

page 29

records ['rekɔ:dz]	Daten, Unterlagen, Dokumentation
gap year ['gæp jɪə]	*Jahr zwischen Schulabschluss und Studienbeginn*
gender ['dʒendə]	Geschlecht

page 30

to **promote** [prə'məʊt]	fördern
to **support sth.** [sə'pɔ:t]	etw *(Argument, etc.)* untermauern
to **leaf through** ['li:f θru:]	durchblättern
appropriate [ə'prəʊpriət]	passend, angemessen
fortnight ['fɔ:tnaɪt]	vierzehn Tage
hot air balloon [ˌhɒt eə bə'lu:n]	Heißluftballon
to **cruise** [kru:z]	eine Kreuzfahrt/Schiffsreise machen
cruise [kru:z]	Kreuzfahrt
to **rule sth. out** [ˌru:l 'aʊt]	etw ausschließen
to **be struck on sth.** [bi 'strʌk ɒn]	von etw beeindruckt sein
to **be up to sb.** [bi 'ʌp tə]	bei jdm liegen, jds Entscheidung sein
agreement [ə'gri:mənt]	Zustimmung
preference ['prefrəns]	Vorliebe
rejection [rɪ'dʒekʃn]	Ablehnung, Zurückweisung
to **allocate** ['æləkeɪt]	zuweisen

page 31

departure lounge [dɪ'pɑ:tʃə laʊndʒ]	Abflughalle
to **head** [hed]	unterwegs sein nach, sich aufmachen nach
to **be fed up with sth.** [bi ˌfed 'ʌp wɪð]	von etw die Nase voll haben
to **be starved of sth.** [bi 'stɑ:vd əv]	von etw nicht genug bekommen, nach etw ausgehungert sein
nervous breakdown [ˌnɜ:vəs 'breɪkdaʊn]	Nervenzusammenbruch

UNIT 3

page 32

grooming salon ['gru:mɪŋ sælɒn]	*etwa:* Hundesalon
associate [ə'səʊʃiət]	Teilhaber/in, Partner/in
retailer ['ri:teɪlə]	Einzelhändler/in
pet parent ['pet peərənt]	Tierbesitzer/in, Herrchen/ Frauchen
responsibility [rɪˌspɒnsə'bɪləti]	Aufgabe, Aufgabengebiet, Zuständigkeit
appointment [ə'pɔɪntmənt]	Termin
to brush [brʌʃ]	bürsten
to clip nails [ˌklɪp 'neɪlz]	Nägel schneiden
to perform [pə'fɔ:m]	durchführen, ausführen
to groom [gru:m]	pflegen
benefits *pl.* ['benɪfɪts]	(Sozial-)Leistungen
health plan *AE* ['helθ plæn]	Krankenversicherung
career advancement [kə'rɪə ədvɑ:nsmənt]	beruflicher Aufstieg
phone operator ['fəʊn ɒpəreɪtə]	Telefonist/in
bilingual [ˌbaɪ'lɪŋgwəl]	zweisprachig
ambulatory ['æmbjulətri]	ambulant
surgery ['sɜ:dʒəri]	Chirurgie, OP
switchboard operator ['swɪtʃbɔ:d ɒpəreɪtə]	Telefonist/in
outpatient ['aʊtpeɪʃnt]	ambulante/r Patient/in
outpatient hospital ['aʊtpeɪʃnt hɒspɪtl]	Tagesklinik
requirement [rɪ'kwaɪəmənt]	Anforderung
high volume [ˌhaɪ 'vɒlju:m]	*hier:* mit hohem Patienten-aufkommen
front desk [ˌfrʌnt 'desk]	Rezeption, Empfang
etiquette ['etɪket]	Umgangsformen
reliable [rɪ'laɪəbl]	zuverlässig
Associate's degree [əˌsəʊʃiəts dɪ'gri:]	*Associate*-Abschluss
to appeal to sb. [ə'pi:l tə]	jdn ansprechen, jdn reizen

page 33

to face sth. [feɪs]	vor etw stehen, mit etw konfrontiert sein/werden, sich einer Sache stellen (müssen)
turmoil ['tɜ:mɔɪl]	Aufruhr, Durcheinander
Spaniard ['spænjəd]	Spanier/in
to flee for ['fli: fə]	flüchten nach
wine merchant ['waɪn mɜ:tʃənt]	Weinhändler/in, Weinhandel/-handlung
unexpected(ly) [ˌʌnɪk'spektɪd]	unerwartet
overall [ˌəʊvər'ɔ:l]	allgemein, Gesamt-
boom-to-bust [ˌbu:m tə 'bʌst]	wirtschaftlich instabil *(wörtlich: von Boom zu Bankrott)*
native country [ˌneɪtɪv 'kʌntri]	Heimatland
far apart [ˌfɑ:r ə'pɑ:t]	weit (voneinander) entfernt
longer-term [ˌlɒŋgə 'tɜ:m]	längerfristig
to exceed [ɪk'si:d]	übertreffen
university-educated [ˌju:nɪ'vɜ:səti edʒukeɪtɪd]	mit Universitätsausbildung
shortage ['ʃɔ:tɪdʒ]	Mangel, Knappheit
to draw [drɔ:]	anziehen, anlocken
skilled [skɪld]	(gut) ausgebildet
on track [ɒn 'træk]	auf Kurs
Federal Employment Agency [ˌfedərəl ɪm'plɔɪmənt eɪdʒənsi]	Bundesarbeitsagentur
shortfall ['ʃɔ:tfɔ:l]	Mangel, Defizit
skilled worker [ˌskɪld 'wɜ:kə]	Facharbeiter/in
domestic [də'mestɪk]	einheimisch
thus [ðʌs]	daher, deshalb
to woo [wu:]	(um-, an-)werben
economic crisis [i:kəˌnɒmɪk 'kraɪsɪs]	Wirtschaftskrise
Chamber of Commerce [ˌtʃeɪmbər əf 'kɒmɜ:s]	Handelskammer
informational session [ɪnfəˌmeɪʃənl 'seʃn]	Informationsveranstaltung
emigration [emɪ'greɪʃn]	Auswanderung
major ['meɪdʒə]	groß, bedeutend, wichtig
starting salary ['stɑ:tɪŋ sæləri]	Anfangsgehalt
some [sʌm]	*hier:* ungefähr
permanent contract [ˌpɜ:mənənt 'kɒntrækt]	unbefristeter Vertrag
temporary employment agency [ˌtemprəri ɪm'plɔɪmənt eɪdʒənsi]	Zeitarbeitsagentur
contract ['kɒntrækt]	Vertrag
engineering firm [ˌendʒɪ'nɪərɪŋ fɜ:m]	Ingenieurbüro
in line with sth. [ɪn 'laɪn wɪð]	in Einklang mit etw
spokesperson ['spəʊkspɜ:sn]	Sprecher/in
demand (for sth.) [dɪ'mɑ:nd]	Nachfrage (nach etw)
job centre ['dʒɒbsentə]	Arbeitsamt

page 34

chancellor ['tʃɑ:nsələ]	Kanzler/in
to extend an invitation to sb. [ɪkˌstend ən ɪnvɪ'teɪʃn tə]	jdn einladen
to sense [sens]	spüren
placement agency ['pleɪsmənt eɪdʒənsi]	Arbeitsvermittlung
to grab [græb]	(sich etw) packen, nehmen
to expand [ɪk'spænd]	ausweiten
unique [ju'ni:k]	einzigartig, einmalig
to work closely with sb. [ˌwɜ:k 'kləʊsli wɪð]	eng mit jdm zusammenarbeiten
to sign [saɪn]	unterschreiben, unterzeichnen
to man [mæn]	besetzen, bedienen
to take sth. in stride [ˌteɪk ɪn 'straɪd]	locker mit etw umgehen
temporary ['temprəri]	befristet

to **make it past sth.** [ˌmeɪk ɪt 'pɑːst]	etw überstehen
trial period [ˌtraɪəl 'pɪəriəd]	Probezeit
rapidly ['ræpɪdli]	schnell
chef [ʃef]	Koch/Köchin, Küchenchef/in
to **settle down** [ˌsetl 'daʊn]	sich niederlassen, sesshaft werden

page 35

worrisome ['wʌrɪsəm]	Besorgnis erregend
applicant ['æplɪkənt]	Bewerber/in
considerably [kən'sɪdərəbli]	erheblich, beträchtlich

page 36

to **conduct** [kən'dʌkt]	durchführen
performance [pə'fɔːməns]	Leistung
assessment [ə'sesmənt]	Beurteilung, Bewertung
to **sweat sth.** [swet]	sich um etw Sorgen machen
concern [kən'sɜːn]	Bedenken, Sorge(n)
to **fall behind** [ˌfɔːl bɪ'haɪnd]	zurückbleiben, in Rückstand geraten
anxiety [æŋ'zaɪəti]	Angst, Sorge
chatter ['tʃætə]	Gerede
to **raise sb.** [reɪz]	jdn aufziehen, jdn großziehen
reminder [rɪ'maɪndə]	Mahnung, Erinnerung
astronomically [ˌæstrə'nɒmɪkli]	astronomisch, *hier:* unfassbar, unglaublich
to **release** [rɪ'liːs]	veröffentlichen
lame [leɪm]	lahm, schwach
meaningless ['miːnɪŋləs]	sinnlos, wenig aussagekräftig, unbedeutend
commonsense [ˌkɒmən 'sens]	vernünftig
ranking ['ræŋkɪŋ]	Rangliste
substantial [səb'stænʃl]	erheblich, wesentlich
pack [pæk]	Rudel, Meute
to **lag** [læg]	zurückliegen, hinterherhinken
to **receive top honors** *AE* [rɪˌsiːv ˌtɒp 'ɒnəz]	den ersten Preis bekommen
to **draw a conclusion** [ˌdrɔː ə kən'kluːʒn]	einen Schluss ziehen, eine Schlussfolgerung ziehen
breathless ['breθləs]	atemlos, *hier:* aufgeregt, voreilig
to **declare** [dɪ'kleə]	erklären, ernennen
representative sample [reprɪˌzentətɪv 'sɑːmpl]	repräsentative Stichprobe
to **be up against sth.** [bi 'ʌp əgenst]	einer Sache gegenüberstehen, es mit etw zu tun haben
to **fail to do sth.** [ˌfeɪl tə du]	es nicht schaffen, etw zu tun, etw nicht tun können
to **capture** ['kæptʃə]	erfassen
grade *AE* [greɪd]	Klasse, Klassenstufe
to **fail a test** [ˌfeɪl ə 'test]	eine Prüfung nicht bestehen
life path ['laɪf pɑːθ]	Lebensweg
high-stakes test ['haɪ steɪks 'test]	alles entscheidende Prüfung
curb [kɜːb]	Bordstein, Straßenrand

page 37

undoing [ʌn'duːɪŋ]	Verderben, Untergang
policymaker ['pɒləsimeɪkə]	politische/r Entscheidungsträger/in
to **scramble to do sth.** ['skræmbl tə du]	händeringend versuchen, etw zu tun, sich dringend bemühen, etw zu tun
anaemic [ə'niːmɪk]	kraftlos, blass, blutarm, blutleer
to **address a challenge** [əˌdres ə 'tʃælɪndʒ]	eine Herausforderung annehmen
complacent [kəm'pleɪsnt]	selbstzufrieden, selbstgefällig
to **maintain a perspective** [meɪnˌteɪn ə pə'spektɪv]	alles in Relation sehen
superior [suː'pɪəriə]	überlegen
variety [və'raɪəti]	Vielfalt
legal system [ˌliːgl 'sɪstəm]	Rechtssystem
property rights *pl.* ['prɒpəti raɪts]	Eigentumsrechte
trade [treɪd]	Handel
to **matter to sth.** ['mætə tə]	für etw wichtig sein
competitiveness [kəm'petətɪvnəs]	Wettbewerbsfähigkeit
to **hearten** ['hɑːtn]	ermutigen
to **crunch the numbers** [ˌkrʌntʃ ðə 'nʌmbəz]	die Zahlen durchrechnen
crucially ['kruːʃli]	vor allem
significant [sɪg'nɪfɪkənt]	bedeutend, maßgeblich
pronounced [prə'naʊnst]	ausgeprägt
to **account for sth.** [ə'kaʊnt fə]	etw erklären, etw nachweisen
What's the takeaway? [ˌwɒts ðə 'teɪkəweɪ]	Was sagt uns das?
troubling ['trʌblɪŋ]	beunruhigend
solvable ['sɒlvəbl]	lösbar
to **compete with sb./sth.** [kəm'piːt wɪð]	mit jdm/etw konkurrieren, mit jdm/etw im Wettbewerb stehen
to **swamp** [swɒmp]	überschwemmen
in terms of [ɪn 'tɜːmz əv]	-mäßig, hinsichtlich, was ... betrifft
to **obsess about sth.** [əb'ses əbaʊt]	sich zwanghaft mit etw beschäftigen
gifted ['gɪftɪd]	begabt
US Census Bureau [juː ˌes 'sensəs bjʊərəʊ]	Statistisches Bundesamt der USA
white-collar profession [waɪt ˌkɒlə prə'feʃn]	Angestelltenberuf
core [kɔː]	Kern(-)
to **constrain** [kən'streɪn]	einengen, einschränken
social mobility [ˌsəʊʃl məʊ'bɪləti]	soziale Mobilität
completion [kəm'pliːʃn]	Abschluss, Beendigung
to **earn a degree** [ˌɜːn ə dɪ'griː]	einen Abschluss erwerben
to **outcompete** [ˌaʊtkəm'piːt]	einholen, aus dem Feld schlagen
inequitable [ɪn'ekwɪtəbl]	ungerecht
distribution of wealth [dɪstrɪˌbjuːʃn əv 'welθ]	Vermögensverteilung
prospect ['prɒspekt]	Aussicht

page 38

to **score** [skɔː]	*(Ergebnis)* erzielen
to **arouse** [ə'raʊz]	auslösen, hervorrufen
to **constitute** ['kɒnstɪtjuːt]	ausmachen, bilden
to **administer** [əd'mɪnɪstə]	durchführen
to **recruit** [rɪ'kruːt]	rekrutieren, anwerben
low-wage [ˌləʊ 'weɪdʒ]	schlecht bezahlt, Niedriglohn-
down-hearted [ˌdaʊn 'hɑːtɪd]	entmutigt, niedergeschlagen
indifference [ɪn'dɪfrəns]	Gleichgültigkeit
cautious ['kɔːʃəs]	vorsichtig
to **disagree with sb.** [ˌdɪsə'griː wɪð]	jdm nicht zustimmen

page 39

metaphorical [ˌmetə'fɒrɪkl]	metaphorisch
decisive [dɪ'saɪsɪv]	entscheidend
to **perform** [pə'fɔːm]	abschneiden *(in einer Prüfung, etc.)*, Leistung(en) bringen
to **grant** [grɑːnt]	bewilligen, gewähren
to **poison** ['pɔɪzn]	vergiften

page 40

workforce ['wɜːkfɔːs]	Arbeitskräfte
for instance [fər 'ɪnstəns]	zum Beispiel
to **recognize** ['rekəgnaɪz]	anerkennen, zugeben
upward ['ʌpwəd]	aufwärts, nach oben
jeopardy ['dʒepədi]	Gefahr
to **obtain** [əb'teɪn]	erhalten, bekommen
to **guarantee** [ˌgærən'tiː]	garantieren
forecast ['fɔːkɑːst]	Vorhersage, Prognose
rate [reɪt]	Quote
comparatively [kəm'pærətɪvli]	vergleichsweise, relativ
to **stress** [stres]	betonen
to **let sb. down** [ˌlet 'daʊn]	jdn im Stich lassen, jdn enttäuschen
prerequisite [priː'rekwəsɪt]	Voraussetzung, Bedingung
bureaucratic [ˌbjuərə'krætɪk]	bürokratisch
government-run ['gʌvənmənt rʌn]	staatlich
to **secure sth.** [sɪ'kjuə]	sich etw sichern
manual work [ˌmænjuəl 'wɜːk]	körperliche Arbeit, handwerkliche Arbeit
thereby [ˌðeə'baɪ]	dadurch
lucrative ['luːkrətɪv]	einträglich

page 41

compound ['kɒmpaʊnd]	zusammengesetzt

page 42

labour ['leɪbə]	Arbeit
brief(ly) ['briːf]	kurz
corporation [ˌkɔːpə'reɪʃn]	Unternehmen, Konzern
demographic change [deməˌgræfɪk 'tʃeɪndʒ]	demographischer Wandel
researcher [rɪ'sɜːtʃə]	Forscher/in
threatening ['θretnɪŋ]	bedrohlich
labour market ['leɪbə mɑːkɪt]	Arbeitsmarkt
early retirement [ˌɜːli rɪ'taɪəmənt]	Vorruhestand
condition [kən'dɪʃn]	*hier:* Krankheit
prevention [prɪ'venʃn]	Vorbeugung
urgent(ly) ['ɜːdʒənt]	dringend
supply [sə'plaɪ]	Angebot
to **turn sb. out** [ˌtɜːn 'aʊt]	jdn hervorbringen
overwhelmed [ˌəʊvə'welmd]	überfordert
to **take action** [ˌteɪk 'ækʃn]	Maßnahmen ergreifen
in-house [ˌɪn 'haʊs]	betriebsintern
vital ['vaɪtl]	unerlässlich, lebensnotwendig
to **render** ['rendə]	machen
idle ['aɪdl]	untätig
scarce [skeəs]	knapp
unified ['juːnɪfaɪd]	einheitlich
emerging country [ɪˌmɜːdʒɪŋ 'kʌntri]	Schwellenland

page 43

unemployment benefits [ˌʌnɪm'plɔɪmənt benɪfɪts]	Arbeitslosenunterstützung
ceased operations [ˌsiːst ɒpə'reɪʃnz]	Geschäftsbetrieb eingestellt
vacant ['veɪkənt]	leer stehend
tenant ['tenənt]	Pächter/in, Mieter/in
to **adopt** [ə'dɒpt]	übernehmen, *hier:* ergreifen
practicality [ˌpræktɪ'kæləti]	praktische Durchführbarkeit
to **lower** ['ləʊə]	senken
admission [əd'mɪʃn]	Zulassung
to **enrol** [ɪn'rəʊl]	sich einschreiben
to **eliminate** [ɪ'lɪmɪneɪt]	abschaffen
tuition fee [tjuˈɪʃn fiː]	Studiengebühr

page 44

to **be beset by sth.** [bi bɪ'set baɪ]	von etw heimgesucht werden, von etw befallen sein
pathetic [pə'θetɪk]	jämmerlich, armselig
stodgy ['stɒdʒi]	schwerfällig
to **adapt to sth.** [ə'dæpt tə]	sich an etw anpassen
steady ['stedi]	solide, stabil
reformed [rɪ'fɔːmd]	geläutert, verbessert
to **emerge** [ɪ'mɜːdʒ]	hervortreten, in Erscheinung treten
dominant ['dɒmɪnənt]	beherrschend, vorherrschend
to **account for sth.** [ə'kaʊnt fə]	für etw verantwortlich sein
neat [niːt]	gepflegt
due to ['djuː tə]	aufgrund von
modest ['mɒdɪst]	bescheiden
to **lecture sb.** ['lektʃə]	jdn belehren
to **boast about sth.** ['bəʊst əbaʊt]	mit etw angeben/prahlen

UNIT 4

page 45

bullying ['bʊliɪŋ] — Mobben, Mobbing
bulletin ['bʊlətɪn] — Mitteilung, Posting
horrendous [hɒ'rendəs] — grauenhaft, entsetzlich
to **call sb. names** [ˌkɔːl 'neɪmz] — jdn beleidigen
to **curse** [kɜːs] — fluchen, (jdn) verfluchen
to **sob** [sɒb] — schluchzen
to **commit suicide** [kəˌmɪt 'suːɪsaɪd] — Selbstmord begehen
to **hang oneself** [hæŋ] — sich erhängen
closet ['klɒzɪt] — Wandschrank, Kammer
precious ['preʃəs] — kostbar, wertvoll
to **tackle sth.** ['tækl] — gegen etw vorgehen
to **put sb. behind bars** [ˌpʊt bɪhaɪnd 'bɑːz] — jdn hinter Gitter bringen

page 46

freedom of speech [ˌfriːdəm əf 'spiːtʃ] — Redefreiheit, Recht auf freie Rede
to **wrestle** ['resl] — sich abmühen, zu kämpfen haben
free speech [ˌfriː 'spiːtʃ] — Redefreiheit
civility [sɪ'vɪlɪti] — Anstand, Bürgersinn
a cop on the beat [ə ˌkɒp ɒn ðə 'biːt] — ein Polizist auf Streife
harassment ['hærəsmənt] — Belästigung, Übergriff(e)
police squad [pə'liːs skwɒd] — Polizeitruppe, -einheit, -kommando
to **charge sb. with sth.** ['tʃɑːdʒ wɪð] — Tatvorwurf gegen jdn erheben
to **violate** ['vaɪəleɪt] — *(Gesetz, etc.)* verletzen
terms of service [ˌtɜːmz əf 'sɜːvɪs] — Nutzungsbedingungen
on the front line [ɒn ðə ˌfrʌnt 'laɪn] — an vorderster Front
prominence ['prɒmɪnəns] — Bekanntheit, Stellenwert
arbiter ['ɑːbɪtə] — Instanz
to **determine** [dɪ'tɜːmɪn] — bestimmen
Supreme Court [suˌpriːm 'kɔːt] — *höchster Gerichtshof der USA*
justice ['dʒʌstɪs] — Richter/in
critic ['krɪtɪk] — Kritiker/in
abuse [ə'bjuːs] — Missbrauch, Beschimpfung(en)
to **put sb. at risk** [ˌpʊt ət 'rɪsk] — jdn gefährden
privacy policy ['prɪvəsi pɒlɪsi] — Datenschutz(bestimmungen)
to **threaten (sth. against sb.)** ['θretn] — (jdn mit etw) bedrohen
to **report** [rɪ'pɔːt] — melden, anzeigen
law enforcement authority [ˌlɔː ɪn'fɔːsmənt ɔːθɒrəti] — Strafverfolgungsbehörde
offender [ə'fendə] — Straftäter/in
to **prosecute sb.** ['prɒsɪkjuːt] — jdn strafrechtlich verfolgen
public figure [ˌpʌblɪk 'fɪgə] — Person des öffentlichen Lebens
abusive [ə'bjuːsɪv] — beleidigend, missbräuchlich
to **flag** [flæg] — markieren
intent [ɪn'tent] — Absicht
high-visibility [ˌhaɪ vɪzə'bɪləti] — öffentlichkeitswirksam, mit hoher Außenwirkung

page 47

rogue [rəʊg] — Einzelgänger, schwarzes Schaf
antigay [ˌænti'geɪ] — schwulenfeindlich
threat [θret] — Drohung
to **track sth. down** [ˌtræk 'daʊn] — etw aufspüren, etw ausfindig machen
to **shut sth. down** [ˌʃʌt 'daʊn] — etw schließen
taunt [tɔːnt] — höhnische Bemerkung, Hänselei
incident ['ɪnsɪdənt] — Vorfall
hidden from casual view [ˌhɪdn frəm ˌkæʒuəl 'vjuː] — im Verborgenen
mind-numbing ['maɪnd nʌmɪŋ] — stumpfsinnig
meanness ['miːnnəs] — Gemeinheit(en)
insult ['ɪnsʌlt] — Beleidigung
thorny ['θɔːni] — heikel
to **police** [pə'liːs] — überwachen, kontrollieren
to **decline** [dɪ'klaɪn] — (es) ablehnen
to **surface** ['sɜːfɪs] — auftauchen, aufkommen
repudiation [rɪˌpjuːdi'eɪʃn] — Zurückweisung, Ablehnung
death threat ['deθ θret] — Morddrohung
to **involve** [ɪn'vɒlv] — einbeziehen, beteiligen
to **offend** [ə'fend] — (jdn) beleidigen, (jdn) verletzen, Ärgernis erregen
to **cross the line** [ˌkrɒs ðə 'laɪn] — zu weit gehen, eine/die Grenze überschreiten
supervisor ['suːpəvaɪzə] — Vorgesetzte/r
refusal [rɪ'fjuːzl] — Weigerung
to **seek** [siːk] — versuchen
to **walk a delicate line** [wɔːl ə ˌdelɪkət 'laɪn] — sich auf einem schmalen Grat bewegen
denial [dɪ'naɪəl] — Leugnung
Jew [dʒuː] — Jude/Jüdin
associate dean [əˌsəʊʃiət 'diːn] — stellvertretende/r Dekan/in
thoughtful ['θɔːtfl] — umsichtig, bedacht
soft-spoken [ˌsɒft 'spəʊkən] — zurückhaltend, leise, bescheiden
to **make for sb.** ['meɪk fə] — jdn abgeben, jdn darstellen
unlikely [ʌn'laɪkli] — unwahrscheinlich
enforcer [ɪn'fɔːsə] — Vollzugs-/Vollstreckungsbeamte/r, Gesetzeshüter/in
archaeology major [ˌɑːkɪ'ɒlədʒi meɪdʒə] — jd, der/die Archäologie im Hauptfach studiert (hat)
underbelly ['ʌndəbeli] — Schattenseite
to **handle sth.** ['hændl] — mit etw umgehen, mit etw zurecht kommen

page 48

to **permit** ['pɜːmɪt] — erlauben, gestatten
to **gain** [geɪn] — erlangen, erreichen
to **bring sb. to justice** [ˌbrɪŋ tə 'dʒʌstɪs] — jdn vor Gericht stellen, jdn zur Rechenschaft ziehen
influential [ˌɪnflu'enʃl] — einflussreich
to **take advantage of sth.** [ˌteɪk əd'vɑːntɪdʒ əv] — etw ausnutzen

to **overwhelm** [ˌəʊvəˈwelm]	überwältigen
offensive [əˈfensɪv]	beleidigend
offence [əˈfens]	Straftat
agreement [əˈgriːmənt]	Vereinbarung
rude [ruːd]	unhöflich, unverschämt
seldom [ˈseldəm]	selten
to **try** [traɪ]	(vor Gericht) verhandeln, (jdn) vor Gericht stellen
court of law [ˌkɔːt əv ˈlɔː]	Gericht, Gerichtshof

page 49

to **confiscate** [ˈkɒnfɪskeɪt]	konfiszieren
perpetrator [ˈpɜːpɪtreɪtə]	Täter/in
vicious [ˈvɪʃəs]	boshaft, bösartig
careless [ˈkeələs]	nachlässig, fahrlässig
to **take pains** [ˌteɪk ˈpeɪnz]	sich (große) Mühe geben
to **display** [dɪˈspleɪ]	aufweisen, an den Tag legen
unimaginably [ˌʌnɪˈmædʒɪnəbli]	unvorstellbar
throughout [θruːˈaʊt]	durchwegs
to **come across sth.** [ˌkʌm əˈkrɒs]	auf etw stoßen, etw finden
to **get involved** [ˌget ɪnˈvɒlvd]	sich beteiligen, sich einmischen
drug prevention [ˈdrʌg prɪˈvenʃn]	Suchtprävention

page 50

to **launch** [lɔːntʃ]	starten
to **eclipse sth.** [ɪˈklɪps]	etw in den Schatten stellen
struggle [ˈstrʌgl]	Kampf
to **contain** [kənˈteɪn]	eindämmen, unter Kontrolle bringen
let alone [let əˈləʊn]	geschweige denn
illicit [ɪˈlɪsɪt]	illegal
to **spew** [spjuː]	speien
malignant [məˈlɪgnənt]	bösartig, heimtückisch
glimmer of hope [ˌglɪmər əv ˈhəʊp]	Hoffnungsschimmer
extraordinary [ɪkˈstrɔːdnri]	außergewöhnlich
scourge [skɜːdʒ]	Geißel
Secretary General [ˌsekrətri ˈdʒenrəl]	Generalsekretär/in
resounding failure [rɪˌzaʊndɪŋ ˈfeɪljə]	eklatanter Misserfolg
to **head sth.** [hed]	etw leiten
proven [ˈpruːvn]	erprobt, erwiesen
to **regulate** [ˈregjuleɪt]	(gesetzlich) regeln
to **criminalise** *BE* [ˈkrɪmɪnlaɪz]	kriminalisieren
tycoon [taɪˈkuːn]	(Industrie-)Magnat
to **blast sth.** [blɑːst]	etw scharf kritisieren, etw verreißen
to **drive** [draɪv]	treiben, antreiben, lenken
convenience [kənˈviːniəns]	Bequemlichkeit, Nutzen
courier [ˈkʊriə]	Kurier
availability [əˌveɪləˈbɪləti]	Verfügbarkeit
to **hand** [hænd]	übergeben, überreichen
to **decriminalise** *BE* [diːˈkrɪmɪnəlaɪz]	entkriminalisieren
legal regulation [ˌliːgl regjuˈleɪʃn]	gesetzliche Bestimmungen
to **wrestle sth. from sb.** [ˈresl frəm]	jdm etw entreißen
to **adopt** [əˈdɒpt]	einführen, übernehmen, annehmen
traction [ˈtrækʃn]	Zugkraft
external affairs [ɪkˌstɜːnl əˈfeəz]	auswärtige Angelegenheiten
recession [rɪˈseʃn]	Rezession
costly [ˈkɒstli]	teuer
unsustainable [ˌʌnsəˈsteɪnəˈbl]	nicht tragfähig, unhaltbar
unintended [ˌʌnɪnˈtendɪd]	unbeabsichtigt
savage [ˈsævɪdʒ]	wild, wüst

page 51

on the doorstep [ɒn ðə ˈdɔːstep]	direkt vor der Haustür
narco-cartel [ˌnɑːkəʊ kɑːˈtel]	(*lateinamerikanisches*) Drogenkartell
bullish [ˈbʊlɪʃ]	dickköpfig, (übertrieben) selbstsicher
ally [ˈælaɪ]	Verbündete/r, Bündnispartner/in
to **raise** [reɪz]	erhöhen, *(Thema, etc.)* ansprechen
to **feed** [fiːd]	befeuern
specious [ˈspiːʃəs]	fadenscheinig, hanebüchen
justification [ˌdʒʌstɪfɪˈkeɪʃn]	Rechtfertigung, Begründung
evidence to the contrary [ˌevɪdəns tə ðə ˈkɒntrəri]	gegenteilige Anhaltspunkte/Hinweise
to **emphasise** *BE* [ˈemfəsaɪz]	betonen
seizure [ˈsiːʒə]	Beschlagnahme
arrest [əˈrest]	Verhaftung
declining [dɪˈklaɪnɪŋ]	rückläufig, zurückgehend
zero tolerance [ˌzɪərəʊ ˈtɒlərəns]	Nulltoleranz
blunt(ly) [blʌnt]	unverblümt, rundweg
to **reject** [rɪˈdʒekt]	zurückweisen, ablehnen
to **cut** [kʌt]	senken
jail [dʒeɪl]	Gefängnis
approach [əˈprəʊtʃ]	Ansatz, Herangehensweise
downside [ˈdaʊnsaɪd]	Nachteil(e), Kehrseite
prohibition [ˌprəʊɪˈbɪʃn]	Verbot
trillion [ˈtrɪljən]	Billion
in terms of [ɪn ˈtɜːmz əv]	in Form von
wreckage [ˈrekɪdʒ]	Trümmer
home insurance [ˌhəʊm ɪnˈʃʊərəns]	Hausversicherung
arguably [ˈɑːgjuəbli]	möglicherweise, wohl
to **urge** [ɜːdʒ]	drängen, auffordern
to **counter sth.** [ˈkaʊntə]	einer Sache entgegenwirken
to **pretend** [prɪˈtend]	so tun, als ob
once [wʌns]	ehemals
to **push sb. aside** [ˌpʊʃ əˈsaɪd]	jdn verdrängen
estimate [ˈestɪmət]	Schätzung
bonanza [bəˈnænzə]	Goldgrube
ballot initiative [ˈbælət ɪnɪʃətɪv]	Wählerinitiative
test case [ˈtest keɪs]	Präzedenzfall

evidence ['evɪdəns]	Beweis(e), Nachweis, Hinweis(e), Indizien
criminal justice overcrowding [ˌkrɪmɪnl ˌdʒʌstɪs əʊvə'kraʊdɪŋ]	Überbeanspruchung der Justizbehörden
to **step up** [ˌstep 'ʌp]	vortreten
to **be loath to do sth.** [bi ˌləʊθ tə du]	etw nur sehr ungern tun
to **brand** [brænd]	brandmarken, stigmatisieren, beschimpfen
hysteria [hɪ'stɪəriə]	Hysterie
to **remove sth. from the equation** [rɪˌmu:v frəm ðə ɪ'kweɪʒn]	etw ausklammern, etw außen vor lassen
public health [ˌpʌblɪk 'helθ]	Gesundheitswesen, öffentliche Gesundheit
to **shatter** ['ʃætə]	zerschmettern, zerschlagen
smokescreen ['sməʊkskri:n]	Vorwand, Nebelkerze
to **prohibit** [prə'hɪbɪt]	verbieten
to **dupe** [dj:up]	überlisten, hinters Licht führen

page 52

in view of [ɪn 'vju: əv]	angesichts
matter-of-fact [ˌmætərə'fækt]	sachlich
to **monopolize** [mə'nɒpəlaɪz]	monopolisieren
to **deter** [dɪ'tɜ:]	abschrecken
drug cartel ['drʌg kɑ:tel]	Drogenkartell
imprisonment [ɪm'prɪznmənt]	Inhaftierung
to **assume** [ə'sju:m]	übernehmen
tax revenues ['tæks revənju:z]	Steuereinnahmen
prison inmate ['prɪzn ɪnmeɪt]	Gefängnisinsasse/-in
conviction [kən'vɪkʃn]	Verurteilung
voter ['vəʊtə]	Wähler/in
rehab facility ['ri:hæb fəsɪləti]	Therapieeinrichtung
sceptical (of sth.) ['skeptɪkl]	skeptisch (in Bezug auf etw)
enthusiastic [ɪnˌθju:zi'æstɪk]	begeistert, enthusiastisch

page 53

attempt [ə'tempt]	Versuch
evil ['i:vl]	Übel
to **shift into a new phase** [ˌʃɪft ɪntu ə ˌnju: 'feɪz]	einen neuen Abschnitt einleiten
once and for all [ˌwʌns ən fər 'ɔ:l]	ein- für allemal
narcotics [nɑ:'kɒtɪks]	Betäubungsmittel
on-going ['ɒngəʊɪŋ]	anhaltend, fortdauernd
to **aim** [eɪm]	darauf abzielen
to **neglect** [nɪ'glekt]	vernachlässigen
at first glance [ət ˌfɜ:st 'glɑ:ns]	auf den ersten Blick
to **convey** [kən'veɪ]	vermitteln
to **tend to do sth.** ['tend tə du]	dazu neigen, etw zu tun
to **favour** ['feɪvə]	befürworten
to **conceal** [kən'si:l]	kaschieren, verdecken
spread [spred]	Verbreitung
resolution [ˌreʒə'lu:ʃn]	Entschluss, Beschluss
xenophobia [ˌzenə'fəʊbiə]	Fremdenfeindlichkeit, Fremdenhass
havoc ['hævək]	Chaos, Verwüstung
pay-rise ['peɪ raɪz]	Lohnerhöhung
ingredient [ɪn'gri:diənt]	Zutat, Inhaltsstoff
vehicle ['vi:əkl]	Fahrzeug
temper ['tempə]	Naturell, Wut, Laune
proposal [prə'pəʊzl]	Vorschlag
merit ['merɪt]	Vorzug
to **implement** ['ɪmplɪmənt]	umsetzen, anwenden, durchführen
harsh [hɑ:ʃ]	hart

page 54

juvenile delinquency [ˌdʒu:vənaɪl dɪ'lɪŋkwənsi]	Jugendkriminalität
to **sentence sb.** ['sentəns]	jdn (zu etw) verurteilen, das Strafmaß für jdn bestimmen
to **convict sb.** [kən'vɪkt]	jdn schuldig sprechen, jdn verurteilen
judge [dʒʌdʒ]	Richter/in
to **be faced with sth.** [bi 'feɪst wɪð]	mit etw konfrontiert sein
just [dʒʌst]	gerecht
humane [hju:'meɪn]	human
repeat offender [rɪˌpi:t ə'fendə]	Wiederholungstäter/in
mandatory ['mændətəri]	gesetzlich vorgeschrieben
prison sentence ['prɪzn sentəns]	Gefängnisstrafe, Haftstrafe
parole [pə'rəʊl]	Bewährung
burglary ['bɜ:gləri]	Einbruchdiebstahl
assault [ə'sɔ:lt]	Körperverletzung
rape [reɪp]	Vergewaltigung
drug trafficking ['drʌg træfɪkɪŋ]	Drogenhandel
to **post a bond** [ˌpəʊst ə 'bɒnd]	eine Kaution hinterlegen
to **release sb.** [rɪ'li:s]	jdn auf freien Fuß setzen
on bail [ɒn 'beɪl]	auf Kaution
pending trial [ˌpendɪŋ 'traɪəl]	bis zum Prozess
lenient ['li:niənt]	mild
suspended sentence [səˌspendɪd 'sentəns]	Bewährungsstrafe
fine [faɪn]	Geldstrafe
community service [kə'mju:nəti sɜ:vɪs]	gemeinnützige Arbeit, Sozialdienst
first-time offender [ˌfɜ:st taɪm ə'fendə]	Ersttäter/in, nicht Vorbestrafte/r
petty crime [ˌpeti 'kraɪm]	Bagatelldelikt(e)
anti-social behaviour [ænti ˌsəʊʃl bɪ'heɪvjə]	abweichende (antisoziale) Verhaltensweise(n)
release [rɪ'li:s]	Freilassung, Entlassung
to **reintegrate** [ˌri:'ɪntɪgreɪt]	wiedereingliedern
ex-convict [ˌeks 'kɒnvɪkt]	Strafentlassene/r, ehemalige/r Strafgefangene/r
to **reoffend** [ˌri:ə'fend]	wieder straffällig werden
criminologist [ˌkrɪmɪ'nɒlədʒɪst]	Kriminologe/-in

prosecutor ['prɒsɪkju:tə]	Strafverfolger/in, Staatsanwalt/-anwältin
deterrent [dɪ'terənt]	Abschreckungsmittel
underlying causes [ʌndəˌlaɪɪŋ 'kɔ:sɪz]	zugrundeliegende Ursachen
broken families [ˌbrəʊkən 'fæməliz]	zerrüttete Familien(verhältnisse)
social inequality [ˌsəʊʃl ɪnɪ'kwɒləti]	soziale Ungleichheiten
white-collar crime [waɪt ˌkɒlə 'kraɪm]	Wirtschaftskriminalität
bribery ['braɪbəri]	Bestechung
tax evasion ['tæks ɪveɪʒn]	Steuerhinterziehung
greed [gri:d]	Habgier
boredom ['bɔ:dəm]	Langeweile
injustice [ɪn'dʒʌstɪs]	Ungerechtigkeit
social order [ˌsəʊʃl 'ɔ:də]	Gesellschaftsordnung, Sozialordnung
big-time criminal [ˌbɪg taɪm 'krɪmɪnl]	Schwerkriminelle/r
to **be to blame** [bi tə 'bleɪm]	schuld sein, die Schuld tragen
to **be obliged to do sth.** [bi ə'blaɪdʒd tə du]	etw tun müssen
to **make ends meet** [meɪk ˌendz 'mi:t]	über die Runden kommen
parental supervision [pəˌrentl su:pə'vɪʒn]	elterliche Aufsicht
maturity [mə'tʃʊərəti]	Reife
to **exert** [ɪg'zɜ:t]	ausüben
peer pressure [ˌpɪə 'preʃə]	Gruppenzwang, Gruppendruck
shoplifting ['ʃɒplɪftɪŋ]	Ladendiebstahl
truancy ['tru:ənsi]	Schulschwänzen
binge-drinking ['bɪndʒ drɪŋkɪŋ]	Alkoholexzesse, Komasaufen
graphic ['græfɪk]	anschaulich
to **differentiate** [ˌdɪfə'renʃieɪt]	unterscheiden, differenzieren
objectionable [əb'dʒekʃnəbl]	anstößig, bedenklich
to **get a grip on sth.** [ˌget ə 'grɪp ɒn]	etw in den Griff bekommen
to **place sb. on probation** [ˌpleɪs ɒn prə'beɪʃn]	jds Strafe zur Bewährung aussetzen
first-hand [ˌfɜ:st 'hænd]	direkt, am eigenen Leib
ordeal [ɔ:'di:l]	Qual, Martyrium, Leid
reduced sentence [rɪˌdju:st 'sentəns]	vermindertes Strafmaß, Strafmilderung
counselling session ['kaʊnsəlɪŋ seʃn]	Beratungstermin, Therapiesitzung
to **be eligible for sth.** [bi 'elɪdʒəbl fə]	für etw in Frage kommen
early parole [ˌɜ:li pə'rəʊl]	vorzeitige Haftentlassung

page 55

property ['prɒpəti]	Eigentum
life sentence ['laɪf sentəns]	lebenslange Freiheitsstrafe
severe [sɪ'vɪə]	hart, streng
rapist ['reɪpɪst]	Vergewaltiger/in
burglar ['bɜ:glə]	Einbrecher/in

page 56

motoring offence [ˌməʊtərɪŋ ə'fens]	Verkehrsdelikt
handling ['hændlɪŋ]	Hehlerei
vehicle theft ['vi:əkl θeft]	Fahrzeugdiebstahl

page 57

to **prove sth.** [pru:v]	sich als etw erweisen
to **lock sb. up** [ˌlɒk 'ʌp]	jdn einsperren
to **detain sb.** [dɪ'teɪn]	jdn in Haft nehmen
juvenile justice system [ˌdʒu:vənaɪl 'dʒʌstɪs sɪstəm]	Jugendstrafrecht
criminal charge [ˌkrɪmɪnl 'tʃɑ:dʒ]	Anklage
to **wind up** [ˌwaɪnd 'ʌp]	landen, enden
tangled ['tæŋgld]	verstrickt, verwickelt
up close [ˌʌp 'kləʊs]	aus nächster Nähe, detailliert, genau
youth unit ['ju:θ ju:nɪt]	*hier:* Jugendstrafanstalt
to **skip school** [ˌskip 'sku:l]	die Schule schwänzen
curfew ['kɜ:fju:]	Ausgangssperre
to **invoke sth** [ɪn'vəʊk]	etw anwenden, auf etw zurückgreifen
sanction ['sæŋkʃn]	Sanktion, Zwangsmittel
wound [wu:nd]	Wunde
scar [skɑ:]	Narbe
detention [dɪ'tenʃn]	Haft, Gewahrsam
detention center *AE* [dɪ'tenʃn sentə]	Haftanstalt, Gefängnis
heart attack ['hɑ:t ətæk]	Herzinfarkt
to **have a fight** [həv ə 'faɪt]	sich (heftig) streiten
to **charge sb. with sth.** ['tʃɑ:dʒ wɪð]	jdn einer Sache anklagen
second degree murder [ˌseknd dɪˌgri: 'mɜ:də]	Totschlag
behind bars [bɪhaɪnd 'bɑ:z]	hinter Gittern
to **lock down** [ˌlɔk 'daʊn]	einschließen, abschließen
limp [lɪmp]	schlaff
to **stab sb. to death** [ˌstæb tə 'deθ]	jdn erstechen
juvenile ['dʒu:vənaɪl]	Jugendliche/r
on technicalities [ɒn ˌteknɪ'kælɪtiz]	aus formalen Gründen
to **violate probation** [ˌvaɪəleɪt prə'beɪʃn]	gegen Bewährungsauflagen verstoßen
longtime ['lɒŋtaɪm]	langjährig, erfahren
to **be truant** [bi 'tru:ənt]	die Schule schwänzen
court order [ˌkɔ:t 'ɔ:də]	Gerichtsbeschluss, gerichtliche Verfügung
authority [ɔ:θɒrəti]	Vollmacht, Befugnis
district attorney *AE* [ˌdɪstrɪkt ə'tɜ:ni]	Bezirksstaatsanwalt, Generalstaatsanwalt
to **devote sth. to sb./sth.** [dɪ'vəʊt]	etw auf/für jdn/etw verwenden
at gunpoint [ət 'gʌnpɔɪnt]	mit vorgehaltener Waffe
cashier [kæ'ʃɪə]	Kassierer/in
to **pickpocket** ['pɪkpɒkɪt]	*(Taschendieb/in:)* stehlen
income tax ['ɪnkʌm tæks]	Einkommensteuer
to **turn sb. in** [ˌtɜ:n 'ɪn]	jdn anzeigen

page 58

juvenile ['dʒu:vənaɪl]	Jugendliche/r
empathy ['empəθi]	Mitgefühl
alienated ['eɪliəneɪtɪd]	entfremdet
guidance ['gaɪdəns]	Führung, Anleitung, Orientierungshilfe

UNIT 5

page 59

quota ['kwəʊtə]	Quote
parenting ['peərəntɪŋ]	elterliche Fürsorge, Kindererziehung
battle of the sexes [ˌbætl əv ðə 'seksɪz]	Geschlechterkampf
ageism ['eɪdʒɪzəm]	Altersdiskriminierung

page 60

to **be better off** [bi ˌbetər 'ɒf]	(finanziell) besser gestellt sein
steadily ['stedɪli]	kontinuierlich, ständig
bias ['baɪəs]	Vorurteil(e), Einseitigkeit, Verzerrung
ceiling ['si:lɪŋ]	(Zimmer-)Decke
maternity leave [mə'tɜ:nəti li:v]	Mutterschaftsurlaub
hard-won [ˌhɑ:d'wʌn]	mühsam erkämpft
to **get by** [ˌget 'baɪ]	zurechtkommen
negotiating skills *pl.* [nɪ'gəʊʃieɪtɪŋ skɪlz]	Verhandlungsgeschick
to **put up with sth.** [ˌpʊt 'ʌp wɪð]	etw ertragen, etw hinnehmen
to **make allowances for sb.** [meɪk ə'laʊənsɪz fə]	jdm Zugeständnisse machen, auf jdn Rücksicht nehmen
lion's share [ˌlaɪənz 'ʃeə]	Löwenanteil
infamous ['ɪnfəməs]	berühmt-berüchtigt
shift [ʃɪft]	Schicht
to **be delegated sth.** [bi 'delɪgeɪtɪd]	etw übertragen bekommen
burden ['bɜ:dn]	Last, Belastung
life-expectancy ['laɪf ɪkspektənsi]	Lebenserwartung
ageing ['eɪdʒɪŋ]	alternd, älter werdend
in-laws *pl.* ['ɪn lɔ:z]	Schwiegereltern
carer ['keərə]	Pfleger/in, Betreuer/in
to **be supposed to do sth.** [bi sə'pəʊzd tə du]	etw tun sollen
longevity [lɒn'dʒevəti]	Langlebigkeit, hohe Lebensdauer
population pyramid	Bevölkerungspyramide
fertility [fə'tɪləti]	Fruchtbarkeit, Geburtenrate
childcare facility ['tʃaɪldkeə fəsɪləti]	Kinderbetreuungseinrichtung
it remains to be seen [ɪt rɪˌmeɪnz tə bi 'si:n]	es bleibt abzuwarten

page 61

to **encounter** [ɪn'kaʊntə]	begegnen
to **appoint sb.** [ə'pɔɪnt]	jdn einstellen, jdn berufen
solely ['səʊlli]	allein, ausschließlich
root [ru:t]	Wurzel, Stamm
no mean achievement [nəʊ ˌmi:n ə'tʃi:vmənt]	beachtliche Leistung
counterpart ['kaʊntəpɑ:t]	Pendant
subheading ['sʌbhedɪŋ]	Zwischenüberschrift

page 62

gender gap ['dʒendə gæp]	Geschlechterkonflikt, Kluft zwischen den Geschlechtern
to **add a novel twist to sth.** [æd ə ˌnɒvl 'twɪst tə]	etw aufpeppen, sich etwas Neues einfallen lassen für etw
time-use survey ['taɪm ju:s sɜ:veɪ]	Zeitbudgeterhebung
pollster ['pəʊlstə]	Meinungsforscher/in
to **stand out** [ˌstænd 'aʊt]	herausstechen
apparently [ə'pærəntli]	anscheinend
to **do laundry** [du 'lɔ:ndri]	Wäsche waschen
to **figure** ['fɪgə]	vermuten, glauben
gathering ['gæðərɪŋ]	Treffen, Zusammenkunft
to **tend to be sth.** ['tend tə bi:]	eher/tendenziell etw sein
intriguing [ɪn'tri:gɪŋ]	faszinierend, verblüffend
unsettling [ˌʌn'setlɪŋ]	verstörend, beunruhigend
stark [stɑ:k]	krass, überdeutlich
pattern ['pætn]	Muster
to **cut back on sth.** [ˌkʌt 'bæk ɒn]	etw einschränken

page 63

to **fall short** [ˌfɔ:l 'ʃɔ:t]	unzureichend sein
to **devote** [dɪ'vəʊt]	widmen
to **dust** [dʌst]	abstauben
dust [dʌst]	Staub
breakthrough ['breɪkθru:]	Durchbruch
to **come up with sth.** [ˌkʌm 'ʌp wɪð]	sich etw einfallen lassen, auf etw kommen
well-adjusted [ˌwel ə'dʒʌstɪd]	wohlerzogen
sort of ['sɔ:t əv]	irgendwie
narrow ['nærəʊ]	eng, beschränkt
ambition [æm'bɪʃn]	Ziel
to **flood** [flʌd]	strömen
workforce ['wɜ:kfɔ:s]	arbeitende Bevölkerung
to **come to grips with sth.** [ˌkʌm tə 'grɪps wɪð]	mit etw klarkommen, etw in den Griff bekommen
preschool [ˌpri:'sku:l]	Kindergarten, Vorschule
to **figure out** [ˌfɪgər 'aʊt]	herausfinden, verstehen
on average [ɒn 'ævərɪdʒ]	im Durchschnitt
to **perceive** [pə'si:v]	wahrnehmen

page 64

dull [dʌl]	langweilig
to **have one's work cut out for one** [həv wɜ:k ˌkʌt 'aʊt fə]	viel zu tun haben
to **veer off** [ˌvɪər 'ɒf]	vom Kurs abkommen
impact ['ɪmpækt]	Aufprall

page 65

fuse [fju:z]	Zündschnur
to **age** [eɪdʒ]	altern
share [ʃeə]	Anteil
temporary blip [ˌtemprəri 'blɪp]	vorübergehende Störung

to **counterbalance** [ˌkaʊntəˈbæləns]	ausgleichen, aufwiegen
to **predict** [prɪˈdɪkt]	vorhersagen
to **level out** [ˌlevl ˈaʊt]	sich einpendeln, sich einpegeln
to **magnify** [ˈmægnɪfaɪ]	vergrößern
to **swell the ranks** [ˌswel ðə ˈræŋks]	die Reihen auffüllen
pensioner [ˈpenʃənə]	Rentner/in
drop [drɒp]	Rückgang, Einbruch

page 66

to **take a knock** [ˌteɪk ə ˈnɒk]	einen Knacks bekommen, einen Schlag versetzt bekommen
resilient [rɪˈzɪliənt]	stabil, robust
to **kill sb. off** [ˌkɪl ˈɒf]	jdn sterben lassen, jdn töten
to **be due to do sth.** [bi ˈdjuː tə du]	etw tun werden
to **triple** [ˈtrɪpl]	sich verdreifachen
macroeconomic [ˌmækrəʊˌiːkəˈnɒmɪk]	makroökonomisch
to **suggest** [səˈdʒest]	*hier:* behaupten, sagen, nahelegen
labour force [ˈleɪbə fɔːs]	erwerbstätige Bevölkerung
to **shrink** [ʃrɪŋk]	schrumpfen
output growth [ˈaʊtpʊt ɡrəʊθ]	Produktionswachstum
ratio [ˈreɪʃiəʊ]	Verhältnis
to **deteriorate** [dɪˈtɪəriəreɪt]	sich verschlechtern
to **maintain sb.** [meɪnˈteɪn]	jdn unterhalten, jdn versorgen
bulk [bʌlk]	Großteil, Hauptanteil
to **swallow sth. up** [ˌswɒləʊ ˈʌp]	etw schlucken
generous [ˈdʒenərəs]	großzügig
to **be inclined to do sth.** [bi ɪnˈklaɪnd tə du]	dazu neigen, etw zu tun
care [keə]	Pflege, Betreuung
respectively [rɪˈspektɪvli]	beziehungsweise
to **halve** [hɑːv]	sich halbieren
to **swell** [swel]	anschwellen
populous [ˈpɒpjələs]	bevölkerungsreich
spending [ˈspendɪŋ]	Ausgaben
relentless(ly) [rɪˈlentləs]	unentwegt, unaufhaltsam
to **mask** [mɑːsk]	kaschieren, verdecken

page 67

disproportionate [ˌdɪsprəˈpɔːʃnət]	unverhältnismäßig
modest [ˈmɒdɪst]	mäßig, maßvoll
principal [ˈprɪnsəpl]	Haupt-
same-sex [ˌseɪm ˈseks]	gleichgeschlechtlich

page 68

to **grey** [ɡreɪ]	ergrauen
to **get engaged** [ɡet ɪnˈɡeɪdʒd]	sich verloben
to **turn sour** [ˌtɜːn ˈsaʊə]	sich verschlechtern, unangenehm werden
vow [vaʊ]	Schwur, Gelöbnis, Versprechen
until death us do part [ʌntɪl ˌdeθ ʌs du ˈpɑːt]	bis dass der Tod uns scheidet

page 69

fair [feə]	Messe
to **touch wood** [ˌtʌtʃ ˈwʊd]	auf Holz klopfen
tasting [ˈteɪstɪŋ]	Verkostung
to **put sb. off sth.** [ˌpʊt ˈɒf]	jdm etw verleiden, jdn von etw abhalten
commitment [kəˈmɪtmənt]	Verpflichtung, Bindung
newly-wed [ˈnjuːli wed]	frisch verheiratet, jung vermählt
by profession [baɪ prəˈfeʃn]	von Beruf
to **accompany** [əˈkʌmpəni]	begleiten
lasting [ˈlɑːstɪŋ]	dauerhaft, nachhaltig

page 70

to **weed out** [ˌwiːd ˈaʊt]	aussortieren
to **bother doing sth.** [ˈbɒðə]	sich die Mühe machen, etw zu tun
to **dog-sit** [ˈdɒɡ sɪt]	den Hund hüten

UNIT 6

page 71

to **settle** [ˈsetl]	sich niederlassen
neighbouring [ˈneɪbərɪŋ]	Nachbar-, benachbart
to **pen sb. in** [ˌpen ˈɪn]	jdn einsperren, jdn einpferchen
oppression [əˈpreʃn]	Unterdrückung
the Blessed Land [ðə ˌblesɪd ˈlænd]	das Gelobte Land
to **huddle close** [ˌhʌdl ˈkləʊs]	sich eng aneinander drängen
to **hang on to sth.** [ˌhæŋ ˈɒn tə]	an etw festhalten
to **say grace** [ˌseɪ ˈɡreɪs]	das Tischgebet sprechen
to **unfurl** [ʌnˈfɜːl]	entfalten, auseinander falten
My Country, 'Tis of Thee (I Sing) [maɪ ˌkʌntri ˌtɪz əv ˈðiː aɪ ˌsɪŋ]	Mein Land, von dir ist's, dass ich singe *(patriotisches Lied der USA von 1831)*
liberty [ˈlɪbəti]	Freiheit
statue [ˈstætʃuː]	Statue

page 72

ethnic diversity [ˌeθnɪk daɪˈvɜːsəti]	ethnische Vielfalt, Völkervielfalt
origin [ˈɒrɪdʒɪn]	Herkunft
mean [miːn]	gemein, fies
menacing [ˈmenəsɪŋ]	bedrohlich
to **pick sth. apart** [ˌpɪk əˈpɑːt]	etwa: etw auseinandernehmen
feature [ˈfiːtʃə]	Gesichtszug
race [reɪs]	Rasse
tan [tæn]	*(Haut:)* braun
ancestry [ˈænsestri]	Vorfahren
to **span the globe** [ˌspæn ðə ˈɡləʊb]	den Globus umspannen
mulatto [mjuːˈlætəʊ]	Mulatte/-in
to **be tinged with sth.** [bi ˈtɪndʒd wɪð]	einen Beigeschmack/ Anklang von etw haben

shame [ʃeɪm] | Schande, Scham
to **confirm** [kən'fɜːm] | bestätigen
affirmation [ˌæfɜː'meɪʃn] | Bekräftigung, Bestätigung
mutual ['mjuːtʃuəl] | gemeinsam, gegenseitig
lineage ['lɪniɪdʒ] | Abstammung, Herkunft
to **erupt** [ɪ'rʌpt] | ausbrechen
cheers *pl.* [tʃɪəz] | Jubel
mixed race [ˌmɪkst 'reɪs] | gemischtrassig
multiracial [ˌmʌlti'reɪʃl] | gemischtrassig
biracial [baɪ'reɪʃl] | gemischtrassig
crop (of sth.) [krɒp] | Gruppe (von etw)
to **come of age** [ˌkʌm əv 'eɪdʒ] | erwachsen werden
vanguard ['væŋɡɑːd] | Vorhut
to **be in the midst of sth.** [bi ɪn ðə 'mɪdst əv] | mitten in etw sein
shift [ʃɪft] | Wandel, Veränderung
intermarriage [ˌɪntə'mærɪdʒ] | Mischehe
color line *AE* ['kʌlə laɪn] | Rassenschranke
fluid ['fluːɪd] | fließend, vage
sense of identity [ˌsens əv aɪ'dentəti] | Identitätsgefühl
to **affirm** [ə'fɜːm] | bekräftigen
to **portray sth. as sth.** [pɔː'treɪ] | etw als etw darstellen
pitiable ['pɪtiəbl] | bemitleidenswert
to **blend** [blend] | mischen
to **transcend sth.** [træn'send] | über etw hinausgehen
bigotry ['bɪɡətri] | Fanatismus
prejudice ['predʒudɪs] | Vorurteil(e)
affirmative action [əˌfɜːmətɪv 'ækʃn] | aktive Förderung von Minderheiten/positive Diskriminierung
stratification [ˌstrætɪfɪ'keɪʃn] | (soziale) Schichtenbildung, Stratifikation
at the expense of sb./sth. [ət ði ɪk'spens əv] | auf Kosten von jdm/etw
notion ['nəʊʃn] | Idee, Gedanke, Vorstellung
panacea [ˌpænə'siːə] | Allheilmittel, Patentlösung
transcendence [træn'sendəns] | Überwindung
tribe [traɪb] | (Volks-)Stamm
Balkanization [ˌbɔːlkənaɪ'zeɪʃn] | Balkanisierung *(Zerfall eines größeren in viele Kleinstaaten)*
to **tear sb. apart** [ˌteər ə'pɑːt] | jdn auseinanderreißen
to **have a say** [ˌhəv ə 'seɪ] | mitreden (können), ein Mitspracherecht haben
ambiguous [æm'bɪɡjuəs] | mehrdeutig, unklar
ubiquitous [juː'bɪkwɪtəs] | allgegenwärtig

page 73

icebreaker ['aɪsbreɪkə] | *etw, das die Stimmung auflockert*
to **label** ['leɪbl] | etikettieren, bezeichnen
Peruvian [pə'ruːviən] | peruanisch
to **be in awe of sth.** [bi ˌɪn 'ɔː əv] | Ehrfurcht vor etw haben
to **unwind** [ˌʌn'waɪnd] | sich entspannen, abschalten
supportive [sə'pɔːtɪv] | verständnisvoll
advocacy ['ædvəkəsi] | Eintreten (für etw), Engagement
to **counter** ['kaʊntə] | entgegnen, kontern
amid [ə'mɪd] | inmitten, unter
neo-Classical [ˌniːəʊ 'klæsɪkl] | klassizistisch
spouse [spaʊz] | Ehegatte/Ehegattin
prominent ['prɒmɪnənt] | deutlich sichtbar
to **conceptualize sth.** [kən'septʃuəlaɪz] | etw in Begriffe fassen
to **gloss sth. over** [ˌɡlɒs 'əʊvə] | etw vertuschen, etw überdecken
circumstances *pl.* ['sɜːkəmstaːnsɪz] | (Lebens-)Umstände

page 74

bigot ['bɪɡət] | Eiferer, Fanatiker/in
to **pretend to do sth.** [prɪ'tend] | vorgeben, etw zu tun
to **be rife with sth.** [bi 'raɪf wɪð] | voll von etw sein
to **impose sth.** [ɪm'pəʊz] | etw verhängen, etw auferlegen, etw anordnen
ban (on sth.) [bæn] | Verbot (von etw)
to **advocate sth.** ['ædvəkeɪt] | für etw eintreten
deportation [ˌdiːpɔː'teɪʃn] | Ausweisung
asylum seeker [ə'saɪləm siːkə] | Asylsuchende/r
implication [ˌɪmplɪ'keɪʃn] | Folge, Konsequenz
to **preach** [priːtʃ] | predigen

page 75

to **legislate** ['ledʒɪsleɪt] | Gesetze erlassen
to **fare** [feə] | abschneiden, ergehen
instinctive [ɪn'stɪŋktɪv] | instinktiv
commonplace ['kɒmənpleɪs] | alltäglich, gewöhnlich
routinely [ruː'tiːnli] | routinemäßig
to **abuse** [ə'bjuːz] | beleidigen, beschimpfen
boarding house ['bɔːdɪŋ haʊs] | Wohnheim, Pension
infamously ['ɪnfəməsli] | schändlich, berüchtigt
to **bar sb. from sth.** [bɑː] | jdn von etw ausschließen
brazen ['breɪzn] | schamlos, dreist
act [ækt] | Gesetz
on the grounds of sth. [ɒn ðə 'ɡraʊndz əv] | aufgrund von etw
legislation [ˌledʒɪs'leɪʃn] | Gesetzgebung, Gesetze
civil offence [ˌsɪvl ə'fens] | zivilrechtliches Vergehen
criminal offence [ˌkrɪmɪnl ə'fens] | strafrechtliches Vergehen, Straftat
landmark ['lændmɑːk] | Meilenstein
foundation [faʊn'deɪʃn] | Fundament, Grundlage, Grundstein
subsequent ['sʌbsɪkwənt] | nachfolgend, folgend
duty ['djuːti] | Pflicht
to **alter** ['ɔːltə] | sich ändern
overt(ly) [əʊ'vɜːt] | offen (gezeigt)
to **be regarded as sth.** [bi rɪ'ɡɑːdɪd əz] | als etw gelten, für etw erachtet werden
to **vote** [vəʊt] | *hier:* stimmen
clash [klæʃ] | Auseinandersetzung

to **obliterate** [əb'lɪtəreɪt]	auslöschen
Home Office ['həʊm ɒfɪs]	*brit. Innenministerium*
to **come a long way** [kʌm ə ˌlɒŋ 'weɪ]	es weit bringen
to **cease sth.** [si:s]	etw beenden, etw einstellen
blatant ['bleɪtnt]	eklatant, unverhohlen
grave [greɪv]	groß, ernsthaft, schwer
infant mortality ['ɪnfənt mɔ:tæləti]	Säuglingssterblichkeit
senior ['si:niə]	höher(rangig)
civil service [ˌsɪvl 'sɜ:vɪs]	Staatsdienst, öffentlicher Dienst
judiciary [dʒu'dɪʃəri]	der Richterstand
barrier ['bæriə]	Hindernis
progress ['prəʊgres]	Fortschritt, Fortkommen

page 76

political force [pəˌlɪtɪkl 'fɔ:s]	politische Kraft
to **force sth. down sb.'s throat** [fɔ:s ˌdaʊn sʌmbədiz 'θrəʊt]	jdm etw aufzwingen
diverse [daɪ'vɜ:s]	vielfältig
to **spill blood** [ˌspɪl 'blʌd]	Blut vergießen
segregated ['segrɪgeɪtɪd]	getrennt, isoliert
testament (to sth.) ['testəmənt]	Beweis (für etw)
Member of Parliament (MP) [ˌmembər əf 'pɑ:ləmənt]	Parlamentsabgeordnete/r
to **combat sth.** ['kɒmbæt]	etw bekämpfen
council estate ['kaʊnsl ɪsteɪt]	Siedlung mit Sozialwohnungen
abuse [ə'bju:s]	Beschimpfungen, Gewalt
swath [sweɪð]	Streifen, Landstrich, Gegend
virtually ['vɜ:tʃuəli]	praktisch
make-up ['meɪkʌp]	Zusammensetzung
borough ['bʌrə]	Stadtbezirk
pressing ['presɪŋ]	dringlich, dringend
right-wing [ˌraɪt 'wɪŋ]	(politisch) rechts, rechtsgerichtet
flaw [flɔ:]	Mangel
to **prevail** [prɪ'veɪl]	herrschen, vorherrschen

page 77

drawback ['drɔ:bæk]	Nachteil
to **be an asset** [bi ən 'æset]	wertvoll sein
representation [ˌreprɪzen'teɪʃn]	Vertretung
vast [vɑ:st]	weit, groß
to **address sth.** [ə'dres]	etw *(Problem, etc.)* angehen
tension ['tenʃn]	Spannung
concerted [kən'sɜ:tɪd]	vereint, gemeinsam
disobedience [ˌdɪsə'bi:diəns]	Ungehorsam
council ['kaʊnsl]	Stadtrat, Bezirksrat
to **deny** [dɪ'naɪ]	bestreiten, leugnen

page 78

barbed-wire fence [bɑ:bd ˌwaɪə 'fens]	Stacheldrahtzaun
leaky ['li:ki]	undicht
to **stow oneself away** [ˌstəʊ ə'weɪ]	als blinder Passagier reisen, sich als blinder Passagier verstecken
desperate ['despərət]	verzweifelt
to **abandon** [ə'bændən]	verlassen
drought [draʊt]	Dürre
barren ['bærən]	unfruchtbar, öde
uninhabitable [ˌʌnɪn'hæbɪtəbl]	unbewohnbar
famine ['fæmɪn]	Hungersnot
dust bowl ['dʌst bəʊl]	Trockengebiet
plain [pleɪn]	Ebene
persecution [ˌpɜ:sɪ'kju:ʃn]	Verfolgung
pilgrim ['pɪlgrɪm]	Pilger/in
displaced person [dɪsˌpleɪst 'pɜ:sn]	Vertriebene/r, Flüchtling
to **bear witness to sth.** [ˌbeə 'wɪtnəs tə]	etw bezeugen, von etw zeugen
to **refer to sb./sth. as sth.** [rɪ'fɜ: tə]	jdn/etw als etw bezeichnen
to **apply to sb./sth.** [ə'plaɪ tə]	für jdn/etw gelten
ruthless ['ru:θləs]	skrupellos
human trafficker [ˌhju:mən 'træfɪkə]	Menschenhändler/in
to **exploit** [ɪk'splɔɪt]	ausbeuten, ausnutzen
settler ['setlə]	Siedler/in
resentment [rɪ'zentmənt]	Unmut, Groll, Ressentiment
custom ['kʌstəm]	Sitte, Brauch
melting pot ['meltɪŋ pɒt]	Schmelztiegel
to **assimilate to sth.** [ə'sɪməleɪt tə]	sich an etw anpassen
citizenship ['sɪtɪznʃɪp]	Staatsbürgerschaft
influx ['ɪnflʌks]	Strom, Zustrom
to **naturalize** ['nætʃrəlaɪz]	einbürgern
economic decline [i:kəˌnɒmɪk dɪ'klaɪn]	Konjunkturrückgang, Wirtschaftskrise, -flaute
to **accuse sb. of sth.** [ə'kju:z]	jdn einer Sache beschuldigen
host country ['həʊst kʌntri]	Gastland
supremacy [su:'preməsi]	Überlegenheit, Vormacht(stellung)

page 79

alienation [ˌeɪliə'neɪʃn]	Entfremdung
self-assertive [ˌself ə'sɜ:tɪv]	selbstbewusst
to **confine sb. to sth.** [kən'faɪn]	jdn auf etw beschränken, jdn in etw einsperren
to **proclaim** [prə'kleɪm]	(öffentlich) erklären
asset ['æset]	Vorteil, Wert, Plus
enrichment [ɪn'rɪtʃmənt]	Bereicherung
broadening ['brɔ:dnɪŋ]	Erweiterung
to **put sth. forward** [ˌpʊt 'fɔ:wəd]	etw vorbringen, etw zur Diskussion stellen
deplorable [dɪ'plɔ:rəbl]	erbärmlich, furchtbar
obstacle ['ɒbstəkl]	Hindernis
resident ['rezɪdənt]	Bewohner/in, Einwohner/in
benefit ['benɪfɪt]	Vorteil, Nutzen
timid ['tɪmɪd]	schüchtern
uniformity [ˌju:nɪ'fɔ:məti]	Einheitlichkeit, Eintönigkeit

page 80

legal residency [ˌliːɡl ˈrezɪdənsi]	Aufenthaltsgenehmigung, -recht
contentious [kənˈtenʃəs]	umstritten, kontrovers
divisive [dɪˈvaɪsɪv]	polarisierend, entzweiend
large-scale [ˈlɑːdʒ skeɪl]	groß, in großem Umfang/ Maßstab
misconception [ˌmɪskənˈsepʃn]	falsche Vorstellung(en), irrige Annahme(n)
to **overestimate** [ˌəʊvərˈestɪmeɪt]	überschätzen
to **arm** [ɑːm]	bewaffnen, ausrüsten
respondent [rɪˈspɒndənt]	Befragte/r
to **prime sb. with sth. for sth.** [praɪm]	jdn mit etw auf etw vorbereiten
headquartered [ˌhedˈkwɔːtəd]	mit Sitz in
ill-informed [ˌɪlɪnˈfɔːmd]	schlecht informiert
to **poll sb.** [pəʊl]	jdn befragen
to **comprise** [kəmˈpraɪz]	ausmachen, umfassen
vexing [ˈveksɪŋ]	verzwickt
labor market *AE* [ˈleɪbə mɑːkɪt]	Arbeitsmarkt
assimilation [əˌsɪməˈleɪʃn]	Anpassung, Assimilierung
enforcement [ɪnˈfɔːsmənt]	Durchsetzung, *Überwachung der Einhaltung von Gesetzen*
constituent [kənˈstɪtjuənt]	Wähler/in (eines Wahlkreises)
to **reveal** [rɪˈviːl]	enthüllen, zeigen
to **benefit** [ˈbenɪfɪt]	profitieren
social-security measures *pl.* [ˌsəʊʃl sɪˈkjʊərəti meʒəz]	Sozialversicherungsleistungen
poll [pəʊl]	Umfrage
participant [pɑːˈtɪsɪpənt]	Teilnehmer/in
to **ease** [iːz]	lindern
hardship [ˈhɑːdʃɪp]	Not
to **correlate** [ˈkɒrəleɪt]	(miteinander) in Beziehung stehen, korrelieren
to **shift** [ʃɪft]	verändern
perception [pəˈsepʃn]	Wahrnehmung
albeit [ɔːlˈbiːɪt]	wenn auch
marginal(ly) [ˈmɑːdʒɪnl]	geringfügig
broad-brush [ˈbrɔːd brʌʃ]	*hier:* sehr allgemein formuliert
xenophobic [ˌzenəˈfəʊbɪk]	fremdenfeindlich
sentiment [ˈsentɪmənt]	Ansicht(en), Meinung(en)
nuanced [ˈnjuːɑːnst]	differenziert
docile [ˈdəʊsaɪl]	fügsam
labor *AE* [ˈleɪbə]	Arbeitskräfte
asylum application [əˈsaɪləm æplɪkeɪʃn]	Asylantrag

page 81

educationalist [ˌedʒuˈkeɪʃnəlɪst]	Pädagoge/-in
to **hit the headlines** [ˌhɪt ðə ˈhedlaɪnz]	Schlagzeilen machen
compulsory [kəmˈpʌlsəri]	obligatorisch
remedial class [rɪˌmiːdiəl ˈklɑːs]	Förderkurs
to **catch up with sb.** [ˌkætʃ ˈʌp wɪð]	aufholen, jdn einholen

page 82

to **be sworn into office** [bi ˌswɔːn ɪntu ˈɒfɪs]	den Amtseid ablegen
the promised land [ðə ˌprɒmɪst ˈlænd]	das gelobte Land
fluent(ly) [ˈfluːənt]	fließend
to **outdo sb.** [ˌaʊtˈduː]	jdn übertreffen
to **monitor** [ˈmɒnɪtə]	überwachen, kontrollieren
overhaul [ˈəʊvəhɔːl]	Revision
to **opt for sth.** [ˈɒpt fə]	sich für etw entscheiden

UNIT 7

page 84

to **read up on sth.** [ˌriːd ˈʌp ɒn]	sich über etw informieren
pundit [ˈpʌndɪt]	Experte/-in
delivery system [dɪˈlɪvəri sɪstəm]	Bereitstellungssystem
geek-speak [ˈɡiːk spiːk]	Technik-Jargon
to **lose sight of sth.** [ˌluːz ˈsaɪt əv]	etw aus den Augen verlieren
to **bear sth. out** [ˌbeər ˈaʊt]	etw bestätigen
newspaper circulation [ˈnjuːzpeɪpə sɜːkjəleɪʃn]	Zeitungsauflage(n)
newscast [ˈnjuːzkɑːst]	Nachrichtensendung
rating [ˈreɪtɪŋ]	*hier:* Einschaltquote
to **be in decline** [bi ɪn dɪˈklaɪn]	zurückgehen, sinken
immune to sth. [ɪˈmjuːn tə]	immun gegen etw
insulated [ˈɪnsjuleɪtɪd]	isoliert
boom-and-bust cycle [ˌbuːm ən ˈbʌst saɪkl]	Zyklus von Hochkonjunktur und Krisen
mortgage [ˈmɔːɡɪdʒ]	Hypothek
draft [drɑːft]	Einberufung
sacrifice [ˈsækrɪfaɪs]	Opfer, Opferbereitschaft
freshman [ˈfreʃmən]	Student/in im ersten Studienjahr
to **place the blame with sb.** [ˌpleɪs ðə ˈbleɪm wɪð]	jdm die Schuld geben
trade [treɪd]	Gewerbe
degree [dɪˈɡriː]	Abschluss

page 85

to **staff** [stɑːf]	(mit Personal) besetzen
metro(politan) [ˌmetrəˈpɒlɪtən]	großstädtisch, Stadt-
daily [ˈdeɪli]	*hier:* Tageszeitung
to **approach** [əˈprəʊtʃ]	sich nähern, zugehen auf
mindset [ˈmaɪndset]	Mentalität, Denkweise
to **be raised on sth.** [bi ˈreɪzd ɒn]	mit etw aufwachsen
to **keep up with sth.** [ˌkiːp ˈʌp wɪð]	mit etw mithalten
to **axe sb.** [æks]	jdn entlassen, jdn feuern
bankrupt [ˈbæŋkrʌpt]	pleite
legacy media [ˈleɡəsi miːdiə]	traditionelle Medien *(im Gegensatz zu den Neuen Medien)*

hand-wringing ['hænd rɪŋɪŋ]	Händeringen
purveyor [pə'veɪə]	Lieferant/in
workable ['wɜːkəbl]	durchführbar
avid ['ævɪd]	begeistert, leidenschaftlich, eifrig
doable ['duːəbl]	durchführbar
to **capture sb.'s attention** [,kæptʃər ə'tenʃn]	jds Aufmerksamkeit gewinnen
to **occupy** ['ɒkjupaɪ]	besetzen, einnehmen

page 86

measurement ['meʒəmənt]	Maß
legal agreement [,liːgl ə'griːmənt]	rechtswirksame Vereinbarung

page 87

formerly ['fɔːməli]	vormals, ehemals
to **set on fire** [,set ɒn 'faɪə]	anzünden, in Brand setzen
stall [stɔːl]	(Markt-)Stand
to **prompt** [prɒmpt]	hervorrufen, veranlassen
broadcaster ['brɔːdkɑːstə]	Sender
media outlet ['miːdiə aʊtlet]	Medium, Sender, Presseorgan
to **suppress** [sə'pres]	unterdrücken
airing ['eərɪŋ]	Ausstrahlung, Sendung
to **undergo** [,ʌndə'gəʊ]	sich unterziehen, durchmachen
coverage ['kʌvərɪdʒ]	Berichterstattung, Bericht(e)
on the ground [ɒn ðə 'graʊnd]	vor Ort
to **put sth. into practice** [,pʊt ɪntə 'præktɪs]	etw in die Tat/Praxis umsetzen
culmination [,kʌlmɪ'neɪʃn]	Höhepunkt
realisation *BE* [,rɪəlaɪ'zeɪʃn]	Erkenntnis
swift(ly) [swɪft]	schnell, rasch
to **cover sth.** ['kʌvə]	über etw berichten
to **draw upon sth.** ['drɔː əpɒn]	auf etw zurückgreifen, aus etw schöpfen
trusted ['trʌstɪd]	bewährt, zuverlässig
credibility [,kredə'bɪləti]	Glaubwürdigkeit
to **submit** [səb'mɪt]	einreichen
to **verify** ['verɪfaɪ]	prüfen
snippet ['snɪpɪt]	Nachrichtenschnipsel
to **gauge** [geɪdʒ]	messen, abschätzen, beurteilen
vox pop(uli) [,vɒks 'pɒpjulaɪ]	Volkes Stimme, öffentliche Meinung
to **solicit sth.** [sə'lɪsɪt]	etw erbitten
lead [liːd]	*hier:* Hinweis, Anhaltspunkt, Spur
raw material [,rɔː mə'tɪəriəl]	Rohmaterial, Rohstoff

page 88

to **distil** [dɪ'stɪl]	destillieren
to **do away with sth.** [,duː ə'weɪ wɪð]	etw abschaffen
editor ['edɪtə]	Redakteur/in
to **show sth. up** [,ʃəʊ 'ʌp]	etw (deutlich) zeigen, etw deutlich machen
torrent ['tɒrənt]	Flut, Schwall, (reißender) Strom
co-founder ['kəʊfaʊndə]	Mitbegründer/in
curation [kjʊə'reɪʃn]	Pflege *(von Daten, etc.)*
mindless ['maɪndləs]	stumpfsinnig
hybrid ['haɪbrɪd]	gemischt, Misch-
founder ['faʊndə]	Gründer/in
to **insist** [ɪn'sɪst]	beteuern, (darauf) bestehen
merely ['mɪəli]	lediglich, bloß
to **trigger** ['trɪgə]	auslösen
to **broadcast** ['brɔːdkɑːst]	senden

page 89

to **air** [eə]	senden, ausstrahlen
controversial [,kɒntrə'vɜːʃl]	umstritten, strittig
topical ['tɒpɪkl]	aktuell
distribution (department) [,dɪstrɪ'bjuːʃn dɪpɑːtmənt]	Vertrieb, Versand
unequal [ʌn'iːkwəl]	ungleich, unterschiedlich
species ['spiːʃiːz]	Art, Spezies
announcement [ə'naʊnsmənt]	Erklärung, Ankündigung
to **break the news to sb.** [,breɪk ðə 'njuːz tə]	jdm die/eine Nachricht überbringen

page 90

tavern ['tævən]	Schenke
gossip ['gɒsɪp]	Klatsch, Tratsch
invention [ɪn'venʃn]	Erfindung
steam-powered ['stiːm paʊəd]	dampfbetrieben
printing press ['prɪntɪŋ pres]	Druckerpresse
broadsheet ['brɔːdʃiːt]	seriöse Tageszeitung *(eigentlich ein großes Zeitungsformat, etwa 29,5 × 23,5 Zoll)*
tabloid ['tæblɔɪd]	Boulevardzeitung *(kleines Zeitungsformat, etwa 17 × 11 Zoll)*
ownership ['əʊnəʃɪp]	Besitz
to **disseminate** [dɪ'semɪneɪt]	verbreiten
readership ['riːdəʃɪp]	Leserschaft
newsstand ['njuːzstænd]	Zeitungskiosk
licence fee ['laɪsns fiː]	Rundfunkgebühr
turn of the millennium [,tɜːn əv ðə mɪ'leniəm]	Jahrtausendwende
fundamental(ly) [,fʌndə'mentl]	grundlegend, wesentlich
to **recreate** [,riːkri'eɪt]	nachbilden, neu schaffen
opinionated [ə'pɪniəneɪtɪd]	rechthaberisch
partisan [,pɑːtɪ'zæn]	voreingenommen
establishment [ɪ'stæblɪʃmənt]	Gründung, Einrichtung
humiliation [hjuː,mɪli'eɪʃn]	Erniedrigung
viewing figures ['vjuːɪŋ fɪgəz]	Zuschauerzahlen
celebrity [sə'lebrəti]	Prominente/r
sensationalist [sen'seɪʃənəlɪst]	sensationslüstern
insensitive [ɪn'sensətɪv]	unsensibel, instinktlos

breach [bri:tʃ]	Verletzung, Verstoß
acquaintance [ə'kweɪntəns]	Bekannte/r
to **circulate** ['sɜ:kjəleɪt]	verbreiten
copyright ['kɒpiraɪt]	Urheberrecht
violation [ˌvaɪə'leɪʃn]	Verletzung, Verstoß
online theft [ˌɒnlaɪn 'θeft]	Online-Diebstahl
to **discourage sb. from sth.** [dɪs'kʌrɪdʒ]	jdn von etw abhalten
creator [kri'eɪtə]	Urheber/in

page 91

competition [ˌkɒmpə'tɪʃn]	Konkurrenz
to **embarrass sb.** [ɪm'bærəs]	jdn bloßstellen
piracy ['paɪrəsi]	Piraterie, Datendiebstahl
to **bring sth. about** [ˌbrɪŋ ə'baʊt]	etw herbeiführen, zu etw führen
intrusion [ɪn'tru:ʒn]	Eingriff, Eindringen

page 92

access (to sth.) ['ækses]	Zugriff (auf etw)
addicted to sth. [ə'dɪktɪd tə]	von etw abhängig, nach etw süchtig
addict ['ædɪkt]	Abhängige/r, Süchtige/r
addiction [ə'dɪkʃn]	Abhängigkeit, Sucht
disorder [dɪs'ɔ:də]	Störung
excessive [ɪk'sesɪv]	übermäßig
obsessive [əb'sesɪv]	zwanghaft
to **interfere with sth.** [ˌɪntə'fɪə wɪð]	etw beeinträchtigen
nutrition [nju'trɪʃn]	Ernährung, Nahrung
weight gain ['weɪt geɪn]	Gewichtszunahme
weight loss ['weɪt lɒs]	Gewichtsabnahme
gaming site ['geɪmɪŋ saɪt]	Spiele-Website
brain [breɪn]	Gehirn
to **impair** [ɪm'peə]	beeinträchtigen
decision-making ability [dɪˌsɪʒn meɪkɪŋ ə'bɪləti]	Entscheidungsfähigkeit
to **devote sth. to sth.** [dɪ'vəʊt]	etw *(Zeit)* auf etw verwenden
to **turn to sth.** ['tɜ:n tə]	sich einer Sache zuwenden
temporarily ['temprərəli]	vorübergehend
loneliness ['ləʊnlinəs]	Einsamkeit
to **evaporate into thin air** [ɪˌvæpəreɪt ɪntə ˌθɪn 'eə]	sich in Luft auflösen
to **meditate** ['medɪteɪt]	meditieren
breathing exercise ['bri:ðɪŋ eksəsaɪz]	Atemübung
counselling ['kaʊnsəlɪŋ]	Beratung, (psychologische/soziale) Therapie
coping skills ['kəʊpɪŋ skɪlz]	Bewältigungsstrategie(n)
to **let off steam** [let ˌɒf 'sti:m]	Dampf ablassen
to **resort to sth.** [rɪ'zɔ:t tə]	auf etw zurückgreifen, zu etw greifen
compulsive [kəm'pʌlsɪv]	zwanghaft
to **take note** [ˌteɪk 'nəʊt]	aufpassen
emotional state [ɪˌməʊʃənl 'steɪt]	Gefühlszustand

to **reveal** [rɪ'vi:l]	preisgeben
intimate ['ɪntɪmət]	intim
intellectual property [ɪntəˌlektʃʊəl 'prɒpəti]	geistiges Eigentum
legal action [ˌli:gl 'ækʃn]	rechtliche Schritte, Rechtsmittel
copyright holder ['kɒpiraɪt həʊldə]	Urheberrechtsinhaber/in

page 93

to **lurk** [lɜ:k]	lauern
to **address sb.** [ə'dres]	jdn ansprechen

page 94

victim ['vɪktɪm]	Opfer
fraud [frɔ:d]	Betrug
to **be on the alert** [bi ɒn ði ə'lɜ:t]	wachsam sein
taxpayer ['tækspeɪə]	Steuerzahler/in
to **drop the matter** ['drɒp ðə mætə]	die Angelegenheit auf sich beruhen lassen

UNIT 8

page 95

carbon dioxide [ˌkɑ:bən daɪ'ɒksaɪd]	Kohlendioxid
carbon footprint [ˌkɑ:bən 'fʊtprɪnt]	CO_2-Fußabdruck
fossil fuel ['fɒsl fju:əl]	fossiler Brennstoff
component [kəm'pəʊnənt]	Bestandteil
greenhouse gas [ˌgri:nhaʊs 'gæs]	Treibhausgas
to **pollute** [pə'lu:t]	verschmutzen
global warming [ˌgləʊbl 'wɔ:mɪŋ]	Erderwärmung
appliance [ə'plaɪəns]	Elektrogerät
fan [fæn]	Ventilator

page 96

dull [dʌl]	langweilig, farblos, fad
stride [straɪd]	(großer) Schritt
to **power** ['paʊə]	mit Energie versorgen, antreiben
to **eliminate** [ɪ'lɪmɪneɪt]	beseitigen, überflüssig machen
to **burn sth.** [bɜ:n]	etw verbrennen
coal [kəʊl]	Kohle
natural gas [ˌnætʃrəl 'gæs]	Erdgas
nuclear power [ˌnju:kliə 'paʊə]	Kernkraft
peak oil [ˌpi:k 'ɔɪl]	Ölfördermaximum
off guard [ˌɒf 'gɑ:d]	unvorbereitet
to **abandon sth.** [ə'bændən]	etw aufgeben, etw hinter sich lassen
convenience [kən'vi:niəns]	Annehmlichkeit
mighty ['maɪti]	äußerst, unheimlich
a stiff price [ə ˌstɪf 'praɪs]	ein hoher Preis
to **play out** [ˌpleɪ 'aʊt]	*hier:* sich auswirken
underwhelming [ˌʌndə'welmɪŋ]	nicht gerade überwältigend, wenig berauschend

panel ['pænl]	Ausschuss, Gremium
to **aim at sth.** ['eɪm ət]	auf etw abzielen, etw bezwecken
to **detail** ['di:teɪl]	(einzeln) aufführen, ausführlich beschreiben, informieren über
piddling ['pɪdlɪŋ]	lächerlich (gering)
electric grid [ɪˌlektrɪk 'grɪd]	Stromnetz
to **start operating** [ˌstɑ:t 'ɒpəreɪtɪŋ]	in Betrieb gehen
tempting ['temptɪŋ]	verlockend
unequivocal [ˌʌnɪ'kwɪvəkl]	eindeutig, zweifelsfrei
multitude ['mʌltɪtju:d]	Vielzahl
profitable ['prɒfɪtəbl]	rentabel
peak [pi:k]	*hier:* Fördermaximum
to **loom** [lu:m]	drohen, bedrohlich näher rücken

page 97

stringent ['strɪndʒənt]	streng
firm [fɜ:m]	fest, hart, unverrückbar
to draw a line [ˌdrɔ: ə 'laɪn]	einen Strich ziehen
utility company [ju:'tɪləti kʌmpəni]	Versorgungsunternehmen

page 98

conflicting [kən'flɪktɪŋ]	widersprüchlich
intention [ɪn'tenʃn]	Absicht
to **transmit** [træns'mɪt]	übertragen
to **substitute** ['sʌbstɪtju:t]	ersetzen
quadrillion [kwɒ'drɪljən]	Billarde
British thermal unit (BTU) [ˌbrɪtɪʃ ˌθɜ:ml 'ju:nɪt]	*Maßeinheit f. Energie im englischsprachigen Raum, ca. 1055J*
projection [prə'dʒekʃn]	Hochrechnung, Prognose
hydro energy [ˌhaɪdrəʊ 'enədʒi]	Wasserkraft

page 99

waste disposal ['weɪst dɪspəʊzl]	Müllentsorgung, Abfallentsorgung
packaging ['pækɪdʒɪŋ]	Verpackung
to **leave sth. a long way off** [ˌli:v ə lɒŋ ˌweɪ 'ɒf]	etw in weite Ferne rücken
wrapper ['ræpə]	Verpackung, Beutel, Tüte
covering ['kʌvərɪŋ]	Verpackung, Folie
proportion [prə'pɔ:ʃn]	Teil, Anteil
to **strangle** ['stræŋgl]	ersticken, strangulieren
gaudy ['gɔ:di]	grell
coat [kəʊt]	Schicht, Decke
impermeable [ɪm'pɜ:miəbl]	(wasser)dicht
to **float** [fləʊt]	(im Wasser) treiben
to **clog sth. up** [ˌklɒg 'ʌp]	etw verstopfen
sea creature ['si: kri:tʃə]	Meerestier
to **flutter** ['flʌtə]	flattern
to **pile up** [ˌpaɪl 'ʌp]	sich stapeln
noxious ['nɒkʃəs]	giftig, schädlich
to **dispose of sth.** [dɪ'spəʊz əv]	etw entsorgen, sich einer Sache entledigen
unmatched [ˌʌn'mætʃt]	unerreicht
landfill ['lændfɪl]	Mülldeponie
to **clutter sth. up** [ˌklʌtər 'ʌp]	etw mit etw übersäen
underestimate [ˌʌndər'estɪmeɪt]	zu geringe Schätzung
contiguous [kən'tɪgjuəs]	benachbart
goods *pl.* [gʊdz]	Waren, Güter
property ['prɒpəti]	Eigenschaft
durable ['djʊərəbl]	haltbar
flexible ['fleksəbl]	biegsam
to **shatter** ['ʃætə]	zerspringen

page 100

film [fɪlm]	Folie
spoilage ['spɔɪlɪdʒ]	Verderb (von Nahrungsmitteln)
harvest ['hɑ:vɪst]	Ernte
the developed world [ðə dɪˌveləpt 'wɜ:ld]	*etwa:* die Industrienationen
tray [treɪ]	Schale
widespread ['waɪdspred]	verbreitet
lifespan ['laɪfspæn]	Lebensdauer
to **shrinkwrap** ['ʃrɪŋkræp]	mit Schrumpffolie umwickeln, in Schrumpffolie einschweißen
diet ['daɪət]	Ernährung
inert [ɪ'nɜ:t]	verfalls-/reaktionsbeständig, inert
to **bury** ['beri]	vergraben, begraben
counterintuitive [ˌkaʊntərɪn'tju:ɪtɪv]	auf den ersten Blick unlogisch/widersinnig
to **sequester** [sɪ'kwestə]	binden, speichern
to **grip** [grɪp]	ergreifen, fesseln
throwaway society [ˌθrəʊəweɪ sə'saɪəti]	Wegwerfgesellschaft
nappy ['næpi]	Windel
biodegradable [ˌbaɪəʊdɪ'greɪdəbl]	biologisch abbaubar
cornstarch ['kɔ:nstɑ:tʃ]	Maisstärke
additive ['ædətɪv]	Zusatz(stoff)
to **break sth. down** [ˌbreɪk 'daʊn]	etw zersetzen, etw abbauen
on the go [ɒn ðə 'gəʊ]	unterwegs
self-imposed [ˌself ɪm'pəʊzd]	selbst auferlegt
incineration [ɪnˌsɪnə'reɪʃn]	Müllverbrennung
plant [plɑ:nt]	Anlage, Werk, Fabrik
assurance [ə'ʃʊərəns]	Zusage, Garantie, Beteuerung
damaging ['dæmɪdʒɪŋ]	schädlich
hierarchy ['haɪərɑ:ki]	Hierarchie
to **propose** [prə'pəʊz]	vorschlagen
to **unite** [ju'naɪt]	sich zusammenschließen
to **fund** [fʌnd]	finanzieren
to **recover** [rɪ'kʌvə]	zurückholen

page 101

minute ['maɪ'nju:t]	winzig
to **conserve** [kən'sɜ:v]	konservieren

page 102

recovery [rɪ'kʌvəri]	Wiedergewinnung
harmful ['hɑ:mfl]	schädlich
health-giving ['helθ gɪvɪŋ]	gesundheitsfördernd
to **store** [stɔ:]	lagern

deforestation [diː,fɒrɪ'steɪʃn]	Abholzung, Waldzerstörung, Entwaldung
to **take sth. into account** [,teɪk ɪntu ə'kaʊnt]	etw berücksichtigen

page 103

to **reshape** [,riː'ʃeɪp]	umgestalten
to **seize** [siːz]	ergreifen
power plant ['paʊə plɑːnt]	Kraftwerk
feasible ['fiːzəbl]	machbar, durchführbar
to **soar** [sɔː]	in die Höhe schnellen, sprunghaft ansteigen
in abundance [ɪn ə'bʌndəns]	reichlich, im Übermaß
hydroelectric energy [haɪdrəʊɪ,lektrɪk 'enədʒi]	Wasserkraft
dam [dæm]	Staudamm
to **ferment** [fə'ment]	gären
agricultural [,ægrɪ'kʌltʃərəl]	landwirtschaftlich
crops *pl.* [krɒps]	Ernte, (Nutz-)Pflanzen, Früchte
grain [greɪn]	Getreide
large-scale ['lɑːdʒskeɪl]	Massen-, in großem Maßstab
solar power [,səʊlə 'paʊə]	Sonnenenergie
windmill ['wɪndmɪl]	Windmühle
latitude ['lætɪtjuːd]	Breite
to **deplete** [dɪ'pliːt]	(sich) erschöpfen, dezimieren
to **speed up** [,spiːd 'ʌp]	beschleunigen
adoption [ə'dɒpʃn]	Einführung
fate [feɪt]	Schicksal
extinction [ɪk'stɪŋkʃn]	Ausrottung

page 104

energy supply ['enədʒi səplaɪ]	Energieversorgung
soil [sɔɪl]	Erdreich, Erdboden
to **trap** [træp]	einschließen
greenhouse effect ['griːnhaʊs ɪfekt]	Treibhauseffekt
pulp [pʌlp]	Zellstoff
farmland ['fɑːmlænd]	Ackerland
to **extract sth. from sth.** ['ɪkstrækt]	etw einer Sache entziehen
capture ['kæptʃə]	Rückhaltung
biodiversity [,baɪəʊdaɪ'vɜːsəti]	Artenvielfalt
sea level ['siː levl]	Meeresspiegel
to conserve sth. [kən'sɜːv]	etw einsparen, mit etw sparsam umgehen
non-polluting [,nɒn pə'luːtɪŋ]	umweltfreundlich
biofuel [,baɪəʊ'fjuːəl]	Biokraftstoff
reflection [rɪ'flekʃn]	Widerspiegelung
sophisticated [sə'fɪstɪkeɪtɪd]	raffiniert, ausgeklügelt
domestic waste [də,mestɪk 'weɪst]	Hausmüll
non-returnable [,nɒn rɪ'tɜːnəbl]	Einweg-
deposit [dɪ'pɒzɪt]	Pfand
designated ['dezɪgneɪtɪd]	(dafür) vorgesehen
leftover food [,leftəʊvə 'fuːd]	Essensreste
to **incinerate** [ɪn'sɪnəreɪt]	verbrennen
hazardous waste [,hæzədəs 'weɪst]	Sondermüll
disinfectant [,dɪsɪn'fektənt]	Desinfektionsmittel
to **educate sb. to do sth.** ['edʒukeɪt]	jdn dazu erziehen, etw zu tun

page 105

to **cut down** [,kʌt 'daʊn]	*(Baum)* fällen
gradual ['grædʒuəl]	allmählich
poisonous ['pɔɪzənəs]	giftig

page 106

to **endanger** [ɪn'deɪndʒə]	gefährden
pollutant [pə'luːtənt]	Schadstoff
to **promote** [prə'məʊt]	fördern, unterstützen
enterprise ['entəpraɪz]	Unternehmen
reliable [rɪ'laɪəbl]	verlässlich

UNIT 9

page 107

refugee camp [,refju'dʒiː kæmp]	Flüchtlingslager
urgent ['ɜːdʒənt]	dringlich

page 108

starvation [stɑː'veɪʃn]	Verhungern
malnutrition [,mælnjuː'trɪʃn]	Unterernährung
epidemic disease [epɪ,demɪk dɪ'ziːz]	Epidemie
present-day [,preznt 'deɪ]	gegenwärtig
vast [vɑːst]	riesig
supply [sə'plaɪ]	Vorrat, Vorkommen
natural resources *pl.* [,nætʃrəl rɪ'sɔːsɪz]	natürliche Rohstoffe
to **gain wealth** [,geɪn 'welθ]	reich werden
exploitation [,eksplɔɪ'teɪʃn]	Ausbeutung
indigenous [ɪn'dɪdʒənəs]	eingeboren
destiny ['destəni]	Schicksal, Bestimmung
colonial power [kə'ləʊniəl 'paʊə]	Kolonialmacht
to **fail to do sth.** [feɪl]	(es) versäumen, etw zu tun
sufficient [sə'fɪʃnt]	genügend, ausreichend
well [wel]	Brunnen
water line ['wɔːtə laɪn]	Wasserleitung
political entity [pə,lɪtɪkl 'entəti]	politische Einheit, Staatsgebilde
to **displace** [dɪs'pleɪs]	vertreiben
boundary ['baʊndri]	Grenze
arbitrary ['ɑːbɪtrəri]	willkürlich
civil war [,sɪvl 'wɔː]	Bürgerkrieg
in turn [ɪn 'tɜːn]	seiner-/ihrerseits, wiederum
impoverished [ɪm'pɒvərɪʃt]	verarmt

inhospitable [ˌɪnhɒ'spɪtəbl]	unwirtlich
to **migrate** [maɪ'greɪt]	abwandern, (fort)ziehen
newcomer ['nju:kʌmə]	Neuankömmling
sprawling ['sprɔ:lɪŋ]	sich ausbreitend, ausufernd
abominable [ə'bɒmɪnəbl]	grässlich, fürchterlich
brain drain ['breɪn dreɪn]	*Abwanderung hochqualifizierter Arbeitskräfte*
industrialized country [ɪnˌdʌstriəlaɪzd 'kʌntri]	Industrienation, -staat
(foreign) aid [ˌfɒrən 'eɪd]	Hilfe, Entwicklungshilfe
subsidy ['sʌbsədi]	Subvention, Finanzhilfe
loan [ləʊn]	Darlehen
protective import tariff [prəˌtektɪv 'ɪmpɔ:t 'tærɪf]	Einfuhr-Schutzzoll
produce ['prɒdju:s]	(landwirtschaftliche) Erzeugnisse
plight [plaɪt]	Notlage, Elend
to **subsidize** ['sʌbsɪdaɪz]	subventionieren, fördern
to **force sb. out of business** [ˌfɔ:s aʊt əv 'bɪznəs]	jdn vom Markt drängen
undernourished [ˌʌndə'nʌrɪʃt]	unterernährt
to **starve to death** [ˌstɑ:v tə 'deθ]	verhungern
debt relief ['det rɪli:f]	Schuldenerlass
protective trade policies [prəˌtektɪv 'treɪd 'pɒləsiz]	Handelsbarrieren
sewer system ['su:ə sɪstəm]	Kanalisation(ssystem)

page 109

to **lend itself to sth.** [lend]	sich für etw eignen
habitation [ˌhæbɪ'teɪʃn]	Besiedlung
exit ['eksɪt]	Abwanderung
to **borrow** ['bɒrəʊ]	borgen, leihen
supply and demand [səˌplaɪ ən dɪ'mɑ:nd]	Angebot und Nachfrage
to **be in short supply** [bi ɪn ˌʃɔ:t sə'plaɪ]	knapp sein
to **cut off supply** [kʌt ˌɒf sə'plaɪ]	den Nachschub abschneiden
to **pool** [pu:l]	zusammenlegen, vereinigen
tax relief ['tæks rɪli:f]	Steuererleichterung, -nachlass
relief fund [rɪ'li:f fʌnd]	Hilfsfonds
sigh of relief [ˌsaɪ əv rɪ'li:f]	Seufzer der Erleichterung

page 110

infertile [ɪn'fɜ:taɪl]	unfruchtbar
to **support** [sə'pɔ:t]	*hier:* ernähren
to **project** [prə'dʒekt]	schätzen, hochrechnen, prognostizieren
sobering ['səʊbərɪŋ]	ernüchternd
demographer [dɪ'mɒgrəfə]	Demograph/in
council ['kaʊnsl]	Rat
to **feed sb.** [fi:d]	jdn ernähren
to **be better off** [bi ˌbetər 'ɒf]	besser dran sein
revision [rɪ'vɪʒn]	Korrektur, Nachbesserung
slight [slaɪt]	leicht
to **stagnate** [stæg'neɪt]	stagnieren
to **be caught up in sth.** [bi ˌkɔ:t 'ʌp ɪn]	in etw verstrickt sein
abortion [ə'bɔ:ʃn]	Abtreibung
sex education [ˌseks edʒu'keɪʃn]	Sexualerziehung, -kunde
meddling ['medlɪŋ]	Einmischung
birth control ['bɜ:θ kəntrəʊl]	Verhütungsmittel, Empfängnisverhütung
to **call for sth.** ['kɔ:l fə]	etw fordern
to **empower sb.** [ɪm'paʊə]	jdn/jds Rechte stärken
contraceptive [ˌkɒntrə'septɪv]	Verhütungsmittel
donor ['dəʊnə]	Spender/in
to **revise** [rɪ'vaɪz]	korrigieren, nachbessern
forecasting ['fɔ:kɑ:stɪŋ]	Prognose, Vorhersage
to **caution** ['kɔ:ʃn]	warnen
caveat ['kævi:æt]	Vorbehalt
to **skyrocket** ['skaɪrɒkɪt]	in die Höhe schnellen, explodieren
to **quintuple** ['kwɪntʊpl]	sich verfünffachen
to **quadruple** ['kwɒdrʊpl]	sich vervierfachen
to **prove sth.** [pru:v]	sich als etw erweisen
implicit [ɪm'plɪsɪt]	unausgesprochen, (stillschweigend) vorausgesetzt
questionable ['kwestʃənəbl]	fragwürdig, fraglich
assumption [ə'sʌmpʃn]	Annahme, Voraussetzung

page 111

epidemic [ˌepɪ'demɪk]	Epidemie
sustainable [sə'steɪnə'bl]	vertretbar, haltbar
voluntary ['vɒləntri]	freiwillig
devastating ['devəsteɪtɪŋ]	verheerend
prevalence ['prevələns]	Verbreitung, Vorherrschen, Prävalenz
immunodeficiency [ɪˌmju:nəʊdɪ'fɪʃnsi]	Immunschwäche
to **turn out to be sth.** [ˌtɜ:n 'aʊt]	sich als etw erweisen
drug regimen ['drʌg redʒɪmən]	Arzneimitteltherapie
death rate ['deθ reɪt]	Sterblichkeit
survival [sə'vaɪvl]	Überleben
heartening ['hɑ:tnɪŋ]	ermutigend
lack [læk]	Mangel
dearth (of sth.) [dɜ:θ]	Mangel (an etw)
trial ['traɪəl]	Versuch
literate ['lɪtərət]	des Lesens und Schreibens kundig
imprecise [ˌɪmprɪ'saɪs]	ungenau
unanimous [ju'nænɪməs]	einstimmig
unwillingness [ʌn'wɪlɪŋnəs]	Widerwille, mangelnde Bereitschaft

page 112

to **exercise caution** [ˌeksəsaɪz 'kɔ:ʃn]	Vorsicht walten lassen
to **be a foregone conclusion** [ə ˌfɔ:gɒn kən'klu:ʒn]	von vornherein feststehen

imminent ['ɪmɪnənt]	bevorstehend
unfounded [ˌʌn'faʊndɪd]	unbegründet
regardless of [rɪ'gɑ:dləs əv]	ungeachtet
birth rate ['bɜ:θ reɪt]	Geburtenrate
to **secure sth.** [sɪ'kjuə]	etw sicherstellen
objective [əb'dʒektɪv]	Ziel

page 113

humanitarian [ˌhju:mænɪ'teəriən]	humanitär
jointly ['dʒɔɪntli]	gemeinsam
to **award sth.** [ə'wɔ:d]	etw *(Preis, etc.)* verleihen
struggle ['strʌgl]	Kampf, Eintreten (für etw)
to **profile** ['prəʊfaɪl]	porträtieren

page 114

much-needed [ˌmʌtʃ 'ni:dɪd]	dringend benötigt, dringend erforderlich
crusade [kru:'seɪd]	Kreuzzug, Kampagne
paramount ['pærəmaʊnt]	Haupt-, höchste/r/s, oberste/r/s
slavery ['sleɪvəri]	Sklaverei
totalitarianism [təʊˌtælə'teəriənɪzəm]	Totalitarismus
brutality [bru:'tæləti]	Brutalität
to **inflict sth. on sb.** [ɪn'flɪkt]	jdm etw zufügen
sex trafficking ['seks træfɪkɪŋ]	Menschenhandel, Frauenhandel
acid ['æsɪd]	Säure
bride burning ['braɪd bɜ:nɪŋ]	Brautverbrennung
to **hold sth. up** [ˌhəʊld 'ʌp]	etw stützen, etw tragen
aspiration [ˌæspə'reɪʃn]	(angestrebtes) Ziel, Wunschdenken
slice [slaɪs]	Teil
uneducated [ʌn'edʒukeɪtɪd]	ungebildet, ohne Schulbildung
to **marginalize sb.** ['mɑ:dʒɪnəlaɪz]	jdn ins Abseits drängen
to **be mired in sth.** [be 'maɪəd ɪn]	in (einem Sumpf von) etw stecken
to **be riven by sth.** [bi 'rɪvn baɪ]	von etw zerrissen/ zerfressen sein
to **awake to sth.** [ə'weɪk tə]	sich einer Sache bewusst werden
to **observe** [əb'zɜ:v]	beobachten
muddy ['mʌdi]	matschig
back alley [ˌbæk 'æli]	Gasse, Seitengasse
to **dissolve into sth.** [dɪ'zɒlv ɪntə]	sich in etw auflösen
deadbeat ['dedbi:t]	nichtsnutzig, Nichtstuer/in
to **accumulate sth.** [ə'kju:mjəleɪt]	etw anhäufen
blunt [blʌnt]	direkt, unverblümt
to **raise the stakes** [ˌreɪz ðə 'steɪks]	*etwa:* die Situation verschärfen
shattered ['ʃætəd]	am Boden zerstört
to **sign up with sth.** [ˌsaɪn 'ʌp wɪð]	einer Sache beitreten, sich bei etw anmelden
schooling ['sku:lɪŋ]	Schulbesuch, Schulbildung
to **tolerate** ['tɒləreɪt]	tolerieren
embroidery [ɪm'brɔɪdəri]	Stickerei
merchant ['mɜ:tʃənt]	Händler/in
to **pay sth. off** [ˌpeɪ 'ɒf]	etw abbezahlen

page 115

awakening [ə'weɪkənɪŋ]	Erwachen
obscure [əb'skjʊə]	unklar
to **outline** ['aʊtlaɪn]	beschreiben, skizzieren, umreißen
human rights violation [ˌhju:mən 'raɪts vaɪəleɪʃn]	Menschenrechtsverletzung
to **claim** [kleɪm]	*(Menschenleben)* fordern
skewed [skju:d]	verzerrt, verdreht
battlefield ['bætlfi:ld]	Schlachtfeld
to **mourn sb.** [mɔ:n]	jdn betrauern, jdn beweinen
for want of sth. [fə 'wɒnt əv]	weil etw fehlt
beneficiary [ˌbenɪ'fɪʃəri]	Nutznießer
assets *pl.* ['æsets]	Vermögen(swerte)
consequently ['kɒnsɪkwəntli]	folglich, deshalb
involvement [ɪn'vɒlvmənt]	Beteiligung
to **undermine** [ˌʌndə'maɪn]	untergraben
child sponsorship ['tʃaɪld spɒnsəʃɪp]	Patenschaft
foreign assistance [ˌfɒrən ə'sɪstəns]	Entwicklungshilfe
lubricant ['lu:brɪkənt]	Schmiermittel
crankcase ['kræŋkkeɪs]	Kurbelgehäuse
to **amount to sth.** [ə'maʊnt tə]	einer Sache gleichkommen, sich auf etw belaufen
to **glide** [glaɪd]	gleiten
odds [ɒdz]	Widrigkeiten, Aussichten
misguided [ˌmɪs'gaɪdɪd]	Fehl-
resourcefulness [rɪ'sɔ:sflnəs]	Einfallsreichtum, Findigkeit
to **let sth. go to waste** [let ˌgəʊ tə 'weɪst]	etw ungenutzt lassen
miracle ['mɪrəkl]	Wunder
scale [skeɪl]	Maßstab
to **pay off** [ˌpeɪ 'ɒf]	sich lohnen

page 116

to **derive sth. from sth.** [dɪ'raɪv]	etw *(Nutzen, etc.)* aus etw ziehen

page 117

extensive [ɪk'stensɪv]	ausführlich
to **sponsor sb.** ['spɒnsə]	jdn fördern
to **come of age** [ˌkʌm əv 'eɪdʒ]	volljährig werden, erwachsen werden
to **donate** [dəʊ'neɪt]	spenden
to **volunteer to do sth.** [ˌvɒlən'tɪə]	sich bereit erklären, etw zu tun, etw freiwillig tun
allowance [ə'laʊəns]	Taschengeld
return [rɪ'tɜ:n]	Rendite
interest ['ɪntrəst]	Zins(en)
obesity [əʊ'bi:səti]	Fettleibigkeit

page 118

congressman ['kɒŋgresmən]	Kongressabgeordneter
issue ['ɪʃu:]	Angelegenheit, Thema
decade ['dekeɪd]	Jahrzenht
powerful ['paʊəfl]	machtvoll

slave labour ['sleɪv lɪbə]	Sklavenarbeit
support [sə'pɔːt]	Unterstützung
to force sb. to do sth. [fɔːs]	jdn zu etw zwingen
to be willing to do sth. ['wɪlɪŋ]	bereit sein etw zu tun
scepticism ['skeptɪsɪzəm]	Skepsis
antagonism [æn'tægənɪzəm]	Feindseligkeit
interference [ˌɪntə'fɪərəns]	Einmischung
in the foreseeable future [ɪn ðə fɔːˌsiːəbl 'fjuːtʃə]	in absehbarer Zeit

page 119

to maintain [meɪn'teɪn]	warten, instand halten
oil refinery ['ɔɪl rɪfaɪnəri]	Ölraffinerie
crude oil [ˌkruːd 'ɔɪl]	Rohöl
dirt-poor [ˌdɜːt 'pʊə]	bitterarm
fully-fledged [ˌfʊl 'fledʒd]	voll entwickelt
insurgency [ɪn'sɜːdʒənsi]	Aufstand, Aufruhr
to make a contribution [ˌmeɪk ə ˌkɒntrɪ'bjuːʃn]	einen Beitrag leisten

UNIT 10

page 120

to starve for sth. ['stɑːv fə]	sich nach etw sehnen
to restore [rɪ'stɔː]	wiederherstellen
competitive [kəm'petətɪv]	konkurrenzfähig
homogenization [həˌmɒdʒənaɪ'zeɪʃn]	Angleichung
commodity [kə'mɒdəti]	(Handels-)Ware, Rohstoff

page 121

to apply [ə'plaɪ]	zutreffen
disparat ['dɪspərət]	verschieden
to charge [tʃɑːdʒ]	stürmen
to outduel sb. [ˌaʊt'djuːəl]	jdn aus dem Feld schlagen
R&D (Research and Development) [ˌɑː ən 'diː, rɪˌsɜːtʃ ən dɪ'veləpmənt]	Forschung und Entwicklungs(abteilung)
salvation [sæl'veɪʃn]	Rettung, Erlösung
despondent [dɪ'spɒndənt]	bedrückt, mutlos, niedergeschlagen
pittance ['pɪtəns]	Hungerlohn
shift of power [ˌʃɪft əf 'paʊə]	Kräfteverschiebung, Machtverschiebung
unprecedented [ʌn'presɪdentɪd]	nie dagewesen
(bare) necessities [ˌbeə nə'sesətiz]	die lebensnotwendigen Dinge
spending power ['spendɪŋ paʊə]	Kaufkraft
to splurge on sth. ['splɜːdʒ ɒn]	für etw (mit vollen Händen) viel Geld ausgeben
bonanza [bə'nænzə]	Goldgrube, unerwartet großer Gewinn
consumer goods *pl.* [kən'sjuːmə gʊdz]	Konsumgüter
copper ['kɒpə]	Kupfer
cotton ['kɒtn]	Baumwolle
sales [seɪlz]	Umsatz, Verkaufszahlen
continued [kən'tɪnjuːd]	anhaltend
emerging [ɪ'mɜːdʒɪŋ]	aufkommend, aufstrebend, Schwellen-
to descend into sth. [dɪ'send ɪntə]	in etw verfallen, in etw (hinab-/ver-)sinken
capital equipment ['kæpɪtl ɪkwɪpmənt]	Investitionsgüter, Kapitalausstattung
to spread [spred]	sich ausbreiten
to strengthen ['streŋθn]	sich verstärken
to purchase ['pɜːtʃəs]	kaufen
chamber of minerals and energy [ˌtʃeɪmbər əv ˌmɪnərəlz ənd 'enədʒi]	Handelskammer für Mineralien und Energie
expanding exports [ɪkˌspændɪŋ 'ekspɔːts]	steigende Exporte

page 122

to dine out [ˌdaɪn 'aʊt]	essen gehen
quest (for sth.) [kwest]	Streben (nach etw)
to absorb [əb'sɔːb]	aufnehmen, integrieren, abschöpfen
overhaul ['əʊvəhɔːl]	Überdenken, Anpassung
economic order [iːkəˌnɒmɪk 'ɔːdə]	Wirtschaftsordnung
economic power [iːkəˌnɒmɪk 'paʊə]	Wirtschaftsmacht
to challenge ['tʃælɪndʒ]	herausfordern
to surpass [sə'pɑːs]	überholen
depressed [dɪ'prest]	(*Wirtschaft:*) angeschlagen, kriselnd
to pose a threat to sb./sth. [ˌpəʊz ə 'θret tə]	eine Gefahr/Bedrohung für jdn/etw darstellen
job security [ˌdʒɒb sɪ'kjʊərəti]	Arbeits(platz)sicherheit
to pity ['pɪti]	bemitleiden

page 123

dominance ['dɒmɪnəns]	Vorherrschaft
inevitable [ɪn'evɪtəbl]	unvermeidlich
budget deficit [ˌbʌdʒɪt 'defɪsɪt]	Haushaltsdefizit
to run a deficit [ˌrʌn ə 'defɪsɪt]	ein Defizit aufweisen
lower middle class [ˌləʊə 'mɪdl klɑːs]	untere Mittelklasse
currency ['kʌrənsi]	Währung

page 124

to impact sb./sth. ['ɪmpækt]	sich auf jdn/etw auswirken, Folgen für jdn/etw haben
interconnectedness [ˌɪntəkə'nektɪdnəs]	Vernetzung
vastly ['vɑːstli]	gewaltig
welfare services *pl.* [ˌwelfeə 'sɜːvɪsɪz]	soziale Einrichtungen
sanitation [ˌsænɪ'teɪʃn]	Müll- und Abwasserentsorgung
to maintain [meɪn'teɪn]	aufrecht erhalten
multinational corporation [mʌltiˌnæʃnəl ˌkɔːpə'reɪʃn]	internationaler Konzert, Multi

erosion [ɪ'rəʊʒn] — Abbau, Erosion
social justice [ˌsəʊʃl 'dʒʌstɪs] — soziale Gerechtigkeit
to **impoverish sb.** [ɪm'pɒvərɪʃ] — jdn verarmen lassen
flow [fləʊ] — Fluss
International Monetary Fund (IMF) [ɪntəˌnæʃnəl ˌmʌnɪtri 'fʌnd] — Internationaler Währungsfonds (IWF)
World Trade Organization (WTO) [ˌwɜ:ld 'treɪd ɔ:gənaɪzeɪʃn] — Welthandelsorganisation (WHO)
to **enhance** [ɪn'hɑ:ns] — verstärken, fördern
theft of intellectual property [ˌθeft əv ɪntəˌlektʃʊəl 'prɒpəti] — geistiger Diebstahl
to **disrupt** [dɪs'rʌpt] — stören, behindern
to **stave sb. off** [ˌsteɪv 'ɒf] — jdn abwehren, jdn zurückhalten
restriction [rɪ'strɪkʃn] — Beschränkung
to **amount to sth.** [ə'maʊnt tə] — auf etw hinauslaufen
recolonization [ˌri:kɒlənaɪ'zeɪʃn] — erneute Kolonisierung
to **force sth. upon sb.** ['fɔ:s əpɒn] — jdm etw aufzwingen
profound(ly) [prə'faʊnd] — tiefgreifend
uniqueness [ju'ni:knəs] — Einzigartigkeit
to **diminish** [dɪ'mɪnɪʃ] — verkleinern, schmälern
proponent [prə'pəʊnənt] — Befürworter
to **wipe sth. out** [ˌwaɪp 'aʊt] — auslöschen, zunichte machen

page 125

uninterrupted [ˌʌnˌɪntə'rʌptɪd] — ununterbrochen, unterbrechungsfrei
supplies [sə'plaɪz] — Versorgungsgüter, Nachschub
rotten ['rɒtn] — verdorben, korrupt
nuclear reactor [ˌnju:kliə ri'æktə] — (Kern-)Reaktor
to **dictate sth. to sb.** [dɪk'teɪt] — jdm etw aufzwingen
indisputable [ˌɪndɪ'spju:təbl] — unstrittig
privileged ['prɪvəlɪdʒd] — privilegiert
gradually ['grædʒuəli] — allmählich, nach und nach
reform-minded [rɪˌfɔ:m'maɪndɪd] — reformorientiert
to **be subjected to sth.** [bi səb'dʒektɪd tə] — einer Sache unterworfen sein

page 126

to **put sth. to work** [ˌpʊt tə 'wɜ:k] — etw einsetzen, etw nutzen
arms proliferation ['ɑ:mz prəlɪfəreɪʃn] — Weiterverbreitung von Waffen
geopolitics [ˌdʒi:əʊ'pɒlətɪks] — Geopolitik
to **deploy** [dɪ'plɔɪ] — einsetzen, aufstellen, aufbieten
franchisee [ˌfræntʃaɪ'zi:] — Lizenznehmer
saturated ['sætʃəreɪtɪd] — gesättigt
outlet ['aʊtlet] — Verkaufstelle, Geschäft, Filiale
appetite for sth. ['æpɪtaɪt] — Verlangen nach etw
fare [feə] — Kost
disposable [dɪ'spəʊzəbl] — verfügbar
line [laɪn] — Warteschlange
to **operate sth.** ['ɒpəreɪt] — etw betreiben
to **pave the way** [ˌpeɪv ðə 'weɪ] — den Weg ebnen
to **flourish** ['flʌrɪʃ] — gedeihen, florieren
trickle ['trɪkl] — kleiner, aber stetiger Strom
to **trail behind sth.** [ˌtreɪl bɪ'haɪnd] — hinter etw zurückbleiben
discretionary spending [dɪˌskreʃnri 'spendɪŋ] — Konsumausgaben, Ermessensausgaben
unburdened by sth. [ʌn'bɜ:dnd baɪ] — von etw unbelastet
hangover ['hæŋəʊvə] — Nachwirkung(en)
consumer debt [kən'sju:mə det] — private Überschuldung
medical bills *pl.* ['medɪkl bɪlz] — Gesundheitskosten
health care system ['helθ keə sɪstəm] — Gesundheitssystem
flawed [flɔ:d] — mangelhaft, mit Mängeln behaftet
to **socialize** ['səʊʃəlaɪz] — vergesellschaften
flat [flæt] — pauschal
property ['prɒpəti] — Immobilie(n)
legacy ['legəsi] — Erbe

page 127

foray ['fɒreɪ] — Vorstoß
to **stumble** ['stʌmbl] — stolpern
to **anticipate** [æn'tɪsɪpeɪt] — vorhersehen, mit etw rechnen
stock [stɒk] — Fond
pouch [paʊtʃ] — Beutel
a sure bet [ə ˌʃʊə 'bet] — eine sichere Sache
broth [brɒθ] — Brühe, Bouillon
to **turn out** [ˌtɜ:n 'aʊt] — sich herausstellen
from scratch [frəm 'skrætʃ] — von Grund auf
earnings *pl.* ['ɜ:nɪŋz] — Einkünfte, Einkommen
to **attribute sth. to sth.** [ə'trɪbju:t] — etw einer Sache zuschreiben
deck of cards [ˌdek əv 'kɑ:dz] — Kartensatz, -spiel, -stapel
cord [kɔ:d] — Kabel
suspect ['sʌspekt] — Verdächtige/r

page 128

to **lag behind** [ˌlæg bɪ'haɪnd] — hinterherhinken, hinter etw zurückbleiben
unaffected [ˌʌnə'fektɪd] — unbeeinträchtigt, unberührt
aftermath ['ɑ:ftəmæθ] — Nachwirkung(en)

page 129

interdependence [ˌɪntədɪ'pendəns] — wechselseitige Abhängigkeit, Verflechtung
agent ['eɪdʒənt] — Protagonist/in
ruling party [ˌru:lɪŋ 'pɑ:ti] — Regierungspartei
composite ['kɒmpəzɪt] — zusammengesetzt, gemischt
yapping ['jæpɪŋ] — Gekläffe, große Sprüche
cultural mould [ˌkʌltʃərəl 'məʊld] — kulturelle Prägung

deleterious [ˌdelə'tɪəriəs]	schädlich
urban ['ɜ:bən]	städtisch, Stadt-
artificial [ˌɑ:tɪ'fɪʃl]	künstlich
to **breed** [bri:d]	hervorrufen
law and order [ˌlɔ: ənd 'ɔ:də]	Recht und Ordnung
gun toting ['gʌn təʊtɪŋ]	verbreiteter Schusswaffenbesitz/-gebrauch
to **resist sth.** [rɪ'zɪst]	einer Sache widerstehen
dean [di:n]	Dekan/in
to **link up with sth.** [ˌlɪŋk 'ʌp wɪð]	sich mit etw verknüpfen (lassen)
to **inherit** [ɪn'herɪt]	erben
to **humiliate** [hju:'mɪlieɪt]	erniedrigen
to **regain** [rɪ'geɪn]	wiedererlangen
to **recover sth.** [rɪ'kʌvə]	etw wiederfinden
to **erode away** [ɪˌrəʊd ə'weɪ]	abtragen, verwittern, wegfressen
to **infect** [ɪn'fekt]	anstecken, infizieren
tendency ['tendənsi]	Neigung
to **restate** [ˌri:'steɪt]	noch einmal sagen, neu formulieren
in shame [ɪn 'ʃeɪm]	beschämt
to **bow down to sth.** [ˌbaʊ 'daʊn tə]	sich einer Sache beugen
valid ['vælɪd]	gültig, begründet, berechtigt
to **place emphasis on sth.** [ˌpleɪs 'emfəsɪs ɒn]	etw betonen, etw hervorheben
subordinate [sə'bɔ:dɪnət]	zweitrangig
athletics [æθ'letɪks]	Sport
funding ['fʌndɪŋ]	Finanzierung, Mittel

page 130

penetration [ˌpenɪ'treɪʃn]	Durchdringung

page 131

to **marvel at sth.** ['mɑ:vl ət]	über etw staunen
tremendous [trɪ'mendəs]	ungeheuer
to **be eager to do sth.** [bi 'i:gə tə]	etw unbedingt tun wollen
semi-skilled [ˌsemi'skɪld]	angelernt
to **restructure** [ˌri:'strʌktʃə]	umgestalten, umstrukturieren
income gap ['ɪnkʌm gæp]	Einkommensschere
to **apply sth.** [ə'plaɪ]	etw anwenden

UNIT 11

page 133

clash of interest [ˌklæʃ əv 'ɪntrəst]	Interessenkonflikt
differing ['dɪfərɪŋ]	verschieden, unterschiedlich
state security [ˌsteɪt sɪ'kjʊərəti]	Staatssicherheit
rule [ru:l]	Herrschaft
contagion [kən'teɪdʒən]	ansteckende Krankheit, Seuche, negativer Einfluss
to **unfold** [ʌn'fəʊld]	sich abspielen, sich entwickeln
connectivity [ˌkɒnek'tɪvəti]	Vernetzung, Verbindungen
to **flatten** ['flætn]	ebnen, einebnen
diffusion [dɪ'fju:ʒn]	Verbreitung
fiber-optic cable [ˌfaɪbər ɒptɪk 'keɪbl]	Glasfaserkabel
bandwidth ['bændwɪdθ]	Bandbreite
uprising ['ʌpraɪzɪŋ]	Aufstand
to **pump sth. out** [ˌpʌmp 'aʊt]	etw herauspumpen
atrocities *pl.* [ə'trɒsətiz]	Gräueltaten
grievance ['gri:vəns]	Groll, Klage
aspiration [ˌæspə'reɪʃn]	Ambition, Bestrebung

page 134

vivid ['vɪvɪd]	anschaulich
crackdown ['krækdaʊn]	scharfes Vorgehen
to **shoot sth.** [ʃu:t]	*(Foto, Film:)* etw aufnehmen
to **posit** ['pɒzɪt]	postulieren, aufstellen
orderly ['ɔ:dəli]	geordnet
the sweet spot [ðə 'swi:t spɒt]	der optimale Punkt
to **collaborate** [kə'læbəreɪt]	zusammenarbeiten
revolutionary [ˌrevə'lu:ʃənəri]	Revolutionär/in
to **empower sb.** [ɪm'paʊə]	jdn stärken, jdn (zu etw) ermächtigen
to **meld** [meld]	verschmelzen
to **resemble** [rɪ'zembl]	ähneln
dignity ['dɪgnəti]	Würde
by whim [baɪ 'wɪm]	nach Belieben
to **exaggerate** [ɪg'zædʒəreɪt]	übertreiben
to **undervalue** [ˌʌndə'vælju:]	unterschätzen
spark [spɑ:k]	Funke
to **vent sth.** [vent]	etw (frei) äußern
oppressive [ə'presɪv]	repressiv, tyrannisch
outpouring of emotions [aʊtˌpɔ:rɪŋ əv ɪ'məʊʃnz]	Gefühlsausbruch
dissent [dɪ'sent]	Widerspruch, Unzufriedenheit
to **attain** [ə'teɪn]	erlangen
self-respect [ˌself rɪ'spekt]	Selbstachtung

page 135

to **squash** [skwɒʃ]	zerquetschen, zunichte machen
predominance [prɪ'dɒmɪnəns]	Vorherrschaft
trading nation ['treɪdɪŋ neɪʃn]	Handelsnation
venue ['venju:]	Stätte, Veranstaltungsort
barbarity [bɑ:'bærəti]	Barbarei
law enforcement ['lɔ: ɪnfɔ:smənt]	Durchsetzung von Gesetzen, Gesetzesvollzug
lawlessness ['lɔ:ləsnəs]	Gesetzlosigkeit, Gesetzwidrigkeit
legitimate [lɪ'dʒɪtɪmət]	rechtmäßig, legitim
rogue government [ˌrəʊg 'gʌvənmənt]	Schurkenstaat
tyrant ['taɪrənt]	Tyrann
suppression [sə'preʃn]	Unterdrückung
to **uncover** [ʌn'kʌvə]	aufdecken, entdecken, enthüllen

at grass roots level [ət 'grɑ:s ru:ts levl]	an der Basis
to **press for sth.** ['pres fə]	auf etw drängen
ingenuity [ˌɪndʒə'nju:əti]	Einfallsreichtum, Phantasie
common good [ˌkɒmən 'gʊd]	Gemeinwohl

page 136

rule of law [ˌru:l əv 'lɔ:]	Rechtsstaatlichkeit
majority rule [mə'dʒɒrəti ru:l]	Mehrheitsregierung
oil exploration ['ɔɪl eksplǝreɪʃn]	Ölsuche
adequate(ly) ['ædɪkwət]	angemessen
to **stage** [steɪdʒ]	veranstalten, organisieren
to **intervene** [ˌɪntə'vi:n]	einschreiten, intervenieren

page 137

undersecretary-general [ʌndəˌsekrətri 'dʒenrəl]	Untergeneralsekretär
humanitarian affairs [hju:mænɪˌteəriən ə'feəz]	Menschenrechtsfragen, humanitäre Angelegenheiten
to **confront sth.** [kən'frʌnt]	einer Sache begegnen, einer Sache trotzen
to **reaffirm** [ri:ə'fɜ:m]	erneut bekräftigen
to **tear sth. down** [ˌteə 'daʊn]	etw niederreißen, etw einreißen
torturer ['tɔ:tʃərə]	Folterer, Folterknecht
mourner ['mɔ:nə]	Trauernde/r
to **underscore** [ˌʌndə'skɔ:]	unterstreichen
folly ['fɒli]	Unsinn, Aberwitz
principled ['prɪnsəpld]	prinzipienfest, prinzipientreu
accountability [əˌkaʊntə'bɪləti]	Verantwortlichkeit, Rechenschaft
torture ['tɔ:tʃə]	Folter
detainee [ˌdi:teɪ'ni:]	Gefangene/r, Häftling
rigorous ['rɪgərəs]	rigoros, konsequent
well-resourced [ˌwel rɪ'sɔ:st]	gut (mit Mitteln) ausgestattet
intelligence service [ɪn'telɪdʒəns sɜ:vɪs]	Geheimdienst
detention [dɪ'tenʃn]	Haft, Internierung
rendition [ren'dɪʃŋ]	Auslieferung
willingly ['wɪlɪŋli]	bereitwillig
the moral high ground [ðə ˌmɒrəl ˌhaɪ 'graʊnd]	moralische Überlegenheit
legitimacy [lɪ'dʒɪtɪməsi]	Rechtmäßigkeit
lawful ['lɔ:fl]	rechtmäßig, gesetzmäßig
to **bend** [bend]	beugen
to **enshrine** [ɪn'ʃraɪn]	festschreiben, verankern
torture chamber ['tɔ:tʃə tʃeɪmbə]	Folterkammer
to **be unanimous in sth.** [bi ju'nænɪməs ɪn]	sich in einer Sache einig sein
vigorous ['vɪgərəs]	energisch, leidenschaftlich
rally (around sth.) ['ræli]	Demonstration, Eintreten (für etw)
to **massacre** ['mæsəkə]	niedermetzeln
to **smash** [smæʃ]	zertrümmern, einschlagen
to **unleash** [ʌn'li:ʃ]	entfesseln, auslösen
occupation [ˌɒkju'peɪʃn]	Besetzung
guidance ['gaɪdəns]	Führung, Orientierung
ranks *pl.* [ræŋks]	Reihen
freedom of expression [ˌfri:dəm əv ɪk'spreʃn]	Recht auf freie Meinungsäußerung
recruitment [rɪ'kru:tmənt]	Anwerbung

page 138

to **trump** [trʌmp]	übertrumpfen
homegrown ['həʊmgrəʊn]	heimisch
betrayal [bɪ'treɪəl]	Verrat
to **get away with sth.** [ˌget ə'weɪ wɪð]	mit etw (straflos) davonkommen
stain [steɪn]	Makel
administration [ədˌmɪnɪ'streɪʃn]	Regierung
official [ə'fɪʃl]	Beamte/r
to **authorize** ['ɔ:θəraɪz]	genehmigen, zulassen
to **investigate sb.** [ɪn'vestɪgeɪt]	Ermittlungen gegen jdn anstellen
interrogation [ɪnˌterə'geɪʃn]	Verhör, Vernehmung
to **haunt sb.** [hɔ:nt]	jdn verfolgen
successive [sək'sesɪv]	die nachfolgende/n
hypocrisy [hɪ'pɒkrəsi]	Heuchelei
to **expose** [ɪk'spəʊz]	entlarven, aufdecken
to **honor sb.** *AE* ['ɒnə]	jdn ehren, jdm Respekt erweisen
to **abide by sth.** [ə'baɪd baɪ]	sich an etw halten

page 139

cruel [kru:əl]	grausam
to **disobey sth.** [ˌdɪsə'beɪ]	etw nicht befolgen
disloyal [dɪs'lɔɪəl]	(jdm gegenüber) illoyal
to **question sb.** ['kwestʃən]	jdn verhören
to **charge sb.** [tʃɑ:dʒ]	jdn anklagen
to **judge sb.** [dʒʌdʒ]	jdn verurteilen, über jdn ein Urteil sprechen
to **eye-witness** ['aɪwɪtnəs]	mit eigenen Augen sehen, Augenzeuge von etw sein
to **tempt sb. into sth.** [tempt]	jdn zu etw verleiten
inappropriate [ˌɪnə'prəʊpriət]	unangemessen
ill-advised [ˌɪl əd'vaɪzd]	unklug, schlecht beraten
deliberate(ly) [dɪ'lɪbərət]	absichtlich
constitution [ˌkɒnstɪ'tju:ʃn]	Verfassung
state of emergency [ˌsteɪt əv ɪ'mɜ:dʒənsi]	Ausnahmezustand, Notstand
to **curtail** [kɜ:'teɪl]	einschränken, beschneiden

page 140

resolution [ˌreʒə'lu:ʃn]	Lösung
heterogeneous [ˌhetərə'dʒi:niəs]	heterogen
to **become apparent** [bɪˌkʌm ə'pærənt]	hervortreten, sich zeigen
rivalry ['raɪvlri]	Konkurrenzkampf, Kampf
equitable ['ekwɪtəbl]	gerecht
armed [ɑ:md]	bewaffnet
volatile ['vɒlətaɪl]	unbeständig, instabil, unberechenbar

to **compound** [kɒm'paʊnd]	verschlimmern
inherently [ɪn'hɪərəntli]	grundsätzlich, an sich
dictatorship [dɪk'teɪtəʃɪp]	Diktatur
for good [fə 'gʊd]	endgültig, ein für allemal
emergence [ɪ'mɜ:dʒəns]	Aufkommen
to **attain sth.** [ə'teɪn]	an etw gelangen
weapons of mass destruction [ˌwepənz əv ˌmæs dɪ'strʌkʃn]	Massenvernichtungswaffen
nuclear proliferation [ˌnju:kliə prəlɪfə'reɪʃn]	Verbreitung/Weitergabe von Kernwaffen
rife (with sth.) [raɪf]	voll (von etw)
atomic bomb [əˌtɒmɪk 'bɒm]	Atombombe
military might [ˌmɪlətri 'maɪt]	militärische (Über-)Macht
to **wage war** [ˌweɪdʒ 'wɔ:]	Krieg führen
constitutional law [kɒnstɪˌtju:ʃənl 'lɔ:]	Staatsrecht, Verfassungsrecht
persuasive [pə'sweɪsɪv]	überzeugend
to **sway** [sweɪ]	beeinflussen
due process of law [dju: ˌprəʊses əv 'lɔ:]	ordentliches Gerichtsverfahren
to **deny sb. sth.** [dɪ'naɪ]	jdm etw verweigern
to **censor** ['sensə]	zensieren
confidential [ˌkɒnfɪ'denʃl]	vertraulich
sovereignty ['sɒvrənti]	Souveränität
to **defuse** [ˌdi:'fju:z]	entschärfen

page 141

to **unveil** [ˌʌn'veɪl]	enthüllen, aufdecken
clandestine [klæn'destɪn]	geheim
ample ['æmpl]	reichlich, groß
armed struggle [ˌɑ:md 'strʌgl]	bewaffneter Kampf
disillusioned [ˌdɪsɪ'lu:ʒnd]	ernüchtert, enttäuscht, desillusioniert
utmost ['ʌtməʊst]	äußerste/r/s
to **inject sth. into sth.** [ɪn'dʒekt]	etw einer Sache verleihen
generosity [ˌdʒenə'rɒsəti]	Großzügigkeit
inconceivable [ˌɪnkən'si:vəbl]	unvorstellbar, undenkbar

page 142

to **spark** [spɑ:k]	entzünden, entfachen

page 143

to **step down** [ˌstep 'daʊn]	zurücktreten
to **misname** [mɪs'neɪm]	unzutreffend benennen
to **oust sb.** [aʊst]	jdn absetzen
to **run its course** [ˌrʌn ɪts 'kɔ:s]	seinen (vollen) Verlauf nehmen
to **temper** ['tempə]	mildern
ally ['ælaɪ]	Alliierte/r
alliance [ə'laɪəns]	Allianz
ballot box ['bælət bɒks]	Wahlurne
victory ['vɪktəri]	Sieg
to **pledge** [pledʒ]	geloben
outlook ['aʊtlʊk]	Perspektive, Einstellung
to **throng** [θrɒŋ]	drängen
to **cast your ballot** [ˌkɑ:st jɔ: 'bælət]	seine Stimme abgeben
in decline [ɪn dɪ'klaɪn]	im Niedergang
leverage ['li:vərɪdʒ]	Einfluss; die Fähigkeit, Druck auszuüben
to **defy sb.** [dɪ'faɪ]	jdm trotzen, sich jdm widersetzen
to **propel** [prə'pel]	antreiben, vorantreiben
accountable [ə'kaʊntəbl]	verantwortlich, rechenschaftspflichtig
to **constitute** ['kɒnstɪtju:t]	darstellen, sein
to **be bound to do sth.** [bi 'baʊnd tə du:]	etw tun werden
to **spell trouble** [ˌspel 'trʌbl]	nichts Gutes bedeuten, Ärger bedeuten
trade barrier ['treɪd bæriə]	Handelsschranken
adversely ['ædvɜ:sli]	negativ
to **champion sth.** ['tʃæmpiən]	für etw eintreten, sich für etw einsetzen

page 144

upheaval [ʌp'hi:vl]	Aufruhr
authoritarian [ɔ:ˌθɒrɪ'teəriən]	autoritär
to **voice** [vɔɪs]	äußern, zum Ausdruck bringen
irreversible [ˌɪrɪ'vɜ:səbl]	unumkehrbar
bullet-proof ['bʊlɪtpru:f]	schusssicher
negotiator [nɪ'gəʊʃieɪtə]	Unterhändler/in
settlement ['setlmənt]	Einigung
rescue agency ['reskju: eɪdʒənsi]	Rettungsdienst

UNIT 12

page 146

optical character recognition (OCR) [ˌɒptɪkl 'kærəktə rekəgnɪʃn]	optische Zeichenerkennung
to **multiply** ['mʌltɪplaɪ]	vervielfältigen, multiplizieren
a billionfold [ə 'bɪliənfəʊld]	milliardenfach
triage ['tri:ɑ:ʒ]	Sichtung, Triage
gene [dʒi:n]	Gen
to **clone** [kləʊn]	klonen

page 147

to **be resistant to sth.** [bi rɪ'zɪstənt tə]	sich einer Sache widersetzen
extension [ɪk'stenʃn]	Ausweitung, Verlängerung
to **wax philosophical** [ˌwæks fɪlə'sɒfɪkl]	ins Philosophieren geraten, herumphilosophieren
destructive [dɪ'strʌktɪv]	zerstörerisch
to **transcend** [træn'send]	über sich hinausgehen

page 148

worthwhile [ˌwɜ:θ'waɪl]	lohnend, interessant
hunter gatherer [ˌhʌntə 'gæðərə]	Jäger und Sammler
sterile ['steraɪl]	steril

to **foster** ['fɒstə]	fördern
divide [dɪ'vaɪd]	Kluft
to **depict** [dɪ'pɪkt]	darstellen
faith (in sb./sth.) [feɪθ]	Glaube (an jdn/etw)
precision [prɪ'sɪʒn]	Genauigkeit, Präzision

page 149

to **upend** [ʌp'end]	verkehren, auf den Kopf stellen
to **occur** [ə'kɜː]	geschehen, stattfinden
solitary ['sɒlətri]	einzeln, einsam
to **progress** [prə'gres]	fortschreiten, voranschreiten
pace [peɪs]	Tempo
to **conceive** [kən'siːv]	konzipieren
high achiever [ˌhaɪ ə'tʃiːvə]	leistungsstarke Person
struggler ['strʌglə]	*jd, der mit Schwierigkeiten zu kämpfen hat*
to **harness** ['hɑːnɪs]	nutzen
zip code *AE* ['zɪp kəʊd]	Postleitzahl
legislature ['ledʒɪsleɪtʃə]	Legislative
to **proliferate** [prə'lɪfəreɪt]	stark zunehmen, wuchern
trade association ['treɪd əsəʊsieɪʃn]	Wirtschaftsverband, Fachverband
fraction ['frækʃn]	Bruchteil
to **make one's case** [ˌmeɪk wʌnz 'keɪs]	für seine Sache werben
statehouse ['steɪthaʊs]	Parlamentsgebäude
to **back sb.** [bæk]	jdn unterstützen
contribution [ˌkɒntrɪ'bjuːʃn]	(finanzielle) Zuwendung
school district [ˌskuːl 'dɪstrɪkt]	Schulbezirk

page 150

to **clamber** ['klʌmbə]	klettern
to **pad** [pæd]	tappen
recess *AE* ['riːses]	Pause *(in der Schule)*
to **average** ['ævərɪdʒ]	im Durchschnitt sein/haben
the bulk [ðə 'bʌlk]	der größte Teil, der Löwenanteil
to **mimic** ['mɪmɪk]	nachahmen
dissection [dɪ'sekʃn]	Sektion, Sezieren
brick-and-mortar [ˌbrɪk ən 'mɔːtə]	konventionell
unstable [ʌn'steɪbl]	labil
turnover ['tɜːnəʊvə]	Fluktuation
misstep [ˌmɪs'step]	Fehltritt
needy ['niːdi]	bedürftig

page 151

to **envision** [ɪn'vɪʒn]	(sich etw) vorstellen

page 152

inventiveness [ɪn'ventɪvnəs]	Erfindungsreichtum
watershed invention [ˌwɔːtəʃed ɪn'venʃn]	*etwa:* bahnbrechende Erfindung
study ['stʌdi]	Forschung
tissue ['tɪʃuː]	Gewebe
tailor-made [ˌteɪlə'meɪd]	maßgeschneidert
incurable [ɪn'kjʊərəbl]	unheilbar
genetic engineering [dʒəˌnetɪk ˌendʒɪ'nɪərɪŋ]	Gentechnik
pesticide ['pestɪsaɪd]	Schädlingsbekämpfungsmittel, Pestizid
to **eradicate** [ɪ'rædɪkeɪt]	ausrotten
pest [pest]	Schädling
to **be suspicious of sth.** [bi sə'spɪʃəs əv]	einer Sache gegenüber misstrauisch sein
to **tinker with sth.** ['tɪŋkə wɪð]	an etw herumbasteln, an etw herumpfuschen
to **prophesy** ['prɒfəsaɪ]	voraussagen
blood stream ['blʌd striːm]	Blutbahn, Blutkreislauf
cellular ['seljʊlə]	Zell-
to **prolong** [prə'lɒŋ]	verlängern
drone [drəʊn]	Drohne

page 153

in dire straits [ɪn ˌdaɪə 'streɪts]	in großen Schwierigkeiten, in einer Notlage

page 154

embryonic [ˌembri'ɒnɪk]	embryonal
to **coax sb./sth. into doing sth.** [kəʊks]	jdn/etw dazu bringen, etw zu tun
to **ignite** [ɪg'naɪt]	entzünden
to **pursue** [pə'sjuː]	verfolgen
to **derive sth. from sth.** [dɪ'raɪv]	etw aus etw gewinnen
rejection [rɪ'dʒekʃn]	Abstoßung *(eines transplantierten Organs)*
to **cure** [kjʊə]	heilen
to **reestablish** [ˌriːɪ'stæblɪʃ]	*(Funktion)* wiederaufnehmen
acceleration [əkˌselə'reɪʃn]	Beschleunigung
to **do the trick** [ˌdu ðə 'trɪk]	seinen Zweck erfüllen, funktionieren

page 155

unstoppable [ˌʌn'stɒpəbl]	nicht aufzuhalten, nicht zu verhindern
consolation prize [ˌkɒnsə'leɪʃn praɪz]	Trostpreis
to **swoop** [swuːp]	hinabstürzen, nach unten fliegen
to **tether** ['teðə]	anbinden, festbinden
tidal power [ˌtaɪdl 'paʊə]	Gezeitenkraft
scale model ['skeɪl mɒdl]	maßstabsgetreues Modell
to **discard** [dɪs'kɑːd]	wegwerfen
husk [hʌsk]	Schale, Hülse
sugarcane ['ʃʊgəkeɪn]	Zuckerrohr
pontoon [pɒn'tuːn]	Ponton
pomegranate ['pɒmɪgrænɪt]	Granatapfel
buoyancy ['bɔɪənsi]	Auftrieb
stain-absorbing ['steɪn əbsɔːbɪŋ]	fleckabsorbierend
moth [mɒθ]	Motte
holey ['həʊli]	löchrig
felting needle ['feltɪŋ niːdl]	Filznadel
to **poke** [pəʊk]	stoßen
garment ['gɑːmənt]	Kleidungsstück

patch [pætʃ]	Flicken
rug [rʌg]	Teppich
to **add a twist to sth.** [ˌæd ə 'twɪst tə]	etw aufpeppen
turtleneck ['tɜːtlnek]	Rollkragenpullover
to **eat one's heart out** [ˌiːt wʌnz 'hɑːt aʊt]	vor Neid erblassen
squat [skwɒt]	gedrungen
flesh-and-blood [ˌfleʃ ən 'blʌd]	aus Fleisch und Blut
daunting ['dɔːntɪŋ]	beängstigend, beunruhigend
hydrogen age ['haɪdrədʒən eɪdʒ]	Wasserstoffzeitalter
introductory [ˌɪntrə'dʌktəri]	einführend

page 156

nuclear fusion [ˌnjuːkliə 'fjuːʒn]	Kernfusion
to **decipher** [dɪ'saɪfə]	entschlüsseln
genome ['dʒiːnəʊm]	Genom
dreadful ['dredfl]	scheußlich
to **be on display** [bi ɒn dɪ'spleɪ]	ausgestellt/dargestellt werden

A–Z word list

Dieses Wörterverzeichnis enthält alle Wörter in **Focus on Success Erweiterte Ausgabe 3rd edition** in alphabetischer Reihenfolge. Nicht aufgeführt sind internationale Wörter wie *hotel*, *e-mail* usw.
Wörter, die in den Hörverständnisübungen vorkommen, sind mit einem *T*, und Wörter, die in den *Files*, mit einem *F* hinter der Seitenzahl gekennzeichnet.

4 × 4 *21* Allradfahrzeug

A

to **abandon** *78* verlassen; **~ sth.** *96* etw aufgeben, etw hinter sich lassen
to **abide by sth.** *138* sich an etw halten
abominable *108* grässlich, fürchterlich
abortion *110* Abtreibung
to **absorb** *122* aufnehmen, integrieren, abschöpfen
abundance, in ~ *103T* reichlich, im Übermaß
abuse *46* Missbrauch, Beschimpfung(en); *76* Beschimpfungen, Gewalt
to **abuse** *75* beleidigen, beschimpfen
abusive *46* beleidigend, missbräuchlich
acceleration *154T* Beschleunigung
access (to sth.) *92T* Zugriff (auf etw)
to **accompany** *69* begleiten
accomplishment *17F* Leistung
according to *7* nach, gemäß
account, to **take sth. into ~** *102* etw berücksichtigen
to **account for sth.** *26* etw ausmachen; *37* etw erklären, etw nachweisen; *44* für etw verantwortlich sein
accountability *137* Verantwortlichkeit, Rechenschaft
accountable *143T* verantwortlich, rechenschaftspflichtig
to **accumulate sth.** *114* etw anhäufen
to **accuse sb. of sth.** *78* jdn einer Sache beschuldigen
accustomed, to **be ~ to sth.** *18* an etw gewohnt sein
achievement *6* Leistung, Errungenschaft, Erfolg; **no mean ~** *61* beachtliche Leistung
achiever, high ~ *149* leistungsstarke Person
acid *114* Säure
acquaintance *90* Bekannte/r
to **acquire** *20* kaufen
acre *20* Morgen *(ca. 4047 qm)*
act *75* Gesetz
action, affirmative ~ *72* aktive Förderung von Minderheiten/positive Diskriminierung; **legal ~** *92* rechtliche Schritte, Rechtsmittel; to **take ~** *42T* Maßnahmen ergreifen
adage *10* Sprichwort
to **adapt** *13* anpassen; **~ to sth.** *44* sich an etw anpassen
to **add to sth.** *24* zu etw beitragen, etw vergrößen
addict *92T* Abhängige/r, Süchtige/r
addicted to sth. *92T* von etw abhängig, nach etw süchtig
addiction *92T* Abhängigkeit, Sucht
additive *100* Zusatz(stoff)
to **address: ~ sb.** *93* jdn ansprechen; **~ sth.** *77* etw *(Problem, etc.)* angehen; **~ a challenge** *37* eine Herausforderung annehmen
adequate(ly) *136* angemessen
to **administer** *38* durchführen
administration *138* Regierung
admission *43* Zulassung
to admit sth. *118T* etw zugeben, gestehen
to **adopt** *43* übernehmen, *hier:* ergreifen; *50* einführen, übernehmen, annehmen
adoption *103T* Einführung
advancement, career ~ *32* beruflicher Aufstieg
advantage, to **take ~ of sth.** *48* etw ausnutzen
advent *24* Aufkommen, Beginn
adventurous *21* abenteuerlustig
adversely *143* negativ
to **advocate sth.** *74* für etw eintreten
advocacy *73* Eintreten (für etw), Engagement
affair, external ~s *50* auswärtige Angelegenheiten; **humanitarian ~s** *137* Menschenrechtsfragen, humanitäre Angelegenheiten
to **affect** *9* beeinträchtigen; *14* beeinflussen; *53* betreffen
to **affirm** *72* bekräftigen
affirmation *72* Bekräftigung, Bestätigung
affirmative action *72* aktive Förderung von Minderheiten/positive Diskriminierung
affluence *10* Wohlstand, Überfluss
affordable *24* erschwinglich, bezahlbar
aftermath *128* Nachwirkung(en)
to **age** *65* altern
age, to **come of ~** *72* erwachsen werden; *117* volljährig werden
ageing *60* alternd, älter werdend
ageism *59* Altersdiskriminierung
agent *129T* Protagonist/in
to **aggravate** *26* verschlimmern
agreement *30* Zustimmung; *48* Vereinbarung: **legal ~** *86* rechtswirksame Vereinbarung
agricultural *103T* landwirtschaftlich
(foreign) aid *108* Hilfe, Entwicklungshilfe
to **aim** *53* darauf abzielen; **~ at sth.** *96* auf etw abzielen, etw bezwecken
to **air** *89* senden, ausstrahlen
air, to **evaporate into thin ~** *92T* sich in Luft auflösen
aircraft *27* Flugzeug
airing *87* Ausstrahlung, Sendung
albeit *80T* wenn auch
alert, to **be on the ~** *94* wachsam sein
alienated *58* entfremdet
alienation *79* Entfremdung
alliance *143T* Allianz
to **allocate** *30* zuweisen
allowance *117* Taschendgeld; to **make ~s for sb.** *60* jdm Zugeständnisse machen, auf jdn Rücksicht nehmen
all-time high *26* historischer Höchststand
ally *51* Verbündete/r, Bündnispartner/in; *143T* Alliierte/r
alone, let ~ *50* geschweige denn
to **alter** *75* sich ändern
ambiguous *72* mehrdeutig, unklar
ambition *8* Ehrgeiz; *63* Ziel

ambulatory *32* ambulant
amid *73* inmitten, unter
to **amount to sth.** *115* einer Sache gleichkommen, sich auf etw belaufen; *124* auf etw hinauslaufen
ample *141* reichlich, groß
anaemic *37* kraftlos, blass, blutarm, blutleer
ancestry *72* Vorfahren
announcement *89* Erklärung, Ankündigung
annoyed *18* genervt, verärgert
antagonism *118* Feindseligkeit
to **anticipate** *127* vorhersehen, mit etw rechnen
antigay *47* schwulenfeindlich
anti-social behaviour *54* abweichende (antisoziale) Verhaltensweise(n)
anxiety *36* Angst, Sorge, Angstzustände
anxious *10* besorgt, beunruhigt, bang
apart, far ~ *33* weit (voneinander) entfernt
apparent *7* offensichtlich, deutlich (sichtbar); to **become ~** *140* hervortreten, sich zeigen
apparently *62* anscheinend
appeal *8* Anziehungskraft, Reiz
to **appeal to sb.** *32* jdn ansprechen, jdn reizen
to **appear** *18* scheinen
appetite for sth. *126* Verlangen nach etw
appliance *95* Elektrogerät
applicant *35* Bewerber/in
to **apply** *121* zutreffen; **~ sth.** *131* etw anwenden; **~ to sb./sth.** *78* für jdn/etw gelten
to **appoint sb.** *61* jdn einstellen, jdn berufen
appointment *32* Termin
to **appreciate** *19F* zu schätzen wissen
approach *51* Ansatz, Herangehensweise
to **approach** *85* sich nähern, zugehen auf; **~ sth.** *16T* sich einer Sache nähern
appropriate *30* passend, angemessen
arbiter *46* Instanz
arbitrary *108* willkürlich
archaeology major *47* jd, der/die Archäologie im Hauptfach studiert (hat)
arguably *51* möglicherweise, wohl
to **arm** *80T* bewaffnen, ausrüsten
armed *140* bewaffnet
armed struggle *141* bewaffneter Kampf
arms proliferation *126* Weiterverbreitung von Waffen
to **arouse** *38* auslösen, hervorrufen
arrest *51* Verhaftung
artificial *129T* künstlich
as it were *14* sozusagen, gewissermaßen
aspiration *114* (angestrebtes) Ziel, Wunschdenken; *133* Ambition, Bestrebung
assault *54* Körperverletzung
to **assert** *17F* geltend machen
assessment *36* Beurteilung, Bewertung, Einschätzung
asset *79* Vorteil, Wert, Plus; **income ~** *21* *etwa:* Aktivposten, der Einkommen ermöglicht; to **be an ~** *77* wertvoll sein
assets *115* Vermögen(swerte)
to **assimilate to sth.** *78* sich an etw anpassen
assimiliation *80T* Anpassung, Assimilierung
assistance, foreign ~ *115* Entwicklungshilfe
to **associate** *24* in Verbindung bringen, assoziieren
associate *32* Teilhaber/in, Partner/in; **~ dean** *47* stellvertretende/r Dekan/in; **A~'s degree** *32* Associate-Abschluss
to **assume** *17F* davon ausgehen, annehmen; *52* übernehmen
assumption *110* Annahme, Voraussetzung
assurance *100* Zusage, Garantie, Beteuerung
astronomically *36* astronomisch, *hier:* unfassbar, unglaublich
asylum application *80* Asylantrag
asylum seeker *74* Asylsuchende/r
athletics *129* Sport
atomic bomb *140* Atombombe
atrocities *133* Greueltaten
to **attain** *134* erlangen; **~ sth.** *140* an etw gelangen
attempt *53* Versuch
to **attempt sth.** *7* etw versuchen, etw wagen
attention, to **capture sb.'s ~** *85* jds Aufmerksamkeit gewinnen
to **attribute sth. to sth.** *127* etw einer Sache zuschreiben
authoritarian *144* autoritär
to **authorize** *138* genehmigen, zulassen
availability *50* Verfügbarkeit
average, on ~ *63* im Durchschnitt
to **average** *150* im Durchschnitt sein/haben
aviation *26* Luftfahrt, Flugverkehr
avid *85* begeistert, leidenschaftlich, eifrig
to **awake to sth.** *114* sich einer Sache bewusst werden
awakening *115* Erwachen
to **award sth.** *113* etw *(Preis, etc.)* verleihen
aware, to **be ~ of sth.** *20* sich einer Sache bewusst sein
awe, to **be in ~ of sth.** *73* Ehrfurcht vor etw haben
to **axe sb.** *85* jdn entlassen, jdn feuern

B

baby formula *16T* Babynahrung
to **back sb.** *149* jdn unterstützen
back alley *114* Gasse, Seitengasse
bail, on ~ *54* auf Kaution
to **balance** *9* ausgleichen; **~ sth. with sth.** *20* etw mit etw vereinbaren, etw mit etw auf einen Nenner bringen
Balkanization *72* Balkanisierung *(Zerfall eines größeren in viele Kleinstaaten)*
balloon, hot air ~ *30T* Heißluftballon
ballot, to **cast your ~** *143T* seine Stimme abgeben
ballot box *143T* Wahlurne
ballot initiative *51* Wählerinitiative
bamboo *20* Bambus
ban (on sth.) *74* Verbot (von etw)
to **ban** *28* verbieten, abschaffen
bandwidth *133* Bandbreite
bank account *12* Bankkonto
bankrupt *85* pleite
bankruptcy *17F* Bankrott
bar, to **put sb. behind ~s** *45* jdn hinter Gitter bringen
to **bar sb. from sth.** *75* jdn von etw ausschließen
barbarity *135* Barbarei
barbed-wire fence *78* Stacheldrahtzaun
the bare necessities *121* die lebensnotwendigen Dinge
barren *78* unfruchtbar, öde
barrier *75* Hindernis; **trade ~** *143* Handelsschranken
battle of the sexes *59* Geschlechterkampf
battlefield *115* Schlachtfeld
beat, a cop on the ~ *46* ein Polizist auf Streife
beaten, off the ~ track *20* abseits ausgetretener Pfade
to **bear: ~ sth. out** *84* etw bestätigen; **~ witness to sth.** *78* etw bezeugen, von etw zeugen

behaviour, anti-social ~ *54* abweichende (antisoziale) Verhaltensweise(n); to **engage in a ~** *10* ein Verhalten an den Tag legen
belief *12* Überzeugung
beneficiary *115* Nutznießer
to **bend** *137* beugen
to **benefit** *80T* profitieren; **~ sb.** *24* jdm zugute kommen, jdm nützen
benefit *79* Vorteil, Nutzen
benefits *32* (Sozial-)Leistungen
beset, to **be ~ by sth.** *44* von etw heimgesucht werden, von etw befallen sein
bet, a sure ~ *127* eine sichere Sache
betrayal *138* Verrat
better, to **be ~ off** *60* (*finanziell*) besser gestellt sein; *110* besser dran sein
beyond *10* jenseits
bias *60* Vorurteil(e), Einseitigkeit, Verzerrung
bigot *74* Eiferer, Fanatiker/in
bigotry *72* Fanatismus
big-time criminal *54* Schwerkriminelle/r
bilingual *32* zweisprachig
bill, medical ~s *126* Gesundheitskosten
a billionfold *146* milliardenfach
binge-drinking *54* Alkoholexzesse, Komasaufen
biodegradable *100* biologisch abbaubar
biodiversity *104* Artenvielfalt
biofuel *104* Biokraftstoff
biracial *72* gemischtrassig
birth control *110* Verhütungsmittel, Empfängnisverhütung
birth rate *112* Geburtenrate
blame, to **be to ~** *54* schuld sein, die Schuld tragen; to **place the ~ with sb.** *84* jdm die Schuld geben
to **blast sth.** *50* etw scharf kritisieren, etw verreißen
blatant *75* eklatant, unverholen
to **blend** *72* mischen
the Blessed Land *71* das Gelobte Land
blessing, to **count one's ~s** *17F* dankbar sein (für das, was man hat)
blip, temporary ~ *65* vorübergehende Störung
bliss *10* Glück, Glückseligkeit
blissful *11* glückselig, glücklich
blood, flesh-and-~ *155F* aus Fleisch und Blut; to **spill ~** *76* Blut vergießen
blood stream *152* Blutbahn, Blutkreislauf
blue *14* deprimiert
blunt *114* direkt, unverblümt
blunt(ly) *51* unverblümt, rundweg
to **board** *26* (*Flugzeug*) besteigen
boarding house *75* Wohnheim, Pension
to **boast about sth.** *44* mit etw angeben/prahlen
bonanza *51* Goldgrube; *121* unerwartet großer Gewinn
bond, to **post a ~** *54* eine Kaution hinterlegen
boom-and-bust cycle *84* Zyklus von Hochkonjunktur und Krisen
boom-to-bust *33* wirtschaftlich instabil *(wörtlich: von Boom zu Bankrott)*
to **boost** *12* steigern, fördern
boredom *54* Langeweile
borough *76* Stadtbezirk
to **borrow** *109* borgen, leihen
to **bother** *9* stören, belästigen; **~ doing sth.** *70* sich die Mühe machen, etw zu tun
bound, to **be ~ to do sth.** *143* etw tun werden
boundary *108* Grenze
to **bow down to sth.** *129T* sich einer Sache beugen
brain *92T* Gehirn
brain drain *108 Abwanderung hochqualifizierter Arbeitskräfte*
to **brand** *51* brandmarken, stigmatisieren, beschimpfen
brazen *75* schamlos, dreist
breach *90* Verletzung, Verstoß
to **break: ~ sth. down** *100* etw zersetzen, etw abbauen; **~ the news to sb.** *89* jdm die/eine Nachricht überbringen
breakthrough *63* Durchbruch
breathing exercise *92T* Atemübung
breathless *36* atemlos, *hier:* aufgeregt, voreilig
to **breed** *9* brüten; *129T* hervorrufen
bribery *54* Bestechung
brick-and-mortar *150* konventionell
bride burning *114* Witwenverbrennung
brief(ly) *42* kurz
to **bring sth. about** *91* etw herbeiführen, zu etw führen
brink, on the ~ of sth. *20* kurz vor etw
British thermal unit (BTU) *98 Maßeinheit f. Energie im englischsprachigen Raum, ca. 1055J*
broad-brush *80T hier:* sehr allgemein formuliert
to **broadcast** *88* senden
broadcaster *87* Sender
broadening *79* Erweiterung
broadsheet *90* seriöse Tageszeitung *(eigentlich ein großes Zeitungsformat, etwa 29,5 x 23,5 Zoll)*
broken families *54* zerrüttete Familien(verhältnisse)
broth *127* Brühe, Bouillon
to **brush** *32* bürsten
brush, broad-~ *80T hier:* sehr allgemein formuliert
brutality *114* Brutalität
to **budge** *11* sich bewegen, sich von der Stelle rühren
budget deficit *123* Haushaltsdefizit
bulk *66* Großteil, Hauptanteil; **the ~** *150* der größte Teil, der Löwenanteil
bulletin *45* Mitteilung, Posting
bullet-proof *144* schusssicher
bullish *51* dickköpfig, (übertrieben) selbstsicher
bullying *45* Mobben, Mobbing
buoyancy *155F* Auftrieb
burden *60* Last, Belastung
bureaucratic *40* bürokratisch
burglar *55* Einbrecher
burglary *54* Einbruchdiebstahl
to **burn sth.** *96* etw verbrennen
to **bury** *100* vergraben, begraben
bust, boom-and-~ cycle *84* Zyklus von Hochkonjunktur und Krisen
bust, boom-to-~ *33* wirtschaftlich instabil *(wörtlich: von Boom zu Bankrott)*
by-product *16T* Nebenprodukt

C

calamity *16T* Unheil, Katastrophe
to **call: ~ for sth.** *110* etw fordern; **~ sb. names** *45* jdn beleidigen
campaigner *7* Aktivist/in
canvas *21* Leinwand
capital equipment *121* Investitionsgüter, Kapitalausstattung
capture *104* Rückhaltung
to **capture** *36* erfassen; **~ sb.'s attention** *85* jds Aufmerksamkeit gewinnen
carbon dioxide *95* Kohlendioxid
carbon footprint *95* CO_2-Fußabdruck
care *66* Pflege, Betreuung
career advancement *32* beruflicher Aufstieg
careless *49* nachlässig, fahrlässig, unvorsichtig
carer *60* Pfleger/in, Betreuer/in
cartel, drug ~ *52* Drogenkartell; **narco-~** 51 (lateinamerikanisches) Drogenkartell
case, to **make one's ~** *149* für seine Sache werben
cashier *57* Kassierer/in

to **cast your ballot** *143T* seine Stimme abgeben
casual, hidden from ~ view *47* im Verborgenen
to **catch up with sb.** *81* aufholen, jdn einholen
caught up, to **be ~ in sth.** *110* in etw verstrickt sein
cause *11* Anlass; **underlying ~s** *54* zugrundeliegende Ursachen
to **caution** *110* warnen
caution, to **exercise ~** *112* Vorsicht walten lassen
cautious *38* vorsichtig
caveat *110* Vorbehalt
to **cease sth.** *75* etw beenden, etw einstellen
ceased operations *43* Geschäftsbetrieb eingestellt
ceiling *60* (Zimmer-)Decke
celebrity *90* Prominente/r
cellular *152* Zell-
to **censor** *140* zensieren
census, US C~ Bureau *37* Statistisches Bundesamt der USA
chain *19* Kette
to **challenge** *122* herausfordern
challenge, to **address a ~** *37* eine Herausforderung annehmen
Chamber of Commerce *33* Handelskammer
Chamber of Minerals and Energy *121* Handelskammer für Mineralien und Energie
to **champion sth.** *143* für etw eintreten, sich für etw einsetzen
chancellor *34* Kanzler/in
to **charge** *121* stürmen; **~ sb.** *139* jdn anklagen; **~ sb. with sth.** *46* jdn mit etw beauftragen; **~ sth. for sth.** *8* etw *(Preis, Gebühr)* für etw verlangen; **~ extra** *8* einen Aufpreis verlangen
chatter *36* Gerede
cheerful *14* vergnügt, gut gelaunt
cheers *72* Jubel
chef *34* Koch/Köchin, Küchenchef/in
child sponsorship *115* Patenschaft
childcare facility *60* Kinderbetreuungseinrichtung
chlorine *27* Chlor
to **circulate** *90* verbreiten
circumstances *73* (Lebens-)Umstände
to **cite** *11* anführen, zitieren
citizen *24* Bürger/in
citizenship *78* Staatsbürgerschaft
civil offence *75* zivilrechtliches Vergehen
civil service *75* Staatsdienst, öffentlicher Dienst
civil war *108* Bürgerkrieg
civility *46* Anstand, Bürgersinn
to **claim** *10* behaupten, erklären, verkünden; *115 (Menschenleben)* fordern
to **clamber** *150* klettern
clandestine *141* geheim
clash *75* Auseinandersetzung
clash of interest *133* Interessenkonflikt
climate change *7* Klimawandel
to **clip nails** *32* Nägel schneiden
to **clog** *10* verstopfen; **~ sth. up** *99* etw verstopfen
to **clone** *146* klonen
closely: ~ related to *12* eng verbunden mit; to **work ~ with sb.** *34* eng mit jdm zusammenarbeiten
closet *45* Wandschrank, Kammer
cloud nine, on ~ *15* auf Wolke sieben
to **clutter sth. up** *99* etw mit etw übersäen
coal *96* Kohle
coat *99* Schicht, Decke
to **coax sb./sth. into doing sth.** *154T* jdn/etw dazu bringen, etw zu tun
co-founder *88* Mitbegründer/in
to **collaborate** *134* zusammenarbeiten
collar, white-~ crime *54* Wirtschaftskriminalität; **white-~ profession** *37* Angestelltenberuf
colonial power *108* Kolonialmacht
color line *AE 72* Rassenschranke
to **combat sth.** *76* etw bekämpfen
to **come: ~ about** *21* entstehen; **~ across sth.** *49* auf etw stoßen, etw finden; **~ up with sth.** *63* sich etw einfallen lassen, auf etw kommen
comforts *18* Annehmlichkeiten; **modern ~** *22* moderne Annehmlichkeiten
commerce, Chamber of C~ *33* Handelskammer
to **commit** *54 (Tat)* begehen
commitment *69T* Verpflichtung, Bindung
commodity *120* (Handels-)Ware, Rohstoff
common *14* gemeinsam
common denominator *14* gemeinsamer Nenner
common good *135* Gemeinwohl
commonplace *75* alltäglich, gewöhnlich
commonsense *36* vernünftig
community service *54* gemeinnützige Arbeit, Sozialdienst
commute *10* Arbeitsweg, Pendelstrecke/-zeit
comparatively *40* vergleichsweise, relativ
compelling *7* spannend, mitreißend; *26* zwingend, überzeugend
to **compete with sb./sth.** *37* mit jdm/etw konkurrieren, mit jdm/etw im Wettbewerb stehen
competition *91* Konkurrenz
competitive *12* wettwerbsorientiert, leistungsorientiert; *120* konkurrenzfähig
competitiveness *37* Wettbewerbsfähigkeit, Konkurrenzfähigkeit
complacent *37* selbstzufrieden, selbstgefällig
completion *7* Vervollständigung, Ergänzung; *37* Abschluss, Beendigung
component *95* Bestandteil
composite *129T* zusammengesetzt, gemischt
compound *41* zusammengesetzt
to **compound** *140* verschlimmern
comprehensive *13* umfassend
to **comprise** *80T* ausmachen, umfassen
compulsive *92T* zwanghaft
compulsory *81* obligatorisch
to **conceal** *53* kaschieren, verdecken
to **concede** *26* zugestehen
to **conceive** *149* konzipieren
to **conceptualize sth.** *73* etw in Begriffe fassen
concern *28* Anliegen, Angelegenheit; *36* Bedenken, Sorge(n), Befürchtung; **~ for sth.** *20* Sorge um etw, Rücksicht auf etw
concerned *9* besorgt
concerted *77* vereint, gemeinsam
to **conclude** *17F* folgern, den Schluss ziehen, zu dem Schluss kommen
conclusion, to **be a foregone ~** *112* von vornherein feststehen; to **draw a ~** *36* einen Schluss ziehen, eine Schlussfolgerung ziehen
to **condemn** *10* verurteilen
condition *42T* Krankheit
to **condition** *11* konditionieren
to **conduct** *36* durchführen
confidence *7* Selbstvertrauen, Zuversicht
confidential *140* vertraulich
to **confine sb. to sth.** *79* jdn auf etw beschränken, jdn in etw einsperren
conflicting *98* widersprüchlich
to **confirm** *72* bestätigen
to **confiscate** *49* beschlagnahmen, konfiszieren
to **confront sth.** *137* einer Sache begegnen, einer Sache trotzen

congested *24* verstopft
congestion, traffic ~ *10* Verkehrsstau
congressman *118* Kongressabgeordneter
connectivity *133* Vernetzung, Verbindungen
conscious *26* bewusst; to **be ~ of sth.** *17F* sich einer Sache bewusst sein
consequently *115* folglich, deshalb
conservation *9* Schutz, Naturschutz
to **conserve** *24* schützen, bewahren; *101* konservieren; **~ sth.** *104T* etw einsparen, mit etw sparsam umgehen
to **consider: ~ sth. sth.** *etw für etw halten, etw als etw (an)sehen; to* **be ~ed sth.** *15* als etw gelten
considerably *35* erheblich, beträchtlich
considerate *17F* aufmerksam, rücksichtsvoll
consolation prize *155* Trostpreis
to **consist of sth.** *6* aus/in etw bestehen
constituent *80T* Wähler/in (eines Wahlkreises)
to **constitute** *38* ausmachen, bilden; *143* darstellen, sein
constitution *139* Verfassung
constitutional law *140* Staatsrecht, Verfassungsrecht
to **constrain** *37* einengen, einschränken
construction *27* Bau
consumer debt *126* private Überschuldung
consumer goods *121* Konsumgüter
consumption *10* Konsum, Verbrauch
contagion *133* ansteckende Krankheit, Seuche, negativer Einfluss
to **contain** *50* eindämmen, unter Kontrolle bringen
content *14* zufrieden
content *46* Inhalt
contented *14* zufrieden, wunschlos glücklich
contentious *80T* umstritten, kontrovers
contentment *14* Zufriedenheit
contest *10* Wettbewerb, Wettstreit
contiguous *99* benachbart
continued *121* anhaltend
contraceptive *110* Verhütungsmittel
contract *33* Vertrag; **permanent ~** *33* unbefristeter Vertrag
contrary, evidence to the ~ *51* gegenteilige Anhaltspunkte/Hinweise
to **contribute** *8* beitragen
contribution *7* Beitrag; *149 (finanzielle)* Zuwendung; to **make a ~** *119* einen Beitrag leisten
controversial *89* umstritten, strittig
convenience *50* Bequemlichkeit, Nutzen; *96* Annehmlichkeit
to **convey** *53* vermitteln
conveyor belt *19* Förderband
to **convict sb.** *54* jdn schuldig sprechen, jdn verurteilen
conviction *52* Verurteilung
convincing *13* überzeugend
cop, a ~ on the beat *46* ein Polizist auf Streife
coping skills *92T* Bewältigungsstrategie(n)
copper *121* Kupfer
copyright *90* Urheberrecht
copyright holder *92* Urheberrechtsinhaber/in
coral reef *20* Korallenriff
cord *127* Kabel
core *37* Kern(-)
cornstarch *100* Maisstärke
corporation *42* Unternehmen, Konzern; **multinational ~** *124* internationaler Konzert, Multi
to **correlate** *80T* (miteinander) in Beziehung stehen, korrelieren
costly *50* teuer
cotton *121* Baumwolle
council *77* Stadtrat, Bezirksrat; *110* Rat
council estate *76* Siedlung mit Sozialwohnungen
to **counsel** *16T* raten
counselling session *54* Beratungstermin, Therapiesitzung
counselling *92T* Beratung, (psychologische/soziale) Therapie
to **count one's blessings** *17F* dankbar sein (für das, was man hat)
to **counter** *73* entgegnen, kontern; **~ sth.** *51* einer Sache entgegenwirken
to **counterbalance** *65* ausgleichen, aufwiegen
counterintuitive *100* auf den ersten Blick unlogisch/widersinnig
counterpart *61* Pendant
courier *50* Kurier
course, to run its ~ *143T* seinen (vollen) Verlauf nehmen
court of law *48* Gericht, Gerichtshof
coverage *87* Berichterstattung, Bericht(e)
to **cover sth.** *87* über etw berichten
covering *99* Verpackung, Folie
covertly *16T* verdeckt, insgeheim
crab *16T* Krebs
crackdown *134* scharfes Vorgehen
crammed *10* vollgestopft
crankcase *115* Kurbelgehäuse
crate *21* Kiste
craze *23* Wahn, Modeerscheinung
creator *90* Urheber/in
creature, living ~ *9* Lebewesen; **sea ~** *99* Meerestier
credibility *87* Glaubwürdigkeit
crime, petty ~ *54* Bagatelldelikt(e); **white-collar ~** *54* Wirtschaftskriminalität
criminal, big-time ~ *54* Schwerkriminelle/r
criminal justice overcrowding *51* Überbeanspruchung der Justizbehörden
criminal offence *75* strafrechtliches Vergehen, Straftat
to **criminalise** *BE 50* kriminalisieren
criminologist *54* Kriminologe/-in
crisis, economic ~ *33* Wirtschaftskrise
criterion (*pl.* -a) *19* Kriterium
critic *46* Kritiker/in
to **criticize** *16* kritisieren
crop (of sth.) *72* Gruppe (von etw)
crops *103T* Ernte, (Nutz-)Pflanzen, Früchte
to **cross the line** *47* zu weit gehen, eine/die Grenze überschreiten
crowded *25* überfüllt
to **crowd** *26* füllen, sich drängen
crucially *37* vor allem
crude oil *119* Rohöl
cruel *139* grausam
cruise *30T* Kreuzfahrt
to **cruise** *30T* eine Kreuzfahrt/Schiffsreise machen
to **crunch the numbers** *37* die Zahlen durchrechnen
crusade *26* Kreuzzug, Feldzug; *114* Kampagne
culmination *87* Höhepunkt
culprit *11* Schuldige/r, Übeltäter, *hier auch:* Sündenbock
cultural immersion programme *20 Programm zum Kennenlernen einer Kultur vor Ort*
cultural mould *129T* kulturelle Prägung
curation *88* Pflege *(von Daten, etc.)*
curb *36* Bordstein, Straßenrand
to **curb** *26* eindämmen, beschränken, begrenzen
to **cure** *154T* heilen
to **curl up** *19F* sich zusammenrollen
currency *123* Währung
current *7* Strömung
currently *20* im Moment, aktuell
to **curse** *45* fluchen, (jdn) verfluchen
to **curtail** *139* einschränken, beschneiden
custodian *21* Hüter/in, Wächter/in
custom *78* Sitte, Brauch

to **cut** *51* senken; ~ **back on sth.** *62* etw einschränken; ~ **down** *105* *(Baum)* fällen; ~ **off supply** *109* den Nachschub abschneiden
cut out, to have one's work ~ for one *64* viel zu tun haben
cycle, boom-and-bust ~ *84* Zyklus von Hochkonjunktur und Krisen
cyclone *20* Wirbelsturm, Zyklon

D

daily *85* *hier:* Tageszeitung
dam *103T* Staudamm
damaging *100* schädlich
daunting *155* beängstigend, beunruhigend
daylight *19* Tageslicht, *hier:* Tagesanbruch
deadbeat *114* nichtsnutzig, Nichtstuer/in
to **deal with sb.** *7* mit jdm zu tun haben, mit jdm zurechtkommen
dean *129T* Dekan/in; **associate ~** *47* stellvertretende/r Dekan/in
dearth (of sth.) *111* Mangel (an etw)
death, until ~ us do part *68* bis dass der Tod uns scheidet; to **starve to ~** *108* verhungern
death rate *111* Sterblichkeit
death threat *47* Morddrohung
debt *10* Schuld(en); **consumer ~** *126* private Überschuldung
debt relief *108* Schuldenerlass
decade *118T* Jahrzehnt
to **decipher** *156* entschlüsseln
decision-making ability *92T* Entscheidungsfähigkeit
decisive *39* entscheidend
deck of cards *127* Kartensatz, -spiel, -stapel
to **declare** *36* erklären, ernennen
to **decline** *12* zurückgehen, abnehmen; *47* (es) ablehnen
decline, economic ~ *78* Konjunkturrückgang, Wirtschaftskrise, -flaute; **in ~** *143T* im Niedergang; to **be in ~** *84* zurückgehen, sinken
declining *51* rückläufig, zurückgehend
decriminalise *BE* *50* entkriminalisieren
deeply ingrained *26* tief verwurzelt
deep-rooted *28* tief verwurzelt
to **default on sth.** *27* mit etw *(Zahlung)* im Verzug sein
default setting *14* Standardeinstellung
defeat *9* Niederlage(n)
defender *23* Verteidiger
deficit, budget ~ *123* Haushaltsdefizit; to **run a ~** *123* ein Defizit aufweisen
deforestation *102* Abholzung, Waldzerstörung, Entwaldung
to **defuse** *140* entschärfen
to **defy sb.** *143T* jdm trotzen, sich jdm widersetzen
degree *84* Abschluss; **Associate's ~** *32* Associate-Abschluss; to **earn a ~** *37* einen Abschluss erwerben
delegated, to be ~ sth. *60* etw übertragen bekommen
deleterious *129T* schädlich
deliberate(ly) *139* absichtlich
delicate *20* empfindlich; to **walk a ~ line** *47* sich auf einem schmalen Grat bewegen
delinquency, juvenile ~ *54* Jugendkriminalität
delinquent, juvenile ~ *57* jugendliche/r Straftäter/in
delivery system *84* Bereitstellungssystem
demand *27* Forderung
demand (for sth.) *33* Nachfrage (nach etw)
demographer *110* Demograph/in
demographic change *42T* demographischer Wandel
denial *47* Leugnung
denominator, common ~ *14* gemeinsamer Nenner
to **deny** *77* bestreiten, leugnen; ~ **sb. sth.** *140* jdm etw verweigern
departure lounge *31* Abflughalle
to **depend heavily on sth.** *11* sehr von etw abhängen
to **depict** *148* darstellen
to **deplete** *103T* (sich) erschöpfen, dezimieren
deplorable *79* erbärmlich, furchtbar
to **deploy** *126* einsetzen, aufstellen, aufbieten
deportation *74* Ausweisung
deposit *104* Pfand
depressed *122* *(Wirtschaft:)* angeschlagen, kriselnd
to **derive sth. from sth.** *116* etw *(Nutzen, etc.)* aus etw ziehen; *154T* etw aus etw gewinnen
to **descend into sth.** *121* in etw verfallen, in etw (hinab-/ver-) sinken
to **deserve** *8* verdienen
designated *104* (dafür) vorgesehen
to **desire sth.** *13* sich etw wünschen
desire (for sth.) *13* Wunsch (nach etw), Verlangen (nach etw)
despair *11* Verzweiflung, Hoffnungslosigkeit
desperate *78* verzweifelt
despite *11* trotz
despondent *121* bedrückt, mutlos, niedergeschlagen
destiny *108* Schicksal, Bestimmung
destruction, weapons of mass ~ *140* Massenvernichtungswaffen
destructive *147* zerstörerisch
to **detail** *96* (einzeln) aufführen, ausführlich beschreiben, informieren über
detainee *137* Gefangene/r, Häftling
detention *137* Haft, Internierung
to **deter** *52* abschrecken
to **deteriorate** *66* sich verschlechtern
to **determine** *46* bestimmen
deterrent *54* Abschreckungsmittel
devastating *111* verheerend
the developed world *100* *etwa:* die Industrienationen
development *24* Bau, Bauprojekt
to **devise** *11* ausarbeiten, erfinden
to **devote** *63* widmen; ~ **sth. to sth.** *92T* etw *(Zeit)* auf etw verwenden
dichotomy *26* Zwiespalt, Gegensatz
to **dictate sth. to sb.** *125* jdm etw aufzwingen
dictatorship *140* Diktatur
diet *100* Ernährung
to **differentiate** *54* unterscheiden, differenzieren
differing *133* verschieden, unterschiedlich
diffusion *133* Verbreitung
dignity *134* Würde
to **diminish** *124* verkleinern, schmälern
to **dine** *19* speisen, dinieren, essen; ~ **out** *122* essen gehen
dire straits, in ~ *153* in großen Schwierigkeiten, in einer Notlage
directed at sb. *17F* an/auf jdn gerichtet
dirt-poor *119* bitterarm
to **disagree with sb.** *38* jdm nicht zustimmen
to **disapprove of sth.** *12* etw ablehnen
disconnect *11* Diskrepanz, Bruch
discontent *14* Unzufriedenheit
to **discard** *155F* wegwerfen
to **discourage sb. from sth.** *90* jdn von etw abhalten
discrepancy *12* Diskrepanz
discretionary spending *126* Konsumausgaben, Ermessensausgaben
disease, epidemic ~ *108* Epidemie

disillusioned *141* ernüchtert, enttäuscht, desillusioniert
disinfectant *104* Desinfektionsmittel
disloyal *139* (jdm gegenüber) illoyal
to **dismiss** *25* abtun, wegschicken, entlassen
disobedience *77* Ungehorsam
to **disobey sth.** *139* etw nicht befolgen
disorder *92T* Störung
disparate *121* verschieden
dispirited *14* entmutigt
to **displace** *108* vertreiben
displaced person *78* Vertriebene/r, Flüchtling
display, to **be on ~** *156* ausgestellt/dargestellt werden
to **display** *49* aufweisen, an den Tag legen
disposable *126* verfügbar
disposal, waste ~ *99* Müllentsorgung, Abfallentsorgung
to **dispose of sth.** *99* etw entsorgen, sich einer Sache entledigen
disproportionate(ly) *67* unverhältnismäßig
to **disrupt** *124* stören, behindern
dissection *150* Sektion, Sezieren
to **disseminate** *90* verbreiten
dissent *134* Widerspruch, Unzufriedenheit
to **dissolve into sth.** *114* sich in etw auflösen
distant *23* enfernt
to **distil** *88* destillieren
distribution (department) *89* Vertrieb, Versand
distribution of wealth *37* Vermögensverteilung
diverse *76* vielfältig
diversity, ethnic ~ *72* ethnische Vielfalt, Völkervielfalt
divide *148* Kluft
divisive *80T* polarisierend, entzweiend
divorcee *11* Geschiedene/r
to **do: ~ away with sth.** *88* etw abschaffen; **~ withouth sb./sth.** *7* ohne jdn/etw auskommen
doable *85* durchführbar
docile *80* fügsam
doer *17F* Handelnde/r
to **dog-sit** *70* den Hund hüten
domestic *33* einheimisch
domestic waste *104* Hausmüll
dominance *123* Vorherrschaft
dominant *44* beherrschend, vorherrschend
to **donate** *117* spenden
donor *110* Spender/in
doorstep, on the ~ *51* direkt vor der Haustür
dorm (room) *20* Schlafsaal
to **dot the coast** *20* entlang der Küste verstreut sein
doubtful *12* zweifelhaft
down in the dumps *15* niedergeschlagen, deprimiert
downcast *14* niedergeschlagen
down-hearted *38* entmutigt, niedergeschlagen
downside *51* Nachteil(e), Kehrseite
draft *84* Einberufung
to **drain** *20* abfließen
drain, brain ~ *108 Abwanderung hochqualifizierter Arbeitskräfte*
to **draw** *33* anziehen, anlocken; **~ upon sth.** *87* auf etw zurückgreifen, aus etw schöpfen
drawback *77* Nachteil
dreadful *156* scheußlich
to **dribble** *8* sabbern, tropfen
drive *20* Schub, Aktion, Antrieb, Schwung
to **drive** *50* treiben, antreiben, lenken
drone *152* Drohne
drop *65* Rückgang, Einbruch
to **drop the matter** *94* die Angelegenheit auf sich beruhen lassen
drought *78* Dürre
drug cartel *52* Drogenkartell
drug prevention *49* Suchtprävention
drug regimen *111* Arzneimitteltherapie
drug trafficking *54* Drogenhandel
due, to **be ~ to do sth.** *66* etw tun werden
due process of law *140* ordentliches Gerichtsverfahren
due to *44* aufgrund von
dull *64* langweilig; *96* farblos, fad
dumps, down in the ~ *15* niedergeschlagen, deprimiert
to **dupe** *51* überlisten, hinters Licht führen
durable *99* haltbar
to **dust** *63* abstauben
dust *63* Staub
dust bowl *78* Trockengebiet
duty *75* Pflicht

E

eager, to **be ~ to do sth.** *131* etw unbedingt tun wollen
early parole *54* vorzeitige Haftentlassung
early retirement *42T* Vorruhestand
to **earn a degree** *37* einen Abschluss erwerben
earnings *127* Einkünfte, Einkommen; **foreign exchange ~** *24* Deviseneinnahmen
earthquake-proof *16T* erdbebensicher
to **ease** *80T* lindern
to **eat one's heart out** *155F* vor Neid erblassen
to **eclipse sth.** *50* etw in den Schatten stellen
eco-friendly *20* umweltfreundlich
ecologist *9* Umweltforscher/in, Ökologe/-in
economic crisis *33* Wirtschaftskrise
economic decline *78* Konjunkturrückgang, Wirtschaftskrise, -flaute
economic growth *24* Wirtschaftswachstum
economic order *122* Wirtschaftsordnung
economic power *122* Wirtschaftsmacht
economist *10* Wirtschaftswissenschaftler/in
ecosystem *20* Ökosystem
ecotourism *24* Ökotourismus
eco-traveler *AE 24* Ökotourist/in
ecstasy *14* Begeisterung, Ekstase
edge, rough around the ~s *21* kantig, ungeschliffen
to **edit** *28* redigieren
editor *88* Redakteur/in
editorial staff *17* Redaktion
to **educate sb. to do sth.** *104* jdn dazu erziehen, etw zu tun
educated *12* gebildet, ausgebildet
educationalist *81* Pädagoge/-in
effort *6* Bemühung, Anstrengung, Leistung
elaborate *10* ausgefeilt, aufwändig
elderly *22* älter, betagt
to **elect** *12* wählen
election, presidential ~ *57T* Präsidentschaftswahlen
electric grid *96* Stromnetz
to **elevate** *11* anheben
eligible, to **be ~ for sth.** *54* für etw in Frage kommen
to **eliminate** *43* abschaffen; *96* beseitigen, überflüssig machen
elsewhere *10* anderswo
to **embarrass sb.** *91* jdn bloßstellen
to **embrace** *16T* annehmen
embroidery *114* Stickerei
embryonic *154T* embryonal
to **emerge** *24* aufkommen, entstehen; *44* hervortreten, in Erscheinung treten
emergence *140* Aufkommen
emergency *19* Notfall
emerging *121* aufkommend, aufstrebend, Schwellen-
emerging country *42* Schwellenland

emigration *33* Auswanderung
to **emit** *24* ausstoßen, emittieren
emotional state *92* Gefühlszustand
empathy *58* Mitgefühl
emphasis, to **place ~ on sth.** *129* etw betonen, etw hervorheben
to **emphasise** *BE 51* betonen
employment agency, temporary ~ *33* Zeitarbeitsagentur
to **empower sb.** *110* jdn/jds Rechte stärken; *134* jdn (zu etw) ermächtigen
to **encounter** *61* begegnen
to **encourage** *24* fördern, anregen
end, to **make ~s meet** *54* über die Runden kommen
to **endanger** *106* gefährden
energy supply *104* Energieversorgung
enforcement *80T* Durchsetzung, *Überwachung der Einhaltung von Gesetzen;* **law ~** *135* Durchsetzung von Gesetzen, Gesetzesvollzug; **law ~ authority** *46* Strafverfolgungsbehörde
enforcer *47* Vollzugs-/Vollstreckungsbeamte/r, Gesetzeshüter/in
to **engage: ~ with sb.** *21* mit jdn in Dialog treten, mit jdm ins Gespräch kommen; **~ in a behaviour** *10* ein Verhalten an den Tag legen
engaged, to **get ~** *68* sich verloben
engine *24* Lokomotive, Motor
engineering *40* Technik, Ingenieurwesen, Maschinenbau
engineering firm *33* Ingenieurbüro
to **enhance** *14* fördern, steigern; *124* verstärken, fördern
enrichment *79* Bereicherung
to **enrol** *43* sich einschreiben, anmelden
to **enshrine** *137* festschreiben, verankern
to **ensure** *20* sicherstellen, gewährleisten
enterprise *106* Unternehmen; **social ~** *21* soziales Unternehmen
enthusiastic *52* begeistert, enthusiastisch
entire *16T* gesamt, ganz
entitled, to **be ~ to sth.** *28* zu etw berechtigt sein, auf etw einen Anspruch haben
entitlement *26* Anspruch
entity, political ~ *108* politische Einheit, Staatsgebilde
entrepreneur *27* Unternehmer/in
environmentalist *26* Umweltschützer/in
to **envision** *151* (sich etw) vorstellen
epidemic *111* Epidemie; **~ disease** *108* Epidemie
equation *14* Gleichung; to **remove sth. from the ~** *51* etw ausklammern, etw außen vor lassen
equipment *10* Ausrüstung, Geräte; **capital ~** *121* Investitionsgüter, Kapitalausstattung
equitable *140* gerecht
equivalent *24* Gegenwert, Entsprechung
to **eradicate** *152* ausrotten
to **erode away** *129T* abtragen, verwittern, wegfressen
erosion *124* Abbau, Erosion
to **erupt** *72* ausbrechen
the essentials *17* die wesentlichen Dinge
establishment *90* Gründung, Einrichtung
estate, council ~ *76* Siedlung mit Sozialwohnungen
estimate *51* Schätzung
to **estimate** *11* schätzen
ethnic diversity *72* ethnische Vielfalt, Völkervielfalt
etiquette *32* Umgangsformen
to **evaporate into thin air** *92T* sich in Luft auflösen
evasion, tax ~ *54* Steuerhinterziehung
eventually *27* irgendwann (einmal), schließlich
evidence *51* Beweis(e), Nachweis, Hinweis(e), Indizien
evidence to the contrary *51* gegenteilige Anhaltspunkte/Hinweise
evil *53* Übel
to **evolve** *21* entstehen, sich entwickeln
to **exaggerate** *134* übertreiben
to **exceed** *33* übertreffen
exception *60* Ausnahme
excessive *92T* übermäßig
ex-convict *54* Strafentlassene/r, ehemalige/r Strafgefangene/r
excuse *26* Ausrede
to **exercise caution** *112* Vorsicht walten lassen
to **exert** *54* ausüben
exhaustion *19* Erschöpfung
exit *109* Abwanderung
to **expand** *34* ausweiten
expanding exports *121* steigende Exporte
expectancy, life ~ *10* Lebenserwartung
expense, at the ~ of sb./sth. *72* auf Kosten von jdm/etw
expertise *17F* Kompetenz, Sachverstand, Fachwissen
to **exploit** *78* ausbeuten, ausnutzen
exploitation *108* Ausbeutung
explorer *19* Entdecker/in
to **expose** *138* entlarven, aufdecken
to **express** *6* ausdrücken
expression, freedom of ~ *137* Recht auf freie Meinungsäußerung
expressly *27* ausdrücklich
to **extend an invitation to sb.** *34* jdn einladen
extension *147* Ausweitung, Verlängerung
extensive *117* ausführlich
extent *24* Ausmaß, Umfang
external affairs *50* auswärtige Angelegenheiten
extinction *103* Ausrottung
to **extract sth. from sth.** *104* etw einer Sache entziehen
extraordinary *50* außergewöhnlich
to **eye-witness** *139* mit eigenen Augen sehen, Augenzeuge von etw sein

F

to **face sth.** *33* vor etw stehen, mit etw konfrontiert sein/werden, sich einer Sache stellen (müssen)
faced, to **be ~ with sth.** *54* mit etw konfrontiert sein
fad *23* Modeerscheinung, kurzlebiger Trend
to **fail** *16T* scheitern, versagen; **~ to do sth.** *36* es nicht schaffen, etw zu tun; etw nicht tun können; *108* (es) versäumen, etw zu tun; **~ a test** *36* eine Prüfung nicht bestehen
failure *16T* Scheitern, Versagen; **resounding ~** *50* eklatanter Misserfolg
fair *69* Messe
faith (in sb./sth.) *148* Glaube (an jdn/etw)
to **fall: ~ behind** *36* zurückbleiben, in Rückstand geraten; **~ short** *63* unzureichend sein
familiar *21* vertraut
famine *78* Hungersnot
fan *95* Ventilator
far apart *33* weit (voneinander) entfernt
fare *9* Fahrpreis; *126* Kost
to **fare** *75* abschneiden, ergehen
farmland *104* Ackerland
fate *103* Schicksal
to **favour** *53* befürworten
feature *72* Gesichtszug
fed up, to **be ~ with sth.** *31* von etw die Nase voll haben
Federal Employment Agency *33* Bundesarbeitsagentur
federation *26* Verband

fee, licence ~ *90* Rundfunkgebühr; **tuition ~** *43* Studiengebühr
to **feed** *51* befeuern; **~ sb.** *110* jdn ernähren; **~ on sth.** *10* sich von etw ernähren, *hier:* von etw gespeist werden
to **feel let down** *15* (von jdm/etw) enttäuscht sein
feelgood quotient *11* etwa: Wohlfühlquotient
felting needle *155F* Filznadel
fence, barbed-wire ~ *78* Stacheldrahtzaun
to **ferment** *103T* gären
fertility *60* Fruchtbarkeit, Geburtenrate
fiber-optic cable *133* Glasfaserkabel
to **figure** *62* vermuten, glauben; **~ out** *63* herausfinden, verstehen
figure, public ~ *46* Person des öffentlichen Lebens
figures *10* Zahlen
film *100* Folie
final draft *28* endgültige Fassung
finding *11* Ergebnis
fine *54* Geldstrafe
to **fire** *11* (Personal) entlassen
fire, to **set on ~** *87* anzünden, in Brand setzen
firm *97* fest, hart, unverrückbar
first-hand *54* direkt, am eigenen Leib
first-time offender *54* Ersttäter/in, nicht Vorbestrafte/r
fit, survival of the ~test *12* Überleben der bestangepassten Individuen
to **flag** *46* markieren
flat *10 hier:* auf gleichem Niveau; *126* pauschal
to **flatten** *133* ebnen, einebnen
flaw *76* Mangel
flawed *126* mangelhaft, mit Mängeln behaftet
fledged, fully-~ *119* voll entwickelt
to **flee sth.** *24* fliehen, flüchten
flesh-and-blood *155F* aus Fleisch und Blut
flexible *99* biegsam
to **float** *99* (im Wasser) treiben
to **flock** *24* strömen
to **flood** *63* strömen
to **flourish** *126* gedeihen, florieren
flow *124* Fluss
fluent(ly) *82* fließend
fluid *72* fließend, vage
to **flutter** *99* flattern
folly *137* Unsinn, Aberwitz
food for thought *19F* Denkanstoß/-anstöße
foolhardy *23* tollkühn, verwegen
for good *140* endgültig, ein für allemal
for want of sth. *115* weil etw fehlt
foray *127* Vorstoß
force, labour ~ *66* erwerbstätige Bevölkerung; **political ~** *76* politische Kraft
to **force: ~ sth. upon sth.** *76* jdm etw aufzwingen; **~ sb. out of business** *108* jdn vom Markt drängen; **~ sb. to do sth.** jdn zu etwas zwingen
forecast *40* Vorhersage, Prognose
forecasting *110* Prognose, Vorhersage
foregone, to **be a ~ conclusion** *112* von vornherein feststehen
foreign aid *108* Entwicklungshilfe
foreign assistance *115* Entwicklungshilfe
foreign exchange earnings *24* Deviseneinnahmen
foreseeable, in the ~ future *118* in absehbarer Zeit
foresight *20* Voraussicht, Weitblick
formerly *87* vormals, ehemals
fortnight *30T* vierzehn Tage
fossil fuel *95* fossiler Brennstoff
to **foster** *148* fördern
foundation *21* Stiftung; *75* Fundament, Grundlage, Grundstein; to **lay the ~** *24* den Grundstein legen
founder *88* Gründer/in
fraction *149* Bruchteil
to **frame** *18* einrahmen
franchisee *126* Lizenznehmer
frantically *8* wie wild, wie verrückt
fraud *94* Betrug
free speech *46* Redefreiheit
freedom of expression *137* Recht auf freie Meinungsäußerung
freedom of speech *46* Redefreiheit, Recht auf freie Rede
frequency *17F* Häufigkeit
freshman *84* Student/in im ersten Studienjahr
freshness *17F* Originalität, Frische
front desk *32* Rezeption, Empfang
front line, on the ~ *46* an vorderster Front
frontier *26* Grenze
frothy *26* schäumend
to **fuel** *26* anheizen, anfachen
fulfilling *14* erfüllend
fully-fledged *119* voll entwickelt
to **fund** *100* finanzieren
fund, relief ~ *109* Hilfsfonds
fundamental(ly) *14* grundlegend; *90* wesentlich
funding *129* Finanzierung, Mittel
fuse *65* Zündschnur

G

gain *10* Gewinn
to **gain** *48* erlangen, erreichen; **~ wealth** *108* reich werden
to **gamble** *12* spielen, wetten
gaming site *92T* Spiele-Website
gap: gender ~ *62* Geschlechterkonflikt, Kluft zwischen den Geschlechtern; **income ~** *131* Einkommensschere
gap year *29 Jahr zwischen Schulabschluss und Studienbeginn*
garment *155F* Kleidungsstück
gas-guzzling *27* spritfressend
gasoline *AE 11* Benzin, Sprit
to **gather** *21* sich versammeln; **~ sth.** *17F* etw sammeln
gatherer, hunter ~ *148* Jäger und Sammler
gathering *62* Treffen, Zusammenkunft
gaudy *99* grell
to **gauge** *87* messen, abschätzen, beurteilen
GDP *9* BIP (Bruttoinlandsprodukt)
geek-speak *84* Technik-Jargon
gender *29* Geschlecht
gender gap *62* Geschlechterkonflikt, Kluft zwischen den Geschlechtern
gene *146* Gen
to **generate** *10* erzeugen
generosity *141* Großzügigkeit
generous *66* großzügig
genetic engineering *152* Gentechnik
genome *156* Genom
genuine *24* echt, authentisch, wahr
geopolitics *126* Geopolitik
geothermally-heated *26* mit Erdwärmeheizung
to **get: ~ away with sth.** *138* mit etw (straflos) davonkommen; **~ by** *60* zurechtkommen; **~ on with sth.** *9* mit etw weiterkommen
gifted *37* begabt
glance, at first ~ *53* auf den ersten Blick
to **glide** *115* gleiten
glider *7* Segelflugzeug
gliding *7* Segelfliegen
glimmer of hope *50* Hoffnungsschimmer
global warming *95* Erderwärmung
globe, to **span the ~** *72* den Globus umspannen
gloom *14* Trübsinn, düstere Stimmung
to **gloss sth. over** *73* etw vertuschen, etw überdecken
go, on the ~ *100* unterwegs

to **go places** *19* herumkommen, reisen
goal *17F* Ziel
godson *8* Patensohn
good, for ~ *140* endgültig, ein für allemal
goods *99* Waren, Güter
gossip *90* Klatsch, Tratsch
government, non-~(al) organization *22* Nichtregierungsorganisation; **rogue ~** *135* Schurkenstaat
government-run *40* staatlich
to **grab** *34* (sich etw) packen, nehmen
grace, to **say ~** *71T* das Tischgebet sprechen
grade *AE 36* Klasse, Klassenstufe
gradual(ly) *105* allmählich; *125* nach und nach
grain *103T* Getreide
grand *10* prachtvoll, imposant; *17* groß, großartig
to **grant** *39* bewilligen, gewähren
graphic *54* anschaulich
grassroots *20* Basis-; **at ~ level** *135* an der Basis
grateful *17F* dankbar
gratitude *6* Dankbarkeit
grave *75* groß, ernsthaft, schwer
greed *54* Habgier
greenhouse effect *104* Treibhauseffekt
greenhouse gas *95* Treibhausgas
green-minded *26* umwelt(schutz) orientiert
to **grey** *68* ergrauen
grid, electric ~ *96* Stromnetz
grievance *133* Groll, Klage
grimace *27* Grimasse
to **grip** *100* ergreifen, fesseln
grip, to **come to ~s with sth.** *63* mit etw klarkommen, etw in den Griff bekommen; to **get a ~ on sth.** *54* etw in den Griff bekommen
gripping *7* fesselnd
to **groom** *32* pflegen
grooming salon *32 etwa:* Hundesalon
gross *16T* brutto; **G~ Domestic Product** *9* Bruttoinlandsprodukt
ground, on the ~ *87* vor Ort; **on the ~s of sth.** *75* aufgrund von etw
growth, economic ~ *24* Wirtschaftswachstum; **output ~** *66* Produktionswachstum
to **guarantee** *40* garantieren
guard, off ~ *96* unvorbereitet
guardian *21* Hüter/in
guidance *58* Führung, Anleitung, Orientierungshilfe; *137* Führung, Orientierung
guidebook *19* Reiseführer
gulf *24* Golf
gunpoint, at ~ *57* mit vorgehaltener Waffe
gun toting *129T* verbreiteter Schusswaffenbesitz/-gebrauch

H

habitation *109* Besiedlung
hair dryer *19* Fön
to **halve** *66* sich halbieren
handling *56* Hehlerei
to **hand** *50* übergeben, überreichen; **~ sth. over** *21* etw (über-)geben
hand, first-~ *54* direkt, am eigenen Leib
to **handle sth.** *47* mit etw umgehen, mit etw zurecht kommen
hands-on *22* praktisch, praxisnah
hand-wringing *85* Händeringen
to **hang: ~oneself** *45* sich erhängen; **~ on to sth.** *71T* an etw festhalten
hangover *126* Nachwirkung(en)
harassment *46* Belästigung, Übergriff(e)
hardship *80T* Not
hardware store *27* Eisenwarenhandlung, Baumarkt
hard-won *60* mühsam erkämpft
harmful *102* schädlich
to **harness** *149* nutzen
harsh *53* hart, aggressiv, rau, streng
harvest *100* Ernte
to **haunt sb.** *138* jdn verfolgen
to **have a say** *72* mitreden (können), ein Mitspracherecht haben
havoc *53* Chaos, Verwüstung
hazardous waste *104* Sondermüll
to **head** *31* unterwegs sein nach, sich aufmachen nach; **~ sth.** *50* etw leiten
headline, to **hit the ~s** *81* Schlagzeilen machen
headquartered *80T* mit Sitz in
heady *23* berauscht
health *17F* Gesundheit; **public ~** *51* Gesundheitswesen, öffentliche Gesundheit
health care *11* Gesundheitsfürsorge, Gesundheitswesen; **~ system** *126* Gesundheitssystem
health plan *AE 32* Krankenversicherung
health-giving *102* gesundheitsfördernd
heart, to **eat one's ~ out** *155F* vor Neid erblassen; to **make your ~ sing** *14* das Herz höher schlagen lassen, jdn von Herzen glücklich machen
to **hearten** *37* ermutigen
heartening *111* ermutigend
heedless *23* achtlos, unachtsam
herder *21* Hirte/-in
heritage *21* Erbe
heterogeneous *140* heterogen
hidden from casual view *47* im Verborgenen
hierarchy *100* Hierarchie
high *14* Hochstimmung; **all-time ~** *26* historischer Höchststand; to **be in ~ spirits** *13* bei bester Laune sein
high achiever *149* leistungsstarke Person
high ground, the moral ~ *137* moralische Überlegenheit
high volume *32 hier:* mit hohem Patientenaufkommen
high-stakes test *36* alles entscheidende Prüfung
high-visibility *46* öffentlichkeitswirksam, mit hoher Außenwirkung
highly visible *47* öffentlichkeitswirksam, mit hoher Außenwirkung
to **hire sb.** *19* jdn engagieren
to **hit the headlines** *81* Schlagzeilen machen
to **hold: ~ on to sth.** *20 hier:* etw behalten; **~ sth. up** *114* etw stützen, etw tragen
holey *155F* löchrig
home insurance *51* Hausversicherung
Home Office *75 brit. Innenministerium*
homegrown *138* heimisch
homeless *21* obdachlos; **the ~** *21* Obdachlose
homogenization *120* Angleichung
honesty *23* Ehrlichkeit
honor, to **receive top ~s** *AE 36* den ersten Preis bekommen
to **honor sb.** *AE 138* jdn ehren, jdm Respekt erweisen
hoplessness *9* Aussichtslosigkeit, Hoffnungslosigkeit
horrendous *45* grauenhaft, entsetzlich
hospitality industry *20* Gastgewerbe
host country *78* Gastland
host family *21* Gastfamilie
hot air balloon *30T* Heißluftballon
household waste *26* Haushaltsmüll
housing *11* Wohnungen, Wohnungsbau, Wohungsmarkt
to **huddle close** *71T* sich eng aneinander drängen
human rights violation *115* Menschenrechtsverletzung
human trafficker *78* Menschenhändler/in
humane *54* human
humanitarian *113* humanitär

humanitarian affairs *137* Menschenrechtsfragen, humanitäre Angelegenheiten
to **humiliate** *129T* erniedrigen
humiliation *90* Erniedrigung
hunter gatherer *148* Jäger und Sammler
husk *155F* Schale, Hülse
hybrid *88* gemischt, Misch-
hydro energy *98* Wasserkraft
hydroelectric energy *103T* Wasserkraft
hydroelectric plant *26* Wasserkraftwerk
hydrogen age *155* Wasserstoffzeitalter
hypocrisy *138* Heuchelei
hysteria *51* Hysterie

I

icebreaker *73 etw, das die Stimmung auflockert*
identity, sense of ~ *72* Identitätsgefühl
idle *42T* untätig
to **ignite** *154T* entzünden
ill-advised *139* unklug, schlecht beraten
ill conceived *24* schlecht durchdacht, schlecht geplant
ill-informed *80T* schlecht informiert
illicit *50* illegal
immediate *11* unmittelbar
immersion, cultural ~ programme *20 Programm zum Kennenlernen einer Kultur vor Ort*
imminent *112* bevorstehend
immune to sth. *84* immun gegen etw
immunodeficiency *111* Immunschwäche
impact *9* Auswirkung(en), Einfluss, Folgen; *64* Aufprall
to **impact sb./sth.** *124* sich auf jdn/etw auswirken, Folgen für jdn/etw haben
to **impair** *92T* beeinträchtigen
impatient *8* ungeduldig
impermeable *99* (wasser)dicht
to **implement** *53* umsetzen, anwenden, durchführen
implication *74* Folge, Konsequenz
implicit *110* unausgesprochen, (stillschweigend) vorausgesetzt
to **impose sth.** *74* etw verhängen, etw auferlegen, etw anordnen
to **impoverish sb.** *124* jdn verarmen lassen
impoverished *108* verarmt
imprecise *111* ungenau
imprisonment *52* Inhaftierung
inaccessible *23* unzugänglich
inappropriate *139* unangemessen
incentive *9* Anreiz
incident *47* Vorfall
to **incinerate** *104* verbrennen
incineration *100* Müllverbrennung
inclined, to **be ~ to do sth.** *66* dazu neigen, etw zu tun
income *11* Einkommen; **source of ~** *21* Einkommensquelle
income asset *21 etwa:* Aktivposten, der Einkommen ermöglicht
income gap *131* Einkommensschere
income tax *57* Einkommensteuer
inconceivable *141* unvorstellbar, undenkbar
to **incorporate** *21* aufnehmen, einbauen, einbeziehen
incurable *152* unheilbar
independent streak *7* Unabhängigkeitsdrang
indicator *8* Gradmesser, Indikator
indifference *38* Gleichgültigkeit
indigenous *108* eingeboren
indisputable *125* unstrittig
industrialized country *108* Industrienation, -staat
inequality *11* Ungleichheit; **social ~** *54* soziale Ungleichheiten
inequitable *37* ungerecht
inert *100* verfalls-/reaktionsbeständig, inert
inevitable *123* unvermeidlich
infamous *60* berühmt-berüchtigt
infamously *75* schändlich, berüchtigt
infant mortality *75* Säuglingssterblichkeit
to **infect** *129T* anstecken, infizieren
infertile *110* unfruchtbar
to **inflate** *18* aufblasen
to **inflict sth. on sb.** *114* jdm etw zufügen
influential *48* einflussreich
influx *78* Strom, Zustrom
informational session *33* Informationsveranstaltung
ingenuity *135* Einfallsreichtum, Phantasie
ingrained, deeply ~ *26* tief verwurzelt
ingredient *53* Zutat, Inhaltsstoff
inherently *140* grundsätzlich, an sich
to **inherit** *129T* erben
inhospitable *108* unwirtlich
in-house *42T* betriebsintern
to **inject sth. into sth.** *141* etw einer Sache verleihen
injustice *54* Ungerechtigkeit, Unrecht
in-laws *60* Schwiegereltern
inmate, prison ~ *52* Gefängnisinssasse/-in
innocent *52* unschuldig
insane *10* wahnsinnig, verrückt
insecurity *10* Verunsicherung, Unsicherheit
insensitive *90* unsensibel, instinktlos
to **insist** *88* beteuern, (darauf) bestehen
inspiring *12* anregend, inspirierend
instance, for ~ *40* zum Beispiel
instinctive *75* instinktiv
insulated *84* isoliert
insult *47* Beleidigung
insurance, home ~ *51* Hausversicherung
insurgency *119* Aufstand, Aufruhr
integral part *24* wesentlicher Bestandteil
intellectual property *92* geistiges Eigentum; **theft of ~** *124* geistiger Diebstahl
intelligence service *137* Geheimdienst
intense(ly) *23* intensiv, stark
intent *46* Absicht
intention *98* Absicht
interconnectedness *124* Vernetzung
interdependence *129T* wechselseitige Abhängigkeit, Verflechtung
interest *117* Zins(en)
to **interfere with sth.** *92T* etw beeinträchtigen
interference *118* Einmischung
intermarriage *72* Mischehe
International Monetary Fund (IMF) *124* Internationaler Währungsfonds (IWF)
interrogation *138* Verhör, Vernehmung
to **intervene** *136* einschreiten, intervenieren
interviewee *14* Befragte/r
intimate *92* intim
intriguing *62* faszinierend, verblüffend
introductory *155* einführend
intrusion *91* Eingriff, Eindringen
to **invent** *28* erfinden
invention *90* Erfindung
inventiveness *152* Erfindungsreichtum
to **investigate sb.** *138* Ermittlungen gegen jdn anstellen
invitation, to **extend an ~ to sb.** *34* jdn einladen
to **involve** *11* mit sich bringen, zur Folge haben; *47* einbeziehen, beteiligen
involved, to get ~ *49* sich beteiligen, sich einmischen
involvement *115* Betiligung

irreversible *144* unumkehrbar
issue: special ~ *17* Sonderausgabe, Sonderheft; *118T* Angelegenheit, Thema

J

jail *51* Gefängnis
jeopardy *40* Gefahr
Jew *47* Jude/Jüdin
job centre *33* Arbeitsamt
job security *122* Arbeits(platz) sicherheit
job tenure *11* Anstellungsdauer
to **join** *13* beitreten
jointly *113* gemeinsam
to **jolt** *27* aufrütteln, schockieren
Jones, to **keep up with the ~es** *12 etwa:* mit den Nachbarn mithalten
judge *54* Richter/in
to **judge** *18* urteilen; **~ sb.** *139* jdn verurteilen, über jdn ein Urteil sprechen
judiciary *75* der Richterstand
just *54* gerecht
justice *46* Richter/in; to **bring sb. to ~** *48* jdn vor Gericht stellen, jdn zur Rechenschaft ziehen
justification *51* Rechtfertigung, Begründung
to **justify** *6* rechtfertigen, begründen
juvenile *58* Jugendliche/r; **~ delinquency** *54* Jugendkriminalität; **~ delinquent** *57* jugendliche/r Straftäter/in

K

to **keep: ~ sth. up** *26* etw beibehalten; **~ up with sth.** *85* mit etw mithalten; **~ up with the Joneses** *12 etwa:* mit den Nachbarn mithalten
to **kill sb. off** *66* jdn sterben lassen, jdn töten
kindness *17F* Freundichkeit, Liebenswürdigkeit
knock, to **take a ~** *66* einen Knacks bekommen, einen Schlag versetzt bekommen

L

to **label** *73* etikettieren, bezeichnen
labor *AE* *80* Arbeitskräfte
labour *42* Arbeit; **slave ~** *118T* Sklavenarbeit
labour force *66* erwerbstätige Bevölkerung
labour market (labor market *AE***)** *42T* Arbeitsmarkt
lack *111* Mangel
to **lack sth.** *7* (zu) wenig von etw haben; *19F* etw nicht haben
to **lag** *36* zurückliegen, hinterherhinken; **~ behind** *128* hinterherhinken, hinter etw zurückbleiben
lame *36* lahm, schwach
landfill *99* Mülldeponie
landmark *75* Meilenstein
large-scale *80T* groß, in großem Umfang/Maßstab; *103T* Massen-
lasting *69* dauerhaft, nachhaltig
latitude *103T* Breite
to **launch** *50* starten
laundry *19* Wäsche; to **do ~** *62* Wäsche waschen
law, court of ~ *48* Gericht, Gerichtshof; **due process of ~** *140* ordentliches Gerichtsverfahren; **rule of ~** *136* Rechtsstaatlichkeit; **~ and order** *129T* Recht und Ordnung; **to pass a ~** *12* ein Gesetz verabschieden/erlassen
law enforcement *135* Durchsetzung von Gesetzen, Gesetzesvollzug; **~ authority** *46* Strafverfolgungsbehörde
lawful *137* rechtmäßig, gesetzmäßig
lawlessness *135* Gesetzlosigkeit, Gesetzwidrigkeit
lead *87 hier:* Hinweis, Anhaltspunkt, Spur
to **lead the way** *20* die Richtung weisen, es vormachen
leadership *12* Führung
to **leaf through** *30* durchblättern
leaky *78* undicht
leave, maternity ~ *60* Mutterschaftsurlaub
to **leave sth. a long way off** *99* etw in weite Ferne rücken
to **lecture sb.** *44* jdn belehren
leftover food *104* Essensreste
legacy *126* Erbe
legacy media *85* traditionelle Medien *(im Gegensatz zu den Neuen Medien)*
legal action *92* rechtliche Schritte, Rechtsmittel
legal agreement *86* rechtswirksame Vereinbarung
legal regulation *50* gesetzliche Bestimmugen
legal residency *80* Aufenthaltsgenehmigung, -recht
legal system *37* Rechtssystem
to **legislate** *75* Gesetze erlassen
legislation *75* Gesetzgebung, Gesetze
legislature *149* Legislative
legitimacy *137* Rechtmäßigkeit
legitimate *135* rechtmäßig, legitim
leisure *10* Freizeit
to **lend iteself to sth.** *109* sich für etw eignen
lenient *54* mild, nachsichtig
to **let: ~ sb. down** *40* jdn im Stich lassen, jdn enttäuschen; to **feel let down** *15* (von jdm/etw) enttäuscht sein; **~ go of sth.** *9* sich von etw lösen, etw vernachlässigen; **~ off steam** *92T* Dampf ablassen
let alone *50* geschweige denn
level *11* Niveau, Grad
to **level out** *65* sich einpendeln, sich einpegeln
leverage *143T* Einfluss; die Fähigkeit, Druck auszuüben
liberty *71T* Freiheit
licence fee *90* Rundfunkgebühr
life expectancy *10* Lebenserwartung
life path *36* Lebensweg
life sentence *55* lebenslange Freiheitsstrafe
lifespan *100* Lebensdauer
lifetime, of a ~ *8* einmalig
light-deprived *26* von Lichtmangel betroffen
light-hearted *14* heiter, unbekümmert
likewise *10* ebenso, gleichermaßen
line *126* Warteschlange; **in ~ with sth.** *33* in Einklang mit etw; to **cross the ~** *47* zu weit gehen, eine/die Grenze überschreiten; **to draw a ~** *97* einen Strich ziehen; to **walk a delicate ~** *47* sich auf einem schmalen Grat bewegen
lineage *72* Abstammung, Herkunft
to **link up with sth.** *129T* sich mit etw verknupfen (lassen)
lion's share *60* Löwenanteil
literally *21* buchstäblich
literate *111* des Lesens und Schreibens kundig
littered, to **be ~ with sth.** *20* mit etw übersät sein
living *21* lebendig; **~ creature** *9* Lebewesen
living, to **make a ~ out of sth.** *7* mit etw seinen Lebensunterhalt bestreiten
loan *108* Darlehen
loath, to **be ~ to do sth.** *51* etw nur sehr ungern tun
local *19* Einheimische/r
locale *26* Ort, Örtlichkeit, Region
loneliness *92T* Einsamkeit
longer-term *33* längerfristig
longevity *60* Langlebigkeit, hohe Lebensdauer
long-haul flight *26* Langstreckenflug
long-term *35* langfristig

to **loom** *96* drohen, bedrohlich näher rücken
loss *14* Verlust
a **loved one** *14* nahestehender Mensch
to **lower** *43* senken
lower middle class *123* untere Mittelklasse
low-wage *38* schlecht bezahlt, Niedriglohn-
lubricant *115* Schmiermittel
lucrative *40* einträglich
to **lurk** *93* lauern

M

macroeconomic *66* makroökonomisch
to **magnify** *65* vergrößern
to **maintain** *119* warten, instand halten; *124* aufrecht erhalten; **~ sb.** *66* jdn unterhalten, jdn versorgen
major *33* groß, bedeutend, wichtig
majority *11* Mehrheit
majority rule *136* Mehrheitsregierung
to **make: ~ for sb./sth.** *47* jdn/etw abgeben, jdn/etw darstellen; **~ it past sth.** *34* etw überstehen; **~ one's case** *149* für seine Sache werben
make-up *76* Zusammensetzung
malignant *50* bösartig, heimtückisch
malnutrition *108* Unterernährung
to **man** *34* besetzen, bedienen
to **mandate** *11* (gesetzlich) vorschreiben
mandatory *54* gesetzlich vorgeschrieben
manners *22* Manieren, Umgangsformen
manual work *40* körperliche Arbeit, handwerkliche Arbeit
marginal(ly) *80T* geringfügig
to **marginalize sb.** *114* jdn ins Abseits drängen
marital status *12* Familienstand
to **marvel at sth.** *131* über etw staunen
to **mask** *66* kaschieren, verdecken
to **massacre** *137* niedermetzeln
massive *24* riesig, gewaltig, enorm
to **match sth.** *11* mit etw übereinstimmen
match, to **be a good ~ for sb./sth.** *7* gut zu jdm/etw passen
maternity leave *60* Mutterschaftsurlaub
to **matter** *18* wichtig sein; **~ to sth.** *37* für etw wichtig sein
matter, no ~ *11* ungeachtet, ganz egal; to **drop the ~** *94* die Angelegenheit auf sich beruhen lassen
matter-of-fact *52* sachlich
maturity *54* Reife
mean *72* gemein, fies; **no ~ achievement** *61* beachtliche Leistung
meaningless *36* sinnlos, wenig aussagekräftg, unbedeutend
meanness *47* Gemeinheit(en)
means *24* Mittel, Möglichkeit
to **measure** *14* messen
measure *22* Maßnahme; **social-security ~s** *80T* Sozialversicherungsleistungen; to **take ~s** *22* Maßnahmen ergreifen
measurement *86* Maß
meddling *110* Einmischung
media, legacy ~ *85* traditionelle Medien *(im Gegensatz zu den Neuen Medien)*
media outlet *87* Medium, Sender, Presseorgan
median *11* mittlere/r/s
mediation *22* Vermittlung
medical bills *126* Gesundheitskosten
to **meditate** *92T* meditieren
to **meet a need** *10* ein Bedürfnis befriedigen
to **meld** *134* verschmelzen
melting pot *78* Schmelztiegel
Member of Parliament MP) *76* Parlamentsabgeordnete/r
menacing *72* bedrohlich
merchant *114* Händler/in; **wine ~** *33* Weinhändler/in, Weinhandel/-handlung
merely *88* lediglich, bloß
merit *53* Vorzug
metaphorical *39* metaphorisch
metro(politan) *85* großstädtisch, Stadt-
midst, to **be in the ~ of sth.** *72* mitten in etw sein
might, military ~ *140* militärische (Über-)Macht
mighty *96* äußerst, unheimlich
to **migrate** *108* abwandern, (fort) ziehen
millennium, turn of the ~ *90* Jahrtausendwende
military might *140* militärische (Über-)Macht
to **mimic** *150* nachahmen
to **mind** *8* etw dagegen haben
mind *23* Bewusstsein; **peace of ~** *14* innerer Friede, Seelenfrieden
mindless *88* stumpfsinnig
mind-numbing *47* stumpfsinnig
mindset *85* Mentalität, Denkweise
minute *101* winzig
miracle *115* Wunder
mired, to **be ~ in sth.** *114* in (einem Sumpf von) etw stecken
misconception *80T* falsche Vorstellung(en), irrige Annahme(n)
miserable *14* elend, unglücklich
misguided *115* Fehl-
misleading *12* irreführend
to **misname** *143T* unzutreffend benennen
misstep *150* Fehltritt
mixed race *72* gemischtrassig
mobility, social ~ *37* soziale Mobilität
modern comforts *22* moderne Annehmlichkeiten
modest *11* klein, unerheblich; *44* bescheiden; *67* mäßig, maßvoll
to **monitor** *82* überwachen, kontrollieren
to **monopolize** *52* monopolisieren
mood *13* Stimmung, Laune
moon, over the ~ *15* (vor Freude) ganz aus dem Häuschen
the moral high ground *137* moralische Überlegenheit
mortality, infant ~ *75* Säuglingssterblichkeit
mortar, brick-and-~ *150* konventionell
mortgage *84* Hypothek
moth *155F* Motte
motoring offence *56* Verkehrsdelikt
mould, cultural ~ *129T* kulturelle Prägung
mountain range *18* Gebirgszug
to **mourn sb.** *115* jdn betrauern, jdn beweinen
mourner *137* Trauernde/r
much-needed *114* dringend benötigt, dringend erforderlich
muddy *114* matschig
mulatto *72* Mulatte/-in
multinational corporation *124* internationaler Konzert, Multi
to **multiply** *146* vervielfältigen, multiplizieren
multiracial *72* gemischtrassig
multitude *96* Vielzahl
to **mute** *10* dämpfen
mutual *72* gemeinsam, gegenseitig

N

name, to **call sb. ~s** *45* jdn beleidigen
napkin *19* Serviette
nappy *100* Windel
narco-cartel *51* (lateinamerikanisches) Drogenkartell
narcotics *53* Betäubungsmittel
narrow *63* eng, beschränkt
native country *33* Heimatland

natural gas *96* Erdgas
natural resources *108* natürliche Rohstoffe
to **naturalize** *78* einbürgern
neat *44* gepflegt
necessarily, not ~ *8* nicht unbedingt
(bare) necessities *121* die lebensnotwendigen Dinge
need, to meet a ~ *10* ein Bedürfnis befriedigen
needy *150* bedürftig
to **neglect** *53* vernachlässigen
negotiating skills *60* Verhandlungsgeschick
negotiator *144* Unterhändler/in
neighbouring *71* Nachbar-, benachbart
neo-Classical *73* klassizistisch
nerve-wrecking *8* nervenaufreibend
nervous breakdown *31* Nervenzusammenbruch
to **nestle** *20* sich schmiegen, eingebettet sein
newcomer *108* Neuankömmling
newly-wed *69T* frisch verheiratet, jung vermählt
news, to **break the ~ to sb.** *89* jdm die/eine Nachricht überbringen
newscast *84* Nachrichtensendung
newspaper circulation *84* Zeitungsauflage(n)
newsstand *90* Zeitungskiosk
niche market *24* Nischenmarkt
no ... whatsoever *118T* nicht der/die/das geringste, überhaupt keine/r/s
no matter *11* ungeachtet, ganz egal
nomad *21* Nomade/-in
nomadic *21* Nomaden-
non-government(al) organization *22* Nichtregierungsorganisation
non-polluting *104* umweltfreundlich
non-returnable *104* Einweg-
not necessarily *8* nicht unbedingt
note, to **take ~** *92T* aufpassen
to **notice** *17* feststellen
notion *72* Idee, Gedanke, Vorstellung
novelist *11* Romanautor/in
noxious *99* giftig, schädlich
nuanced *80T* differenziert
nuclear fusion *156* Kernfusion
nuclear power *96* Kernkraft
nuclear proliferation *140* Verbreitung/Weitergabe von Kernwaffen
nuclear reactor *125* (Kern-)Reaktor
number, to **crunch the ~s** *37* die Zahlen durchrechnen
numbing, mind-~ *47* stumpfsinnig
numerous *24* zahlreich
nutrition *92T* Ernährung, Nahrung

O

obesity *117* Fettleibigkeit
objectionable *54* anstößig, bedenklich
objective *112* Ziel
obligation *28* Verpflichtung
obliged, to **be ~ to do sth.** *54* etw tun müssen
to **obliterate** *75* auslöschen
obscure *115* unklar
to **observe** *114* beobachten
to **obsess about sth.** *37* sich zwanghaft mit etw beschäftigen
obsessive *92T* zwanghaft
obstacle *79* Hindernis
to **obtain** *40* erhalten, bekommen
occupation *137* Besetzung
to **occupy** *20* einnehmen; *85* besetzen
to **occur** *14* vorkommen, sich ereignen; *149* geschehen, stattfinden
odds *115* Widrigkeiten, Aussichten; to **be at ~ with oneself** *14* mit sich hadern, mit sich selbst uneins sein
off: ~ guard *96* unvorbereitet; **~ the beaten track** *20* abseits ausgetretener Pfade; to **be better ~** *60* (finanziell) besser gestellt sein; *110* besser dran sein
offence *48* Straftat; **criminal ~** *75* strafrechtliches Vergehen, Straftat; **motoring ~** *56* Verkehrsdelikt
to **offend** *47* (jdn) beleidigen, (jdn) verletzen, Ärgernis erregen
offender *46* Straftäter/in; **first-time ~** *54* Ersttäter/in, nicht Vorbestrafte/r; **repeat ~** *54* Wiederholungstäter/in
offensive *48* beleidigend
official *138* Beamte/r; **party ~** *161* Parteifunktionär/in
oil, peak ~ *96* Ölfördermaximum
oil exploration *136* Ölsuche
oil refinery *119* Ölraffinerie
once *51* ehemals
once and for all *53* ein für allemal
on-going *53* anhaltend, fortdauernd
online theft *90* Online-Diebstahl
to **operate: ~ sth.** *126* etw betreiben; to **start ~ing** *96* in Betrieb gehen
operation, ceased ~s *43* Geschäftsbetrieb eingestellt
operator, switchboard ~ *32* Telefonist/in; **tour ~** *24* Reiseveranstalter
opinionated *90* rechthaberisch
opponent *51* Gegner/in
oppression *71* Unterdrückung
oppressive *134* repressiv, tyrannisch
to **opt for sth.** *82* sich für etw entscheiden
optical character recognition (OCR) *146* optische Zeichenerkennung
ordeal *54* Qual, Martyrium, Leid
order, economic ~ *122* Wirtschaftsordnung; **public ~** *10* öffentliche Ordnung; **social ~** *54* Gesellschaftsordnung, Sozialordnung; **law and ~** *129T* Recht und Ordnung
orderly *134* geordnet
origin *72* Herkunft
otherwise *24* auch
to **oust sb.** *143T* jdn absetzen
outcome *16T* Ergebnis, Resultat
to **outcompete** *37* einholen, aus dem Feld schlagen
to **outdo sb.** *82* jdn übertreffen
to **outduel sb.** *121* jdn aus dem Feld schlagen
to **outlaw** *11* (gesetzlich) verbieten
outlet *21* Ventil, Betätigungsfeld; *126* Verkaufstelle, Geschäft, Filiale
to **outline** *115* beschreiben, skizzieren, umreißen
outlook *143T* Perspektive, Einstellung
outpatient *32* ambulante/r Patient/in
outpatient hospital *32* Tagesklinik
outpouring of emotions *134* Gefühlsausbruch
output growth *66* Produktionswachstum
overall *33* allgemein, Gesamt-
to **overcome** *27* überwinden, hinwegkommen über
overcrowding *24* Überfüllung; **criminal justice ~** *51* Überbeanspruchung der Justizbehörden
to **overestimate** *80T* überschätzen
overhaul *82* Revision; *122* Überdenken, Anpassung
overpriced *24* überteuert
overt(ly) *75* offen (gezeigt)
to **overuse sth.** *7* etw zu viel/oft gebrauchen
to **overwhelm** *48* überwältigen
overwhelmed *42T* überfordert
ownership *90* Besitz

P

pace *149* Tempo
pack *36* Rudel, Meute
package holiday *24* Pauschalurlaub
packaging *99* Verpackung
to **pad** *150* tappen
pain, to **take ~s** *49* sich (große) Mühe geben

panacea *72* Allheilmittel, Patentlösung
panel *96* Ausschuss, Gremium
paramount *114* Haupt-, höchste/r/s, oberste/r/s
paraphernalia *10* Zubehör, Utensilien
parental supervision *54* elterliche Aufsicht
parenting *59* elterliche Fürsorge, Kindererziehung
parliamentarian *Abgeordnete/r*
parole *54* Bewährung
participant *80T* Teilnehmer/in
particularly *11* insbesondere, besonders
partisan *90* voreingenommen
party, ruling ~ *129T* Regierungspartei
party official *16T* Parteifunktionär/in
to **pass a law** *12* ein Gesetz verabschieden/erlassen
patch *155F* Flicken
paternalistic *11* bevormundend, paternalistisch
path *17F* Weg; **life ~** *36* Lebensweg
pathetic *44* jämmerlich, armselig
patient *8* geduldig
pattern *62* Muster
to **pave the way** *126* den Weg ebnen
to **pay: ~ off** *115* sich lohnen; **~ sth. off** *114* etw abbezahlen
pay-rise *53* Lohnerhöhung
peace of mind *14* innerer Friede, Seelenfrieden
peak *96 hier:* Fördermaximum
peak oil *96* Ölfördermaximum
peer pressure *54* Gruppenzwang, Gruppendruck
to **pen sb. in** *71* jdn einsperren, jdn einpferchen
pending trial *54* bis zum Prozess
pendulum *14* Pendel
penetration *130* Durchdringung
pensioner *65* Rentner/in
to **perceive** *23* wahrnehmen
perception *80T* Wahrnehmung
to **perform** *32* durchführen, ausführen; *39* abschneiden *(in einer Prüfung, etc.)*, Leistung(en) bringen; **~ sth.** *17F* etw ausführen
performance *36* Leistung
permanent contract *33* unbefristeter Vertrag
to **permit** *48* erlauben, gestatten
perpetrator *49* Täter/in
persecution *78* Verfolgung
perspective, to **maintain a ~** *37* alles in Relation sehen
persuasive *140* überzeugend
Peruvian *73* peruanisch
pest *152* Schädling
pesticide *152* Schädlingsbekämpfungsmittel, Pestizid
pet parent *32* Tierbesitzer/in, Herrchen/Frauchen
petty crime *54* Bagatelldelikt(e)
philosophical, to **wax ~** *147* ins Philosophieren geraten, herumphilosophieren
phone operator *32* Telefonist/in
physical *17F* körperlich, physisch
to **pick sth. apart** *72 etwa:* etw auseinandernehmen
to **pickpocket** *57 (Taschendieb/in:)* stehlen
picture, the big ~ *17F* das große Ganze
piddling *96* lächerlich (gering)
to **pile up** *99* sich stapeln
pilgrim *78* Pilgerer/-in
pillar, main ~ *103T* tragende Säule
piracy *91* Piraterie, Datendiebstahl
pitiable *72* bemitleidenswert
pittance *121* Hungerlohn
to **pity** *122* bemitleiden
placement agency *34* Arbeitsvermittlung
to **plague** *17F* plagen, heimsuchen
plain *8* einfach, schlicht; *78* Ebene
plant *100* Anlage, Werk, Fabrik; **power ~** *103T* Kraftwerk
to **play out** *96 hier:* sich auswirken
to **pledge** *143T* geloben
to **please sb.** *17F* jdm gefallen, jdn zufrieden stellen
pleasure *10* Vergnügen
plight *108* Notlage, Elend
to **plummet** *12* (drastisch) fallen, abstürzen
point, to **make a ~ to do sth.** *17F* es sich zur Aufgabe machen, etw zu tun; darauf Wert legen, etw zu tun
to **point out** *10* darauf hinweisen
to **poison** *39* vergiften
poisonous *105* giftig
to **poke** *155F* stoßen
to **police** *47* überwachen, kontrollieren
police squad *46* Polizeitruppe, -einheit, -kommando
policies *11* Strategien, Programme
policy *16T* Politik, Vorgehensweise
policymaker *37* Politiker/in, politische/r Entscheidungsträger/in
political entity *108* politische Einheit, Staatsgebilde
political force *76* politische Kraft
poll *80T* Umfrage
to **poll sb.** *80T* jdn befragen
pollster *62* Meinungsforscher/in
pollutant *106* Schadstoff
to **pollute** *95* verschmutzen
polluting, non-~ *104* umweltfreundlich
pomegranate *155F* Granatapfel
pontoon *155F* Ponton
to **pool** *109* zusammenlegen, vereinigen
populated, sparsely ~ *23* dünn besiedelt
population pyramid *60* Bevölkerungspyramide
populous *66* bevölkerungsreich
to **portray sth. as sth.** *72* etw als etw darstellen
to **pose a threat to sb./sth.** *122* eine Gefahr/Bedrohung für jdn/etw darstellen
posh *21* schick, vornehm
to **posit** *134* postulieren, aufstellen
possessions *10* Besitztümer; Hab und Gut
to **post a bond** *54* eine Kaution hinterlegen
potty *7* verrückt, plemplem
pouch *127* Beutel
poverty *24* Armut
to **power** *96* mit Energie versorgen, antreiben
power *26* Strom; **colonial ~** *108* Kolonialmacht; **economic ~** *122* Wirtschaftsmacht; **shift of ~** *121* Kräfteverschiebung, Machtverschiebung; **spending ~** *121* Kaufkraft
powerful *118T* machtvoll
power plant *103T* Kraftwerk
power supply *26* Stromversorgung
practicality *43* praktische Durchführbarkeit
practice *28* Praktik; to **put sth. into ~** *87* etw in die Tat/Praxis umsetzen
to **preach** *74* predigen
to **precede** *16T* vorausgehen, vorangehen
precious *45* kostbar, wertvoll
precision *148* Genauigkeit, Präzision
to **predict** *65* vorhersagen
predominance *135* Vorherrschaft
preference *30* Vorliebe
prejudice *72* Vorurteil(e)
preoccupied *17* besorgt
preparation *17* Vorbereitung
prerequisite *40* Voraussetzung, Bedingung
preschool *63* Kindergarten, Vorschule
present-day *108* gegenwärtig
to **preserve** *20* erhalten, bewahren, schützen
to **press for sth.** *135* auf etw

drängen
pressing *76* dringlich, dringend
presumably *10* vermutlich
to **pretend** *51* so tun, als ob; ~ **to do sth.** *74* vorgeben, etw zu tun
pretty *7* ziemlich
to **prevail** *76* herrschen, vorherrschen
prevalence *111* Verbreitung, Vorherrschen, Prävalenz
prevention *42T* Vorbeugung; **drug** ~ *49* Suchtprävention
pricey *26* teuer
to **pride oneself of sth.** *20* auf etw stolz sein, sich etw auf etw zugute halten
primarily *16T* hauptsächlich
to **prime sb. with sth. for sth.** *80T* jdn mit etw auf etw vorbereiten
principal *67* Haupt-
principled *137* prinzipienfest, prinzipientreu
printing press *90* Druckerpresse
prison inmate *52* Gefängnisinssasse/-in
prison sentence *54* Gefängnisstrafe, Haftstrafe
pristine *20* makellos, unberührt
privacy *23* Privatsphäre
privacy policy *46* Datenschutz(bestimmungen)
privileged *125* privilegiert
probation, to place sb. on ~ *54* jds Strafe zur Bewährung aussetzen
process, due ~ **of law** *140* ordentliches Gerichtsverfahren
to **proclaim** *79* (öffentlich) erklären
produce *108* (landwirtschaftliche) Erzeugnisse
profession, by ~ *69* von Beruf
to **profile** *113* porträtieren
profitable *96* rentabel
profound(ly) *124* tiefgreifend
progress *75* Fortschritt, Fortkommen
to **progress** *149* fortschreiten, voranschreiten
to **prohibit** *51* verbieten
prohibition *51* Verbot
to **project** *110* schätzen, hochrechnen, prognostizieren
projection *98* Hochrechnung, Prognose
to **proliferate** *149* stark zunehmen, wuchern
proliferation, nuclear ~ *140* Verbreitung/Weitergabe von Kernwaffen; **arms** ~ *126* Weiterverbreitung von Waffen
to **prolong** *152* verlängern
prom *8* Promenade
prominence *46* Bekanntheit, Stellenwert
prominent *73* deutlich sichtbar
the promised land *82* das gelobte Land
promising *12* vielversprechend
to **promote** *30* fördern; *106* unterstützen
promotion *8* Beförderung
to **prompt** *87* hervorrufen, veranlassen
pronounced *37* ausgeprägt
proof *14* Beweis(e)
to **propel** *143T* antreiben, vorantreiben
properly *13* richtig, angemessen
property *27* Grundstück; *55* Eigentum; *99* Eigenschaft; *126* Immobilie(n); **intellectual** ~ *92* geistiges Eigentum; **theft of intellectual** ~ *124* geistiger Diebstahl
property rights *37* Eigentumsrechte
to **prophesy** *152* voraussagen
proponent *124* Befürworter
proportion *99* Teil, Anteil
proposal *53* Vorschlag
to **propose** *100* vorschlagen
to **prosecute sb.** *46* jdn strafrechtlich verfolgen
prosecutor *54* Strafverfolger/in, Staatsanwalt/-anwältin
prospect *37* Aussicht
prosperity *10* Wohlstand
prosperous *11* wohlhabend
protective import tariff *108* Einfuhr-Schutzzoll
protective trade policies *108* Handelsbarrieren
to **prove:** ~ **sth.** *110* sich als etw erweisen; ~ **one's worth** *8* sich beweisen, seine Stärke unter Beweis stellen
proven *50* erprobt, erwiesen
to **provide** *11* bieten, zur Verfügung stellen, liefern
public figure *46* Person des öffentlichen Lebens
public health *51* Gesundheitswesen, öffentliche Gesundheit
public order *10* öffentliche Ordnung
to **publish** *17* veröffentlichen, herausbringen
pulp *104* Zellstoff
to **pump sth. out** *133* etw herauspumpen
pundit *84* Experte/-in
to **purchase** *121* kaufen
purchasing power *11* Kaufkraft
to **pursue** *154T* verfolgen
pursuit (of sth.) *26* Jagd (nach etw)
purveyor *85* Lieferant/in
to **push:** ~ **sb. aside** *51* jdn verdrängen
to **put:** ~ **forward** *79* etw vorbringen, etw zur Diskussion stellen; ~ **sb. off sth.** *69T* jdm etw verleiden, jdn von etw abhalten; ~ **up with sth.** *60* etw ertragen, etw hinnehmen, sich etw gefallen lassen

Q

quadrillion *98* Billarde
to **quadruple** *110* sich vervierfachen
quest (for sth.) *122* Streben (nach etw)
to **question sb.** *139* jdn verhören
questionable *110* fragwürdig, fraglich
to **quintuple** *110* sich verfünffachen
to **quit** *8* kündigen, aufgeben
quota *59* Quote
quote *6* Zitat
quotient, feelgood ~ *11 etwa:* Wohlfühlquotient

R

R&D (Research and Development) *121* Forschung und Entwickluns(sabteilung)
race *72* Rasse; **mixed** ~ *72* gemischtrassig
rage, to **be all the** ~ *21* der letzte Schrei sein
to **raise** *26 (Frage, etc.)* aufwerfen; *51* erhöhen, *(Thema, etc.)* ansprechen; ~ **sb.** *36* jdn aufziehen, jdn großziehen; ~ **the stakes** *114 etwa:* die Situation verschärfen
raised, to **be** ~ **on sth.** *85* mit etw aufwachsen
rally (around sth.) *137* Demonstration, Eintreten (für etw)
random *17F* willkürlich, beliebig
to **rank** *11* einen Platz *(in einer Rangliste)* einnehmen
ranking *36* Rangliste
ranks *137* Reihen; to **swell the** ~ *65* die Reihen auffüllen
rape *54* Vergewaltigung
rapid(ly) *34* schnell
rapist *55* Vergewaltiger
rarely *18* selten
rash *23* impulsiv, unbesonnen
rat race *10* erbarmungsloser Überlebenskampf
rate *40* Quote, Anteil; **death** ~ *111* Sterblichkeit
to **rate** *10* einschätzen, bewerten, einstufen
rather *7* ziemlich
rating *84 hier:* Einschaltquote
ratio *66* Verhältnis
raw material *87* Rohmaterial, Rohstoff

to **reach out to sb.** *21* jdn zu erreichen versuchen
to **read up on sth.** *84* sich über etw informieren
readership *90* Leserschaft
to **reaffirm** *137* erneut bekräftigen
real estate *12* Immobilien
realisation *BE* *87* Erkenntnis
recess *AE* *150* Pause *(in der Schule)*
recession *50* Rezession
reckless *20* leichtsinnig, unbesonnen, rücksichtslos
reclusive *23* zurückgezogen
to **recognize** *40* anerkennen, zugeben
recolonization *124* erneute Kolonisierung
recommendation *16* Empfehlung
records *29* Daten, Unterlagen, Dokumentation
to **recover** *100* zurückholen; **~ sth.** *17F* etw wiedererlangen; *129T* etw wiederfinden
recovery *102* Wiedergewinnung
to **recreate** *90* nachbilden, neu schaffen
to **recruit** *38* rekrutieren, anwerben
recruitment *137* Anwerbung
reduced sentence *54* vermindertes Strafmaß, Strafmilderung
redundant, to **be made ~** *12* (betriebsbedingt) entlassen werden
to **re-engineer** *11* umarbeiten, umorganisieren
to **reestablish** *154T* *(Funktion)* wiederaufnehmen
to **refer: ~ to sth.** *12* sich auf etw beziehen, auf etw verweisen; **~ to sb./sth. as sth.** *78* jdn/etw als etw bezeichnen
reflection *104* Widerspiegelung
reformed *44* geläutert, verbessert
reform-minded *125* reformorientiert
refugee camp *107* Flüchtlingslager
refusal *47* Weigerung
to **refuse** *26* sich weigern
to **regain** *129T* wiedererlangen
regard, with ~ to *12* hinsichtlich, bezüglich
regarded, to **be ~ as sth.** *75* als etw gelten, für etw erachtet werden
regardless of *24* ganz gleich, egal (wie); *112* ungeachtet
regimen, drug ~ *111* Arzneimitteltherapie
to **regulate** *50* (gesetzlich) regeln
regulation, legal ~ *50* gesetzliche Bestimmugen
regulations *27* Vorschriften, Bestimmungen
rehab facility *52* Therapieeinrichtung
to **reintegrate** *54* wiedereingliedern
to **reject** *51* zurückweisen, ablehnen
rejection *30* Ablehnung, Zurückweisung; *154T* Abstoßung *(eines transplantierten Organs)*
related, closely ~ to *12* eng verbunden mit
release *27* Freisetzung; *54* Freilassung, Entlassung
to **release** *24* freisetzen; *36* veröffentlichen; **~ sb.** *54* jdn auf freien Fuß setzen
relentless(ly) *66* unentwegt, unaufhaltsam
reliability *23* Zuverlässigkeit
reliable *32* zuverlässig; *106* verlässlich
relief, debt ~ *108* Schuldenerlass; **sigh of ~** *109* Seufzer der Erleichterung; **tax ~** *109* Steuererleichterung, -nachlass
relief fund *109* Hilfsfonds
to **remain: it ~s to be seen** *60* es bleibt abzuwarten
remedial class *81* Förderkurs
reminder *36* Mahnung, Erinnerung
remote *20* entlegen
to **remove sth. from the equation** *51* etw ausklammern, etw außen vor lassen
to **render** *42T* machen
rendition *137* Auslieferung
renewable *26* erneuerbar
to **reoffend** *54* wieder straffällig werden
renowned for sth. *20* für etw berühmt, für etw bekannt
repeat offender *54* Wiederholungstäter/in
to **replace** *8* ersetzen, austauschen
to **replant** *20* neu anpflanzen
to **report** *46* melden, anzeigen
representation *77* Vertretung
representative sample *36* repräsentative Stichprobe
repudiation *47* Zurückweisung, Ablehnung
requirement *32* Anforderung
rescue agency *144* Rettungsdienst
researcher *42T* Forscher/in
to **resemble** *134* ähneln
resentment *78* Unmut, Groll, Ressentiment
to **reshape** *103T* umgestalten
residency, legal ~ *80* Aufenthaltsgenehmigung, -recht
resident *79* Bewohner/in, Einwohner/in
resilient *66* stabil, robust
to **resist sth.** *129T* einer Sache widerstehen
resistant, to **be ~ to sth.** *147* sich einer Sache widersetzen
resolution *53* Entschluss, Beschluss; *140* Lösung
resort *20* Ferienanlage; *24* Urlaubsort, Ferienort
to **resort to sth.** *92T* auf etw zurückgreifen, zu etw greifen
resounding failure *50* eklatanter Misserfolg
resourcefulness *115* Einfallsreichtum, Findigkeit
resources *20* Ressourcen, Schätze
respect, in this ~ *28* in dieser Hinsicht
respectively *66* beziehungsweise
respondent *80T* Befragte/r
responsibility *32* Aufgabe, Aufgabenngebiet, Zuständigkeit
to **restate** *129T* noch einmal sagen, neu formulieren
to **restore** *120* wiederherstellen
restriction *124* Beschränkung
to **restructure** *131* umgestalten, umstrukturieren
retailer *32* Einzelhändler/in
to **retire** *27* sich zur Ruhe setzen
return *117* Rendite
returnable, non-~ *104* Einweg-
to **reveal** *80T* enthüllen, zeigen; *92* preisgeben
revenue, tax ~s *52* Steuereinnahmen
to **review** *17F* überprüfen, begutachten, durcharbeiten
to **revise** *110* korrigieren, nachbessern
revision *110* Korrektur, Nachbesserung
revolutionary *134* Revolutionär/in
reward *17F* Belohnung, Gewinn
rife (with sth.) *140* voll (von etw); to **be ~ with sth.** *74* voll von etw sein
right-wing *76* (politisch) rechts, rechtsgerichtet
rigorous *137* rigoros, konsequent
rise, steep ~ *57T* steiler Anstieg
rising air *7* aufsteigende Luft(strömung)
risk, to **put sb./sth. at ~** *46* jdn/etw gefährden
rivalry *140* Konkurrenzkampf, Kampf
riven, to be ~ by sth. *114* von etw zerrissen/zerfressen sein
rogue *47* Einzelgänger, schwarzes Schaf, Schurke
rogue government *135* Schurkenstaat
role model *27* Vorbild
root *61* Wurzel, Stamm
rotten *125* verdorben, korrupt

rough: ~ around the edges *21* kantig, ungeschliffen
roughly *16T* ungefähr
routinely *75* routinemäßig
rude *48* unhöflich, unverschämt
rug *155F* Teppich
rule *133* Herrschaft; **majority ~** *136* Mehrheitsregierung; **~ of law** *136* Rechtsstaatlichkeit
to **rule sth. out** *30T* etw ausschließen
ruling party *129T* Regierungspartei
rumour *8* Gerücht
to **run its course** *143T* seinen (vollen) Verlauf nehmen
runner-up *13* Zweitplatzierte/r
rural *21* ländlich
ruthless *78* skrupellos

S

sacrifice *84* Opfer, Opferbereitschaft
to **sacrifice** *10* opfern
salary, starting ~ *33* Anfangsgehalt
sales *121* Umsatz, Verkaufszahlen
salvation *121* Rettung, Erlösung
same-sex *67* gleichgeschlechtlich
sample, representative ~ *36* repräsentative Stichprobe
sanitation *124* Müll- und Abwasserentsorgung
saturated *126* gesättigt
savage *50* wild, wüst
say, to **have a ~** *72* mitreden (können), ein Mitspracherecht haben
saying *10* Sprichwort, Redensart
scale *115* Maßstab
scale model *155F* maßstabsgetreues Modell
scarce *42T* knapp
scarlet macaw *9* der Hellrote Ara *(südamerik. Papgeienart)*
sceptical (of sth.) *52* skeptisch (in Bezug auf etw)
scepticism *118* Skepsis
scholar *10* Gelehrte/r, Wissenschaftler/in
school district *149* Schulbezirk
schooling *114* Schulbesuch, Schulbildung
to **score** *38* *(Ergebnis)* erzielen
scourge *50* Geißel
to **scramble to do sth.** *37* händeringend versuchen, etw zu tun, sich dringend bemühen, etw zu tun
scratch, from ~ *127* von Grund auf
sea creature *99* Meerestier
sea level *104* Meeresspiegel
seaside *8* (am) Meer
seasonal *24* saisonal, saisonabhängig
secluded *20* abgeschieden
Secretary General *50* Generalsekretär/in
to **secure sth.** *40* sich etw sichern; *112* etw sicherstellen
to **seek** *17F* suchen; *47* versuchen; **~ sth. out** *17F* etw ausfindig machen
seemingly *20* anscheinend
segregated *76* getrennt, isoliert
to **seize** *103T* ergreifen
seizure *51* Beschlagnahme
seldom *48* selten
self-assertive *79* selbstbewusst
self-catering holiday apartment *24* Ferienwohnung für Selbstversorger
self-defeating *10* das Gegenteil bewirkend, kontraproduktiv
self-imposed *100* selbst auferlegt
self-respect *134* Selbstachtung
semi-skilled *131* angelernt
senior *75* höher(rangig)
sensationalist *90* sensationslüstern
to **sense** *34* spüren
sense of identity *72* Identitätsgefühl
to **sentence sb.** *54* jdn (zu etw) verurteilen, das Strafmaß für jdn bestimmen
sentence, life ~ *55* lebenslange Freiheitsstrafe; **prison ~** *54* Gefängnisstrafe, Haftstrafe; **reduced ~** *54* vermindertes Strafmaß, Strafmilderung; **suspended ~** *54* Bewährungsstrafe
sentiment *80T* Ansicht(en), Meinung(en)
to **sequester** *100* binden, speichern
service, community ~ *54* gemeinnützige Arbeit, Sozialdienst; **intelligence ~** *137* Geheimdienst; **welfare ~** *124* soziale Einrichtungen; **terms of ~** *46* Nutzungsbedingungen
to **set: ~ sth. aside (for sth.)** *17F* etw vorsehen (für etw); **~ on fire** *87* anzünden, in Brand setzen
to **settle** *71* sich niederlassen; **~ down** *34* sich niederlassen, sesshaft werden
settlement *144* Einigung
settler *78* Siedler/in
severe *55* hart, streng
sewage *20* Abwasser
sewer system *108* Kanalisation(ssystem)
sex, battle of the ~es *59* Geschlechterkampf; **same-~** *67* gleichgeschlechtlich
sex education *110* Sexualerziehung, -kunde
sex trafficking *114* Menschenhandel, Frauenhandel
shame *72* Schande, Scham; **in ~** *129T* beschämt
share *65* Anteil; **lion's ~** *60* Löwenanteil
to **shatter** *51* zerschmettern, zerschlagen; *99* zerspringen
shattered *114* am Boden zerstört
shelter *10* Behausung, Unterkunft
to **shift** *80T* verändern; **~ into a new phase** *53* einen neuen Abschnitt einleiten
shift *60* Schicht; *72* Wandel, Veränderung; **~ of power** *121* Kräfteverschiebung, Machtverschiebung
to **shine** *14* glänzen
to **shoot sth.** *134* *(Foto, Film:)* etw aufnehmen
shoplifting *54* Ladendiebstahl
shore *22* Küste
shoreline *20* Küsten(linie)
shortage *33* Mangel, Knappheit
shortfall *33* Mangel, Defizit
short-term *14* kurzfristig
to **show sth. up** *88* etw (deutlich) zeigen, etw deutlich machen
to **shrink** *66* schrumpfen
to **shrinkwrap** *100* mit Schrumpffolie umwickeln, in Schrumpffolie einschweißen
to **shut sth. down** *47* etw schließen
sigh of relief *109* Seufzer der Erleichterung
sight, to **lose ~ of sth.** *84* etw aus den Augen verlieren
to **sign** *34* unterschreiben, unterzeichnen; **~ up with sth.** *114* einer Sache beitreten, sich bei etw anmelden
significant *37* bedeutend, maßgeblich
significantly *26* bezeichnenderweise
similar *10* ähnlich
to **sin** *28* sündigen
to **sink: sb.'s heart ~s** *15* jdm wird bang, jdm wird das Herz schwer
skewed *115* verzerrt, verdreht
skilled *33* (gut) ausgebildet
skilled worker *33* Facharbeiter/in
to **skim** *22* *(Text)* überfliegen
to **skimp on sth.** *16T* an etw sparen, mit etw knausern
to **skyrocket** *110* in die Höhe schnellen, explodieren
slave labour *118T* Sklavenarbeit
slavery *114* Sklaverei
sleet *26* Schneeregen
slice *114* Teil
slight *110* leicht

sloping hill *20* sanft ansteigender Hügel
slump *11* starker Rückgang, Krise
to **smash** *137* zertrümmern, einschlagen
smokescreen *51* Vorwand, Nebelkerze
smooth *7* glatt, ruhig, sanft
snippet *87* Nachrichtenschnipsel
to **soar** *103T* in die Höhe schnellen, sprunghaft ansteigen
to **sob** *45* schluchzen
sobering *110* ernüchternd
social enterprise *21* soziales Unternehmen
social inequality *54* soziale Ungleichheiten
social justice *124* soziale Gerechtigkeit
social mobility *37* soziale Mobilität
social order *54* Gesellschaftsordnung, Sozialordnung
social-security measures *80T* Sozialversicherungsleistungen
to **socialize** *126* vergesellschaften
society *21* Gesellschaft
soft-spoken *47* zurückhaltend, leise, bescheiden
soil *104* Erdreich, Erdboden
solar panel *27* Solarmodul
solar power *103T* Sonnenenergie
solar-powered *19* solarbetrieben
solely *61* allein, ausschließlich
to **solicit sth.** *87* etw erbitten
solitary *149* einzeln, einsam
solvable *37* lösbar
some *33* *hier:* ungefähr
sophisticated *104* raffiniert, ausgeklügelt
sorry, to **be in a ~ state of affairs** *8* in einem jämmerlichen Zustand sein, ganz schön heruntergekommen sein
sort of *63* irgendwie
sour, to turn ~ *68* sich verschlechtern, unangenehm werden
source of income *21* Einkommensquelle
southernmost *20* südlichste/r/s
sovereignty *140* Souveränität
spacious *21* geräumig
to **span the globe** *72* den Globus umspannen
Spaniard *33* Spanier/in
spark *134* Funke
to **spark** *142* entzünden, entfachen
sparsely populated *23* dünn besiedelt
special issue *17* Sonderausgabe, Sonderheft
speciality *19* Spezialität
species *89* Art, Spezies
specious *51* fadenscheinig, hanebüchen
speech, free ~ *46* Redefreiheit; **freedom of ~** *46* Redefreiheit, Recht auf freie Rede
to **speed up** *103T* beschleunigen
to **spell trouble** *143* nichts Gutes bedeuten, Ärger bedeuten
spending *66* Ausgaben
spending, discretionary ~ *126* Konsumausgaben, Ermessensausgaben
spending power *121* Kaufkraft
to **spew** *50* speien
to **spill blood** *76* Blut vergießen
spirit *11* Geist
spirits *14* Stimmung; to **be in high ~** *13* bei bester Laune sein
to **split** *13* (sich) aufteilen
to **splurge on sth.** *121* für etw (mit vollen Händen) viel Geld ausgeben
spoilage *100* Verderb (von Nahrungsmitteln)
spokesperson *33* Sprecher/in
to **sponsor sb.** *117* jdn fördern
sponsorship, child ~ *115* Patenschaft
spouse *73* Ehegatte
to **spot** *18* erkennen
spot, black ~ *57T* Makel
sprawling *108* sich ausbreitend, ausufernd
spread *53* Verbreitung
to **spread** *121* sich ausbreiten; **~ sth. out** *17F* etw verteilen
to **spring up** *21* aus dem Boden sprießen/schießen
squad, police ~ *46* Polizeitruppe, -einheit, -kommando
to **squash** *135* zerquetschen, zunichte machen
squat *155F* gedrungen
to **staff** *85* (mit Personal) besetzen
staff, editorial ~ *17* Redaktion
staff meeting *17* *hier:* Redaktionssitzung
stage *14* Phase
to **stage** *136* veranstalten, organisieren
to **stagnate** *110* stagnieren
stain *138* Makel
stain-absorbing *155F* fleckabsorbierend
stake, high-~s test *36* alles entscheidende Prüfung; to **be at ~** *26* auf dem Spiel stehen; to **raise the ~s** *114* *etwa:* die Situation verschärfen
stall *87* (Markt-)Stand
to **stand out** *62* herausstechen
stark *62* krass, überdeutlich
to **start operating** *96* in Betrieb gehen
starting salary *33* Anfangsgehalt
starvation *108* Verhungern
to **starve: ~ for sth.** *120* sich nach etw sehnen; **~ to death** *108* verhungern
starved, to **be ~ of sth.** *31* von etw nicht genug bekommen, nach etw ausgehungert sein
state *14* Zustand, Verfassung; **emotional ~** *92* Gefühlszustand; **~ of emergency** *139* Ausnahmezustand, Notstand; to **be in a sorry ~ of affairs** *8* in einem jämmerlichen Zustand sein, ganz schön heruntergekommen sein
state security *133* Staatssicherheit
statehouse *149* Parlamentsgebäude
statue *71* Statue
status, marital ~ *12* Familienstand
to **stave sb. off** *124* jdn abwehren, jdn zurückhalten
steadily *60* kontinuierlich, ständig
steady *44* solide, stabil
steam-powered *90* dampfbetrieben
to **stem from sth.** *17F* auf etw zurückzuführen sein, von etw herrühren
to **step: ~ down** *143T* zurücktreten; **~ up** *51* vortreten
steppe *21* Steppe
sterile *148* steril
to **stick to sth.** *9* sich an etw halten, an etw festhalten
stickler, to **be a ~ for sth.** *27* es mit etw sehr genau nehmen
a stiff price *96* ein hoher Preis
stock *127* Fond
stodgy *44* schwerfällig
to **store** *102* lagern
to **stow oneself away** *78* als blinder Passagier reisen, sich als blinder Passagier verstecken
to **strangle** *99* ersticken, strangulieren
stratification *72* (soziale) Schichtenbildung, Stratifikation
streak, independent ~ *7* Unabhängigkeitsdrang
stream, blood ~ *152* Blutbahn, Blutkreislauf
to **strengthen** *121* sich verstärken
to **stress** *40* betonen
stride *96* (großer) Schritt; to **take sth. in ~** *34* locker mit etw umgehen
stringent *97* streng
to **strive for sth.** *10* nach etw streben
struck, to **be ~ on sth.** *30T* von etw beeindruckt sein
structure *21* Gerüst, Rahmen

struggle *50* Kampf; *113* Eintreten (für etw)
to **struggle** *20* kämpfen, sich abmühen
struggler *149 jd, der mit Schwierigkeiten zu kämpfen hat*
stuck, to **be ~** *10* festsitzen
study *152* Forschung
to **stumble** *127* stolpern
stunning *20* fantastisch, umwerfend
to **subdue** *10* unterdrücken
subdued *11* gedämpft
subheading *61* Zwischenüberschrift
subjected, to **be ~ to sth.** *125* einer Sache unterworfen sein
to **submit** *87* einreichen
subordinate *129* zweitrangig
subsequent *75* nachfolgend, folgend
to **subsidize** *108* subventionieren, fördern
subsidy *108* Subvention, Finanzhilfe
substantial *36* erheblich, wesentlich
to **substitute** *98* ersetzen
suburbia *10* Vorstädte, Wohnsiedlungen am Stadtrand
succession *15* Abfolge, Folge
successive *138* die nachfolgende/n
sufficient *108* genügend, ausreichend
sugarcane *155F* Zuckerrohr
to **suggest** *11* darauf hindeuten; *66* nahelegen, *hier:* behaupten, sagen
suicide *45* Selbstmord
to **suit sth.** *7* zu etw passen
sun-deprived, to be ~ *27* mit wenig Sonne auskommen müssen
sun worshipper *26* Sonnenanbeter/in
superior *37* überlegen
supervision, parental ~ *54* elterliche Aufsicht
supervisor *47* Vorgesetzte/r
supplies *125* Versorgungsgüter, Nachschub
supply *42* Angebot; *108* Vorrat, Vorkommen; **energy ~** *104* Energieversorgung; **power ~** *26* Stromversorgung; **~ and demand** *109* Angebot und Nachfrage; to **be in short ~** *109* knapp sein; to **cut off ~** *109* den Nachschub abschneiden
support *118T* Unterstützung
to **support** *110 hier:* ernähren; **~ sth.** *30* etw *(Argument, etc.)* untermauern
supportive *73* verständnisvoll
supposed, to **be ~ to do sth.** *60* etw tun sollen
to **suppress** *87* unterdrücken
suppression *135* Unterdrückung
supremacy *78* Überlegenheit, Vormacht(stellung)
Supreme Court *46 höchster Gerichtshof der USA*
a sure bet *127* eine sichere Sache
surely *10* sicherlich, mit Sicherheit
surf *26* Brandung
to **surface** *47* auftauchen, aufkommen
surgery *32* Chirurgie, OP
to **surpass** *122* überholen
to **surround** *9* umgeben
survey, time-use ~ *62* Zeitbudgeterhebung
survival *111* Überleben; **~ of the fittest** *12* Überleben der bestangepassten Individuen
suspect *127* Verdächtige/r
suspended sentence *54* Bewährungsstrafe
suspicious, to **be ~ of sth.** *152* einer Sache gegenüber misstrauisch sein
sustainability *20* Nachhaltigkeit
sustainable *20* nachhaltig; *111* vertretbar, haltbar
to **swallow sth. up** *66* etw schlucken
to **swamp** *37* überschwemmen
swath *76* Streifen, Landstrich, Gegend
to **sway** *140* beeinflussen
to **sweat sth.** *36* sich um etw Sorgen machen
the sweet spot *134* der optimale Punkt
to **swell** *66* anschwellen; **~ the ranks** *65* die Reihen auffüllen
swift(ly) *87* schnell, rasch
switchboard operator *32* Telefonist/in
to **swoop** *155F* hinabstürzen, nach unten fliegen
sword, two-edged ~ *24* zweischneidiges Schwert
sworn, to **be ~ into office** *82* den Amtseid ablegen
to **sympathize with sth.** *28* Verständnis für etw haben

T

tabloid *90* Boulevardzeitung *(kleines Zeitungsformat, etwa 17 × 11 Zoll)*
to **tackle sth.** *16T* etw angehen, etw in Angriff nehmen; *45* gegen etw vorgehen
tailor-made *152* maßgeschneidert
takeaway, What's the ~? *37* Was sagt uns das?
tan *26* Sonnenbräune; 72 *(Haut:)* braun
tan line *27* Bräunungsstreifen
tangible *21* spürbar, greifbar
tariff, protective import ~ *108* Einfuhr-Schutzzoll
tarp *21* Plane
tasting *69T* Verkostung
taunt *47* höhnische Bemerkung, Hänselei
tavern *90* Schenke
tax, income ~ *57* Einkommensteuer
tax evasion *54* Steuerhinterziehung
tax relief *109* Steuererleichterung, -nachlass
tax revenues *52* Steuereinnahmen
taxpayer *94* Steuerzahler/in
to **tear: ~ sb. apart** *72* jdn auseinanderreißen; **~ sth. down** *137* etw niederreißen, etw einreißen
temper *53* Naturell, Wut, Laune
to **temper** *143T* mildern
temporarily *92T* vorübergehend
temporary *14* vorübergehend; *34* befristet
temporary blip *65* vorübergehende Störung
temporary employment agency *33* Zeitarbeitsagentur
to **tempt: ~ sb. into sth.** *139* jdn zu etw verleiten; to **be ~ed to do sth.** *16T* versucht sein, etw zu tun
tempting *96* verlockend
tenant *43* Pächter/in, Mieter/in
to **tend: ~ to be sth.** *62* eher/tendenziell etw sein; **~ to do sth.** *53* dazu neigen, etw zu tun
tendency *129T* Neigung
tension *77* Spannung
tenure, job ~ *11* Anstellungsdauer
term: in ~s of *37* -mäßig, hinsichtlich, was ... betrifft; *51* in Form von; **in scientific ~s** *14* wissenschaftlich ausgedrückt; **long-~** *35* langfristig; **longer-~** *33* längerfristig; **short-~** *14* kurzfristig
terms of service *46* Nutzungsbedingungen
test case *51* Präzedenzfall
testament (to sth.) *76* Beweis (für etw)
testimony *21* Aussage
to **tether** *155F* anbinden, festbinden
theft, online ~ *90* Online-Diebstahl
theft of intellectual property *124* geistiger Diebstahl
thereby *40* dadurch
thorny *47* heikel
thoughtful *47* umsichtig, bedacht

threat *47* Drohung; **death ~** *47* Morddrohung; to **pose a ~ to sb./sth.** *122* eine Gefahr/Bedrohung für jdn/etw darstellen
to **threaten (sth. against sb)** *46* (jdn mit etw) bedrohen
threatening *42T* bedrohlich
thrill *6* Begeisterung, überwältigendes Gefühl; *8* Nervenkitzel
thrilled to bits *15* (vor Freude) ganz aus dem Häuschen
throat, to force sth. down sb.'s ~ *76* jdm etw aufzwingen
to **throng** *143T* drängen
throughout *49* durchwegs
throughout my life *7* in meinen ganzen Leben, mein ganzes Leben lang
throwaway society *100* Wegwerfgesellschaft
thus *33* daher, deshalb
tidal power *155F* Gezeitenkraft
time, over ~ *10* mit der Zeit; **at ~s** *14* manchmal, bisweilen
time-use survey *62* Zeitbudgeterhebung
timid *79* schüchtern
tinged, to **be ~ with sth.** *72* einen Beigeschmack/Anklang von etw haben
to **tinker with sth.** *152* an etw herumbasteln, an etw herumpfuschen
tissue *152* Gewebe
tolerance, zero ~ *51* Nulltoleranz
to **tolerate** *114* tolerieren
top: on ~ of the world *15* überglücklich; to **receive ~ honors** *AE 36* den ersten Preis bekommen
topical *89* aktuell
topping *8* Garnierung *(z. B. Schokosoße, Nussstreusel)*
torrent *88* Flut, Schwall, (reißender) Strom
torture *137* Folter
torture chamber *137* Folterkammer
torturer *137* Folterer, Folterknecht
totalitarianism *114* Totalitarismus
toting, gun ~ *129T* verbreiteter Schusswaffenbesitz/-gebrauch
to **touch wood** *69T* auf Holz klopfen
tough *12* hart
tour operator *24* Reiseveranstalter
track, on ~ *33* auf Kurs; **off the beaten ~** *20* abseits ausgetretener Pfade
traction *50* Zugkraft
to **track sth. down** *47* etw aufspüren, etw ausfindig machen
trade *37* Handel; *84* Gewerbe; **protective ~ policies** *108* Handelsbarrieren; **World T~ Organization (WTO)** *124* Welthandelsorganisation (WHO)
trade association *149* Wirtschaftsverband, Fachverband
trade barrier *143* Handelsschranken
trading nation *135* Handelsnation
traffic congestion *10* Verkehrsstau
traffic jam *24* Stau
trafficking, drug ~ *54* Drogenhandel
to **trail behind sth.** *126* hinter etw zurückbleiben
to **train as sth.** *9* eine Ausbildung zum/in etw machen
trait *23* Charakterzug
transaction *8* (Geschäfts-)Vorgang
to **transcend** *147* über sich hinausgehen; **~ sth.** *72* über etw hinausgehen
transcendence *72* Überwindung
to **transform** *26* verwandeln, verändern, umgestalten
to **transmit** *98* übertragen
to **trap** *104* einschließen
tray *100* Schale
treatment *51* Behandlung, Therapie
tremendous *131* ungeheuer
triage *146* Sichtung, Triage
trial *111* Versuch; **pending ~** *54* bis zum Prozess
trial period *34* Probezeit
tribe *72* (Volks-)Stamm
trick, to **do the ~** *154* seinen Zweck erfüllen, funktionieren
trickle *126* kleiner, aber stetiger Strom
to **trigger** *88* auslösen
trillion *51* Billion
to **triple** *66* sich verdreifachen
trouble, to spell ~ *143* nichts Gutes bedeuten, Ärger bedeuten
troubling *37* beunruhigend, besorgniserregend
truancy *54* Schulschwänzen
to **trump** *138* übertrumpfen
trust (of sb) *16T* Vertrauen (in jdn)
trusted *87* bewährt, zuverlässig
to **try** *48* (vor Gericht) verhandeln, (jdn) vor Gericht stellen
tuition *21* Unterricht
tuition fee *43* Studiengebühr
turmoil *33* Aufruhr, Durcheinander
to **turn: ~ to sth.** *92T* sich einer Sache zuwenden; **~ sb. in** *57* jdn anzeigen; **~ sb. out** *42* jdn hervorbringen; **~ out** *127* sich herausstellen; **~ out to be sth.** *111* sich als etw erweisen; **~ sour** *68* sich verschlechtern, unangenehm werden
turn, in ~ *108* seiner-/ihrerseits, wiederum
turn of the millennium *90* Jahrtausendwende
turnover *150* Fluktuation
turquoise *20* türkis(farben)
turtleneck *155F* Rollkragenpullover
twist, to add a ~ to sth. *155F* etw aufpeppen; to **add a novel ~ to sth.** sb *62* etw aufpeppen, sich etwas Neues einfallen lassen für etw
to **twist: no matter how you ~ and turn this thing** *27* wie man es (auch) dreht und wendet
two-edged sword *24* zweischneidiges Schwert
tycoon *50* (Industrie-)Magnat
tyrant *135* Tyrann

U

ubiquitous *72* allgegenwärtig
ultimately *11* letztlich, letztendlich
unaffected *128* unbeeinträchtigt, unberührt
unanimous *111* einstimmig; to **be ~ in sth.** *137* sich in einer Sache einig sein
unburdened by sth. *126* von etw unbelastet
unconventional *21* unkonventionell
to **uncover** *135* aufdecken, entdecken, enthüllen
underbelly *47* Schattenseite
underestimate *99* zu geringe Schätzung
to **undergo** *87* sich unterziehen, durchmachen
underlying *11* zugrunde liegend; **~ causes** *54* zugrundeliegende Ursachen
to **undermine** *115* untergraben
underneath *26* unter
undernourished *108* unterernährt
to **underscore** *137* unterstreichen
undersecretary-general *137* Untergeneralsekretär
to **undervalue** *134* unterschätzen
underwhelming *96* nicht gerade überwältigend, wenig berauschend
undoing *37* Verderben, Untergang
uneducated *114* ungebildet, ohne Schulbildung
unemployment benefits *43* Arbeitslosenunterstützung
unequal *89* ungleich, unterschiedlich
unequivocal *96* eindeutig, zweifelsfrei
unexpected(ly) *33* unerwartet
to **unfold** *133* sich abspielen, sich entwickeln
unfounded *112* unbegründet
to **unfurl** *71T* entfalten, auseinander falten
unified *42* einheitlich

uniformity *79* Einheitlichkeit, Eintönigkeit
unimaginably *49* unvorstellbar
uninhabitable *78* unbewohnbar
unintended *50* unbeabsichtigt
uninterrupted *125* ununterbrochen, unterbrechungsfrei
unique *34* einzigartig, einmalig
uniqueness *124* Einzigartigkeit
to **unite** *100* sich zusammenschließen
university-educated *33* mit Universitätsausbildung
to **unleash** *137* entfesseln, auslösen
unless *9* außer wenn, es sei denn
unlikely *47* unwahrscheinlich
to **unlock** *20* entschlüsseln, erschließen
unmatched *99* unerreicht
unprecedented *121* nie dagewesen
unproven *12* unbewiesen
unredeemable *16T* *hier:* unverzeihlich
unsettling *62* verstörend, beunruhigend
unsightly *24* unansehnlich
unspoiled *20* unberührt, unversehrt
unstable *150* labil
unstoppable *155* nicht aufzuhalten, nicht zu verhindern
unsustainable *50* nicht tragfähig, unhaltbar
until death us do part *68* bis dass der Tod uns scheidet
untouched *20* unberührt
to **unveil** *141* enthüllen, aufdecken
unwillingness *111* Widerwille, mangelnde Bereitschaft
to **unwind** *73* sich entspannen, abschalten
up, to **be ~ to sb.** *30T* bei jdm liegen, jds Entscheidung sein; to **be ~ against sth.** *36* einer Sache gegenüberstehen, es mit etw zu tun haben
to **upend** *149* verkehren, auf den Kopf stellen
upheaval *144* Aufruhr
uprising *133* Aufstand
upward *40* aufwärts, nach oben
urban *129T* städtisch, Stadt-
to **urge** *51* drängen, auffordern
urgent(ly) *42* dringend; *107* dringlich
US Census Bureau *37* Statistisches Bundesamt der USA
utility company *97* Versorgungsunternehmen
utmost *141* äußerste/r/s

V

vacant *43* leer stehend
valid *129* gültig, begründet, berechtigt
valley *18* Tal
valuable *24* wertvoll
value *20* Wert
vanguard *72* Vorhut
vast *77* weit, groß; *108* riesig; *124* gewaltig
to **veer off** *64* vom Kurs abkommen
vehicle *53* Fahrzeug; **~ theft** *56* Fahrzeugdiebstahl
vein *7* Ader, Art
to **vent sth.** *134* etw (frei) äußern
venue *135* Stätte, Veranstaltungsort
to **verify** *87* prüfen
vexing *80T* verzwickt
vicious *49* boshaft, bösartig
victim *94* Opfer
victory *143T* Sieg
view, in ~ of *52* angesichts; **in sb.'s ~** *8* nach jds Ansicht/ Meinung
viewing figures *90* Zuschauerzahlen
vigorous *137* energisch, leidenschaftlich
to **violate** *46* *(Gesetz, etc.)* verletzen
violation *90* Verletzung, Verstoß; **human rights ~** *115* Menschenrechtsverletzung
virtually *76* praktisch
visibility, high-~ *46* öffentlichkeitswirksam, mit hoher Außenwirkung
visible, highly ~ *47* öffentlichkeitswirksam, mit hoher Außenwirkung
vital *42T* unerlässlich, lebensnotwendig
vivid *134* anschaulich
to **voice** *144* äußern, zum Ausdruck bringen
volatile *140* unbeständig, instabil, unberechenbar
volcanic *16T* vulkanisch, Vulkan-
volume *19* Band, Buch; **high ~** *32* *hier:* mit hohem Patientenaufkommen
voluntary *111* freiwillig
volunteer *20* Freiwillige/r, ehrenamtlich Tätige/r
to **volunteer to do sth.** *117* sich bereit erklären, etw zu tun, etw freiwillig tun
vote *75* *hier:* stimmen
voter *52* Wähler/in
vow *68* Schwur, Gelöbnis, Versprechen
vox pop(uli) *87* Volkes Stimme, öffentliche Meinung

W

wage *24* Lohn; **low-~** *38* schlecht bezahlt, Niedriglohn-
to **wage war** *140* Krieg führen
walking tour *21* Führung, Rundgang
wanderlust *26* Reiselust
want, for ~ of sth. *115* weil etw fehlt
war, to **wage ~** *140* Krieg führen
warming, global ~ *95* Erderwärmung
waste, domestic ~ *104* Hausmüll; **hazardous ~** *104* Sondermüll; **household ~** *26* Haushaltsmüll; to **let sth. go to ~** *115* etw ungenutzt lassen
waste disposal *99* Müllentsorgung, Abfallentsorgung
waste-treatment facility *20* Kläranlage
to **watch over sb./sth.** *23* sich um jdn/etw kümmern, über jdn/etw wachen
water conservation *20* Wassersparen
water line *108* Wasserleitung
water shortage *24* Wassermangel, Wasserknappheit
watershed invention *152* *etwa:* bahnbrechende Erfindung
to **wax philosophical** *147* ins Philosophieren geraten, herumphilosophieren
way, to **come a long ~** *75* es weit bringen; to **get one's ~** *9* seinen Willen bekommen, (mit etw) durchkommen; to **lead the ~** *20* die Richtung weisen, es vormachen; to **leave sth. a long ~ off** *99* etw in weite Ferne rücken; to **pave the ~** *126* den Weg ebnen
wealth *10* Reichtum, Wohlstand; **~ of sth.** *21* Fülle von etw; **distribution of ~** *37* Vermögensverteilung; to **gain ~** *108* reich werden
weapons of mass destruction *140* Massenvernichtungswaffen
to **weather** *16T* überstehen
to **weed out** *70* aussortieren
to **weigh** *26* gegeneinander abwägen
weight gain *92T* Gewichtszunahme
weight loss *92T* Gewichtsabnahme
welfare *10* Wohl; **~ services** *124* soziale Einrichtungen; **~ state** *11* Wohlfahrtsstaat, Sozialstaat
well *108* Brunnen
well-adjusted *63* wohlerzogen
well-being *10* Wohl, Wohlergehen
well-resourced *137* gut (mit Mitteln) ausgestattet

were, as it ~ *14* sozusagen, gewissermaßen
whim, by ~ *134* nach Belieben
white-collar crime *54* Wirtschaftskriminalität
white-collar profession *37* Angestelltenberuf
wholesome *20* gesund, positiv
wicked *9* böse, schlecht, schlimm
widespread *100* verbreitet
widower *11* Witwer, *hier:* Verwitweter
wilderness *18* Wildnis
wildlife tourism *24* Safari-Tourismus
to **be willing to do sth.** *118T* bereit etw zu tun
willingly *137* bereitwillig
to **win sb. over** *13* jdn umstimmen, jdn überzeugen
windmill *103T* Windmühle
wine merchant *33* Weinhändler/in, Weinhandel/-handlung
to **wipe sth. out** *124* auslöschen, zunichte machen
wisdom *14* Weisheit, Klugheit
wise *23* klug
witness, to **bear ~ to sth.** *78* etw bezeugen, von etw zeugen
to **woo** *33* (um-, an-)werben
wood, to **touch ~** *69T* auf Holz klopfen
work, to **put sth. to ~** *126* etw einsetzen, etw nutzen
workable *85* durchführbar
workforce *40* Arbeitskräfte; *63* arbeitende Bevölkerung
World Trade Organization (WTO) *124* Welthandelsorganisation (WHO)
worrisome *35* besorgniserregend
to **worsen** *10* sich verschlimmern
worth, to **prove one's ~** *8* sich beweisen, seine Stärke unter Beweis stellen
worthwhile *148* lohnend, interessant
wrapper *99* Verpackung, Beutel, Tüte
wreckage *51* Trümmer
to **wrestle** *46* sich abmühen, zu kämpfen haben; **~ sth. from sb.** *50* jdm etw entreißen

X

xenophobia *53* Fremdenfeindlichkeit, Fremdenhass
xenophobic *80T* fremdenfeindlich
yapping *129T* Gekläffe, große Sprüche

Y

to **yell out** *7* (laut) ausrufen, herausschreien
yurt *21* Jurte

Z

zero tolerance *51* Nulltoleranz
zip code *AE* *149* Postleitzahl

Irregular verbs

arise	arose	arisen	*entstehen*
be	was/were	been	*sein*
beat	beat	beaten	*schlagen*
become	became	become	*werden*
begin	began	begun	*starten, anfangen*
bind	bound	bound	*fesseln, binden*
break	broke	broken	*brechen, kaputtmachen*
bring	brought	brought	*bringen*
broadcast	broadcast	broadcast	*senden, ausstrahlen*
build	built	built	*bauen*
burn	burnt (burned)	burnt (burned)	*brennen*
buy	bought	bought	*kaufen*
catch	caught	caught	*fangen*
choose	chose	chosen	*wählen*
come	came	come	*kommen*
cost	cost	cost	*kosten*
cut	cut	cut	*schneiden*
deal	dealt	dealt	*handeln, sich beschäftigen mit*
dig	dug	dug	*graben, bohren*
do	did	done	*tun, machen*
draw	drew	drawn	*zeichnen*
dream	dreamt (dreamed)	dreamt (dreamed)	*träumen*
drink	drank	drunk	*trinken*
drive	drove	driven	*fahren*
eat	ate	eaten	*essen*
fall	fell	fallen	*fallen*
feel	felt	felt	*fühlen*
fight	fought	fought	*(be)kämpfen*
find	found	found	*finden*
fly	flew	flown	*fliegen*
forget	forgot	forgotten	*vergessen*
freeze	froze	frozen	*frieren*
get	got	got	*bekommen*
give	gave	given	*geben*
go	went	gone	*gehen*
grow	grew	grown	*wachsen*
have	had	had	*haben*
hear	heard	heard	*hören*
hide	hid	hidden	*(sich) verstecken*
hit	hit	hit	*schlagen*
hold	held	held	*halten*
hurt	hurt	hurt	*weh tun*
input	input	input	*eingeben*
keep	kept	kept	*behalten*
know	knew	known	*wissen, kennen*
lay	laid	laid	*legen*
lead	led	led	*führen*
learn	learnt	learnt	*lernen*
leave	left	left	*(weg)gehen, (ver)lassen*
let	let	let	*lassen, erlauben*
light	lit	lit	*erleuchten, entzünden*
lose	lost	lost	*verlieren*
make	made	made	*machen, tun*

mean	meant	meant	*bedeuten*
meet	met	met	*treffen*
pay	paid	paid	*bezahlen*
put	put	put	*legen, stellen*
read	read	read	*lesen*
ride	rode	ridden	*fahren, reiten*
rise	rose	risen	*steigen, sich erheben*
ring	rang	rung	*klingeln*
run	ran	run	*laufen, verwalten*
say	said	said	*sagen*
see	saw	seen	*sehen*
seek	sought	sought	*suchen*
sell	sold	sold	*verkaufen*
send	sent	sent	*senden*
set	set	set	*setzen, stellen, legen*
shake	shook	shaken	*schütteln*
show	showed	shown	*zeigen*
shut	shut	shut	*schließen*
sing	sang	sung	*singen*
sink	sank	sunk	*(ver)senken*
sit	sat	sat	*sitzen*
sleep	slept	slept	*schlafen*
smell	smelt (smelled)	smelt (smelled)	*riechen*
speak	spoke	spoken	*sprechen*
speed	sped	sped	*rasen*
spell	spelt (spelled)	spelt (spelled)	*buchstabieren*
spend	spent	spent	*ausgeben*
stand	stood	stood	*stehen*
steal	stole	stolen	*stehlen*
swim	swam	swum	*schwimmen*
take	took	taken	*nehmen*
teach	taught	taught	*unterrichten*
tear	tore	torn	*zerreißen*
tell	told	told	*erzählen*
think	thought	thought	*denken*
throw	threw	thrown	*werfen*
understand	understood	understood	*verstehen*
wake	woke	woken	*wecken*
wear	wore	worn	*tragen*
win	won	won	*gewinnen*
write	wrote	written	*schreiben*

Problem words and false friends

Fremdsprachenlernen ist faszinierend. Man stolpert immer wieder über erstaunliche Dinge. So gibt es im Englischen etwa eine Reihe von Wörtern, die mehrere Bedeutungen haben können (ähnlich wie im Deutschen). Solche Wörter kann man als Problemwörter sehen. Es gibt auch deutsche und englische Wörter, die zwar gleich oder ähnlich aussehen, gleich oder ähnlich klingen, die jedoch ganz verschiedene Bedeutungen haben. Solche Wörter nennt man False Friends – man kann sich auf sie nicht verlassen.

Hier ist eine kleine Auswahl von Problemwörtern und falschen Freunden. Machen Sie sich eine Notiz, wenn Sie derartigen Wörtern begegnen, und ergänzen Sie die Liste. Dann werden Sie diese Wörter gut beherrschen.

NOUNS

brochure	Prospekt, Faltblatt
prospect	(Zukunfts-)Aussicht
chef	(Chef-)Koch
boss	Chef/Chefin (einer Firma)
look	Blick, Aussehen
to watch (v)	ansehen
meaning	Bedeutung
opinion	Meinung
mobile phone *(BE)* **/ cell phone** *(AE)*	Handy
handy (adj.)	praktisch, nützlich, geschickt

ADJECTIVES

actual	eigentlich, tatsächlich
current	aktuell
the latest	die neueste
the last	der/die/das Letzte
last	letzte(r,s), am Ende
at last	endlich, schließlich
sensible	vernünftig
sensitive	sensibel

ADVERBS

actually	eigentlich
currently	zurzeit, momentan
for (two days)	seit (zwei Tagen)
(two days) ago	vor (zwei Tagen)
least	am wenigsten
at least	wenigstens, zumindest
possibly	möglicherweise, vielleicht
eventually	schließlich, endlich

PREPOSITIONS

beside	neben
besides (adv.)	außerdem
next	nächste(r,s)
nearly (adv.)	fast, beinahe

VERBS AND VERB PHRASES

to be lucky to be happy	Glück haben glücklich sein
to become to get	werden bekommen
to blame sb. for to disgrace sb., oneself	jdm die Schuld geben an, für jdn/sich blamieren
to borrow to lend	borgen, ausleihen verleihen
to bring sb./sth to take sb./sth	jdn/etwas mitbringen jdn/etwas irgendwohin bringen
to discuss sth	etwas besprechen
to get up to stand up	aufstehen sich erheben
keep (working) stay (working)	(an der Arbeit) bleiben dranbleiben
to look to look after sb./sth to look for sb./sth to look into sth	aussehen sich um jdn/etwas kümmern nach jdn/etwas suchen etwas untersuchen
to lose to loosen loose (adj.)	verlieren locker machen, lösen locker, nicht fest
to make sth to make sth of ~ to make out	etwas machen, herstellen etwas herstellen aus ~ etwas ausschreiben, entwickeln, entziffern
to mean to think, to believe	bedeuten meinen, glauben
to prove to check (on)	beweisen, sich erweisen als überprüfen, nachprüfen, kontrollieren
to raise to rise	heben hochgehen, aufgehen
to rob to steal	(aus)rauben stehlen, entwenden
to start off to take off	etw. anfangen starten, abheben
to wonder (if ...) to be surprised	sich fragen (ob ...) wundern überrascht sein

Quellenverzeichnis

Titelfoto:
oben/shutterstock/YanLev, shutterstock/Tom Wang, shutterstock/Sergey Nivens, unten/shutterstock/Jeff Whyte

S. 6/1/shutterstock/Monkey Business Images, S. 6/2/shutterstock/mangostock, S. 6/3/shutterstock/Dudarev Mikhail, S. 6/4/shutterstock/Andresr, S. 6/5, shutterstock/wavebreakmedia, S. 7/shutterstock/Alberto Zornetta, S. 8/Alamy/Joe Fox, S. 9/Alamy/imagebroker/Matthias Hauser, S. 10/Alamy/Radius Images, S. 11/shutterstock/Andy Dean Photography, S. 13/Picture Alliance/EPA/Davis Turner, S. 14/1/shutterstock/Yuri Arcurs, S. 14/2/shutterstock/Andresr, S. 16/Corbis/Mohammad Moniruzzaman, S. 17/Andy Singer, S. 18/ODI, S. 19/1/shutterstock/Vladimir Sazonov, S. 19/2/shutterstock/Studio 1One, S. 20/1/shutterstock/Juriah Mosin, S. 20/2/Alamy/Eagle Visions/Craig Lovele, S. 21/1/Picture Alliance/Eric Nathan, S. 21/2/Eugen Rombach, Freiburg, S. 23/1/Corbis/Heide Benser, S. 23/2/shutterstock/lightpoet, S. 23/3/shutterstock/PhotoSky, S. 24/Picture Alliance/Holger Hollermann, S. 25/Alamy/uk retail Alan King, S. 26/Picture Alliance/Bildagentur Huber, S. 27/Picture Alliance/Uwe Gerig, S. 28/Fotofinder/Schapowalow/Huber, S. 29/Benita Epstein, S. 30/1/shutterstock/Graeme Shannon, S. 30/2/shutterstock/Hazan, S. 30/3/shutterstock/Frank 11, S. 30/4/shutterstock/Fottom, S. 32/1/Fotolia/squidmediaro, S. 32/2/shutterstock/StockLite, S. 33/Picture Alliance/EPA/Juanjo Martin, S. 34/Fotofinder/Bildagentur Hamburg/Rainer Waldkirch, S. 36/Alamy/GoGoImages, S. 37/Alamy/David Grossmann, S. 39/1/Fotofinder/allesalltag, S. 39/2/Fotofinder/Fotex/Susa, S. 39/3/shutterstock/Blue Orange Studio, S. 39/4/shutterstock/Sergey Nivens, S. 40/Alamy/Corbis Flirt, S. 42/1/shutterstock/Yuri Arcurs, S. 42/2/shutterstock/Martin Novak, S. 43/1/Cagle Cartoons, S. 43/2/Universal Uclick/Distr.Bulls Press, S. 45/1/shutterstock/Annette Shaff, S. 45/2/shutterstock/S1001, S. 45/3/Corbis/RF/Radius Images, S. 46/Alamy/Marka, S. 47/Alamy/Vicky Kasala, S. 49/Alamy/Larry Lilac, S. 50/Picture Alliance/AFP/dpa/Matias Recart, S. 51/1/CartoonStock/Wilfred Hildonen, S. 56/CartoonStock, S. 60/Alamy, S. 63/Alamy/Picture Partners, S. 65/Alamy/MJ Photography, S. 67/Alamy/Purestock, S. 68/Randy Glasbergen, S. 69/Fotolia/hawi 101, S. 71/1/Picture Alliance/Everett Collection, S. 71/2/Picture Alliance/Juan Medina, S. 71/3/shutterstock/AG Photo, S. 72/Corbis/Jon Feingersh, S. 75/Corbis/Hulton Collection, S. 76/Corbis/Mike Kemp, S. 78/Corbis/Stephanie Maze, S. 80/Andy Singer, S. 83/1/shutterstock/jocic, S. 83/2/shutterstock/Brian Jackson, S. 83/3/shutterstock/Tomislav Pinter, S. 83/4/shutterstock/bloomua, S. 83/5/shutterstock/Coprid, S. 83/6/shutterstock/Falconia, S. 83/7/shutterstock/koya979, S. 84/Picture Alliance/Bildagentur -online, S. 86/1/Alamy/David Pearson, S. 86/2/Alamy/David Hawtin, S. 87/Picture Alliance/Lucas Dolega, S. 90/Alamy/Darren Starling, S. 93/1/Michael Meister, S. 93/2/Randy Glasbergen, S. 95/1/shutterstock/freesoulproduction, S. 95/2/shutterstock/Sergey Panychev, S. 96/Picture Alliance/Sebastian Kahnert, S. 99/Corbis/Ashley Cooper, S. 100/Corbis/Andrew Aitchison, S. 102/Cartoonstock/Clive Goddard, S. 103/Corbis/Mainichi Newspaper, S. 104/Picture Alliance/Photoshot./Wolfgang Bayer, S. 107/1/Picture Alliance/AFP/Peter_Cunliffe-Jones, S. 107/2/Alamy/Jake Lyell, S. 107/3/Alamy/Friedrich Stark, S. 107/4/shutterstock/Jan S., S. 108/1/Picture Alliance/EPA/George Esiri, S. 110/shutterstock, S. 111/Picture Alliance/Ton Koene, S. 114/Picture Alliance/Asianet Pakistan, S. 115/Picture Alliance/Asianet Pakistan, S. 117/1/Dave Granlund, S. 120/1/cagle cartoons/Olle Johansson, S. 120/2/Alamy/John Wreford, S. 120/3/Picture Alliance/Ton Koene, S. 120/4/Milt Prigee, S. 121/shutterstock/zhu difeng, S. 122/Picture Alliance/Bernd Settnik, S. 123/1/Alamy/Davis Pearson, S. 124/Picture Alliance/Bildagentur -online, S. 126/Picture Alliance/Christiane Eisler, S. 128/Picture Alliance/Ralf Freyer, S. 130/1/CartoonStock/Karsten Schley, S. 132/1/Patrick Chappatte, S. 132/2/Alamy/James Fassinger, S. 132/3/Picture Alliance/Maurizio Gambarini, S. 132/4/political Cartoons/Pavel Constantin, S. 133/Picture Alliance/Khaled Elfiqi, S. 135/Picture Alliance/EPA/Arnel Pain, S. 137/Picture Alliance/Stella Pictures, S. 140/Picture Alliance/Mahfouz Abu Turk, S. 142/Cagle cartoons/David Fritzsimmons, S. 145/1/shutterstock/diversepixel, S. 145/2/Getty Images/Noah Clayton, S. 145/3/shutterstock/Mike Heywood, S. 145/4/Getty Images/

Digital Vision/Hiroshi Watanabe, S. 145/5/shutterstock/Dark Geometry Studios, S. 146/Picture Alliance/Globe ZUMA, S. 149/shutterstock/forestpath, S. 152/cartoo Stock/S. Harris, S. 154/1/CartoonStock/Kamagurka, S. 158/1/shutterstock/Antoliy Samara, S. 158/2/shutterstock/Dmitri Maruta, S. 158/3/shutterstock/icyimage, S. 158/4/shutterstock/vipman, S. 159/1/Geek culture/Nitrozac&Snaggy, S. 159/2/cartoonChurch, S. 160/1/Getty Images/Christian Science Monitor, S. 160/2/Photoshot/LFI/Everett, S. 160/3/Picture Alliance/AP/Alex Brandon, S. 161/1/Getty Images/Jeff Fusco, S. 161/2/Firma Minesto, S. 161/3/Getty Images/Don Arnold, S. 162/1/ODI, S. 162/2/ODI, S. 162/3/Getty Images/Park Ji-Hwan, S. 169/1/shutterstock/Asianet Pakistan, S. 184/1/shutterstock/africa924

Texte:
S. 7/S. 8/S. 9/The Guardian, S. 10/The Newsweek, S. 20/www.csmonitor.com, S. 20/S. 21/www.muchbetteradventureS. com, S. 26/Christian Science Monitor/Karin Rives, S. 33/Time, S. 36/Time, S. 45/cbn.com, S. 46/The New York Times/Miguel Helft, S. 51/ New Zealand Herald, S. 62/The New York Times, S. 62/New York Times/David Leonhardt, S. 65/The Economist, S. 72/The New York Times/Susan Saulny, S. 75/The Independent, S. 84/journalism.about.com/Tony Rogers, S. 87/The Economist, S. 97/Maggie Koerth-Baker, S. 99/The Guardian, S. 110/The New York Times/Justin Gillis/Celia W.Dugger, S. 114/The New York Times/Nicholas D.Kristof/Sheryl Wudunn, S. 121/Time, S. 126/The New York Times/Andrew E.Kramer, S. 134/The New York Times/L.Friedman, S. 137/The New York Times/Jan Egeland, S. 146/Time, S. 149/www.thefiscaltimeS. com, S. 163/The New York Times/Mireya Navarro, S. 164/The Economist, S. 165/The New York Times/Eric Weiner

In einigen Fällen war es uns nicht möglich, die Rechteinhaber zu ermitteln. Selbstverständlich werden wir berechtigte Ansprüche im üblichen Rahmen vergüten.

The World

Stand: 2008

Canada & United States of America

Abbreviations CANADA:

NB = New Brunswick
P.E.I. = Prince Edward Island

Abbreviations UNITED STATES:

CT = Connecticut
DE = Delaware
NH = New Hampshire
NJ = New Jersey
MA = Massachusetts
MD = Maryland
PA = Pennsylvania
RI = Rhode Island
VT = Vermont